GOYIM

Program in Judaic Studies
Brown University
BROWN JUDAIC STUDIES
Edited by
Jacob Neusner,
Wendell S. Dietrich, Ernest S. Frerichs, William Scott Green,
Calvin Goldscheider, David Hirsch, Alan Zuckerman

Project Editors (Project)

David Blumenthal, Emory University (Approaches to Medieval Judaism)
William Brinner (Approaches to Judaism and Islam)
Ernest S. Frerichs, Brown University (Dissertations and Monographs)
Lenn Evan Goodman, University of Hawaii (Studies in Medieval Judaism)
William Scott Green, University of Rochester (Approaches to Ancient Judaism)
Norbert Samuelson, Temple University (Jewish Philosophy)
Jonathan Z. Smith, University of Chicago (Studia Philonica)

Number 155
GOYIM
Gentiles and Israelites in Mishnah-Tosefta

by
Gary G. Porton

GOYIM
Gentiles and Israelites in Mishnah-Tosefta

by
Gary G. Porton

Scholars Press
Atlanta, Georgia

GOYIM
Gentiles and Israelites in Mishnah-Tosefta

Library of Congress Cataloging in Publication Data

Porton, Gary G.
  Goyim : gentiles and Israelites in Mishnah-Tosefta.

  (Brown Judaic studies ; no. 155)
  Bibliography: p.
  Includes index.
  1. Gentiles in rabbinical literature.
2. Mishnah--Criticism, interpretation, etc.
3. Tosefta--Criticism, interpretation, etc.
I. Title. II. Series.
BM720.N6P67   1989   296.1'2306   88-30827
ISBN 1-55540-278-X

Printed in the United States of America
on acid-free paper

For

Bill, Rebecca,
Noah, and Ethan

Table of Contents

Acknowledgements

I wish to thank my teacher, Professor Jacob Neusner, University Professor, Ungerleider Distinguished Scholar of Judaic Studies, and Professor of Judaic Studies, Brown University for his help and support with this volume. The reader will discover that the analyses of the pericopae in Mishnah-Tosefta and the general approach to these documents employed in this work are heavily dependent upon Professor Neusner's studies. Without his pioneering investigations of Mishnah, Tosefta, the *midrashim* and the many other texts of the rabbinic corpus, the present study could not have been undertaken. In addition, I wish to express my appreciation for his accepting this work for inclusion in Brown Judaic Studies.

The present volume has been greatly enhanced by the insights of my colleague, Professor Alan Avery-Peck, Director of Jewish Studies, Tulane University. Alan carefully read an earlier version of this text and made many improvements in its style and its argumentation. Alan's comments and corrections have been incorporated on virtually every page, so that it is impossible to acknowledge each of them separately. Suffice it to say that Alan's contributions have been significant, and they have made this a much clearer and more important study than it would have been had he not taken the time to read and comment upon it.

My colleagues, Professor William S. Green, Chairman of the Department of Religious and Classical Studies, Rochester University, and William R. Schoedel, Professor of Religious Studies and the Classic, University of Illinois, read earlier versions of this volume and made several important comments about its content. In addition, I have had numerous conversions with both of these scholars about specific issues and topics discussed below. I have benefited greatly from their insights and published works. I appreciate the fact that both of these pre-eminent scholars have been a source of support and friendship for the last fifteen years.

Professor Edward M. Bruner, Department of Anthropology at the University of Illinois and Professor Harvey M. Choldin, Department of Sociology at the University of Illinois introduced me to the scholarship and literature on ethnic groups which plays an important part in this volume. I wish to acknowledge their support and the time they spent with me while I was working on this study.

I also wish to thank Mr. Jim Gothard of the Language Learning Laboratory at the University of Illinois for his help with the software needed to produce this manuscript and Mr. Dennis Ford of Scholars Press for his advice and help.

The English translations of the verses from the Hebrew Bible are based on *Tanakh: A New Translation of the Holy Scriptures According to the Traditional Hebrew Text* published by the Jewish Publication Society, Philadelphia, New York, and Jerusalem, 1985.

The initial research for this volume was undertaken while I was associated with the Center for Advanced Study at the University of Illinois and with the aid of a fellowship from the John Simon Guggenheim Memorial Foundation. I wish to thank both of these institutions for their support of this project. I could not have completed this work without the research time and funds supplied by these two organizations.

My wife, Fraeda, and our children, Zipporah Rachel and Avraham Reuven, contributed to this volume through their constant support and love. Without their help this work would have never been completed.

This volume is dedicated to my friends and colleagues, William S. Green, Rebecca Fox, and their sons, Noah Fox Green and Ethan Fox Green. For fifteen years Bill has been more than a close friend; he has been a source of intellectual, emotional, and spiritual support and comfort. He has given unselfishly of his time and intellect so that I might grow as a scholar, a teacher, a Jew, and a caring human being. Without his efforts my career and my life would have been much poorer. Rebecca has also been a source of intellectual stimulation and true friendship for the last several years. She is one of the most intellectually challenging and wittiest persons I have ever met, as well as one of the kindest and warmest human beings I have encountered. It is always a joy to spend time with her. Noah has been a constant source of amazement and joy for all of us who know him. His freshness, his honesty, and his humor have made all of our lives richer and better, and Ethan, whom we have just met, has already won our admiration.

Gary G. Porton
27 Tishri, 5749
Champaign, Illinois

Abbreviations

		M	Mishnah
Ahil.	Ahilot	Mal.	Malachai
Arak.	Arakhim	M.Q.	Mo'ed Qatan
A.Z.	Abodah Zarah	M.S.	Ma'aser Sheni
b	Babylonian	Ma.	Ma'aserot
	Talmud	Mak.	Makkot
b.	ben/son of	Maksh.	Makshirim
B.B.	Baba Batra	Meg.	Megillah
B.M.	Baba Mesi'a'	Me'.	Me'ilah
B.Q.	Baba Qama	Men.	Menahot
Bekh.	Bekhorot	Mid.	Middot
Ber.	Berakhot	Miq.	Miqva'ot
Bes.	Besah	Naz.	Nazir
Dem.	Demai	Ned.	Nedarim
Ed.	Eduyot	Neg.	Nega'im
Erub.	'Erubin	Nid.	Niddah
Ex.	Exodus	Num.	Numbers
Dan.	Daniel	Ohol.	Oholot
Deut.	Deuteronomy	Orl.	'Orlah
Gen.	Genesis	Par.	Parah
Git.	Gittin	Pe.	Pe'ah
Hag.	Hagigah	Pes.	Pesahim
Hal.	Hallah	Pis.	Pisha
Hor.	Horayot	Prov.	Proverbs
Hul.	Hullin	Ps.	Psalms
IIKgs.	II Kings	Qid.	Qiddushin
ISam.	I Samuel	R.H.	Rosh HaShanah
IISam.	II Samuel	Sanh.	Sanhedrin
Jer.	Jeremiah	Shab.	Shabbat
Kel.	Kelim	Sheb.	Shebi'it
Kil.	Kila'yim	Shebu	Shebu'ot
Kip.	Kippurim	Sheq.	Sheqalim
Lev.	Leviticus	Sot.	Sotah
		T	Tosefta

Tan.	Ta'anit
Tem.	Temurah
Ter.	Terumot
Toh.	Tohorot
T.Y.	Tebul Yom
Y	Palestinian Talmud
Y.T.	Yom Tob
Yad.	Yadayim
Yeb.	Yebamot
Zab	Zabim
Zeb.	Zebahim

Chapter One:

Introduction

i

The present investigation demonstrates that the pericopae which discuss the gentiles can be used as a means of gaining insight into how the rabbis who stand behind Mishnah-Tosefta defined their cultural and religious systems and their central concepts/symbols. This volume proceeds in two stages. The study begins by analyzing the pericopae in Mishnah-Tosefta which treat the gentiles, and it focuses on what the sages who stand behind these documents thought was significant about the non-Israelites and their interaction with, and relationship, to Israelites. In the second phase those details are employed as a source of information about the rabbis' conceptions of themselves and their culture.

The thesis developed throughout this study is that the men who stand behind Mishnah-Tosefta were in the process of constructing an Israelite ethnic[1] identity in order to differentiate the Israelites from the gentiles who also populated the Land of Israel. This became an especially pertinent project with the destruction of the Jerusalem Temple, the failure of the Bar Kokhba Revolt, the increased influx of gentiles into the Land of Israel, and the social upheaval which resulted from the disruption of Israel's agricultural economy and the general economic decline experienced throughout the Roman world during that period. The organization of Mishnah-Tosefta indicates that their authors arranged their formulation of Israelite identity around a few key concepts/symbols: The Land of Israel, Israel's periods of Sacred Time, The People Israel and their Ethnic Institutions and Practices, The God of Israel, and The Residence of Israel's God.

By studying the various rules and regulations which these documents indicate were, or should be, imposed on the gentiles and Israelites *vis-a-vis* these major images, we find direct information concerning the creation and the

----

[1]For a discussion of the term "ethnic," see below, Chapter Twelve.

maintenance of this ethnic group. In the opinion of the rabbis who transmitted Mishnah-Tosefta, a true Israelite is one who relates to the Land, the People, the Temple, and YHWH in the explicit and circumscribed ways prescribed in these documents. In addition, we find significant indirect information about this identity in the discussions of how the gentiles must act in relationship to these same concepts/symbols, for these pericopae often contrast the ways in which an Israelite does/should confront these images with the manner in which a non-Israelite does/should deal with them. Gentiles are not Israelites, and because of this, they respond to the basic symbols of Israelite culture differently from the fashion in which Israelites confront them; however, they do confront them. Therefore, by examining what gentiles may, or may not, do or how they may, or may not, act in relation to these concepts, we can enhance our understanding of the latter's range of meanings. For example, for Israelites, the holiness of the Land of Israel is expressed in terms of the agricultural rules and the required agricultural gifts which derive from their belief that the Land of Israel originally belonged to YHWH and that their special relationship to YHWH is concretized in his giving them his Land. However, we discover that from the point of view of the people behind Mishnah-Tosefta, gentiles may not simply ignore the holiness of the Land of Israel, even though, as non-Israelites, they do not have a special relationship to this Land or to its "original owner," YHWH. The Land of Israel remains holy to some degree no matter who tills her soil, so that the gentiles, from the Israelite point of view, must acknowledge its sacredness; however, they do so in limited and distinct ways when compared to Israelites. Similarly, some passages indicate that non-Israelites, as well as Israelites, may wish to acknowledge Israel's God, YHWH, through the Temple-cult; however, again each group does so in different ways because the symbol of God's residence means different things to each.

Thus, Mishnah-Tosefta's discussions of the gentile lead us to a more sophisticated understanding of the basic concepts of the culture in which those texts were produced than we would have if we had focused on only passages which treat Israelites. The authors of our documents sought to describe the gentile in terms of the same symbols they employed to define the Israelites, and they did so by explaining how each group responded to these ideas in its own unique manner. In fact, for the authors/editors of our texts, the gentiles are most important *only* when they come into contact with these symbols.

That the gentiles are significant only in terms of the central concepts/symbols of Israelite culture becomes clear when we analyze the literary forms in which the discussions of the gentiles are cast. The gentiles are not an independent or unique object of the rabbis' concern. The sages did not isolate their treatment of the gentiles in one location, nor did they distinguish their discussions of them through novel literary conventions. From the point of view of the editorial process or the literary forms, the gentiles are treated in virtually the same manner as the other topics covered in Mishnah-Tosefta. For the most part, treatments of non-Israelites are scattered throughout our documents and are placed in their present contexts because they serve to illustrate the larger issues expressed in the various chapters and tractates, which ultimately center on what an Israelite must do or how an Israelite should act. The gentiles are important primarily because they serve as a means of emphasizing the unique relationship between Israel as an ethnic unit and the central symbols/concepts which serve to define this group in the minds of the authors of our documents.

This study is unique in its emphasis and its conclusions, so that it is necessary to specify how it differs from other projects which may focus on the relationship and interaction of Israelites and non-Israelites. This is not a study of the Jewish views of Christianity or the interaction of Jews and Christians in the first centuries of the common era.[2] While that is a fascinating and important topic, Mishnah-Tosefta do not allow us to pursue it, for unambiguous references to Christians are difficult to discover in these documents,[3] and the texts do not normally differentiate among non-Israelites who worshipped Jesus, non-Israelites who followed Isis, non-Israelites who adored more than one divinity, and non-Israelites who were atheists. The controversies refer to non-Israelites in general, and, while they distinguish between the gentile *as idolater* and the gentile as farmer, merchant, and the like, they do not clearly and consistently specify the various religions to which the non-Israelites paid their allegiances. This renders it difficult to find clear and explicit references to Christians in our texts, and it also makes it hard to locate discourses on specific non-Christian re-

----

[2]Two recent studies on this problem should be mentioned: Lawrence H. Schiffman, "At the Crossroads: Tannaitic Perspectives on the Jewish-Christian Schism," in E.P. Sanders (ed.), *Jewish and Christian Self-Definition Volume Two* (Philadelphia: 1981) which was expanded into *Who Was A Jew: Rabbinic and Halakhic Perspectives of the Jewish-Christian Schism* (Hoboken: 1985); Alan Segal, *Rebecca's Children: Judaism and Christianity in the Roman World* (Cambridge: 1986).

[3]See Reuven Kimelman, "Birkat Ha-Minim and the Lack of Evidence for an Anti-Christian Jewish Prayer in Late Antiquity," in Sanders, 226-244. Segal, *Rebecca's Children*, 147-160. Alan F. Segal, *Two Powers in Heaven: Early Rabbinic Reports About Christianity and Gnosticism* (Leiden: 1977).

ligions, with the exception of the cult of Mercury.[4]

It is comparably difficult to determine from Mishnah-Tosefta how Israelites and gentiles *actually* interrelated. For this reason, we shall discover what the authors/editors of Mishnah-Tosefta *thought* should, or did, happen and not what actually occurred, and this will allow us to understand how the rabbis behind these texts set about to define Israel, without attempting to ascertain what the texts cannot tell us: How this definition was actually put into practice in everyday life. Accordingly, this is not a sociological study of Palestinian society in the first centuries of the common era. The sages who produced Mishnah-Tosefta collected, edited, revised, and presented their material in ways that do not allow us to move from their work into "the real world." These texts are notoriously uninterested in placing the sages' comments into historical or sociological contexts, so that they provide us with few narratives.[5] Furthermore, the sages' comments have been cast in such a way that *even if* we could demonstrate that they accurately reflect the words and ideas of the rabbis to whom they are attributed, and *even if* they were stated in response to a particular "historical" situation, there are no means of determining exactly what those situations were.[6] In addition, there is nothing which distinguishes a description of something which actually occurred or rulings which were followed in daily life from statements about what should happen or that deal with a law which was mute. For example, the rabbis discuss the cult of Molech, an obscure deity mentioned in the Hebrew Bible, with the same vividness with which they deal with the worship of the Roman deity, Mercury, and they describe the details of the cult of the destroyed Temple in Jerusalem with the same exactness as they set forth the rules for assessing damages, questioning witnesses, or composing mar-

----

[4]Isis and Seraphis are mentioned at least once in Mishnah-Tosefta, but this is atypical. Furthermore, the documents mention the worship of Molech, a foreign divinity mentioned in the Bible whose cult had ended hundreds of years before the texts came into existence. Contrary to what Mishnah-Tosefta suggest, the worship of Molech was not a viable form of religious expression in the first centuries of the common era.

[5]For example, in sharp contrast to other literary creations of the first centuries of the common era, Mishnah-Tosefta provide us with few examples of Pronouncement Stories; Gary G. Porton, "The Pronouncement Story in Tannaitic Literature: A Review of Bultmann's Theory," in Robert C. Tannehill (ed.), *Pronouncement Stories Semia*, XX, (1981), 81-99.

[6]On the problems of placing the rabbinic statements in a "historical" context and of discovering anything about the personalities and lives of the Tannaim, see William S. Green, "What's in a Name?—The Problematic of Rabbinic 'Biography,'" in William S. Green (ed.), *Approaches to Ancient Judaism: Theory and Practice* (Missoula: 1978), 77-96. See also the studies of particular Tannaim listed below in Chapter Five, note 1.

riage certificates. Separating what existed only in the minds of our authors from what occurred in "real life" is impossible; therefore, this work does not claim to contribute to our understanding of how Israelites and non-Israelites treated one another when they met in the street, did business in the market-place, or confronted one another in the courts. It only seeks to describe what Mishnah-Tosefta have to say about such interpersonal activities.[7]

The present volume limits itself to an analysis and study of the discussions of the gentile which appear in Mishnah-Tosefta because they are the earliest rabbinic texts, and because the definition of the "Israelite" they initiate in response to their interpretation of the events of the first two centuries of the common era sets the agenda for Judaism which continues until today. Furthermore, these documents are distinctive and differ significantly from other types of Jewish literature composed before and after them, as well as those authored close to the time of their final editing. For this reason, this work does not present a history of the development of Jewish views of the gentiles.[8] No attempt has been made to compare the descriptions of the gentiles found in Mishnah-Tosefta with those found in previous Jewish texts--such as the Bible--contemporary authors--such as Philo or Josephus--or latter rabbinic sources--such as the *Tannaitic midrashim* or the *talmudim*. While this is an important issue which needs to be investigated, this can be accomplished only after each text has been analyzed in its own terms. Different documents cannot be compared until they have been individually studied in ways which allow them to be juxtaposed to one another. While the results of the present work provide data which should be placed into conjunction with findings from other sources, at present, there are no similar studies of other texts which supply information which can be accurately compared to the details amassed here, or to the conclusions arrived at in this investigation.

Because the present volume is interested in what the discussions of the gentile found in Mishnah-Tosefta tell us about the creation of a definition of the Israelite ethnic unit through the examination of how Israelites and gentiles respond to the central concepts/symbols of the cultural and religious systems which they compose, this investigation does not attempt to elucidate all of the

---

[7]Mishnah-Tosefta do not provide us with adequate information to produce a work such as Wayne Meeks, *The First Urban Christians* (New Haven: 1983).

[8]For an introductory discussion of the relationship between the Jews and gentiles during the period of the Second Temple, see Shaye J.D. Cohen, *From The Maccabees to the Mishnah* (Philadelphia: 1987), 27-59, especially 46-49. For a summary of the relationship between Jews and non-Jews in Mishnah, see 216-217.

details of Tannaitic *halakhah* concerning the gentile. Because the present volume does not focus on the topic of the gentile in and of itself, the specifics of the laws discussed in our pericopae are covered only when they are relevant for our agenda. While the minutiae of rabbinic law are interesting and important in their own right, they are not necessarily always germane for the goals of this work. Furthermore, the tendency among halakhic studies is to blur the distinctions among the various rabbinic texts and to accept later interpretations of earlier texts as accurate representations of what the earlier sources meant. Because the present study focuses solely on information gathered from Mishnah-Tosefta, the techniques employed by scholars who follow the "halakhic approach" are not always helpful.[9]

To summarize: The present volume analyzes the references to the gentiles in Mishnah-Tosefta with an eye to ascertaining what these pericopae can tell us about the earliest rabbinic definition of the Israelite ethnic unit. It does not attempt to do more than this, nor does it accomplish less.

ii

Following the lead of Jacob Neusner,[10] this work studies Mishnah and Tosefta as related documents[11] which can be interpreted in their own terms. In this it differs from the majority of scholarly works that have interpreted Mish-

----

[9]On the techniques, accomplishments, and limits of the "halakhic approach" see the two works by Schiffman cited above in note 1 and Yehezkel Cohen, *The Attitude to the Gentile in the Halacha and in Reality in the Tannaitic Period* (Unpublished doctoral dissertation, Hebrew University, 1975).

[10]Jacob Neusner, *A History of the Mishnaic Law of Purities* (Leiden: 1974-1977), I-XXII; Jacob Neusner, *A History of the Mishnaic Law of Holy Things* (Leiden: 1979), I-VI; Jacob Neusner, *A History of the Mishnaic Law of Women* (Leiden: 1979-1980), I-V; Jacob Neusner, *A History of the Mishnaic Law of Appointed Times* (Leiden: 1981-1983), I-V; Jacob Neusner, *A History of the Mishnaic Law of Damages* (Leiden: 1983-1985), I-V.

[11]This study assumes that these texts are the products of those cited in them, not of the Gaonic or medieval periods. If it can be demonstrated that this is not true, much of what follows would need to be revised. Further, while I agree with those who suggest that we need to establish an accurate text of Mishnah-Tosefta, and in fact, the entire rabbinic corpus, I have not attempted to do so in this study. For the most part, the available textual variants are insignificant for our purposes. Nor do I enter into the fruitless discussion of the nature of the "official" text of Mishnah. On this latter issue, see Saul Lieberman, *Hellenism in Jewish Palestine: Studies in the Literary Transmission Beliefs and Manners of Palestine in the I Century B.C.E.--IV Century C.E.* (New York: 1950), 83-99. On the need for critical editions of the rabbinic texts, see Peter Schaefer, "Research into Rabbinic Literature: An Attempt to Define the Status Quaestionis," *Journal of Jewish Studies*, XXXVII, 2 (Autumn, 1986), 139-152.

nah, a Palestinian document edited in the first quarter of the third century of the common era, in light of the Babylonian and Palestinian Talmuds and the Gaonic and Medieval commentators. The underlying assumptions of the scholars who produced these studies is that rabbinic thought comprises an organic unity in which a statement in any text, or made at any point in time, is useful in correctly understanding every other document or statement. Therefore, a twelfth century comment on the Talmud or Mishnah is viewed as accurately representing what the earlier collection meant to say. In distinction to these other scholars, Neusner has exegeted Mishnah in light of itself, with some reference to information gleaned from Tosefta, a Palestinian text which was probably edited shortly after Mishnah. This approach allows us to ascertain *what Mishnah says* and to separate this from what later documents and figures *claim it says*.[12]

Focusing on Mishnah-Tosefta allows us to gaze into minds of the men who are seen by themselves and by later generations as the creators of rabbinic Judaism through the windows of its earliest literary creations. However, these sages comprised only one segment of the Palestinian Israelite community of their era, and all the information we amass about their thoughts is filtered through the intellects of those who were the final editors of these documents. Although not the work of one hand,[13] Mishnah is a fairly well-edited collection of Tannaitic statements which exhibits its own concerns and agenda,[14] and it is our earliest source of information which unambiguously can be attributed to the Palestinian rabbis of the first centuries of the common era. Because the final editorial activity was so thorough, at present, it is impossible to move from what we have now to what stood before it. Although a different text from Mishnah, it appears that the same can be said about Tosefta. Attempts to discover the "original" form a pericope, what a sage actually said, or the "historical" setting in which a *sugya* should be placed are doomed to failure. All we possess is what the sages who created these documents wanted us to have, and we have acquired that information in the forms they determined for us.

----

[12]I do not wish to claim that the later texts do not contain accurate interpretations and explanations of Mishnah-Tosefta. However, because it is impossible to separate these from later comments which have been read into the earlier collections, it seems best to have recourse to the later comments as infrequently as possible. At best, the exegetes provide possible meanings of Mishnah-Tosefta from which one can choose, based on a careful reading of Mishnah itself. See Alan J. Peck, *The Priestly Gift in Mishnah: A Study of Tractate Terumot* (Chico: 1981), 26-27.

[13]There is no evidence that Judah the Patriarch or any other single person edited Mishnah, nor is the editorial process clearly understood at this time. On this problem, see Jacob Neusner (ed.), *The Modern Study of the Mishnah* (Leiden: 1973), and Jacob Neusner, *Judaism: The Evidence of the Mishnah* (Chicago: 1981).

[14]See the works of Jacob Neusner cited above in note 10 and Jacob Neusner, *Judaism*.

In addition, we do not know why Mishnah and Tosefta were composed, or how they were meant to function.[15] In the structures they have been transmitted to us, Mishnah-Tosefta are extremely terse. In order to unpack them, one has to know a good deal of information which they do not contain, which they do not fully explicate, or which they assume. However, because they are composed of statements attributed to persons identified as rabbis, it seems reasonable to claim that these texts were composed by people who made up at least a portion of the circle of Palestinian rabbis and that they were written for and directed towards other rabbis, or least towards individuals who were as well informed about the details of rabbinic thought and who shared the same concerns and world-view as did the sages behind our texts. It is doubtful that, on their own, people outside these rabbinic circles could have, or were suppose to have, made sense of these documents. Therefore, in understanding Mishnah-Tosefta, we gain information about the thoughts of only the rabbis who produced these texts; we do not necessarily learn about those Israelites who were not part of the religious/cultural elite or about those segments of the religious/cultural elite who did not share the assumptions of the authors/editors of these collections.

Mishnah-Tosefta are literary creations, and they must be interpreted as such. While I do not wish to suggest that we can definitively and completely understand and interpret the minds and thoughts of the sages who stand behind our texts, I do believe that through these documents we can gain limited insights into what they thought about the nature of the Israelite ethnic unit they sought to create. To achieve our goal, however, we must pay attention to the literary traits of our sources. We cannot ignore the importance of literary conventions or overlook the difficulty of moving, as reader/interpreter, from the texts before us to the minds of those who produced them. However, recently anthropologists have developed methods for understanding a culture through its literary creations, and those techniques will be useful for our study.[16] Thus, even though all we have are literary compositions created over seventeen hundred years ago, we still should be able to move from those texts into the minds of their authors in order to understand what they believed were the essential aspects of the Israelite culture they lived and created.

----

[15]Cf., S. Cohen, 229-230.

[16]See, for example, Harvey E. Goldberg, *Judaism Viewed from Within and From Without: Anthropological Studies* (Albany: 1987); Edward M. Bruner (ed.), *Text, Play and Story: Proceedings, American Ethnological Society* (Washington: 1984); Michael M. J. Fischer, "Ethnicity and the Post-Modern Arts of Memory," James Clifford and George E. Marcus (eds.), *Writing Culture* (Berkeley and Los Angeles: 1986), 194-233.

To summarize: For the purposes of this study, Mishnah-Tosefta best can be seen as a means of entering into the thought-world of a segment of the Palestinian rabbinic community because the contents of these texts reflect and transmit the intellectual images which their authors/editors held. Although these documents appear uninterested in the world around them, the sages to whom most of our comments are attributed could have responded to an important reality of the world in which they lived, for the masters to whom the majority of the attributed *sugyot* are assigned flourished after the Bar Kokhba War, at a period when the gentile presence in Palestine was reaching a new significance.[17] The impression given by our texts is that the sages most concerned with the gentiles lived at a time when the gentiles' presence in Palestine was increasing and when their influence was growing. Thus, these documents seem to provide us with an appropriate way of approaching the gentile as an entity confronting the Israelite ethnic community in the first two centuries of the common era.

iii

This volume contains two sections: Chapters two through five deal with the literary features of our *sugyot*. Chapters six through twelve focus on the meaning of the passages. The first section takes up a variety of literary questions, such as the contexts in which the relevant passages appear, the functions of the references to the gentile within the chapters, tractates, and other contexts, the literary forms in which the pericopae are cast, and the sages to whom they are attributed. These four chapters seek to discover whether or not the structures and functions of the passage which discuss the gentile differ from the other pericopae in Mishnah-Tosefta. They examine whether or not the topic of the gentile engenders any unique literary forms or is limited to specific literary patterns. In addition, they attempt to ascertain if the gentile was discussed because the topic was important in its own right, or because dealing with the gentile served the larger agenda of the contexts in which they appeared. The second section organizes the passages which treat the gentile according to the relevant concepts of Israelite thought and culture, as expressed in Mishnah-Tosefta. This permits our understanding of how the figure of the gentile fits within the com-

----

[17]On this period the best two works remain Michael Avi-Yonah, *The Jews of Palestine: A Political History from the Bar Kokhba War to the Arab Conquest* (New York: 1976), and E. Mary Smallwood, *The Jews under Roman Rule: From Pompey to Diocletian* (Leiden: 1976).

plex of the basic symbols and concepts of rabbinic thought, as found in Mishnah-Tosefta. In these latter seven chapters, the discussions of the gentile are organized around the topics of the Land of Israel, Israelite sacred time, social interaction, the gentile as idolater, the Temple and its cult, and finally, Israelite purity rules. At this point the data on how the gentiles relate to these central ideas of rabbinic Judaism are used to expand our understanding of these images. The analyses make it clear that these were complex symbols with wide ranges of meanings and that a complete understanding of their significance can be gained only after one compares and contrasts the ways in which the gentiles were sup- pose to respond to them with the manners in which the Israelites confronted them. Based on the information amassed in chapters six through eleven, chapter twelve suggests that one way in which to understand the discussions of the gentile in Mishnah-Tosefta is to set them in the context of the creation and maintenance of the Israelites as an ethnic group. Chapter twelve further claims that it is possible to understand the descriptions of the gentiles in Mishnah- Tosefta in terms of any other ethnic group's treatment of the "other."

By categorizing the Israelites in Palestine during the third century of the common era as an ethnic group, I do not mean to negate the religious aspect of their culture; I merely wish to identify it as one aspect of Israel's ethnic identity. We shall see in the final chapter that religion and religious symbols and ideas can be important elements, and even the central elements, in the make up of an ethnic group. What I wish to suggest is only that the Israelites of Late Antiquity can be understood and studied in terms other than solely theological categories,[18] such as God's people, and that the theological/religious categories must be set into the broader context of ethnic identity. This will be explicated fully in the final chapter of this study. While the religious symbols and concepts such as YHWH, his Residence, his Revelation, and his People were the basic categories which informed Mishnah-Tosefta's discussions of many topics, in- cluding the gentile, this does not make Israelite culture or thought solely reli- gious, but rather places the Israelite people in the same category as other ethnic groups. The claims of "chosenness" implied in the discussions of the gentile, YHWH's Land, his Residence, and the like can be seen as typical expressions of ethnicity and not as *uniquely* Israelite attempts to establish their religious supe-

----

[18]For discussions of the ways in which "theological concerns" have dictated the scholar- ly agendas and conclusions with reference to Israel in Late Antiquity, see E.P. Sanders, *Paul and Palestinian Judaism: A Comparison of Patterns of Religion* (Philadelphia: 1977), 1-12. Jacob Neusner, *The Rabbinic Traditions About the Pharisees Before 70* (Leiden: 1971), III, 320-368.

riority. In brief, the conclusions of this work imply that the study of Israel in Late Antiquity should follow the procedures and methods employed for the investigation and understanding of any other people or culture.

Chapter Two:

Mishnaic and Toseftan Essays on the Gentiles

i

The content of a rabbinic passage, like the substance of any other written text, cannot be explicated independently of its contextual setting and its formal literary traits. This is especially true if, like in the case of Mishnah-Tosefta, the material in the document is consciously formulated in terms of a catalogue of a few literary forms which are divided into a number of contextual units of varying sizes.[1] Here, and in the following chapter, the issue of context will be analyzed through the comparison of the content of the passage under consideration with the thematic substance of the *sugyot* which surround it.[2] By examining the meaning of contiguous pericopae, it is possible to determine at least one of the passages' characteristics which induced the editor(s) to combine them into unified wholes. For example, mBerakhot can be divided into seven sections, the first six of which are tightly woven thematic units which in this instance happen to correspond to the standard chapter divisions. Upon inspection, we discover that the compiler(s) of this tractate were concerned mainly with three major topics: The *Shema'*, the *Amidah*, and the ritual aspects of the meal.[3] Therefore,

----

[1]On this see the following: Jacob Neusner, *A History of the Mishnaic Law of Purities* (Leiden: 1974-1977); *A History of the Mishnaic Law of Holy Things* (Leiden: 1979); *A History of the Mishnaic Law of Women* (Leiden: 1979-1980); *A History of the Mishnaic Law of Appointed Times* (Leiden: 1981-1983); *A History of the Mishnaic Law of Damages* (Leiden: 1983-1985); *Judaism: The Evidence of Mishnah* (Chicago: 1981); Martin Jaffe, *Mishnah's Theology of Tithing: A Study of Tractate Maaserot* (Chico: 1981); Peter Haas, *A History of the Mishnaic Law of Agriculture: Tractate Maaser Sheni* (Chico: 1980); Richard Sarason, *A History of the Mishnaic Law of Agriculture. Section Three: A Study of Tractate Demai* (Leiden: 1979); Alan Peck, *The Priestly Gift in Mishnah: A Study of Tractate Terumot* (Chico: 1981). Roger Brooks, *Support for the Poor in the Mishnaic Law of Agriculture: Tractate Peah* (Chico: 1983). Louis Newman, *The Sanctity of the Seventh Year: A Study of Mishnah Tractate Shebiit* (Chico: 1983).
[2]Matters of literary form will be covered in Chapter Four.
[3]Tzvee Zahavy, *The Mishnaic Law of Blessings and Prayers: Tractate Berakhot* (Atlanta: 1987), 7-10.

if the gentiles were a topic of concern to our authors, either in and of themselves or in relationship to other matters interspersed within the various tractates, we would expect to find contextual units within the tractates which point to this fact. The discussions in this and the next chapter will allow us to pursue this point, for we shall ask if the non-Israelite, or particular views of the gentile, provided an issue around which our authors organized their material.

The first significant fact we encounter is that with the exception of *Abodah Zarah*, neither Mishnah nor Tosefta contain a sustained discussion of the gentile. And even *Abodah Zarah* is not completely devoted to the topic of the gentile. Its subject-matter is varied, and portions of the tractate do not focus on the gentile.[4] The non-Israelites were not as major a concern of the authors of our texts as were the agricultural gifts, the holidays, the Israelite family, the court system and the laws of damages, the sacrificial system, and matters of purity. Nor were non-Israelites a topic of interest, such as the *pe'ah*, the *'erub*, the *ketubah*, or the like, which generated a tractate or even a chapter within a tractate outside of *Abodah Zarah*. This, however, should be expected, for Mishnah is a parochial text, devoted primarily to the *internal* concerns of a small group of Palestinian rabbis. Furthermore, it is evident that Mishnah's agenda was shaped as much by the Torah's contents as by the realities of the rabbis' Palestinian environment at the opening of our era,[5] and "the nations of the world" are of little concern to the writers of the Five Books of Moses.[6]

To summarize: Despite the social and political environment in which Mishnah-Tosefta took shape, the issue of the gentile and the ways in which the non-Israelite impinged upon the Israelites' world were not a *major* preoccupation of the authors of the earliest rabbinic texts. The larger setting in which Mishnah-Tosefta took shape was dominated by the non-Israelite, and the rabbis and the people for whom, and to whom, they spoke and over whom they

----

[4]For an outline of the tractate *Abodah Zarah* see Jacob Neusner, *A History of the Mishnaic Law of Damages Part Four, Shebuot, Eduyot, Abodah Zarah, Abot, Horayot. Translation and Explanation* (Leiden: 1985), 139-141. Neusner lists the major topics of the tractate as follows: Commercial relationships with gentiles (1:1-2:7); Idols (3:1-4:7); Libation-wine (4:8-5:12).

[5]Neusner, *Judaism*, 167-229.

[6]The dependence of our authors on the Torah will be seen throughout this study, especially in their choice of terminology. For example, when speaking of non-Israelite slaves, Mishnah-Tosefta talk of Canaanite slaves. Also, our texts discuss Amorites and Ammonites as if they were contemporaries with the rabbis, as well as ancient biblical peoples. Furthermore, the discussion of the *Asherah* which appears throughout Mishnah-Tosefta employs a biblical term and is based on biblical imagery.

exercised, or wished to exercise, authority had contact daily with gentiles. Non-Israelites held ultimate political power, their economic systems affected the Israelites as well as the non-Israelites of Palestine, and their views of the world, and even their modes of expression, appear throughout the early rabbinic documents.[7] This finds expression in the discussions of gentile courts, tax-collectors, and government officials which appear in our texts. Furthermore, we shall find references to wars with Rome, invading troops, and "threatening" soldiers. But these "realities" did not lead the writers of Mishnah-Tosefta to create a significant number of sustained essays on the topic of the gentile.

ii

In the present chapter, we shall examine the few small essays on the gentile which appear in Mishnah and Tosefta. The term "essay" refers to a grouping of two or more contiguous *sugyot*. Outside of *Abodah Zarah*,[8] we encounter only a few small groupings of pericopae which deal with the gentile, with more of these appearing in Tosefta than in Mishnah. MDem. 6:1-2, mTer. 8:11-12, mShab. 1:5-8, mPes. 2:2-3, mGit. 5:8-9, mBekh. 3:1-2, mOhol. 18:7-10, and mMakh. 2:5-9 are the only locations in Mishnah, outside of *Abodah Zarah*, where we discover a juxtaposition of two or more contiguous *sugyot* which discusses the gentile. Some of these essays focus on the gentile, while others center on internal Israelite concerns and refer to the gentile only as a means of making a point about Israelite ritual, law, or custom. MOhol. 18:7-10

---

[7]The literature which supports these claims is vast. See, for example, Saul Lieberman, *Hellenism in Jewish Palestine: Studies in the Literary Transmission Beliefs and Manners of Palestine in the I Century B.C.E.-IV Century C.E.* (New York: 1950); *Greek in Jewish Palestine: Studies in the Life and Manners of Jewish Palestine in the II-IV Centuries C.E.* (New York: 1942); Michael Avi-Yonah, *The Jews of Palestine: A Political History From the Bar Kokhba War to the Arab Conquest* (New York: 1976); E. Mary Smallwood, *The Jews Under Roman Rule: From Pompey to Diocletian* (Leiden: 1976); Martin Hengel, *Judaism and Hellenism: Studies in their Encounter in Palestine during the Early Hellenistic Period*, translated by John Bowden (Philadelphia: 1974); Shmuel Safrai and Menahem Stern (eds.), *The Jewish People in the First Century: Historical Geography, Political History, Cultural and Religious Life and Institutions* (Philadelphia: 1974-1987), 4 Vols.; Emil Schürer, *A History of the Jewish People in the Age of Jesus Christ (175 B.C.-A.D. 135), A New English Version*, revised and edited by Geza Vermes & Fergus Millar (Edinburgh: 1973-1987), 4 Vols.

[8]Because Neusner has dealt with the structure of *Abodah Zarah* in ways which lead to our concern with "essays," I have omitted this tractate from consideration in this and the following chapter.

and mTer. 8:11-12 are concerned with the gentile as a possible source of ritual defilement. MMakh. 2:5-9, mDem. 6:1-2, and mBekh. 3:1-2 deal with situations in which gentiles and Israelites live and work together, so that there is a possibility of ambiguity concerning matters of concern to the Israelite community. MShab. 1:7-9 center on the question of whether or not an Israelite can complete a task on the Sabbath which was begun before the Sabbath. The gentile appears to illustrate the point that the law concerns the Israelite even when he is not the main person engaged in the activity. MPes. 2:1-3 are generated by the prohibition of using leaven after Passover which remained in an Israelite's possession during the holiday, not by the subject of the gentile. The point of mGit. 5:8-9 is that Israelites should attempt to create a peaceful environment in which to live and that this should affect the way they deal with non-Israelites. Thus, we see that the essays on the gentile may have been generated by a perception of the gentile or by an internal Israelite issue which was more fully illustrated by attention to the non-Israelite. However, even though the references to the gentile function in different ways and have different meanings in the several essays, in all of them the appearance of the gentile serves as one of the elements which unites the disparate *sugyot* into larger units.

MOhol. 18:7-10 form an extended discussion of the dwelling-places of the gentiles[9] within the Land of Israel and the likelihood that they are sources of corpse-uncleanness. The *assumption* of the essay is that gentiles might bury their aborted fetuses on their property, so that the area would be considered a grave-area from which an Israelite who enters its confines would become unclean.[10] Chapter Eighteen of mOholot contains two themes: The discussions of

----

[9]Mdwr[wt] hgwym.

[10]MOhol. 18:7 states that the dwelling is unclean and that after a gentile has lived there for forty days, it must be examined, unless an Israelite woman or a slave watched over the gentile. MOhol. 18:8 deals with the places which should be examined: deep drains and foul water (anonymous), dunghills, and loose earth; however, places where a pig or a weasel can penetrate do not need to be examined (Hillelites). MOhol. 18:9 notes that the rules do not apply to colonnades, and Simeon b. Gamliel adds that they do not apply to a gentile city which lies in ruins. MOhol. 18:10 contains an anonymous list of places with which an Israelite need not be concerned with regard to the issue of uncleanness: Arab tents, field-huts, simple tents, fruit-shelters, summer-houses, gate-houses, open space in courtyards, bath-houses, armories, the legion's camp-grounds. Although Mishnah does not specify why gentiles' dwellings are considered to be unclean, the context of mOholot suggests that it relates to the presence of corpses. The reference to forty days in mOhol. 18:7 draws attention to the least amount of time an embryo was believed to be formed in the womb, mNid. 3:7. Thus, it is generally claimed that the gentiles' dwellings were unclean because they disposed of abortions within their drains or similar areas, Bartinoro, *loc. cit.*; Yom Tov, *loc. cit.*; Herbert Danby, *The Mishnah: Translated from the Hebrew with Introduction and Brief Explanatory Notes* (London: reprint 1964), 675, n. 10; Hanokh Albeck, *The Six Orders of the Mishnah: Order Qodashim* (Tel Aviv: reprint 1957), 185; Jacob Neusner, *A History of the Mishnaic Law of Purities Part Four Ohalot. Commentary* (Leiden: 1974), 341. This would

1) the grave areas, begun in the previous section and continued in mOhol. 18:1-6, and 2) the gentiles' residences. A brief aside concerning the liability for tithes, the applicability of the laws of the seventh year, and the cleanness of one who buys a field in Syria opens mOhol. 18:7[11] and serves to link the discussion of the grave-area to the gentiles' dwellings.[12] The issue under consideration is derived from the assumed practices of the gentile and reflects on their character. It is the gentile *qua* gentile which produces this essay, for "obviously" Israelites would not dispose of their aborted fetuses in unmarked graves on their property.

The gentile as a possible source of ritual defilement underlies mTer. 8:11-12; however, at least one of these texts further implies that gentiles could pose a physical threat to Israelites. MTer. 8:11 deals with the possible defilement of heave-offering,[13] while mTer. 8:12 pictures the gentiles as threatening to rape Israelite women.[14] On one level, these cases are different, for one deals with the defilement of heave-offering, while the other treats the defilement of women. On another level, they share a common picture of the non-Israelite. This is illustrated by attention to the literary forms in which the pericopae are cast and the relationship of their context to that of the *sugyot* which surround them. While mTer. 8:11 continues the discussion of things which defile heave-offering, which precedes it,[15] mTer. 8:12 correlates with only mTer. 8:11

----

explain why certain areas are examined and others are not. The texts seem to assume that the gentiles are unconcerned with the Israelite laws of corpse-uncleanness; therefore, the former dispose of their abortions near, or in, their dwellings.

[11]TAhil. 17:7-18:5 expands on the discussion of the Land of the gentiles.

[12]Neusner, *Ohalot*, 328-329.

[13]MTer. 8:11 contains the following dispute: If a man were carrying loaves of heave-offering, and a gentile threatened to defile all of the loaves if the Israelite did not hand over one of them for him to defile, Eliezer says that the Israelite should not hand over one loaf, while Joshua says that he should leave one on a near-by stone. From the point of view of the legal issues involved, Eliezer holds that "the householder may not bear responsibility for the gentile's making unclean a loaf of bread in the status of heave-offering. Should the gentile make all of the loaves unclean, it is not the householder's fault." Joshua holds that "since the loaves are sure to be made unclean, the householder is no longer responsible for them. He may place a loaf on a rock, where assuredly the gentile will make it unclean;" Peck, 245. Cf., William S. Green, *The Traditions of Joshua Ben Hananiah, Part One: The Early Legal Traditions* (Leiden: 1981), 62-63; Jacob Neusner, *Eliezer ben Hyrcanus: The Tradition and the Man* (Leiden: 1973), I, 63-66.

[14]MTer. 8:12 deals with gentiles who threaten to defile an Israelite women: If the gentiles state that if the Israelites do not deliver one woman to them they will defile all of the women present, the one woman may not be delivered.

[15]MTer. 8:8-11 discuss the houseowner's obligation to protect heave-offering in a state of cleanness, and the specific issue under consideration is at what point may the householder believe that he has fulfilled his obligation, so that he no longer needs to concern himself with the purity of the produce he intends to give to the priest. Peck further argues that the underlying issue of mTer. 8:8-12 is the same as the issue behind mTer. 8:1-3. Both sections discuss "the circumstances under which an individual is or is not blameworthy for performing actions which normally are forbidden;" Peck, 243.

through their shared perception of *the gentile* as a source of defilement. The gentile's admonition that he will defile[16] something in the Israelite's possession is perceived by the editor as the unifying factor behind these two *sugyot* which is indicated by the fact that mTer. 8:12 opens with wkn.[17] That the common perception of the gentile unites these pericopae is further illustrated by the fact that mTer. 8:11 and mTer. 8:12 are stylistically dissimilar. The former is part of the Eliezer-Joshua dispute pattern, while the latter is not.[18] Like in the case of mOhol. 18:7-10, here too the unifying theme of this essay reflects an assumption about the gentile *qua* gentile, for Israelites are not sources of ritual defilement merely because they are Israelites.

MMakh. 2:5-9, mDem. 6:1-2, and mBekh. 3:1-2 assume that gentiles and Israelites live and work together, creating possible ambiguous situations from the point of view of Israelite law. MMakh. 2:5-9 focus on items found in a city with a mixed citizenry of Israelites and gentiles.[19] This section argues that in towns with a diverse population, one makes determinations concerning doubtful matters based on the status of the majority of the people who live there.[20]

----

[16]The gentile is seen as a source of levitical uncleanness with regard to the heave-offering; however, any number of things can make heave-offering unclean, mTer. 8:8-10, so that the gentile, *qua* gentile, is not a *unique* source of uncleanness, but only *one of many* possible sources.

[17]Jacob N. Epstein, *Introduction to the Text of the Mishnah*, Second edition (Tel Aviv: 1964), II, 1049.

[18]The opinion in mTer. 8:12 agrees with that attributed to Eliezer in the previous discussions, for the anonymous opinion holds that the Israelite women may not take responsibility for the rape of one of them; Peck, 245.

[19]MMakh. 2:5 opens with 'yr šyśr'l wnkrym drym bh, "a city in which Israelites and gentiles dwell." MMakh. 2:6-8 build on this, and begin with mṣ' bh . . ., 'm rb gwym . . . . "[if] one found in it . . ., if the majority are gentiles . . . ." The form is broken in mMakh. 2:9; however, many still argue that the issue is whether or not the meat which was found belongs to Israelites or gentiles; Hanokh Albeck, *The Six Orders of the Mishnah: Order Tohorot* (Tel Aviv: reprint 1957), 420; Danby, 760; Bartinoro, *loc. cit.* MMakh. 2:10 opens with hmws' prwt bdrk 'm rb mknysyn lbtyhn, "[if] one found produce on the road, if the majority stored [the produce] in their homes." However, the opening issue does not seem to deal with gentiles and Israelites. MMakh. 2:10 does move to our topic with 'wsr šyśr'l wgwym mṭylyn ltwkw, "[If] there was a storehouse into which Israelites and gentiles cast [their produce]." MMakh. 2:11 returns to the topic of prwt, produce, but it does not deal with gentiles.

[20]The individual *sugyot* deal with the three possibilities: An Israelite majority, a gentile majority, an evenly divided population. MMakh. 2:5-6 center around the problem of benefiting from work done on the Sabbath in a town with a population of both Israelites and gentiles. MMakh. 2:5 rules that if gentiles and Israelites dwell in the same city and there is a bath-house which was open and heated for bathing on the Sabbath, the Israelite could bathe immediately after the Sabbath, if the majority of the people in the city were gentiles. However, if the majority were Israelites or if there were an equal number of Israelites and gentiles, the Israelite had to wait enough time for the water to have been heated after the close of the Sabbath. MMakh. 2:6 states that an Israelite may purchase vegetables gathered during the Sabbath but sold at the end of the Sabbath in a city in which the majority of the population were gentiles. If the majority of the population were Israelites or if there

MDem. 6:1-2 form a unit[21] which discusses "whether a man who works some-one else's field and shares the produce with him must tithe that portion of the produce which he gives to the owner."[22] The assumption that Israelites and non-Israelites may work in each other's fields generates this section.[23] The

----

were the same number of Israelites and non-Israelites in the city, the Israelite customer must wait enough time for vegetables to arrive which were picked after the Sabbath. MMakh. 2:7 deals with finding an abandoned child. The child's status follows the status of the majority of the population. However, if the population is evenly divided, the child is assumed to be an Israelite. Judah rules that the child follows the status of those more likely to have abandoned a child. MMakh. 2:8 speaks of lost property. The Israelite needs to proclaim that he has found an object only if the majority of the population are Israelites or if the population of the city is evenly divided between Israelites and gentiles. MMakh. 2:9, even though it is stylistically different from what precedes it, probably follows the same principle: One determines who owns the meat on the basis of the majority of people who possess the particular type of meat. MMakh. 2:10, which also does not follow the style of mMakh. 2:5-8, speaks of a storehouse into which Israelites and gentiles place their produce. The form of this section is a "words-of"-dispute—which is not a common form in Mishnah—Gary G. Porton, *The Traditions of Rabbi Ishmael Part Four: The Materials as a Whole* (Leiden: 1982), 34-39—between Meir and Sages. Meir holds that the produce is considered *demai*-produce if the majority were Israelites or if the people who deposited grain in the storehouse were equally divided between Israelites and gentiles; if the majority were gentiles, the produce is considered un-tithed. Sages state that if only one Israelite used the storehouse, all of the grain is considered *demai*-produce.

[21]MDem. 6:1 opens hmqbl śdh myśr'l mn hnkry wmn hkwty, "One who sharecrops a field for an Israelite, for a gentile, or for a Samaritan." The second unit of mDem. 6:1 opens with hhwkr śdh myśr'l twrm wnwtn lw, "One who leases a field from an Israelite separates heave-offering and [then] gives [the rental price] to him," and this is paralleled stylistically by hhwkr śdh mn hnkry m'śr wnwtn lw, "one who leases a field from a gentile tithes and [then] gives [the rental price] to him," at the beginning of mDem. 6:2. Judah responds to both phrases which open with hhwkr; however, in mDem. 6:1 we read 'mr rby yhwdh, "said R. Judah," while in mDem. 6:2 we find rby yhwdh 'wmr, "R. Judah says." In mDem. 6:1, Judah deals with the tenant farmer, while in mDem. 6:2, he mentions the sharecropper, not the one who leases a field.

[22]MDem. 6:3-5 "deals with the disposition of heave-offering and first tithe between land-lord and sharecropper when one is a priest or Levite and the other is an Israelite." MDem. 6:7-10 "has to do with the division of produce or property jointly owned by two men of different status. However, all three units [MDem. 6:1-2, mDem. 6:3-5, mDem. 6:7-10] deal with the problem of ti-thing produce from jointly owned produce or property;" Sarason, 202-203.

[23]MDem. 6:1 deals with the sharecropper, hmqbl. Because a field which one works as a sharecropper remains the possession of the landowner and the sharecropper works for a certain percentage of the total yield, the sharecropper does not tithe the produce which he gives to the landowner, no matter whether the landowner is an Israelite, a Samaritan, or a gentile; Sarason, 205. MDem. 6:2 raises the issue of the tenant farmer, hhwkr. The tenant farmer pays the landowner a fixed amount of produce regardless of the success or failure of that year's harvest; therefore, because he takes all the risk, he is considered to be the landowner during the period he leased the field. Al-though he does not have to tithe the produce, he uses it to pay for the rental. He has to separate heave-offering from it, because the heave-offering is taken at the threshing floor from all of the grain before the grain would have been delivered to the property's actual owner; Sarason, 205. According to this text, the tithe is taken before the payment is made to the gentile as if all of the produce, in-cluding that paid in rent, belonged to the Israelite. If the Israelite had leased the field from another Israelite, mDem. 6:1, the one who leased the field would not have been required to separate the tithe

gentile--the Samaritan and the Israelite appear with the gentile in only mDem. 6:1--is mentioned in both mDem. 6:1 and mDem. 6:2 because the two texts deal with different types of contracts which allow one to work another's field, and the status of the field's owner--whether he is an Israelite or a gentile--is central to the discussion. MBekh. 3:1-2 offer the instance in which an Israelite purchased an animal from a gentile and did not know whether or not the animal had given birth while it was in the latter's possession. In order to be certain that he does not violate the laws concerning the first-born of an animal, the Israelite must develop the means of determining whether or not the animal he has purchased from the gentile had given birth before he took possession of it.[24] Gentiles are mentioned because it is assumed that Israelites purchased animals from them and that the former were not concerned with the Israelite law of the firstling. Therefore, they could not be relied upon to tell the Israelite whether or not the animal had already produced an offspring. The animal's status is "a matter of doubt," and this unit comes at the end of a section, beginning in mBekh. 2:9, which deals with other "matters of doubt."[25] These texts presuppose that Israelites constantly come into contact with gentiles and that this may produce situations in which the Israelites must make special efforts to ensure that they do not violate accepted Israelite practice. The passages focus on the gentile as non-Israelite; but, this becomes important only in terms of the Israelites' observing their own ethnic traditions. The issues which generated these essays were matters of internal concern to Israelites; the appearance of the gentile serves only to further the pericopae's discussions of these internal concerns.

---

before he made the payment. Sarason argues that in the case of the one who leases the field, the Mishnah distinguishes between the gentile and the Israelite landowner, for the text assumes that gentiles cannot own property in the Land of Israel; Sarason, 206. See also, Daniel Sperber, *Roman Palestine: 200-400, The Land* (Ramat-Gan: 1978), 160-176. Judah's ruling underscores this point, for if an Israelite leased from a gentile a field which originally belonged to an Israelite, the tithe is taken from the grain as if the field had always belonged to an Israelite; Sarason, 205-206.

[24]In mBekh. 3:1, Ishmael states that one may determine this by discovering the age of the animal, while Aqiba moves the discussion in a totally different direction; Gary G. Porton, *The Traditions of Rabbi Ishmael Part One: The Non-Exegetical Materials* (Leiden: 1976), 173-174. In mBekh. 3:2, Simeon b. Gamliel states that if an animal purchased from a gentile is nursing another animal, the Israelite can assume that a mother is caring for her own young.

[25]MBekh. 3:3-4 prohibit the shearing of a firstling, a totally separate issue. Jacob Neusner, *A History of the Mishnaic Law of Holy Things Part Three Hullin, Bekhorot. Translation and Explanation* (Leiden: 1979), 139-140.

Although the topic of the gentile unites mShab. 1:7-9 into a unit, the theme of this section is whether or not on the Sabbath one may complete work which was begun Friday afternoon or before. The appearance of the gentile indicates that if the gentile worker is aided by an Israelite or works for him, the former falls under the rabbinic Sabbath-rules. Although these texts also assume that gentiles and Israelites work and live in close proximity, the issue is the Sabbath, not the nearness of the gentile.[26] Similarly, the issue of mPes. 2:1-3 is the leaven which the gentile possesses, and not the fact that gentiles and Israelites interact.[27] In neither case does the interaction of the gentile and Israelite produce ambiguous situations; rather, the appearance of the gentile serves to underscore the uniqueness of the Israelite in terms of the latter's traditions.

Although mGit. 5:8-9 primarily deal with different classes of Israelites and the necessity of keeping peace among them, gentiles are mentioned at the end of both *sugyot*. MGit. 5:8 states that Israelites should not try to prevent the poor among the gentiles from collecting the gleanings, *leqet*, the forgotten sheaves, or the grain from the corners, *pe'ah*, and mGit. 5:9 teaches that gentiles may be supported in their work during the Sabbatical year and that they should be greeted when met. All of this is done in the interest of peace. The texts assume that gentiles and Israelites interact at various levels, and the passages' goal is to create a peaceful society. In this context, the gentile is seen as just one of the classes of society which inhabits the Land of Israel.

----

[26]MShab. 1:5-8 contain a number of Houses-disputes. MShab. 1:4 states that when the sages were "in the upper room of Hananiah b. Hezekiah b. Gorion, the House of Shammai outnumbered the House of Hillel, and they decreed eighteen things on that day." For a discussion of the problem of the relationship of mShab. 1:4 to the Houses-disputes which follow, see Jacob Neusner, *The Rabbinic Traditions about the Pharisees before 70: Part II, The Houses* (Leiden: 1973), 122-125. Jacob Neusner, *A History of the Mishnaic Law of Appointed Times Part One Shabbat. Translation and Explanation* (Leiden: 1981), 28. In mShab. 1:7, the Shammaites rule that one may not sell anything to a gentile, help him load his beast, or help him put a load on his shoulder unless he can reach "a near-by place" before the Sabbath begins. The Hillelites permit such actions. In mShab. 1:8, the Shammaites rule the an Israelite cannot give hides to a gentile tanner or clothes to a gentile launderer unless the work can be completed before the Sabbath begins. Again, the Hillelites permit such actions. In mShab. 1:9, Simeon b. Gamliel states that in his father's house clothes were given to a gentile launderer only "three days before the Sabbath." According to the Shammaites, an Israelite should not be responsible for anyone's violating the Sabbath, Israelite or non-Israelite. The Hillelites believed that the sanctity of the Sabbath was not in question.

[27]MPes. 2:1 states that an Israelite may sell his leaven to a gentile. MPes. 2:2 allows an Israelite to derive benefit after Passover from leaven which a gentile possessed during Passover, and mPes. 2:3 argues that an Israelite may derive benefit after Passover from leaven which he handed over to a gentile as security for a loan.

iii

Tosefta contains more essays than does Mishnah. TDem. 1:12-14 form a self-contained unit[28] which discusses a storehouse in which Israelites and non-Israelites have stored grain.[29] The gentiles are important because they are non-Israelites who may cause some ambiguity when their actions impinge on those of Israelites. TDem. 1:15-23 "form. . . [a] unit, relating to the issue and cases of mDem. 1:3(A)" which deals with "grain which is not used for food but for seed or fodder. T[osefta], however, introduces an additional variable--the gentile."[30] Thus, Tosefta's texts are only loosely related to Mishnah, and they may have been placed at this point in Tosefta because, like those which precede and follow, their topic is the gentile. This large complex may be divided into smaller units which also focus on the gentile,[31] so that we have here an ex

----

[28]Sarason, 48.

[29]TDem. 1:12 discusses a storehouse into which Israelites and gentiles have placed their produce and how one determines whether or not the produce is considered tithed produce. Meir holds that one goes by the majority of the produce. If the produce is evenly divided, all of it is considered *demai*. Sages hold that all of it is *demai* even if just *one* Israelite put his produce into a storehouse into which gentiles had placed their produce. Sarason notes that tDem. 1:12 appears in mMakh 2:10 "where it is part of a larger construction employing the protasis-pattern *If the majority are X; if the majority are Y; half and half.*" Sarason argues that the unit belongs in tDemai because it builds on Meir's principle found in tDem. 1:9 and because tDem. 1:13 deals with Samaritan produce which was mentioned in tDem. 1:11; Sarason, 48. In tDem. 1:13, Yosi and Judah differ over the nature of the storehouse discussed in tDem. 1:12. Yosi holds it is a private storehouse, while Judah claims it is a royal storehouse. In tDem. 1:14, Joshua b. Qebusai exegetes Num. 19:19--*the clean person shall sprinkle it upon the unclean person*--and states that this means that "one clean person sprinkles even on a hundred unclean persons." Sarason argues that this "is formally similar" to the case of one Israelite's rendering all of the produce in the storehouse *demai*; Sarason, 50-51.

[30]Sarason, 51.

[31]TDem. 1:17 deals with a sown field which has been purchased from a gentile, and tDem. 1:18 states that they do not cooperate with a gentile in sowing untithed produce; Sarason, 51. The gentile is discussed in tDem. 1:15-18 and tDem. 1:20-23. TDem. 1:15 treats produce which one bought for eating, but which he decides to sell, and tDem. 1:16 speaks of produce which one inherited or received as a gift. In both cases, one cannot sell the produce to a gentile unless it has been tithed. As Sarason notes, tDem. 1:15 and tDem. 1:16 "are a well-constructed formal unit. Only the protases differ. . . . The repeated apodosis . . . makes use of a triplet pattern" in which the gentile is included; Sarason, 51. Both tDem. 1:15 and tDem. 1:16 end with l' ymrkm lgwy wl' y'kylm lbhmt 'hrym wl' lbhmt ṣmw 'l' 'm kn 'yśr, "he should not sell it to a gentile, or feed it to other people's livestock, nor to his own livestock, unless he tithed [it]." Sarason holds that tDem. 1:17-18 relate to mDem. 1:3's discussion of seed that has been purchased; Sarason, 52. While tDem. 1:19-21 "form a section on the feeding of cattle (M [Dem]. 1:3A 1)," the gentile appears only in tDem. 1:20-21. One does not tether his animal next to a gentile's animal or give his animal to a gentile to feed because in both cases, the Israelite's animal is likely to eat untithed grain; Sarason, 54. TDem. 1:22-23 form a unit and "ask whether untithed Israelite oil may be used to benefit gentiles or gentile oil used to

tensive collection of passages which discusses the gentile and which is formed from several independent units from the points of view of topic and form. In tDem. 1:15-1:16, the gentile represents the "rest of humanity," that part not included under the title of Israelite.[32] TDem. 1:17-18 deal with the gentile as a possible source of ambiguity concerning the Israelite laws of planting a field with tithed seeds, a practice not followed by non-Israelites. TDem. 1:19-20 again picture the gentiles as non-Israelites; therefore, they feed their animals untithed grain, and the problematic for the passages concerns the permissibility of the gentile's feeding untithed grain to an Israelite's livestock. TDem. 1:22-23 are concerned with an Israelite's use of untithed gentile oil. In general, these passages in the first chapter of tDemai emphasize the point that the gentile is not an Israelite; however, the texts may be divided into those which assume that the contact between Israelites and gentiles may cause some problems from the point of view of Israelite law and those which merely indicate that humanity can be divided into two large groups--Israelites and non-Israelites. In either case, the references to the gentile were not occasioned by Mishnah, but were created by the editor(s) of this section of Tosefta.

TDem. 4:25-27 are related to mDem. 3:4, which appears to have generated the discussion of the gentile in Tosefta. This is yet another section which assumes that Israelites and gentiles interact with regard to grain and produce.[33] TDem. 4:25 forms a unit with tDem. 4:22-4:24. The gentile appears in only tDem. 4:25; however, the reference is occasioned by mDem. 3:4, which Tosefta explains. The point is that gentiles are not Israelites, so that if their grain is mixed with Israelite grain the mixture is considered *demai*. TDem. 4:26-27 speak of an *am-haares*, a Samaritan, and a gentile as the three segments of Palestinian society which may pose a problem with regard to tithed produce. In

----

benefit Israelites;" Sarason, 54. Both TDem. 1:22 and tDem. 1:23 open with gwy š . . . , "a gentile who . . .".

[32]If an Israelite purchases produce for eating, inherits produce, or receives some as a gift, he may not sell it to anyone, including a gentile, until he has separated the tithe.

[33]TDem. 4:25 opens by quoting mDem. 3:4 and adds an anonymous gloss and one attributed to Simeon b. Gamliel and Simeon. If one leaves his produce with a gentile, the anonymous rule states that he worries about the tithes and the seventh-year produce, while the Simeons rule that the gentile's produce is considered *demai*. TDem. 4:26 discusses one who sends his produce with a gentile agent and rules that in this case, one must again worry about tithes and the seventh-year produce, unless the gentile is taking the grain from the threshing floor. TDem. 4:27 rules that if one mills his grain at a gentile's mill, he must be concerned about uncleanness. As Sarason notes, tDem. 4:26-27 "form a small subunit which applies the principle of M[Dem]. 3:4 to additional cases;" Sarason, 144.

these two texts, the Samaritan and the *am-haares* are juxtaposed to the gentile. The former two groups can be trusted with regard to an Israelite's tithed produce, while the gentiles cannot. Here, the gentile *qua* gentile is not trusted.

TDem. 6:12 quotes mDem. 6:10, and tDem. 6:13-14 build on the discussion of the gentile and the proselyte who divided the property they inherited from their father.[34] Again, the point is that Israelites and non-Israelites interact on several levels and in various situations. The problems which these *sugyot* discuss are occasioned by the ambiguous situations created by the fact that gentiles and Israelites can jointly own, or inherit, property.

Israelites and non-Israelites interacted in Syria, and this is the topic of tTer. 2:10-11. The *sugyot* assume that gentiles and Israelites purchase land together or engage in business transactions concerning property. This interaction raises certain ambiguous situations concerning the Israelite laws dealing with agricultural gifts.[35]

TMo'ed 2:14-15 are based on the fact that Israelites and gentiles normally do business together, for the point of the unit is to create a situation in which it is clear that the Israelite is not doing business with a gentile on the Sabbath. The gentile is a non-Israelite; therefore, he does not observe the Israelite holidays.[36]

----

[34]TDem. 6:13 opens with an account of what Onqelos the convert and his brothers did with their father's estate and then moves onto a discussion of the gentile and proselyte who inherited a bath-house. The text then discusses the gentile and Israelite who jointly purchase a house or a bath-house. TDem. 6:14 deals with a city in which there are Israelites and gentiles, Israelite guards and gentile guards, guardians of fully tithed produce, and guardians of untithed produce. The issue is how the guards may divide the produce. TDem. 6:12-14 form a subunit of tDem. 6:8-14 which build on mDem. 6:10. The discussion focuses on property jointly owned by men of different status. The whole unit is a well developed essay which was occasioned by Mishnah.

[35]TTer. 2:9-11 investigate a field purchased in Syria and build on mTer. 1:5's statements concerning produce from outside the Land of Israel. TTer. 2:10 opens by stating that the land an Israelite purchases in Syria is like land purchased in the suburbs of Jerusalem, with regard to tithes and heave-offering, and ends with a dispute between Rabbi and Simeon b. Gamliel concerning the tithes and heave-offering from a field which an Israelite and a gentile jointly purchase in Syria. TTer. 2:11 is concerned with a field which an Israelite purchased in Syria and then sold to a gentile and a gentile who mortgaged his land to an Israelite. The two are related because the point of tTer. 2:11 is that the heave-offering is taken from only crops grown in Syria on land which an Israelite actually owns. Thus tTer. 2:10-11 form a unit. See Peck, 56-57. Both tTer. 2:10 and tTer. 2:11 open with yśr'l śqnh śdh bswry', "[If] an Israelite purchases a field in Syria."

[36]The unit states that since the time of Aqiba, it is permitted for Israelites to take seats by the chairs of gentiles at which they do business on the Sabbath. The rule is illustrated by a story, introduced by m'śh b, in which Gamliel takes a seat by the chair of a gentile in Akko. "They" disapprove, and Gamliel leaves his seat, rather than argue with those present. These passages are unrelated to their context, for they discuss the Sabbath and gentiles, issues which do not appear in those texts which surround them. The major topic of tMo'ed 2:12-13 is doing business on a festival. See Shamai Kanter, *Rabban Gamaliel II: The Legal Traditions* (Chico: 1980), 119-120.

TB.M. 5:14-21 form an extended essay which regulates loan-transactions between Israelites and gentiles. This unit is occasioned by mB.M. 5:6 which states that Israelites may accept a flock from gentiles on "iron terms,"[37] may borrow from them on interest, may lend to them on interest, and may lend one gentile's money to another gentile without the former's knowledge. The Israelites and the gentiles represent two different groups, and their differences are marked out and maintained by the different rules regulating business transactions among Israelites and between Israelites and gentiles.[38]

THul. 1:2-3 assume that Israelites and non-Israelites will be active in contexts which allow them to exchange meat which is being slaughtered. The issue is that this interaction may create ambiguous situations concerning Israelite rules of slaughtering and the Israelites' use of the slaughtered meat.[39]

TBekh. 2:11-13 and tBekh. 2:14-16 quote and build upon mBekh. 3:1

----

[37]Danby defines "iron terms" as "a species of contract in which A sells his flock to B on condition that B shares the profits with A until such time as he has made payment in full, B being solely responsible for all losses sustained;" Danby, 796.

[38]TB.M. 5:14 builds on the reference to "iron terms" and states that a field may be borrowed on "iron terms" even from an Israelite. TB.M. 5:15 claims that a gentile, but not an Israelite, may borrow a *sheqel* and lend out a *sela*. There are two *sheqels* to one *sela*; Danby, 798. TB.M. 5:16 prohibits an Israelite from offering to take the money one Israelite owes to a gentile in order to pay the gentile. TB.M. 5:17 discusses the same case as TB.M. 5:16 but reverses the roles, so that it deals with a gentile who has borrowed from an Israelite. TB.M. 5:18 prohibits an Israelite from paying a gentile a salary and then telling him to lend out the money on interest, but permits a gentile to pay an Israelite and to tell him to lend the money on interest. TB.M. 5:19 discusses an Israelite's money which was left as a bailment with a gentile and a gentile's money left as bailment with an Israelite in terms of whether or not the money can be lent with interest. TB.M. 5:20 speaks about an Israelite who was a guardian for a gentile's estate, a gentile who was a guardian for an Israelite's estate, and the fact that an Israelite may serve as guarantor of a gentile's loan. TB.M. 5:21 deals with loans between an Israelite and a gentile who converted to Judaism.

[39]THul. 1:2 notes that if a gentile finished an act of slaughtering begun by an Israelite, the slaughter is invalid. If an Israelite finished slaughtering something which a gentile began to slaughter, the act is also invalid. Furthermore, if a gentile slaughtered something which does not render the meat *terefah* and an Israelite completes the act of slaughtering, the meat may be used for food. See the comments of Saul Lieberman, *Tosefeth Rishonim: A Commentary based on Manuscripts of the Tosefta and Works of the Rishonim and Midrashim in Manuscripts and rare Editions* (Jerusalem: 1938), II, 219 and Jacob Neusner, *A History of the Mishnaic Law of Holy Things Part Three Hullin, Bekhorot, Translation and Explanation* (Leiden: 1979), 16. THul. 1:3 claims that if the gentile and the Israelite both held the knife, the act of slaughtering is valid. MHul. 1:1 rules that if a gentile slaughters something, it is classified as carrion, and the meat imparts uncleanness through carrying. While the issue of who completes the slaughtering is Tosefta's issue, the reference to the gentile derives from Mishnah.

and mBekh. 3:2, respectively.[40] Although Tosefta's unit is occasioned by Mishnah, it has expanded Mishnah's concerns and created its own essay on the topic of the firstling. Again, the possible interaction between Israelites and gentiles creates ambiguous situations concerning the Israelite laws of the firstling. The texts attempt to set forth guide-lines which overcome this ambiguity.

TGit. 3:13-14, occasioned by mGit. 5:8-9, create a unit which focuses on the need for Israelites and gentiles to live together in peace. The essay assumes the close proximity of the two groups within Palestinian society; however, its focus is on the way in which the Israelites should concern themselves with the welfare of the gentiles.[41]

The Land of Israel is one of the major concepts around which the mishnaic definition of the People Israel is designed, and, as we shall see below, the problem of how the gentile reacts to this symbol becomes important to our writers.[42] TPe. 2:9-11 investigate the claims of the Israelite poor to produce left after harvesting fields with which gentiles had dealings. TPe. 2:9-10 follow the principles of mPe. 4:6[43] which state that the requirement of *pe'ah* depends on who owns the field at the time of harvest and that only Israelites are required to separate *pe'ah*.[44] Although based on a different principle and related to a dif-

----

[40]TBekh. 2:11-13 offer a somewhat different text from mBekh. 3:1, concerning how one determines whether or not the animal he has purchased from a gentile already has given birth; see Porton, *Ishmael*, I, 172-176. TBekh. 2:14-16 cite mBekh. 3:2, concerning the purchase of a nursing animal from a gentile. However, Tosefta suggests that there is doubt whether or not the animal is nursing its own offspring, while Simeon b. Gamliel claims that the Israelite need not worry about this, mBekh. 3:2. TBekh. 2:16 discusses a case related to, but unmentioned in, Mishnah. If a person gives his beast to a gentile to pasture and he found males nursing from an old beast and females nursing from those who had not previously given birth, he does not worry that the gentile brought the offsprings of one animal to another animal. The issue is the same in all the texts--how does one determine if an animal in the possession of a gentile has previously given birth?

[41]TGit. 3:13 states that for the sake of peace, collectors of funds for the poor collect equally from Israelites and gentiles and distribute the funds equally among the poor of the Israelites and the gentiles. TGit. 3:14 adds that Israelites lament and bury gentiles and that they express condolences to gentile mourners, all for the sake of peace. The theme of the section is living in a situation of public peace and order.

[42]See Chapter Six.

[43]Brooks, 78-79. It is likely that mPe. 4:6 provided the occasion for the discussion of the gentile in tPe. 2:9-10. MPe. 4:6 discusses hlqt, the gleaning, hskhh, the forgotten sheaf, and hp'h, the corner, items which appear in tPe. 2:10-11.

[44]TPe. 2:9 examines the sale, between an Israelite and a gentile, of a field of standing corn. The text reviews the three possible cases: 1) A gentile sells a field to an Israelite; 2) an Israelite sells a field to a gentile; 3) a gentile and an Israelite both own the field. TPe. 2:10 discusses the case of a gentile--Erfurt reads "convert"--Saul Lieberman, *Tosefta Ki-fshutah: Order Zera'im, Part One* (New York: 1955), 150-151--who has died and whose property Israelites distribute, and it is based on the same assumptions as tPe. 2:9: If the Israelites took possession of the standing crop, it is exempt from the gleanings, forgotten sheaves, and *pe'ah*, but the tithes must be separated from it. If the unharvested produce is still attached to the ground when the Israelite takes

ferent mishnah,[45] tPe. 2:11[46] was joined to tPe. 2:9-10 because of their common reference to the gentile's connection to the poor person's gifts.[47] The issue which generates this essay is whether or not the gentile is responsible for specific agricultural gifts, all of which in the Torah are related to YHWH's possession of the Land of Israel.

TDem. 6:1-4, 7 expand upon mDem. 6:1-2.[48] However, the major issue is whether or not gentiles must respond to the holy nature of the Land of Is-

----

possession of the field, he is responsible for the gifts to the poor. If the produce is detached from the ground when he takes possession, the Israelite is not responsible for giving the agricultural gifts to the poor.

[45]TPe. 2:11 seems to relate to mPe. 4:9. Brooks notes that tPe. 2:11 "qualifies" the following statement in mPe. 4:9: "Gleanings, forgotten sheaves, and *pe'ah* belonging to a gentile are subject to [the separation of] tithes unless [the gentile] has declared them ownerless property;" Brooks, 82.

[46]TPe. 2:11 states that a gentile's *leqet*, forgotten sheaf, and *pe'ah* are liable for tithes only when the gentile protests if someone other than the poor takes the produce. If the gentile does not protest another's seizing the produce, what the gentile declares ownerless is considered ownerless, so that the crop is not subject to tithes.

[47]TPe. 2:9-10 open with gwy š . . ., "gentile who." *Pe'ah* is the only gift mentioned in tPe. 2:9. TPe. 2:10 ends with a reference to ḥlqt, hškḥh, p'h, and m'śrwt, and these are mentioned in the same order in tPe. 2:11. This section fits into a larger discussion of agricultural gifts for the poor. The phrase p'h l'nyyn, "designation as pe'ah," predominates in the passages surrounding our set; however, it does not appear in our three pericopae. Also, the discussion of *leqet*, forgotten sheaves, and tithes, which appears in tPe. 2:10-11, does not appear in the surrounding context.

[48]Sarason states: "T[Dem]. 6:1-7 comprise a single thematic unit which deals at length with the bases of M[Dem]. 6:1-2 (T. 6:1-5W). . . and then takes up related issues (T. 6:5X-6:7). The major formal articulations in the first part are patterned on, and expand upon, those of M[Dem];" Sarason, 206. TDem. 6:1 opens by quoting mDem. 6:1, he who sharecrops a field for a gentile, and discusses how he gives the tithes. TDem. 6:2 examines tithes from a field which an Israelite divides; see Sarason, 207, for alternate readings. TDem. 6:1 opens with hmqbl sdh mn hgwy, "one who sharecrops a field for the gentile," and tDem. 6:2 opens with hhwlq sdh mn hgwy, "one who divides a field with the gentile," and expands upon Mishnah's discussion of taking tithes from a field which one leases from a gentile. TDem. 6:3 treats the Samaritan and ignores the gentile. TDem. 6:4 builds on the reference to the Roman treasury in tDem. 6:3 and discusses the Samaritan, mentioned in tDem. 6:3, and the gentile, not mentioned in tDem. 6:3. TDem. 6:5-7 comment upon one who sharecrops a field; only tDem. 6:7 refers to a gentile. The latter discusses an Israelite who sharecrops his father's field for a gentile. For the most part, Tosefta's concern with the gentile in tDem. 6:1-2 derives from Mishnah's reference to the non-Israelite in mDem. 6:1-2. MDem. 6:1 opens with hmqbl sdh mysr'l mn hnkry wmn hkwty, "one who sharecrops a field for an Israelite, for a gentile, or for a Samaritan," and mDem. 6:2 opens with hhwkr sdh mn nkry, "one who leases a field from a gentile." Thus, Tosefta's formulation parallels that in Mishnah. The reference in tDem. 6:4 probably relates to the fact that the Samaritan and the gentile are often mentioned together, e.g. in mDem. 6:1, and tDem. 6:7 completes the discussion in tDem. 6:6, for the former talks about a field which is sharecropped for an Israelite, while the latter discusses a field which is sharecropped for a gentile.

rael by separating the tithes. Sarason argues that the this relates to a disagreement among the sages over whether or not gentiles can legally own property
within the Land of Israel.[49] Therefore, the discussion of the non-Israelites
revolves around their relationship to one of the central concepts of mishnaic culture, the Land of Israel.

TTer. 4:12-13, which build on mTer. 3:9,[50] discuss a gentile who separates heave-offering and who sets apart the first-born of a clean animal, the firstborn of an ass, the dough-offering, or second tithe. It is a summary of the rules
concerning a gentile's relationship to Israelite agricultural offerings and the latter's cult.[51]

TKil. 2:15-16 deal with a gentile in the context of the rules concerning
"mixed-kinds" of produce.[52] The important issue throughout is whether or not
the gentile, like the Israelite, must take into account the holy nature of the Land
of Israel.

Exactly how the customs and rules connected with Israelite holy days
applied to non-Israelites was a matter of concern to our authors. This issue was
important because Israelites and gentiles lived in close contact with one another,
and the actions of the members of one group affected the activities of the other
aggregate. TShab. 13:9-12 are concerned with the relationship of the gentile to
the Israelites' Sabbath-laws. The specific subject of this essay is that an Israelite
may not tell a gentile to work for him on the Sabbath.[53] Although tShab. 13:9

----

[49]Sarason, 209.

[50]Peck, 127.

[51]TTer. 4:12 and tTer. 4:13 open with gwy š . . ., "gentile who." TTer. 4:14 deals with
the Samaritan and asks whether he is considered a gentile or an Israelite with reference to the agricultural offerings, so that tTer. 4:14 also contains a reference to the gentile. However, its major concern is the Samaritan.

[52]TKil. 2:15 discusses a gentile who engages in grafting plants to each other, and tKil.
2:16 states that Israelites may not produce "mixed-kinds" with gentiles, except in specific locations.
Mandelbaum notes that tKil. 2:15-16 form a unit "dealing with the . . . problem of benefiting from
diverse-kinds grown by others." He further argues that "these pericopae thus provide a fitting conclusion to T[osefta]'s discussion of diverse-kinds of seeds in Chapters One and Two;" Mandelbaum,
141-142.

[53]TShab. 13:9 quotes mShab. 16:6's discussion of a gentile who came to put out a fire on
the Sabbath and adds a narrative, introduced by m'śh š, in which soldiers from Sepphoris were prevented by Joseph b. Simai of Sihin from putting out a fire in his courtyard. Sages state that he need
not have done this. TShab. 13:10 rules that Israelites may not rent utensils to gentiles on Friday, and
tShab. 13:11 states that they do not send letters with gentiles on Friday. Neither issue is directly related to Mishnah; however, they do treat the general topic of a gentile's working on the Sabbath for
the benefit of an Israelite. TShab. 13:12 quotes mShab. 16:8's ruling that an Israelite may use the
water which a gentile drew for his own beast, but the former may not use water which the latter drew
for the Israelite's animal—Tosefta's dependence on Mishnah is such that the antecedent of "his" in
the phrase "his animal," bhmtw, does not appear in Tosefta, but occurs only in Mishnah—and expands the matter by discussing the gentile's bringing hay to feed his animal. Tosefta concludes that

and tShab. 13:12 quote mShab. 16:6 and mShab. 16:8 respectively, the inclusion of the materials not directly related to the topics in Mishnah suggests that we have a minor collection of passages built around the theme of the gentile's working on the Sabbath for the benefit of Israelites. This same topic is covered in tShab. 17:14-15, which build on mShab. 23:4 and open in similar language;[54] however, the issue is framed differently in each document.[55] The passages, although concerned with working on the Sabbath, are joined together because of their references to the non-Israelite.

TErub. 5:18-19 assume that gentiles and Israelites live together in courtyards, and they focus on the applicability of the laws concerning establishing a common courtyard for the Sabbath if a gentile lives there among the Israelites. MErub. 6:1 appears to be the occasion for this brief essay in Tosefta.[56]

----

the Israelite may use the hay the gentile brought to feed his own animal only if he does not know the gentile. TShab. 13:14 augments the reference in mShab. 16:8 to Gamliel's use of a gangplank placed on the ship by a gentile on the Sabbath. TShab. 13:9-14, with the exception of tShab. 13:13 which deals with how close to the Sabbath one may embark on a trip on a boat, is somewhat related to the situation in tShab. 13:14 and mShab. 17:8, which mention that Gamliel and the elders were on a ship. They form a unit which centers on the gentile's working on the Sabbath for the benefit of an Israelite.

[54]MShab. 23:4 reads gwy šhby' hlylyn bšbt l' yspd bhn yśr'l, "a gentile who brought wailing pipes on a Sabbath—an Israelite may not make a lament with them;" TShab. 17:14 reads gwy šhby' hlylyn bšbyl yśr'l bšbt l' yspd bhn 'wtw yśr'l, "a gentile who brought wailing pipes for a [certain] Israelite on the Sabbath, that Israelite may not make a lament with them."

[55]Mishnah states that the Israelites should not use wailing pipes brought by a gentile on the Sabbath, while Tosefta states that if a gentile brought the pipes for a *particular* Israelite, they may not be used for *that* Israelite. TShab. 17:15 carries this further and states that if a gentile built a coffin and dug a grave for a particular Israelite, that Israelite may not be buried in them; however, another Israelite may be buried in them. Both texts in Tosefta illustrate the principle that an Israelite may not benefit from work which a gentile does for him on the Sabbath; however, one may benefit from work which a gentile does on the Sabbath, if it were not done specifically for him or her. The context is what type of work may be done for a bride or a corpse on the Sabbath, and the reference to the gentile derives from Mishnah, not Tosefta. However, Tosefta expands on Mishnah's issues in its own ways. See Neusner, *Shabbat*, 200-201.

[56]TErub. 5:18 states that a gentile may renounce his share in a courtyard by renting out his property. The discussion of how one gives up his right to the courtyard derives from mErub. 6:1-2. TErub. 5:19 states that for the purposes of carrying on the Sabbath, a courtyard inhabited by a gentile is considered to be the same as a cattle-pen. This builds on mErub. 6:1 in which Meir and Eliezer b. Jacob debate the effect of a gentile's restricting an Israelite's use on the Sabbath of a courtyard in which they both dwell. Mishnah seems to be the occasion for this passage, especially because tErub. 5:20 quotes the end of mErub. 6:1; however, Tosefta has expanded Mishnah's discussion of the gentile in its own ways. See Jacob Neusner, *A History of the Mishnaic Law of Appointed Times Part Two Erubin, Pesahim. Translation and Explanation* (Leiden: 1981), 82-84.

The proximity of Israelites and gentiles generates tPis. 2:5-15, which expand on mPes. 2:2-3. This is a collection of passages which focuses on how one determines to whom leaven, which somehow was related to both an Israelite and a gentile during Passover, belongs. The theme of the unit is the prohibition against the Israelite's using leaven which he possessed during the holiday.[57] Tosefta's essay is much more thorough than the one found in Mishnah.

TB.Q. 1:1-2 explain that gentiles are not the same as Israelites; therefore, the laws of restitution for damages done to property belonging to "children of the covenant," mentioned in mB.Q. 1:2-3, do not apply to the former.[58]

----

[57]TPis. 2:5 notes that if a gentile works in a store belonging to an Israelite and leaven is found in items in the store after Passover, an Israelite cannot derive benefit from the leaven. TPis. 2:6 states that if the store belongs to a gentile and an Israelite works in it, leaven found in the items in the store is permitted to an Israelite after Passover; thus tPis. 2:5 and tPis. 2:6 deal with both sides of the same issue. TPis. 2:7-8 have the same ruling with regard to leaven found in the store, with tPis. 2:7 dealing with an Israelite's store with gentile workers, while tPis. 2:8 treats a gentile's store with Israelite workers. TPis. 2:9 employs much of the same language as mPes. 2:3 with reference to a gentile who lent money to an Israelite on the security of leaven, but Tosefta's version is less ambiguous than that in Mishnah. MPes. 2:3 reads nkry šhlwh 't yśr'l 'l ḥmṣw 'ḥr ḥpsh mtr bhn'h, "a gentile who made a loan to an Israelite on the security of his [the Israelite's] leaven, after Passover, it is permitted [for the Israelite] to derive benefit [from it];" tPis. 2:9 reads nkry šhlwh 't yśr'l 'l ḥmyṣw 'm lw 'm l' b'ty 'd ḥpsh hry hw' mkwr lk mwtr b'kylh w'yn ṣryk lwm bhn'h, "a gentile who made a loan to an Israelite on the security of his leaven, [and] said to him, "If I have not come back to you before Passover, lo, this is sold to you"—it is permitted to eat it, and there is no need to say that he may derive benefit [from it]." TPis. 2:10 is similar to the second part of mPes. 2:3 and discusses the other side of the issue. MPes. 2:3 reads wyśr'l šhlwh 't nkry 'l ḥmṣw 'ḥr ḥpsh 'swr bhn'h, "and an Israelite who made a loan to a gentile on the security of his leaven, after Passover, he may not derive benefit [from it];" tPis. 2:10 reads yśr'l šhlwh 't nkry 'l ḥmyṣw w'm lw 'm l' b'ty qwdm lpsh hry hw' mkwr lk 'ḥr ḥpsh 'swr bhn'h w'yn ṣryk lwm b'kylh, "An Israelite who made a loan to a gentile on the security of his leaven, if he said to him, 'If I have not come back to you before Passover, lo, this is sold to you'—after Passover he is prohibited to derive benefit [from it], and there is no need to mention eating." TPis. 2:11 speaks of a gentile who had leaven in his possession when he came to an Israelite's house. The Israelite need not burn the leaven, unless the gentile deposited it with him. However, if the Israelite placed the leaven in a room/house by itself, he need not burn it. TPis. 2:12 states that if a gentile and an Israelite were traveling together on a boat and the Israelite sold the leaven to the gentile or gave it to him as an unrestricted gift, the Israelite may buy it back after Passover. TPis. 2:13 indicates that an Israelite may tell the gentile to buy more leaven than he intended, in case the Israelite might need it after Passover, and tPis. 2:14 states that an Israelite may rent his ass to a gentile to use to transport leaven. If the Israelite found a sizable amount of leaven on the way that the ass had traveled, he may take it. However, he may not take a small amount. TPis. 2:15 contains a story about Gamliel who was going from Akko to Kezib in which a gentile plays an important role, for he took the bread from Gamliel. TPis. 2:16 is included because it supposedly occurred on the same trip; however, the issues of leaven and Passover are not the subject of tPis. 2:16; rather, it focuses on a vow which a certain person took.

[58]MB.Q. 1:2 indicates that an Israelite is liable for damages done to property belonging to "children of the covenant," and tB.Q. 1:1 quotes this line from Mishnah and explains that this excludes an ox belonging to an Israelite which gored an ox belonging to a gentile. Tosefta's reference to a gentile makes explicit what is implied in Mishnah. Similarly, mB.Q. 1:3 specifies that court proceedings are on the basis of testimony given by freemen and "children of the covenant," and

TB.Q. 4:1-3 deal with the application of the laws concerning the damage done by an ox to oxen owned by gentiles,[59] and they expand upon mB.Q. 4:3 which discusses the ox jointly owned by the Israelite and the sanctuary, as well as an ox of an Israelite or a gentile which damages the other's ox.[60] The point of this essay is that one set of rules applies to members of the Israelite ethnic unit, while another set is used for dealings with a gentile.

THul. 9:2-5, with the exception of tHul. 9:4,[61] form a unit discussing the liability for gifts to the priests. As we would expect, an animal owned by a gentile is not liable for the priestly gifts.[62] The reference to the gentile is found in mHul. 10:3 which states that something slaughtered for a priest or a gentile is exempt, discusses a priest or a gentile who sells the animal to an Israelite, and deals with one who is a partner with the priest and the gentile. However, Tosefta supplements Mishnah and spells out the issues in its own terms. Here

----

tB.Q. 1:2 quotes the line from Mishnah and notes that this excludes gentiles, slaves, and those who are invalid for giving testimony before a court. This unit in Tosefta is based on explaining the phrase "children of the covenant" in Mishnah, and it is Mishnah which leads to Tosefta's explicit mention of the gentile.

[59]TB.Q. 4:1 discusses an ox which is jointly owned by an Israelite and a gentile. If it were an ox which was known to be dangerous, and it gored an Israelite's ox, the owners pay full damages; if it were deemed a harmless ox, the owners pay half-damages. In this case, the ox is treated the same as one which is jointly owned by an Israelite and the sanctuary. However, if the ox belongs to a gentile, and it gored an Israelite's ox, the gentile is required to pay full damages whether it were deemed a harmless or a dangerous ox. TB.Q. 4:2 deals with a gentile's ox which injured another gentile's ox. Even if the gentiles agreed to live according to Israelite law, the owner is responsible for full damages no matter the ox's character, "for the distinction between an ox deemed harmless and one which is an attested danger does not apply in the case of damages done in regard to a gentile." In tB.Q. 4:3, Meir states that if an Israelite's ox gored a gentile's ox, the Israelite is exempt; but, if the gentile's ox gored the Israelite's ox, no matter the ox's character, the gentile must pay the damages from his choicest real estate. However, the text opens with a discussion of an Israelite's ox which gores a Samaritan's ox and a Samaritan's ox which gores an Israelite's ox.

[60]The ox jointly owned by a gentile and an Israelite is found only in Tosefta.

[61]THul. 9:4 does not discuss the gentile; rather, it refers to an Israelite who sold his animal to a priest to slaughter. The priest, Israelite, and gentile are the topics of this section, so that tHul. 9:4 fits into the context, even though it does not refer to the gentile.

[62]THul. 9:2 rules that if one slaughters for the purpose of healing, for food for a gentile, or for food for dogs, the slaughtering is valid, so that the priestly gifts must be given. (The same list appears in tHul. 5:2 in connection with the prohibition against slaughtering an animal and its offspring on the same day.) However, the act of slaughtering by a gentile is invalid, so that the animal is not liable for the priestly gifts, tHul. 9:3. If a priest or gentile sold a beast to an Israelite to slaughter, the beast is liable for the priestly gifts; however, if the beast were in the possession of the gentile or the priest when it was slaughtered, it is not liable. THul. 9:5 adds that a gentile and one who is a partner with a gentile is exempt from the priestly gifts. Furthermore, one who is in partnership with a gentile does not have to bring evidence of the partnership.

the gentile is a non-Israelite who is under no obligation to support the religious elite of the Israelite people.

TNeg. 2:14-15 deal with a bright spot on a gentile,[63] and tNeg. 7:14-15 are based on the assumption that the Israelite laws concerning mildew do not apply to a gentile or his property.[64] TMiq. 6:3-4 treat the acceptability and purity of immersion-pools and bath-houses with which gentiles come into contact.[65] TToh. 11:8-9 deal with the purity of grapes lying on the ground or on leaves with which the gentile has come into contact.[66] These *sugyot* make the point that the purity-laws of the Israelites do not apply to those outside the group.

THul. 5:2-3 discuss the gentile in relationship to the Israelite rule that one cannot slaughter an animal and its offspring on the same day, Lev. 22:28.[67] Here Israelites are different from gentiles, for the latter are not obligated to follow those "folk-customs" which derive from the Israelites' traditions recorded in the Written Torah.

----

[63]The general opinion is that skin-diseases do not render gentiles unclean. The discussion and issues are built upon mNeg. 7:1, much of which is quoted in Tosefta. Only tNeg. 2:14 refers to the gentile; however, tNeg. 2:15 explains the logic of tNeg. 2:14 and expands upon it.

[64]TNeg. 7:14 states that if an Israelite purchases a garment from a gentile, the garment must be examined anew for signs of mildew, and tNeg. 7:15 has the exact same rule for a house. Both are framed in the same language. The references to the gentile are found only in Tosefta, and they are integral to its formulation of the passages.

[65]TMiq. 6:3 discusses the pool at the house of Anath in Rome which was declared unfit because gentiles emptied and filled it. TMiq. 6:4 deals with a bath with gentile attendants. If the filters open onto a private domain, it is unclean. However, if they open onto a public domain, they are clean. If an Israelite entered in the morning and touched the water, it is clean, no matter if gentiles enter and leave the bath. However, if it were locked or designated as private property, it is unclean. The issue of the bath-house is raised in tMiq. 6:3 concerning Gamliel and Onqelos in Ashkelon; however, the issue of the gentile bath attendants is found only in tMiq. 6:4.

[66]TToh. 11:8 states that if an Israelite purchased grapes lying on the ground from gentiles, the Israelite must "do the work in cleanness." If he purchased them from Israelites, he must do the work in uncleanness. If they were lying on leaves, he should prepare them in uncleanness, no matter from whom he purchased them. TToh. 11:9 states that if one eats grapes from a basket or from what is lying on the ground, and the wine spurts on the grapes, it is clean, even in the case of gentiles, and one need not worry about the gentile's having made a libation with the wine. These texts are juxtaposed because they deal with items lying on the ground. I suspect that the reference to the gentile is occasioned by its using the same language as tToh. 11:6, which has a more natural reference to the gentile.

[67]THul. 5:2 states that if one slaughters for the purposes of healing, for consumption by gentiles, or for consumption by dogs, the slaughtering is valid and can be prohibited on account of the prohibition against slaughtering "it and its offspring." THul. 5:3 concludes that a gentile's act of slaughtering is permitted even if it violates the prohibition against slaughtering "it and its offspring," for it is an invalid act of slaughtering which is not subject to any of the Israelite restrictions on slaughtering. The reference to gentiles is found only in Tosefta, not in mHul. 5:3-4.

TShab. 6:1-7:21, which was considered an independent unit in some early rabbinic documents,[68] is a long essay which discusses folk customs and practices which are, or are not, "among the ways of the Amorites." Tosefta appears to be an expansion of mShab. 6:10 in which sages number three things mentioned by Meir as being included among the ways of the Amorites."[69] Describing these practices in terms of a biblical people long since disappeared reflects the rabbinic practice of viewing present concerns in terms of biblical paradigms.[70] The general tone of the passages is that the Amorites practice some "folk-customs" which must be avoided by Israelites.

The unifying theme of tErub. 3:5-8 is the Israelite response to an attack by gentiles on the Sabbath.[71] Similarly, tTan. 3:7-8 point to the period when "the Greek kings" sought to prevent the Israelites' access to Jerusalem.[72] The gentile is here seen as a threat to Israelite society.

TAhil. 18:6-12, except tAhil. 18:9 which returns to the topic of the gentile lands which runs through tAhil. 18:1-5, treat the dwellings of gentiles

----

[68]BShab. 67a refers to the Amorite Chapter cited by a tanna. See Alexander Kohut (ed.), *Aruch Completum sive Lexicon vocabula et res, quae in libris Targumicis, Talmudicis et Midraschicis continentur, explicans auctore Nathane fillo Jehielis* (New York: nd), I, 127. Ginzberg, on the basis of these passages, states that the Amorites "were considered as magicians and sorcerers;" Louis Ginzberg, *The Legends of the Jews* (Philadelphia: reprint 1968), VI, 177-178, n. 34. Meir discusses the ways of the Amorites in Sifra (Weiss 86a) in an exegesis of Lev. 18:3, *[You shall not copy the practices of the Land of Egypt where you dwelt, or of the land of Canaan to which I am taking you;]* nor shall you follow their customs. Kohler, on the basis of this and other passages, writes, "the Canaanites are usually spoken of as the Amorites. . . . To the apocryphal writers of the first and second pre-Christian century they are the main representatives of heathen superstition, loathed as idolaters. . . ;" Kaufmann Kohler, "Amorites—In Rabbinical and Apocryphal Literature" in Isidore Singer (ed.), *The Jewish Encyclopedia* (New York: reprint ND), I, 529-530.

[69]Saul Lieberman, *Tosefta Ki-fshutah: A Comprehensive Commentary on the Tosefta Part III Order Mo'ed* (New York: 1962), 79ff.

[70]Epstein argues that the section should be attributed to R. Yosi; Jacob N. Epstein, *Prolegomena ad Litteras Tannaiticas: Mishna, Tosephta et Interpretationes Halachicas* edited by E.Z. Melamed (Tel Aviv: 1958), 146.

[71]TErub. 3:5 explains how Israelites should respond to a gentile attack. TErub. 3:6 is a story which explains why the law is the way it is. TErub. 3:7 is an aside which deals with the Israelites' besieging a gentile village on the Sabbath during an optional war. TErub. 3:8 returns to the issue of the gentiles' laying siege to an Israelite city. Neusner suggests that the reference in mErub. 4:1 to the gentiles' carrying the Israelite beyond the Sabbath-limit is the occasion for this essay in Tosefta; Neusner, *Erubin*, 57.

[72]TTan. 3:7-8 explain the meaning of Pestle-smugglers and Fig-pressers in mTan. 4:5 with reference to events which happened when the Greek kings set up border-guards on the roads, so that the people could not go up to Jerusalem. A similar story is told about Salmai the Netophathite, not mentioned in Mishnah. The reference to the Greek kings is part of the story found in Tosefta.

and is occasioned by mOhol. 18:7-10.[73] Even though Tosefta's discussion is occasioned by Mishnah, Tosefta contains its own essay in its own style and language.[74]

Some of our essays contain components on unrelated topics, so that the only factor which units the independent elements is the reference to the gentile. TTer. 1:14 is related to mTer. 8:11's discussion of a householder's responsibility to protect heave-offering from being made unclean.[75] TTer. 1:15 contains a narrative, opening with m'sh b, which illustrates the rule in mTer. 1:1, cited at the opening of tTer. 1:15, that a gentile may not separate heave-offering from the produce of an Israelite, even with the latter's permission.[76] The two texts relate to different *mishnayot*; therefore, I assume that have been placed together in Tosefta because of their common references to gentile/heave-offering. However, the shared problem is the gentile's relationship to the holiness of the Land of Israel, as expressed through the Israelite agricultural gifts.

TSheb. 3:12-13 mention the gentile; however, tSheb. 3:12 focuses on renting a field from a gentile during the Sabbatical year, while tSheb. 3:13 centers on finding a grave-area in a gentile's field. Clearly the two texts have been placed in the same context because of their common references to a gentile's field, even though they do not share a common concern.[77]

TQid. 5:10 states that a woman should not be alone with one hundred gentiles and seems to expand upon mQid. 4:12, which rules that a woman may

----

[73]TAhil. 18:6 rules that any person makes the dwelling subject to the purity-laws of corpses and that a Samaritan is equal to a gentile in this regard. In tAhil. 18:7 we learn that they suspend the status of holy things because of the gentile's dwelling. The text also takes up Mishnah's question of how long the gentile must have resided in the dwelling for these concerns to be relevant. TAhil. 18:8 focuses on the person who watches the gentile's dwelling, and tAhil. 18:10-11 expand upon the question of mOhol. 18:8, concerning how and what is examined. TAhil. 18:12 details the types of structures which do and do not fall under this category, which relates to mOhol. 18:9-10; however, each collection phrases the issues differently.

[74]For a comparison of the discussions in Mishnah and Tosefta, see Neusner, *Ohalot*, 340-347.

[75]Peck, 246. In Tosefta the gentile is paired with the Samaritan, for both could render the heave-offering unclean.

[76]In Tosefta, Simeon b. Gamliel agrees with Mishnah, but Isaac rules that a gentile may separate the heave-offering if the Israelite stands near his side; Peck, 46-47.

[77]TSheb. 3:12 states that if an Israelite rents a field from a gentile, he should have the gentile agree to work the field during the Sabbatical year. TSheb. 3:12 seems unrelated to what precedes it in tSheb. 3:11; however, Newman suggests that it "has been inserted here to supplement the discussion of renting fields" which is found in tSheb. 3:11; Newman, 99. TSheb. 3:13 discusses a field which is plowed by a gentile or a Samaritan. Such a field cannot be made a grave-area, for the gentiles and Samaritans do not listen to rabbinic decrees.

be alone with two Israelite men.[78] TQid. 5:11, which may be related to mQid. 3:12,[79] quotes Meir's claim that one couple can produce five different classes of people, and it discusses a gentile whose slaves marry each other. Because tQid. 5:10 and tQid. 5:11 are thematically unrelated and seem to relate to different *mishnayot*, I assume that their common references to the gentile caused them to be placed in a contiguous relationship.

TToh. 8:8 states that if one stuffs his utensils in the wall niches of a bath-house, they are unclean[80] because the gentiles may be questioned about them; that is, the gentiles could see them and perhaps touch them. TToh. 8:9 rules that if one purchases utensils from gentile craftsmen or gives them to a gentile craftsmen, they are unclean with *midras*-uncleanness, but clean of corpse-uncleanness. TToh. 8:8 derives from mToh. 7:7; however, the reference to gentiles appears only in Tosefta. TToh. 8:9, which is related in theme to tToh. 8:8, is not derived from Mishnah. It is possible that the two text were juxtaposed because tToh. 8:8 discusses the gentile last, while tToh. 8:9 opens with a reference to the gentiles.

iv

We have uncovered only a few essays in Mishnah and Tosefta which treat the gentile, and we can conclude that the gentile was not a major topic of concern to the compilers of either document. Although the essays on the non-Israelite are more numerous in Tosefta than in Mishnah, the significance of this fact is unclear. For whatever reason, the agenda of Mishnah allowed for the creation of fewer essays on the gentile than did the program of the creators of Tosefta. In general, the essays in Tosefta are of three types: 1) Generated by a reference to the gentile in Mishnah and closely aligned to Mishnah's discussion; 2) generated by a reference to the gentile in Mishnah, but developed in distinct ways in each collection; 3) independent of Mishnah and engendered by Tosefta's own concerns. This parallels the general scheme of the ways in which Tosefta is related to Mishnah,[81] so that we find in Tosefta what we expect to discover.

----

[78]The reference to gentiles is found in only tQid. 5:10. TQid. 5:9-10 build on mQid. 4:12 and form a unit. The end of tQid. 5:10 is related to the opening of mQid. 4:14.

[79]Jacob Neusner, *A History of the Mishnaic Law of Women Part Four Sotah, Gittin, Qiddushin. Translation and Explanation* (Leiden: 1980), 250-251.

[80]Lieberman, *Tosefeth Rishonim*, IV, 85-86.

[81]Jacob Neusner, *The Tosefta: Its Structure and Its Sources* (Atlanta: 1986), ix.

The essays are not uniform, for they are created from different perspectives. Some of them deal with the gentile *qua* gentile, others deal with the gentile as "other," while still others focus on the gentile as idolater. A few of the essays were engendered by one of these views of the gentile, while others were created from the point of view of the basic concepts/symbols of the Israelite ethnic group. Thus, the gentiles can be the major topic under consideration, or they can be secondary to other concerns. In the latter passages, the gentiles appear only further to develop inherent Israelite concerns. Furthermore, a few *sugyot* are grouped together only because they share references to the gentile, even though their pictures of the gentile are not uniform, and the perspectives from which the gentiles are approached vary.

The existence of the gentile in the Land of Israel stands behind much of the material. However, the proximity of the Israelite and non-Israelite within Palestinian society leads to several different treatments of the gentile. First, the gentile appears as one segment of Palestinian society, or as the symbol for the "other" portion of humanity, not represented by Israelites. In the former instance, we may find references to the Samaritans and/or the *am-haares*, while in the latter, the population is divided between "us" and "them," Israelites and gentiles. However, in both types of *sugyot*, the gentile is an abstraction of all non-Israelites, for in general the *am-haares* and the Samaritan are aligned in opposition to the gentile.

The most common reason for the creation of an essay on the gentiles is that the authors of Mishnah-Tosefta saw them living alongside the Israelites and engaging in business and social activities with them. In the minds of the sages behind these documents, this interaction produced ambiguous situations from the point of view of Israelite customs and laws. For example, how does an Israelite know the status of a gentile's grain with regard to the separation of the agricultural gifts? How can an Israelite determine if the animal he has purchased from a gentile had given birth to an offspring before the transfer of its ownership? In a town with a mixed population, how does one determine the status of objects? Behind these essays are the assumptions that Israelites and non-Israelites follow different customs and act in distinct ways and that Israelites should take this into account when they interact with gentiles.

The essays also indicate that Israelites act in different ways when dealing with fellow Israelites from the manner in which they interact with gentiles. For example, the Israelite laws of damages are divided into two major categories: Those which apply to Israelites, and those which are applicable to gentiles. Similarly, the rules covering financial transactions among Israelites are different from those utilized for financial dealings between Israelites and non-Israelites. These types of essays serve to reinforce the unity of the Israelite people and to differentiate them from the gentiles. They can be considered essays designed to create and to maintain the Israelite ethnic group.

Some of the essays illustrate the relationship of the gentile to the basic concepts/symbols of the Israelite ethnic group. Although these issues will be fully explicated below, it is useful to introduce the topics at this point. The Land of Israel is a complex symbol to which, according to the compilers of Mishnah-Tosefta, gentiles and Israelite must respond, albeit in different ways. The issue is whether or not the holiness of YHWH's land must be taken into account by gentiles, and if so, how they must express it. Similarly, some of our essays begin to explicate the relationship of the non-Israelite to the Israelite concept of purity. Furthermore, the relationship of the gentile to the Israelite cycle of holy time finds expression in our essays.

The essays also illustrate the ability of their authors to differentiate among different aspects of the gentile. For example, the *gentile as idolater* is the subject of some of the essays in *Abodah Zarah*. When viewed in this light, the gentile should be avoided. This is illustrated through the prohibition against eating certain foods prepared by non-Israelites, or through the avoidance of wine with which the gentile has come into contact. The *gentile as other* is the topic of other essays. Here we discover that different laws of damages apply to gentiles than do to Israelites and that different monetary practices are used when one interacts with a gentile or an Israelite. Elsewhere, the lecherous and dangerous nature of the *gentile qua gentile* is the subject of other units of *sugyot*. Finally, we have seen that the gentile as a segment of the Palestinian population is a topic of interest and concern from the point of view of Israelite law and the central concepts/symbol of the Israelite cultural and religious systems.

In brief, these essays set the agenda for what follows, for the basic categories and issues arise in these passages. They also point to the complexity of the problems before us and the different schemes which must be employed to explicate fully the material.

Chapter Three:

Contexts of Singular Passages

i

Above we examined the essays on the gentile. Now we turn to those *sugyot* which are not juxtaposed to others which deal with the non-Israelite in order to discover how these passages fit into their contexts. Do the references to the gentile stand out as awkward in their present settings, or do they relate to the section which surrounds them? Are the pericopae on the gentile carefully worked into the larger unit, such as the chapter, or not? By asking these questions, we can determine whether discussions of the gentile are a natural outcome of the editorial process, or whether they have been included because of their intrinsic interest, even though they did not fit well into their present settings. The *sugyot* from Mishnah will be treated separately from those in Tosefta. The editorial processes which produced Mishnah allow us to organize the discussions of the gentile according to the ways in which they function in the chapters, while the most useful way to deal with the pericopae in Tosefta is to group them according to their relationship to Mishnah, as well as to their surroundings in their own document.

Anticipating the results of this investigation, we shall see that, for the most part, the discussions of the gentile in Mishnah fit well into their contexts, so that the treatments of the non-Israelite generally begin from a concern with a specific Israelite law or ritual. Furthermore, the different pictures of the gentile correspond to those we discovered in the previous chapter: Gentile as other, gentile as idolater, gentile as dangerous, etc. The impression we have at this point is that the gentiles *qua* gentiles were of little concern to the compilers of Mishnah-Tosefta; they were important only from the point of view of the particulars of the cultural system set forth in the concepts and symbols contained in Mishnah and Tosefta.

ii

Introductions to chapters

Several chapters of Mishnah open with references to the gentile, so that the treatment of the non-Israelite introduces the decidedly Israelite-centered mishnaic discussion. Most often, we learn that the rules of the chapter do *not* pertain to the gentile. MBer. 7:1 begins a chapter which focuses on the grace after meals by enumerating who may, and who may not, be included among those who recite the blessings. The gentile, who is excluded, contrasts with the Samaritan, who is included. MTer. 1:1[1] states that a gentile may not give heave-offering from what belongs to an Israelite, even with the latter's consent.[2] The gentile is mentioned along with the deaf-mute, the imbecile, the minor, and the one who separates heave-offering from another's produce to constitute the "five who may not separate heave-offering."[3] MOrl. 1 deals with those trees which are exempt from, or liable to, the laws of the fourth-year produce, and mOrl. 1:2 specifies that the important issue is the tree, not who planted it or owns it: Any tree which bears fruit is included in the biblical injunction, even one planted by a gentile.[4] MErub. 4:1-11 deal with the *'erub* and violating the

----

[1]The first two chapters of mTerumot are based on the assumption that in some cases heave-offering which is improperly separated or which is separated by unfit persons is still consider-ed valid heave-offering. MTer. 1:1-5 offer examples of heave-offering which is *post facto* invalid, while mTer. 1:6-10 deal with cases in which the separation is *post facto* valid; Alan J. Peck, *The Priestly Gift in Mishnah: A Study of Tractate Terumot* (Chico: 1981), 29.

[2]The gentile cannot separate heave-offering from an Israelite's produce for the same rea-son that one Israelite cannot separate heave-offering from another Israelite's produce: One does not have the power to sanctify another person's property. The rule that the gentile cannot separate heave-offering from an Israelite's produce, even if the latter grants him permission to do so, also teaches that a gentile cannot serve as an Israelite's agent; Peck, 32.

[3]MTer. 1:1-3 discuss some of these five; however, the gentile appears only in mTer. 1:1. The non-Israelite is different from the others in the list, and he is excluded for reasons different from those which apply to the others who appear. Peck notes that the deaf-mute, imbecile, and minor "are distinguished from other individuals in that they are not believed to understand the implications of their actions. . . . [I]n separating produce to be heave-offering, the individual designates that pro-duce to be holy. He accomplishes this only if he is conscious of being engaged in a sacred activity. The deaf mute, imbecile and minor, unable to understand the implications of their actions, can not successfully do this;" Peck, 31.

[4]Essner notes that this part of mOrl. 1:2 continues the discussion of mOrl. 1:1, which has been interrupted by the opening sections of mOrl. 1:2. The reference to the gentile is included along with references to a tree planted in the public domain, a tree planted by a robber, a tree planted on a boat, and a tree which sprouts by itself; all of these trees are subject to the laws of *'orlah*. These ex-amples illustrate the point that all fruit trees are liable to the laws of *'orlah*. MOrl. 1:1-2 open the tractate by defining which trees are included under the rule of Lev. 19:23, *When you enter the land and plant any tree for food, you shall regard its fruit as forbidden. Three years it shall be forbidden for you, not to be eaten.* MOrl. 1:1 follows the biblical verse and includes any tree which a person uses for food, while mOrl. 1:2 makes the point that any tree which bears

Sabbath-limit.[5] MErub. 4:1 lists the gentile and an evil spirit as things which might force the Israelite to violate the Sabbath-limit, while mErub. 4:3 mentions someone who crossed the Sabbath-limit for an acceptable reason. Thus mErub. 4:1 and mErub. 4:3 serve as an appropriate introduction to the issues of this chapter.[6] MErub. 6:1-10 focus on the *'erub* and the courtyard. MErub. 6:1's dispute about the validity of an *'erub* in a courtyard in which a gentile lives[7] lays the ground work for mErub. 6:2-4, which treat the *'erub* in which not everyone in the courtyard participates.[8] MBekh. 1:1 and mBekh. 2:1 are parallel pericopae which introduce their respective chapters. The first *sugya* deals with the unborn of an ass, while the second discusses the unborn of cattle.[9] Because the first chapter of mBekhorot treats the redemption of the firstborn of an ass, Ex. 13:11-13, while the second chapter of mBekhorot discusses the firstborn of cattle, Ex. 22:28-29, these texts serve as introductions to their respective chapters of Mishnah.[10] MNeg. 3:1 states that gentiles and resident aliens cannot contract uncleanness from the signs of skin-disease, mNeg. 11:1 rules that gentiles' clothes cannot contract uncleanness from the signs of mildew, and mNeg. 12:1 indicates that gentiles' houses cannot contract uncleanness from signs of mildew. All three passages make the same point: These laws of uncleanness do not apply to non-Israelites. MNeg. 3:1 opens by listing those who

----

fruit is included in the biblical injunction; Howard S. Essner, "The Mishnah Tractate 'Orlah: Translation and Commentary," in William S. Green, *Approaches to Ancient Judaism Volume III: Text as Context in Early Rabbinic Literature* (Chico: 1981), 105, 108-113.

[5]Jacob Neusner, *A History of the Mishnaic Law of Appointed Times Part Two Erubin, Pesahim. Translation and Explanation* (Leiden: 1981), 7.

[6]MErub. 4:1 ends with a discussion of one on a ship, and this issue is expanded in mErub. 4:2.

[7]The anonymous opinion in mErub. 6:1 states that an Israelite cannot erect an *'erub* in a courtyard if gentiles or those who do not accept the validity of the *'erub* live there. Eliezer b. Jacob states that only an Israelite can restrict the actions of another Israelite.

[8]The gentile along with the Israelite who does not accept the validity of the *'erub* are the two possibilities of those who could cause the problems with which the section is concerned.

[9]MBekh. 1:1 states that if an Israelite bought the unborn of an ass from a gentile, sold it to him, an aside in the text notes that this is forbidden, was a joint owner with a gentile, received asses from, or sent asses to, a gentile with the understanding that while one would raise the animals, both would share in the profits, the laws of the firstling do not apply. Mishnah quotes Num. 3:13, *all of the firstborn in Israel*, and notes that the phrase *in Israel* excludes the gentiles. MBekh. 2:1 applies the same laws to the unborn of cattle.

[10]Both texts assume that because the gentile is unconcerned about the rules of the firstling, the Israelite has no way of knowing if an offspring born after the animal was purchased from a gentile is a firstling.

cannot contract uncleanness from the signs of skin-disease and then moves to a discussion of those skin problems which may be certified unclean within two weeks. MNeg. 11 speaks about garments which may become unclean and opens with a comment about the gentile, and mNeg. 12 treats houses which are rendered unclean by mildew and opens with our statement. Thus the appearance of the gentile functions the same throughout the Tractate and serves to introduce the issues of each chapter. In mPar. 2:1, Eliezer rules that an Israelite may not purchase the Red Heifer from a gentile, while sages permit this. Because this chapter of mParah focuses on what determines whether or not the Heifer is acceptable, our pericope serves as an appropriate introduction to the chapter. MMiq. 8 treats those required to use immersion-pools, so that mMiq. 8:1, which distinguishes between immersion-pools inside and outside the Land of Israel and discusses for what forms of uncleanness an Israelite may use gentile immersion-pools outside the Land of Israel,[11] serves as an introduction to the chapter.

In these pericopae, the references to the gentiles serve to illustrate and to refine points of Israelite law and custom. Most often, we discover that gentiles are not Israelites, so that the folk-ways or symbols which distinguish the Israelites are not applicable to non-Israelites. This is the case, for example, in the treatment of the Israelite purity rules, for they do not apply to gentiles. In other instances, the "otherness" of the gentile is irrelevant, for the fulfillment of the regulations does not depend solely on the nature of the persons involved. The fact that the rules of the fourth-year produce apply to all trees, no matter who planted them, illustrates this point. The relevance of the gentile's "otherness" is debated in the discussions of establishing an 'erub in courtyards inhabited by gentiles and Israelites, as well as in the disagreement over whether or not one may purchase a Red Heifer from a gentile. The dangerous character of the gentile is assumed in some of the material concerning the Israelites' violation of the Sabbath-limits. Thus, the few cases in which references to the gentile initiate chapters offer us a variety of pictures of the non-Israelites and make different assumptions concerning the nature and importance of their "otherness." However, despite these different perceptions of the gentile, the passages serve the same literary function, for they all act as proper introductions to their various chapters.

----

[11]The text is ambiguous, for it is unclear if Eliezer discusses gentile immersion-pools within the Land, or the location of Israelite immersion-pools within the Land. Compare Herbert Danby, *The Mishnah: Translated from the Hebrew With Introduction and Brief Explanatory Notes* (Oxford: 1964), 741-742 with Jacob Neusner, *Eliezer Ben Hyrcanus: The Tradition and the Man,* (Leiden: 1973), I, 391.

Opening sugyot which are not introductions

In contrast to the examples given above, references to gentiles may open chapters which treat a assortment of themes. As a result, the opening *sugyot* are not introductions to the *whole* chapter. MShab. 24:1 refers to the gentile,[12] but the chapter covers a number of unrelated topics[13] and contains several literary patterns.[14] Similarly, mNaz. 9:1 does not thematically initiate the chapter, for as Neusner notes, this chapter is a thematic "miscellany."[15] MEd. 5 is divided into four parts which are unified by tradent, not by thematic development.[16] Because mEd. 5:1-5, like mEd. 4:1-12, are "organized around the leniencies of the Shammaites and the strict rulings of the Hillelites,"[17] mEd. 5:1[18] does provide an introduction to a non-thematic trait of the chapter; however, reference to the gentile is incidental to the thematic structure. MHul. 1:1 opens by stating that "all slaughter, and their act of slaughtering is valid except for" the impaired individuals and the gentile, but this aside does not fit in with the major theme of the chapter.[19] MHul. 9:1-8 form a unit discussing connections, and the aside about the gentile interrupts the thematic development of the chapter. According to mHul. 9:1, if an Israelite slaughtered an unclean beast for a gentile, and it still jerks its limbs, it can convey food-uncleanness. It conveys

----

[12]MShab. 24:1 tells us that an Israelite may not carry a purse on the Sabbath. If darkness overtakes an Israelite while he is traveling on Friday night, he must give his purse to a gentile. If there is no gentile with him, he must place the purse on his animal.

[13]Jacob Neusner, *A History of the Mishnaic Law of Appointed Times Part One Shabbat. Translation and Explanation* (Leiden: 1981), 204.

[14]The passage is stylistically different from the other units in this chapter. The others begin with the third person plural infinitive; our passage opens with my s.

[15]Jacob Neusner, *A History of the Mishnaic Law of Women Part Three Nedarim, Nazir. Translation and Explanation* (Leiden: 1980), 192.

[16]Jacob Neusner, *A History of the Mishnaic Law of Damages Part Four Shebuot, Eduyot, Abodah Zarah, Abot, Horayot. Translation and Explanation* (Leiden: 1985), 114.

[17]Jacob Neusner, *The Rabbinic Traditions About the Pharisees Before 70* (Leiden: 1971), II, 337.

[18]The Shammaites declared clean the blood of a gentile woman and the blood of the purifying of a woman who is a leper, while the Hillelites state that "it is like her spittle and her urine." This also appears in mNid. 4:3.

[19]The text does make a distinction between the impaired Israelites, whose act of slaughtering is accepted if a normal Israelite supervises, and the gentile, whose act of slaughter is never valid. Although mHul. 1:1-2 deal with valid and invalid acts of slaughter and could serve as a typical opening of a mishnaic chapter, the complex nature of the chapter prevents mHul. 1:1 from serving as an adequate introduction. Neusner points out the complexity of the formal traits of this chapter and of mHul. 1:1-2 in particular; Jacob Neusner, *A History of the Mishnaic Law of Holy Things Part Three Hullin, Bekhorot. Translation and Explanation* (Leiden: 1979), 12-15.

point of the text is that the animal's status in conveying uncleanness depends on the person slaughtering the animal, and not on the person who owns the animal. Also, an unclean animal slaughtered for a gentile is considered food, so that the rules of food-uncleanness apply to it, even though it cannot serve as food for Israelites.[20] The slaughter of the unclean beast for the gentile is included here because, like the items with which mHul. 9:1 opens, it imparts food-uncleanness, but it does not impart carrion-uncleanness. The discussion of the gentile is introduced by kywṣ' bw, "similarly."[21]

A uniform picture of the gentile emerges from these passages. They all focus on the non-Israelite nature of the gentile and the fact that the Israelite traditions and laws are not applicable to them. In mShab. 24:1 the gentile is a non-Israelite who may engage in activities on the Sabbath which are forbidden to Israelites. Similarly, in mNaz. 9:1 we learn that gentiles, unlike women and slaves, cannot take a Nazirite-vow. In mEd. 5:1, the Houses disagree concerning the nature of a gentile woman's blood, a disagreement based on the fact that gentiles are not Israelites. MHul. 1:1 states that gentiles cannot validly slaughter meat, the assumption being that they are not Israelites; however, they are human beings, for meat slaughtered for them is considered food.

Thematically appropriate references to gentiles

Most of the other appearances of the gentile which occur throughout the rest of Mishnah can be fit into the thematic concerns of the various units. MBer. 8:5-6 deal with the *habddalah*, and in mBer. 8:5 the Houses disagree over the order of the blessings for the lamp, food, spices, and *habddalah* and whether or not the verb "creates" in the blessing over the lights is in the perfect or imperfect tense. MBer. 8:6 carries forth this discussion and tells us that a benediction is not said over a gentile's lamp or spices, a lamp or spices used for the dead, or a lamp or spices used for idolatry, items over which the Houses-dispute did not apply. It is interesting that the text distinguishes between the lamp and spices of gentiles and those used for idolatry. The gentile's lamp and spices are *not* excluded from receiving a blessing because they have a connection to idolatry; rather, they are excluded because they do not belong to an Israelite. While Mishnah does not explain why one cannot recite a blessing over the lamp and spices of the gentile, the *gemara*, bBer. 52b-53a, offers several possibilities. However, these attempts to relate the prohibitions to the gentile as idolater seem

----

[20]Neusner, *Hullin*, 107-108.

[21]Neusner sees mHul. 9:1-2 as forming a unit; Neusner, *Hullin*, 105.

to go against the simple meaning of the *sugya*.[22] According to Mishnah, the benediction must be said by Israelites over their own items. Gentiles are not Israelites; therefore, their lamps and spices are not blessed. This may also be why this matter is not debated by the Houses.[23]

MPe. 2:7 states that if the field were reaped by gentiles without the owner's permission[24] or by robbers, or if ants nibbled the crop, or if a wind or cattle broke it down, the field is exempt from the requirement of *pe'ah*,[25] so that the reference to the gentile fits into the discussion of those who detach the crop from the ground without making it liable for a gift to the poor. The responsibility to share the bounty of YHWH's Land with the poor among his people falls upon only members of his people, Israelites, who are responsible for the crops and their harvest. The same point is made in mPe. 4:6, which rules that if a gentile reaped his field while he was a gentile but converted to Judaism after the field was reaped, the harvested field is not subject to the laws of *pe'ah*, gleanings, or the forgotten sheaf, for these laws are incumbent upon only Israelites.[26] MPe. 4:6-8 seek to define which fields in the Land of Israel are liable to the rules concerning the gifts for the poor,[27] and their underlying principle is that

----

[22]The anonymous text suggests that the gentile's lamp might have been used on the Sabbath; therefore, it would not be proper for the Israelite to recite a blessing over it. Judah, in Rab's name, suggests that a gentile's spices were forbidden because they were used at meals, and gentile meals were normally related to some act of idolatry. The anonymous text notes that Mishnah specifically mentions spices of an idol and rejects Judah's reasoning. Hanina of Sura responds that the last part of Mishnah merely expands upon the earlier one.

[23]Similarly, the benedictions are said by Israelites to their God; therefore, lamps and spices belonging to idols do not receive blessings and are also irrelevant. See the discussion of Jacob Neusner, *Invitation to the Talmud: A Teaching Book*, revised and expanded edition including Hebrew texts (New York: Harper & Row, 1984), 55-58, 63-64.

[24]Roger Brooks, *Support for the Poor in the Mishnaic Law of Agriculture: Tractate Peah* (Chico: 1983), 58, especially n. 23.

[25]The point seems clear: If the Israelite owner of the field did not harvest the crop, it does not fall under the obligations incumbent upon Israelites. As Brooks notes, "Whoever completes the harvest of a field must designate *peah* on behalf of the whole, because he alone controls the grain that grows in the rear corner. As we recall (see M. [Peah] 1:3A-B), only this produce can take on the status of *peah* when left unharvested and then designated by the householder;" Brooks, 59. Neither the robber nor the gentile owns the field or *harvests* it with the permission of the field's owner, and the ant, wind, and cattle cannot have harvested the crop. The secondary issues may be whether or not non-Israelites can validly own property in the Land of Israel. As Brooks notes, mPe. 2:7-8 form a unit which apply the principle in mPe. 1:3 "in exhaustive detail;" Brooks, 59.

[26]The point is made even clearer by Judah's ruling that because the laws of gleanings and the forgotten sheaf apply to the time of the sheaf-binding, and not to the time of harvest, the converted gentile is subject to these, for he was an Israelite at the time the sheaves were bound.

[27]MPe. 4:7 offers a case in which the rule of the forgotten sheaf does not apply, and mPe. 4:8 explains when tithes are not required from a field.

"at the time when it would have been liable it was exempt."[28] MPe. 4:9 states that if the poor collected the gleanings, forgotten sheaf, and pe'ah from a gentile's field, they are liable for tithes, unless the non-Israelite had declared the field to be ownerless property.[29] This text continues the discussion begun in mPe. 4:8, which deals with tithes, and it sets the stage for mPe. 4:10, which contains a dispute between Ishmael and Aqiba who supposedly discusses gleanings,[30] and the discussion of gleanings in mPe. 4:11.[31] Again, the reference to the gentile seems to fit nicely into its environment. Throughout these discussions in mPeah, we learn that only Israelites *are required to* support the poor among YHWH's people from the crops of his Land.

MDem. 3:4 distinguishes between the Samaritan and the *am haares* on the one hand, and the gentile on the other.[32] The last section of the passage begins a discussion, which is taken up in mDem. 3:5-6, concerning the Israelites' responsibility to tithe produce which they give to another person.[33] In both

----

[28]Note that the principle is not stated in mPe. 4:6 and that mPe. 4:7 and mPe. 4:8 do not refer to the *pe'ah* or the gleanings. MPe. 4:3 and mPe. 4:9 are the only places in the chapter, besides mPe. 4:6, which refer to all three items.

[29]We assume that the gentile has not tithed the grain, for these laws are followed correctly by Israelites alone.

[30]Gary G. Porton, *The Traditions of Rabbi Ishmael Part One: The Non-Exegetical Materials* (Leiden: 1976), 27-28.

[31]Grain grown in the Land of Israel is subject to the requirement of tithes, for the important factor is that the grain was grown on the Land which belonged to YHWH, not who owned the field. Therefore, once an Israelite takes possession of the grain, he must pay the tithes to YHWH. Ownerless property, however, is not subject to tithes. The rabbis assume that the gentiles would allow the Israelite poor to collect their due from non-Israelite fields, even though mPe. 4:6 explained that a gentile was not obligated to allow the poor to collect from his field. The point of the passage is to make it clear that tithes depend on where the crop is grown and not on who owns the field. This would follow from mPe. 4:8's discussion of ambiguous cases involving dedicated produce and its liability with regard to tithes. The passage also suggests that at least some gentiles helped the poor among the Israelites, even though they were not obligated to do so according to Israelite law.

[32]If an Israelite brought his properly tithed wheat to a miller who was a Samaritan or an *am-haares*, its condition with respect to tithes and seventh-year produce is unchanged, and the same is true if he gave his grain to them for safe-keeping. However, if the miller were a gentile, the grain is considered to be *demai*-produce. If the person to whom the Israelite gave his grain is a gentile, the anonymous text states the grain is considered to belong to the gentile and is not subject to the laws of tithing. Simeon rules that the produce given to the gentile is considered *demai*-produce.

[33]Sarason poses the question as follows: "If we temporarily give our tithed produce to someone who is not deemed trustworthy in the matter of tithing, do we suspect that the produce which he gives back to us is not our own, but has been exchanged, intentionally or not, with other, untithed produce or with seventh-year produce?" Richard S. Sarason, *A History of the Mishnaic Law of Agriculture Section Three: A Study of Tractate Demai. Part One, Commentary* (Leiden: 1979), 140.

cases, the gentile is not considered to be an Israelite and is not to be trusted with tithed produce,[34] unlike the Samaritan and the *am haareṣ* who, from the point of view Mishnah's authors, are marginal Israelites with regard to tithes. The reference to the gentile fits well into this context, and it serves to include even the "marginal" people in the category of Israelites with reference to respecting the Israelite traditions concerning tithing, while at the same time placing the gentile outside the category of those who are even "marginally" concerned with Israelite agricultural practices. MDem. 5:9 argues that a tithe may be given from grain bought from an Israelite for grain bought from a gentile or a Samaritan, or from grain bought from a gentile or Samaritan for grain bought from an Israelite. This passage fits well into the discussion of mDem. 5:3-11, which speaks about separating tithes from one type of produce for another; however, it is framed in a different literary form from what precedes it.[35] Here the gentile, the Israelite, and the Samaritan are seen as three different types of human beings, so that the grain of one is inherently different from the produce of the others. In this context, the gentile is like the Samaritan, for both are considered to be different "species" of human beings from Israelites. MDem. 6:10 deals with a gentile and a proselyte who inherit from their gentile father.[36] MDem. 6:7-10 form a stylistic and thematic unit which deals with the question of how people of different status divide property, so mDem. 6:10's reference to the gentile seems to fit well here.[37] Again, the gentile represents a distinct class of persons, when compared to Israelites.

MSheb. 5:7 states that a potter may sell five oil-jars and fifteen wine-jars to one Israelite during the seventh year and that he may sell more than this amount to a gentile living inside the Land of Israel, or to an Israelite living out-

----

[34]The gentile miller could have mixed untithed grain with, or according to Sarason, exchanged the tithed grain with the produce of an *am-haareṣ*. In the second case, the gentile could have returned his own, untithed produce; therefore, the produce is definitely untithed. Simeon holds that the grain is considered to be *demai*-produce because although the gentile's produce need not be tithed, it could have been mixed with the tithed produce he received, and any amount of tithed produce renders the untithed grain with which it is mixed *demai*-produce; Sarason, 141.

[35]Sarason, 191. MDem. 5:3-8 deal with the issue of separating tithes from one type of produce for other produce which came from an Israelite who may or may not have separated the tithes. Here, the issue is expanded to include all of those who lived in the Land of Israel--Israelites, Samaritans, and gentiles. Because gentiles do not tithe their produce and Samaritans do not tithe produce which they sell in the market, there is no danger that the produce has been doubly tithed. With regard to produce sold in the market, Samaritans and gentiles are similar; Sarason, 192.

[36]The text rules that the proselyte, who has no automatic right of inheritance, may divide the property, so that his gentile brother takes those things connected with idolatry.

[37]Sarason, 226-229.

side of the Land. MSheb. 5:6-8 deal with the implements that an Israelite may sell to another Israelite during the seventh year;[38] thus, mSheb. 5:7 is related thematically to its context.[39] Gentiles are not Israelites; therefore, they do not observe the rules connected with the Sabbatical year. However, because they are not obligated to follow these Israelite taboos of the seventh year, an Israelite may support the former's activity during that sacred period. MSheb. 4:3 seems to be related to mSheb. 4:2;[40] however, it is repeated in mSheb. 5:9 because other sections of the passage contain the reference to doing things "in the interest of peace." The point of these *sugyot* is that Israelites should work to create a peaceful Palestinian society for all who live in the area.

MTer. 3:9 states that a gentile,[41] like a Samaritan, may validly separate heave-offering, take produce as tithes, or dedicate produce to the Temple.[42] Judah rules that a gentile's vineyard is not subject to the restrictions of fourth-year produce, Lev. 19:24, while sages rule that his vineyard is subject to these restrictions.[43] Furthermore, an anonymous statement teaches us that heave-

----

[38]MSheb. 5:6 contains a list of items which a craftsman may not sell in the seventh year and the general rule that any implement is forbidden whose sole use is one that transgress the law of the seventh year. MSheb. 5:8 includes a Houses-dispute concerning the sale of a plowing heifer and discussions of the sale of produce, the lending of a *se'ah*-measure, and the giving of a small amount of money during the seventh year.

[39]The references to the gentile living inside the Land and to the Israelite living outside of the Land conform to the general rule that one does not sell something which can be used to violate the laws of the seventh year, for the laws are not incumbent upon non-Israelites, no matter where they live, or upon Israelites living outside of the Land of Israel.

[40]Louis E. Newman, *The Sanctity of the Seventh Year: A Study of Mishnah Tractate Shebiit* (Chico: 1983), 98.

[41]Peck, 121, n. 35.

[42]According to this text, a gentile may separate the heave-offering and dedicate produce to the Temple; that is, a non-Israelite may place produce in the category of sanctified goods in the same way as an Israelite. Simeon disagrees and claims that while a gentile may separate heave-offering and give it to a priest, what the gentile has separated does not achieve the same status of sanctified produce as that separated by an Israelite. According to Simeon, "a gentile who separates heave-offering does nothing more than give a gift of produce to a priest. A gentile does not have the ability to remove the true heave-offering required of produce grown in the Land of Israel;" Peck, 123. Thus, the anonymous ruling suggests that there is no distinction between Israelites and non-Israelites with regard to heave-offering, while Simeon holds that gentiles are not Israelites; therefore the former cannot impose sanctity on produce as the latter can.

[43]In brief, the dispute is over what determines whether or not the vineyard is subject to the biblical injunction, Lev. 19:24: Does it depend on who owns the vineyard, or does it depend on the vineyard's location within the Land of Israel, YHWH's land? Judah holds that the important factor is who owns the land. Because land owned by a gentile is not a gift from YHWH to the People Israel, the biblical laws do not apply; Peck, 123. Sages state that any vineyard in the Holy Land, no matter who owns it, is on YHWH's land; therefore, all vineyards are subject to the same law. By deciding that the ownership of the land is not the important factor, sages deny that gentile ownership of land in Israel is an important or a valid reason for removing the land from the status of YHWH's property. Thus, this *may* reflect a denial of the principle that gentiles can validly own property in

offering separated by gentiles imposes the status of heave-offering upon unconsecrated produce with which it is mixed; however, Simeon disagrees. Although in general this chapter of mTerumot deals with problems of determining whether or not the separated heave-offering is valid in several ambiguous situations, our text alone focuses on the issue of the non-Israelite. The general question of this passage is "the status of the non-Israelite as regards the agricultural laws."[44] The references to the gentile play an important role in Mishnah's discussions, for they deal with the problem of which Israelite agricultural rules apply to non-Israelites; therefore, they are appropriate to this context. It is important to note that here some of the sages believed that the non-Israelites must take cognizance of the holiness of the Land of Israel, even though they are not Israelites, and even though they do not recognize YHWH's divinity or his ownership of the Land. MTer. 9:7 rules that if an Israelite were weeding in a gentile's field of leeks, he may make a chance meal from the plants, even though the produce has not been tithed. MTer. 9:6-7 deal with a crop grown from seed of untithed produce.[45] Because a gentile's crop is not subject to tithes, the Israelite may eat a chance meal. The gentile appears because he is not an Israelite, and concerns with tithing do not apply to his crops. Therefore, the gentile's field serves to illustrate the topic under discussion. These pericopae from mTerumot point to the complexity of the gentile's relationship to the Holy Land, an issue which will be discussed more fully below,[46] for they illustrate the disagreement among the sages over whether or not gentiles were required, or allowed, to acknowledge YHWH's ownership of the Land of Israel.

MM.S. 4:4 holds that non-Israelite bondmen or bondwomen, like minor children, cannot act on their own; rather, they act only as their master's agent. On the other hand, Israelite bondmen or bondwomen and children who are not minors can act as independent human beings. MM.S. 4:4 and mM.S. 4:5 form a unit, for both discuss how one may deal with the money related to the second tithe so as to avoid paying the added fifth.[47] The non-Israelite bondmen

----

the Land of Israel.

[44]Peck, 122.

[45]If the seed is integral to the crop, the crop has the same status as the seed; therefore, the crop is considered untithed and unfit for food, even for a chance meal. If, however, the seed is not integral to the crop, the crop has no special status, and it may be consumed as a chance meal; Peck, 262-263.

[46]See Chapter Six.

[47]Peter J. Haas, *A History of the Mishnaic Law of Agriculture: Tractate Maaser Sheni* (Chico: 1980), 129-130.

and bondwomen are included here as examples of those who do not have independent status, so that when they act, it is viewed as if the master, not the slave, performed the deed. This is a new picture of the gentile, for here the adult status of the gentiles is ignored, and they are equated with Israelite children.

MHal. 3:5 holds that if gentiles gave dough to an Israelite to prepare for them, the dough is exempt from the dough-offering.[48] Chapter three of mHallah discusses the types of dough which are exempt from the dough-offering, so that our text fits.[49] MHal. 4:7 contains a dispute between Eliezer and Gamliel concerning whether or not an Israelite must tithe a field which he leased from a gentile in Syria. Eliezer says he must; Gamliel says he need not. At issue is the status of fields in Syria--are they considered part of the Land of Israel or not--an issue which also is discussed in mHal. 4:8.[50] With regard to the dough-offering, the gentile need not recognize the holiness of the Land of Israel, for he is not an Israelite.

MShab. 2:5 rules that if an Israelite extinguishes a lamp on Friday night because he is afraid of "gentiles, thieves or an evil spirit," or if he puts it out so that an ill person is able to sleep, he has not violated the Sabbath. Chapter two centers on the Sabbath-lamp, and our *sugya* fits nicely into this chapter.[51] Here

----

[48]If a gentile gave an Israelite dough for a gift, it is exempt from the offering if it had been rolled out. However, it is liable for the offering if it had not been rolled out. If an Israelite and a gentile prepared dough together, it is exempt from the dough-offering if the Israelite's amount is less than that required for the offering to be removed.

[49]The point of the mishnah is clear: Dough belonging to a gentile is not liable for the dough-offering. Thus, our text fits into its context. If the dough belonged to the gentile at the stage at which it would be liable for the dough-offering, it is not liable; however, if ownership were transferred to an Israelite at the stage at which it is liable, the Israelite must give the dough-offering. The whole is dependent on the Israelite, and a gentile is not an Israelite. This point is again stressed in mHal. 3:6, which states that if a gentile converted to Judaism with dough which had already been rolled out, that is dough which no longer required that the dough-offering be removed from it, he does not have to make the offering; however, if he converted while the dough was still liable for the offering, he must make it after he converts; Alan Avery-Peck, *Mishnah's Division of Agriculture: A History and Theology of Seder Zeraim* (Chico: 1985), 316.

[50]The reference to the gentile is not the central issue of the text; rather, the text focuses on the status of fields in Syria and their comparison to those in the Land of Israel. Cf., Neusner, *Eliezer*, I, 80-81.

[51]MShab. 2:1-3 list those items with which it is permissible to kindle a Sabbath-lamp. MShab. 2:4 describes items which may not be used for a Sabbath-lamp, such as an egg shell. MShab. 2:5 enumerates those situations in which one may extinguish a Sabbath-lamp without violating the Sabbath, and mShab. 2:6 lists the three things, violation of which, cause a woman to die in childbirth. The lighting of the Sabbath-lamp is one of the three items. MShab. 2:7 mentions the three things with which a man must be concerned when darkness is falling on the eve of the Sabbath, and the lighting of the Sabbath-lamp is mentioned. Our text mentions the gentile as one of the three things of which an Israelite is afraid and states that he may extinguish the Sabbath-lamp because of his fear and, we assume, in order to save a life; Neusner, *Shabbat*, 37.

the gentile *qua* gentile is seen as possibly dangerous. MShab. 6:10 contains a reference by Meir or sages concerning the "ways of the Amorites."[52] MShab. 6:8-10 discuss items with which people may go out on the Sabbath, and they open with a form of the Hebrew root ys'. For this reason, mShab. 6:10 fits into its context. MShab. 16:6 states that if a gentile came to put out a fire on the Sabbath, the Israelites may not tell him what to do, "for they are not responsible for his keeping the Sabbath." MShab. 16:1-7 discuss what an Israelite may do if there is a fire on the Sabbath, so that mShab. 16:6 fits into its context.[53] MShab. 16:8[54] provides specific examples which follow the general rule that on the Sabbath, an Israelite may benefit from something which gentiles have provided for themselves, but not from something which they did with the intention of benefiting the Israelite.[55] The same theme is carried forward in mShab. 23:4 with reference to a coffin and grave which had been prepared for a gentile on the Sabbath; these may be used by an Israelite. However, an Israelite may not play a dirge on flutes which a gentile carried on the Sabbath, unless he carried them only a short distance. Neusner entitles mShab. 23:1-24:5 "Seemly behavior on the Sabbath."[56] MShab. 23:4 opens with a general rule about a wedding reception and a funeral at the end of the Sabbath, and the relevant portion builds on the mention of the funeral. The majority of references to the non-Israelite in mShabbat are generated by the recognition that they are not Israelites, so that they do not have to observe the periods of Israelite holy time. However, if gentiles do come into contact with Israelites during the latter's periods of sacred time, the former's actions are restricted, so that *indirectly*, even gentiles are affected by the Israelite periods of sacred time.[57]

MErub. 3:5 tells us that an Israelite may set out two *'erubin* and make it conditional as to which he will use. For example, he may state that if gentiles

----

[52]Robert Goldenberg, *The Sabbath Law of Rabbi Meir* (Ann Arbor: 1978), 23-24. Jacob N .Epstein, *Introduction to the Text of the Mishnah* (Tel Aviv: 1964) II, 1142.

[53]Specifically, the passages tell us when an Israelite may move something from a private to a public domain, on a Sabbath, mShab. 1:1, in order to save it from a fire. For a discussion of general principles, see Neusner, *Shabbat*, 146. The point is that the gentile is not an Israelite; therefore, he does not need to observe the Sabbath.

[54]MShab. 16:6 and mShab. 16:8 are related thematically; however, mShab. 16:7 interposes between them.

[55]Thus, an Israelite may use a lamp which the gentile has provided for himself, water his animals at a trough which the gentile has filled with water for his own animals, and use a gangplank which the gentile erected for himself. Again, the point is that a gentile is not an Israelite and is not obligated to observe the Sabbath.

[56]Neusner, *Shabbat*, 12.

[57]For a further discussion of this issue, see below, Chapter Seven.

come from one direction, he will use the *'erub* he has placed in the other direction.[58] Chapter three takes up the issue of the *'erub* and the Sabbath-limit of a town.[59] While mErub. 3:5 discusses the *'erub* as an extension of a town's Sabbath-limit, mErub. 3:6-9 deal with a new theme which is unrelated to the *'erub*. MErub. 3:5 is related to mErub. 3:4, which Neusner calls a "transition" between the two functions of the *'erub* discussed in this chapter.[60] Here the gentile is seen as a possible danger to the Israelite people. MErub. 7:6 is based on the same principle as mM.S. 4:4, non-Israelite servants cannot serve as an Israelite's agent because they cannot act as independent human beings from the point of view of Israelite law. Thus, an Israelite cannot set up a *shittuf* by means of a non-Israelite servant. Our passage begins the discussion of a *shittuf*[61] which is continued in mErub. 8.[62]

MSheq. 1:5 rules that the half-*sheqel* tax may not be accepted from gentiles or Samaritans, even if they wish to pay it.[63] The gentile and Samaritan are contrasted to women, slaves, and minors who, although not required to pay the half-*sheqel*, may do so if they wish. The gentile and Samaritan are mentioned in order to complete the elements of the population of the Land of Israel. MSheq. 1:5 actually completes the discussion begun in mSheq. 1:3, for mSheq. 1:4 expands on the reference to priests in mSheq. 1:3.[64] By not being allowed to pay the half-*sheqel* tax, the gentiles, and Samaritans, are excluded from the Israelite people. The half-*sheqel* tax was used primarily for the maintenance of the public worship at the Temple,[65] and the maintenance of the ethnic shrine

----

[58]Or if a sage comes from one direction, he will use the *'erub* he has placed in that part of town.

[59]Neusner, *Erubin*, 7. Neusner notes that the *'erub* serves two functions: "The commingling of spaces of courtyards to form one large, private domain for carrying,. . . and the extension, through commingling, of the domain covered by the Sabbath-line of a town, for the purposes of a single individual;" Neusner, *Erubin*, 36. Our text deals with the second issue. Apparently, a person may set out an *'erub* in the opposite direction from the approaching gentiles, so that he may go an additional 2000 cubits in order to avoid them; Neusner, *Erubin*, 45-46.

[60]Neusner, *Erubin*, 38.

[61]A *shittuf* serves to unite dwellings in an alley; Danby, 796.

[62]Neusner, *Erubin*, 97.

[63]As the opening chapter of mSheqalim makes clear, only non-priestly male Israelites must pay the tax. This is derived from Ex. 30:11-16. The gentiles are not Israelites. They are not responsible for the up-keep of the Temple, nor may they participate in the communal-sacrifices; therefore, they may not pay the tax, even if they want to pay it.

[64]Jacob Neusner, *A History of the Mishnaic Law of Appointed Times Part Three Sheqalim, Yoma, Sukkah. Translation and Explanation* (Leiden: 1982), 10-12.

[65]Emil Schürer, *The History of the Jewish People in the Age of Jesus Christ (175 B.C.-A.D. 135)*, A new English Version revised and edited by Geza Vermes, Fergus Millar, and Matthew Black (Edinburg: 1979), II, 270-272.

was naturally obligatory for only the members of the Israelite ethnic group, even if they were slaves, minors, and women. Here the gentile does not even achieve the status of an Israelite child. MSheq. 7:6 states that if a gentile sent a whole-offering together with its drink-offering to the Temple from a region "beyond the sea," they may be offered. However, if he did not send the drink-offering, it is paid for with the communal funds derived from the collection of the half-*sheqel*. Neusner argues that mSheq. 7:6 is a "secondary development" of the issues raised in mSheq. 7:4-5.[66] Even though the gentile does not contribute to the maintenance of the public cult through the half-*sheqel* tax, funds from that tax may be used for offerings made by non-Israelites. The underlying issue is the relationship of the non-Israelite to the Temple and its cult.[67] If they wish, gentiles may make voluntary offerings to YHWH, and the Israelite community is obligated to support the gentile's activities.

MYoma 8:7 notes that if people believe a building collapsed on a person during the Day of Atonement, the rubble may be removed "from above him," even if it is not known for certain that there is a person in the ruin, whether he is alive or dead, or whether he is an Israelite or a gentile. MYoma 8:1-7 discuss actions which are prohibited and permitted on the Day of Atonement, so that our text fits into its context.[68] The gentile is included because he represents that part of humankind not represented by Israelites. Together with the Israelites, gentiles complete the make-up of humanity. By including the gentile in its discussion, the passage makes it clear that the saving of *any* human life overrides the prohibition against working on the Day of Atonement, the main issue of the *sugya*.

MTan. 3:7 states that one may sound the *shofar* on the Sabbath to warn the people that the town is encompassed by gentiles or a flood. Chapter three discusses when the *shofar* is sounded, and mTan. 3:8 specifies that it may be sounded "for any public distress." Therefore, our text fits into is present context.[69] The threatening gentile is also found in mTan. 4:6, which sets forth the fast days which commemorate the disasters which befell the Temple and the city

----

[66]Neusner, *Sheqalim*, 48, 51.

[67]For a further discussion of this matter, see below, Chapter Ten.

[68]Neusner suggests that our text and mYoma 8:6 form an appendix to the discussion begun in mYoma 8:1 and continued to the middle of mYoma 8:6; Neusner, *Sheqalim*, 119.

[69]Here, the threat of the gentiles takes precedence over the observance of the Sabbath. Cf., Jacob Neusner, *A History of the Mishnaic Law of Appointed Times Part Four Besah, Rosh Hashshanah, Taanit, Megillah, Moed Qatan, Hagigah. Translation and Explanation* (Leiden: 1983), 118, 121. Neusner views mTan. 3:5-7 as a unit.

of Jerusalem at the hands of the gentiles. MTan. 4:6-7 deal with the fast days which commemorate the destruction of the Temple. The dangerous gentile is a topic we have frequently encountered above.

MMeg. 4:9 interprets Lev. 18:21[70] to mean that one should not allow his offspring to become a non-Israelite.[71] MMeg. 4:8-9 center on the theme of heresy, so that mMeg. 4:9 fits into its context.[72] Here the text assumes that non-Israelites, by their very nature, reject YHWH.

The fact that marriage with a gentile affects one's Levitical status, even throughout the generations, is made clear in mYeb. 7:5.[73] The general theme of the chapter is the status of a woman married to a priest, with reference to her right to eat the heave-offering,[74] and the reference to the gentile is appropriate to the discussion at hand. The underlying assumption is that an Israelite must marry within the ethnic group; intercourse between an Israelite and a member of another ethnic unit produce offsprings who cannot benefit from the prerogatives granted to members of the Israelite community. MYeb. 16:5 examines the incidental testimony of women and children concerning a person's death. Judah b. Baba states that if a gentile overheard a statement and repeated it in order to give testimony, his evidence is invalid.[75] MYeb. 16:3-6 "present a series of rulings on identifying the corpse,"[76] so that the discussion of a gentile's testimony is relevant in this context. Here gentiles are excluded from consciously participating in the normal procedures of the Israelite judicial system. However, they may *incidentally* take part in the court procedures. The fact that gentiles are not Israelites is manifested in the different ways the former are treated in the latter's judicial system.

----

[70]*Do not allow any of your offspring to be offered up to Molech.* . . .

[71]This is usually taken to mean that one should not have intercourse with a non-Israelite woman.

[72]Neusner, *Besah*, 174.

[73]If an Israelite and a priest married and produced a daughter who married a gentile who produced a male grandchild, the child is a *mamzer*. If the grandmother were an Israelite married to a priest, she may eat the heave-offering; however, if the grandmother were from a priestly family, she may not eat the heave-offering.

[74]MYeb. 7:5-6 discuss "a series of cases in which improper sexual relations do not deprive a priest's daughter of the right to eat heave-offering, or in which there is some ambiguity, in the unfolding generations, first, second, third;" Jacob Neusner, *A History of the Mishnaic Law of Women Part One Yebamot. Translation and Explanation* (Leiden: 1980), 106.

[75]A gentile's testimony on a matter of the status of an Israelite woman is invalid; however, according to the *gemara*, bYeb. 121b, one can believe a gentile if he does not intend to give testimony, but is merely relaying what he heard or saw; Neusner, *Yebamot*, 208.

[76]Neusner, *Yebamot*, 201.

MNed. 3:11 describes gentiles as "the Children of Noah," while Israelites are known as "the Children of Abraham." We are also told that the Bible, specifically Jer. 9:26, ISam. 17:36, and IISam. 1:20, describes the gentiles as "uncircumcised." The above terms are explained so that one can assess an Israelite's vow in which he employs them. Because the main interest of mNed. 3:6-11 is the language of a vow,[77] our text, which defines terms which may be used in a vow, fits into its context. However, the gentiles and the Israelites are viewed as forming different "descent groups," for they go back to different biblical progenitors.

In mNed. 4:3, Eliezer explains that the soul of an unclean animal belongs to YHWH, while its body belongs to man, for the owner may sell an unclean animal to a gentile or feed it to dogs. According to Neusner, mNed. 4:2-3 form a unit, for mNed. 4:3 "depends upon" the opening statement of mNed. 4:2.[78] The reference to the gentile parallels the mention of the dogs to indicate that something is being discarded. The gentiles are seen as "others;" in fact, their being members of the human race is undermined in this passage.

MSot. 9:2 states that if a corpse is found near a frontier, a city in which the majority of the population are gentiles, or a city in which there is no Israelite court, the heifer's neck is not broken.[79] Neusner argues that mSot. 9:1-8 are "essentially autonomous of [their] larger setting;"[80] however, the unit centers on the rite of the heifer, so that our discussion fits its context, for it explains when the rite is not appropriate.

MGit. 1:5 notes that any writ drawn up in gentile registries is valid, even if it were signed by gentiles, except for divorce documents and writs of emancipation. Simeon disagrees and claims that even these legal instruments may be prepared by gentiles, if they are authorized to do so. Neusner sees mGit. 1:4-5, which focus on a comparison between the writ of divorce and the writ of emancipation, as an appendix to mGit. 1:1-3. He further considers mGit. 1:6 to be an appendix to mGit. 1:5,[81] which discusses Samaritan witnesses as well as the gentiles. While the gentile administrative system is seen as independent of that of the Israelite structure, the authority of that system is accepted in this pas-

----

[77]Jacob Neusner, *A History of the Mishnaic Law of Women Part Three Nedarim, Nazir. Translation and Explanation* (Leiden: 1980), 28.

[78]Neusner, *Nedarim*, 37.

[79]Deut. 21.

[80]Jacob Neusner, *A History of the Mishnaic Law of Women Part Four Sotah, Gittin, Qiddushin. Translation and Explanation* (Leiden: 1980), 83.

[81]Neusner, *Sotah*, 123.

sage. Here the compilers of Mishnah recognize the realities of the social and political world in which they lived.

We have seen above that a gentile cannot serve as an Israelite's agent, and this is reaffirmed in mGit. 2:5, which states that a divorce document cannot be delivered by a deaf-mute, an imbecile, a minor, a blind man, or a gentile.[82] The chapter provides "the fundamental rules for the preparation and delivery of a writ of divorce;"[83] therefore, the reference to the gentile is appropriate. While we have encountered *sugyot* in which the gentile does not achieve the status of even an Israelite child, here is considered the same as an Israelite minor.

MGit. 4:6 contains two references to the gentile, each of which is placed here for its own reasons. The first mention of the gentile discourages the sale of an Israelite's slave to a non-Israelite, for if a slave is sold to a gentile, it is declared a freeman.[84] This relates to the theme of slavery introduced in mGit. 4:4. The second section states that Israelites should not purchase ritual objects from gentiles for more than their market value.[85] Here, the text conforms to the pattern of mentioning things which are done in "the interest of peace," a phrase which appears several times in this part of the *sugya*.[86] We have two pictures of the gentile. The former picture describes him as the "other" who is un-qualified to own Israelite slaves; the latter paints him as an unethical human being. Both of these pictures focus on the gentile *qua* gentile, whose non-Israelite nature is the point at issue. MGit. 5:9=mSheb. 5:9. The text appears here because the phrase "interest of peace" occurs in mGit. 5:8-9.

MGit. 9:2 indirectly takes up the issue of whether or not an Israelite woman may marry a non-Israelite: Upon divorcing his wife, an Israelite may stipulate that she may not marry his father, her father, his brother, her brother, a slave, or a gentile. Neusner argues that mGit. 9:1-2+3 form a unit which "takes

----

[82]The others are disqualified because they cannot recite the formula or testify to the validity of the document being transferred from the husband to the wife.

[83]MGit. 2:5-7 "go over the issue of who is fit to write the document (M[Git]. 2:5) and who may deliver it and state the required formula that in his presence, it was written and signed (M[Git]. 2:6-7). Excluded are people whose testimony in an Israelite court is not acceptable;" Neusner, *Sotah*, 133.

[84]Cf., Gary G. Porton, "Forbidden Transactions: Prohibited Commerce with Gentiles in Earliest Rabbinism" in Jacob Neusner and Ernest S. Frerichs (eds.), *"To See Ourselves as Others See Us" Christians, Jews, "Others" in Late Antiquity* (Chico: 1985), 324.

[85]The commentators suggest that this is to discourage the gentiles from stealing these objects and selling them back to Israelites; Hanokh Albeck, *The Six Orders of the Mishnah: Order Nashim* (Tel Aviv: 1959), 283.

[86]Neusner, *Sotah*, 149.

up the question of an incomplete act of divorce, that is, a writ of divorce which leaves the wife subject to the husband's will by prohibiting her from marrying some one man."[87] Above, we have seen the same concern with Israelites' marrying outside of the ethnic group. According to mGit. 9:8, an Israelite court may force a man to divorce his wife; however, gentile justices may not force him to do so, unless they are carrying out the wishes of the Israelite tribunal. The opening of mGit. 9:8 clearly relates to the themes of mGit. 9:6, for both deal with divorce documents upon which we find Hebrew and Greek.[88] Perhaps the mention of Greek occasioned the mention of the gentiles in mGit. 9:8. While recognizing the existence of a non-Israelite judicial system, our text at this point recognizes its authority only if it accedes to the authority of the Israelite courts, perhaps an unrealistic expectation.

MQid. 1:2-3 distinguish between Israelite and non-Israelite slaves with regard to the manner in which they may be acquired by themselves and by others.[89] MQid. 1:1-6 deal with how one acquires an object, and mQid. 1:1-5 share a common style.[90] Thus, the appearance of the gentile slave fits into this context.

MQid. 3:12 again makes it clear that an Israelite cannot contract a valid betrothal or marriage with a gentile. The text further states that the child of a union between an Israelite man and a gentile woman retains the mother's status. As Neusner notes, mQid. 3:12-13 "lay the groundwork for Chapter Four, dealing with the consequence of marriage among various castes and the status of the offspring thereof,"[91] so that the reference to the gentile is appropriate here. MQid. 4:3 states that those mentioned in Deut. 23:1-3, who are "forbidden to enter the

----

[87]Neusner, *Sotah*, 199. The reference to the gentile fits with the reference to the slave, and all of the males listed could be forbidden to the wife; however, the gentile is clearly of a different category from the others, and he may be included here because of the reference to the slave.

[88]Neusner, *Sotah*, 208. Although mGit. 9:7 does not refer to the languages which appear on the writ, it does discuss where on the document the witnesses's signatures should appear, an issue also raised in mGit. 9:6.

[89]The Hebrew slave may be acquired by money or a writ, while the gentile slave may be acquired by money, a writ, or usucaption. Similarly, the manner in which an Israelite slave may secure his freedom is different from the manner in which a gentile slave may acquire his. The Israelite slave, following Ex. 21:2 and Lev. 15:40, is automatically freed after six years of service or upon the arrival of the Jubilee year. The gentile slave, however, is freed only upon payment of money, or upon uttering a writ of indebtedness. What is important is that the two types of slaves are treated differently and that part of this difference results from the Torah's treatment of Israelite and non-Israelite slaves.

[90]The opening clauses employ the root qnh in the Niphal.

[91]Neusner, *Sotah*, 239.

congregation," may intermarry with one another. Judah forbids this practice.[92] Neusner views mQid. 4:1-8 as the principle unit of the chapter, whose point is that "there are diverse groups who may not intermarry by reason of genealogical impairment or imperfection;"[93] thus, the mention of the gentile fits at this point. These passages share the picture of the non-Israelite as essentially an "other" who is fundamentally different from the Israelites.

According to mB.Q. 4:3, if an Israelite's ox gored the ox of a gentile, the Israelite is not culpable.[94] However, if a gentile's ox gores an Israelite's ox, whether the ox were deemed dangerous or not, the gentile must pay full damages. Neusner sees mB.Q. 4:3-4 as a unit, for they "deal with an ox under ownership other than of an ordinary, adult Israelite . . . ,"[95] and the reference to the gentile fits well into this discussion. MB.Q. 4:6 again draws a distinction between Israelites and gentiles: If an ox intended to kill a gentile but killed an Israelite, it is not punished for committing an intentional murder. The contrast between the gentile and the Israelite is only one of three contrasting pairs which appear in the *sugya*. MB.Q. 4:6 fits into its context, for mB.Q. 4:5-9 "in general pay attention to the penalties paid when an ox commits manslaughter."[96]

MB.Q. 8:3 and mB.Q. 8:5 distinguish between Israelite slaves and non-Israelite slaves with respect to the compensation for damages done to them.[97] Neusner labels mB.Q. 8:1-7 "Penalties for assault,"[98] and the contrast drawn between harm done to Israelite and non-Israelite slaves seems appropriate here. The texts here indicate that the distinctions between the Israelites and non-Israelites are maintained by their being treated differently by the Israelite legal and social systems.

----

[92]The text deals with these people because they were mentioned in the Torah. The facts that they no longer existed and that it would have been impossible for the rabbis to regulate their behavior, if they did exist, do not trouble our author(s).

[93]Neusner, *Sotah*, 252.

[94]The basis of the rule is that Ex. 21:35 specifies *his neighbor's ox*, and a gentile is not included among an Israelite's neighbors.

[95]Jacob Neusner, *A History of the Mishnaic Law of Damages Part One Baba Qamma. Translation and Explanation* (Leiden: 1983), 52.

[96]Neusner, *Baba Qamma*, 52.

[97]If an Israelite wounds another person's Israelite or non-Israelite slave, he is liable for the injury, pain, healing, loss of time, and indignity which his act caused. Judah says one is not liable for indignity done to slaves, mB.Q. 8:3. If he wounds his own Israelite slave, he is liable for everything except loss of time; however, if he wounds his own gentile slave, he is not liable for anything. While the texts draw a clear distinction between what one may do to his own gentile slave and Israelite slave, there is no distinction drawn between damage done to another person's slave because both the Israelite and non-Israelite slave are considered the other person's property.

[98]Neusner, *Baba Qamma*, 10-11.

MB.M. 1:5 discusses items found by those who have independent status and those who are not independent of an adult Israelite male; therefore, we find a distinction drawn between a Hebrew and a Canaanite slave.[99] Neusner suggests that mB.M. 1:5 "supplements M. [B.M.] 1:4's interest in the effective acquisition on a man's behalf on the part of his domain,"[100] and the reference to the gentile slave fits well into this context. The point here is that gentiles attain the status of Israelite minors.

MB.M. 5:6 contains a number of rules concerning usury which distinguish between Israelites and non-Israelites.[101] Chapter five opens with definitions of usury and interest, and these remain the major concerns of this series of texts. While mB.M. 5:6 is the only passage which refers to the gentile, its discussion fits well into this chapter. The uniqueness of gentiles when compared to Israelites is maintained by the different financial mores applied when an Israelite is engaged in business transactions with members of the different groups.

MSanh. 7:3 deals with the way in which the Israelite court beheaded people, and it states that they are beheaded "with a sword as the government does." This is a reference to the method of execution attributed to the Roman rulers of Palestine.[102] MSanh. 7:1-3 treat modes of execution, so that our text fits into its context. The text is designed to point to the inhuman cruelty of the non-Israelite authorities.

MSanh. 9:2 mentions a person's liability for manslaughter, and it draws the same distinction between a gentile and an Israelite as did mB.Q. 4:6 with regard to an ox, and both texts employ in the same language.[103] Both *sugyot* illustrate that gentiles make up the part of the human family not covered by Israelites. MSanh. 9:2, along with the end of mSanh. 9:1 and all of mSanh. 9:3,

---

[99]An object found by a person's minor children, his non-Israelite slaves, or his wife belong to him, for they are dependents of Israelite males and have no independent status. However, things found by one's children who are of age, his Hebrew slaves, and his divorced wife belong to them, for they are independent humans.

[100]Jacob Neusner, *A History of the Mishnaic Law of Damages Part Two Baba Mesia. Translation and Explanation* (Leiden: 1983), 16.

[101]An Israelite may accept a flock on "iron-terms" from a gentile, but not from an Israelite, money may be borrowed from, or lent to, a gentile with interest paid or charged, and an Israelite may lend out a gentile's money with the latter's permission.

[102]Hanokh Albeck, *The Six Orders of the Mishnah: Order Neziqin* (Tel Aviv: 1953), 190.

[103]Mtkwn lhrwg . . . . "If a person intended to kill a gentile, but killed an Israelite, he is not culpable for murder."

"discuss[es] the liability to conviction for murder,"[104] and our text seems appropriate in this context.

MSanh. 9:6 prohibits an Israelite from having an Aramean woman as a lover. If an Israelite does take an Aramean lover, the "zealots" may fall on him.[105] As Neusner notes, mSanh. 9:4, 5, and 6 discuss "extra-judicial punishments,"[106] and the situation in which the gentile is mentioned fits into this setting. The passage states that those Israelites who marry outside the ethnic group deserve the harshest of punishments.

According to mSanh. 10:2, Doeg, Balaam, Ahitophel, and Gehazi have no share in the world-to-come. Their exclusion is based on their actions in the Bible, not on their gentile status. The same is true of the generation of the flood and the men of Sodom, mSanh. 10:3. MSanh. 10:1-3 deal with "extra-judicial punishment, at the hands of Heaven,"[107] so that our texts fit into their contexts.[108]

According to Meir[109] in mZeb. 4:5, the laws of refuse, remnant, and uncleanness do not apply to offerings made to the Temple by gentiles, and there is no penalty for slaughtering these offerings at the wrong time, or outside of the Temple-precinct.[110] Neusner argues that "the extended discussion of the role of intention in the invalidation of the sacrifice . . . concludes" with our text,[111] and the reference to gentiles is appropriate here, for they cannot have valid intention from the point of view of mishnaic law. Although gentiles may offer some sacrifices to YHWH, they do so in a manner which distinguishes their offerings from those made by Israelites.[112]

----

[104]Jacob Neusner, *A History of the Mishnaic Law of Damages Part Three Baba Batra, Sanhedrin, Makkot. Translation and Explanation* (Leiden: 1984), 208.

[105]Cf., Num. 25:6-9.

[106]Neusner, *Baba Batra*, 208.

[107]Neusner, *Baba Batra*, 135.

[108]I have not counted this as an essay because more than gentiles are mentioned in this context, and the issue is not the gentile status of those non-Israelites who appear.

[109]Some texts read Simeon; Danby, 473, n. 6; Jacob Neusner, *A History of the Mishnaic Law of Holy Things Part One Zebahim. Translation and Explanation* (Leiden: 1978), 83-86; Naples edition reads Meir. Jerusalem codex Hebr. 4 reads Meir, but has Simeon in parentheses. Paris, Kaufman and Parma read Simeon.

[110]In this text, the application of the sacrificial laws depends on the status of the person who made the offering.

[111]Neusner, *Zebahim*, 84.

[112]For a full discussion of the ways in which gentiles are permitted to respond to YHWH through the Temple-cult and the aspects of the symbol of the Temple to which the gentile can respond, see below, Chapter Ten.

MMen. 9:8 excludes gentiles, slaves, agents, women, deaf-mutes, imbeciles, minors, and the blind from performing the act of the laying on of the hands, a ritual which may be performed by only adult Israelite males acting on their own behalf.[113] Neusner notes that mMen. 9:6-7 "form an autonomous unit shaped in response to form, not substantive considerations: All . . ., except . . ., a triplet."[114] However, mMen. 9:8-9 do focus on a single theme, the rite of the laying on of the hands. In any event, the reference to the gentile is appropriate here. The gentile is equated with the "ritually impaired."

MHul. 2:7 states that an Israelite may slaughter an animal for a gentile; however, Eliezer disagrees with the anonymous rule, arguing that the gentiles' main interest in everything they do is to serve an idol. MHul. 2:7-10 focus on the intentions and motives of the person who slaughters an animal, and mHul. 2:7 is phrased in such a way that it fits into its context.[115] The way in which the *sugya* is composed suggests that the issue was whether or not a gentile *qua* gentile is an idolater. We shall see below that, in general, Mishnah-Tosefta are able to differentiate the *gentile as idolater* from the gentile as farmer, merchant, etc.,[116] so that Eliezer's claim here was not accepted by all of his compatriots.

MHul. 7:2 rules that an Israelite may send to a gentile a thigh which contains the sinew of the hip "because its place is known."[117] Chapter seven focuses on the sinew of the hip, and our text fits nicely into its context. The prohibition against eating the sinew of the hip became a means of marking Israelite identity, and this seems to be the point here.

MHul. 10:3 expands on the principle that only an animal owned by an Israelite is subject to the requirement of the priestly gifts when it is

----

[113]The rite requires intention and knowledge; therefore, our list contains those who cannot have intention or knowledge.

[114]Jacob Neusner, *A History of the Mishnaic Law of Holy Things Part Two Menahot. Translation and Explanation* (Leiden: 1978), 122.

[115]Neusner, *Hullin,* 28.

[116]See below, Chapter Nine.

[117]On the basis of the phrase "because its place is known," some have argued that the issue is the gentile's reselling the hip to an Israelite; Hanokh Albeck, *The Six Orders of the Mishnah: Order Qodashim* (Tel Aviv: reprint 1958), 136; Eli Cashdan, *Hullin: Translated into English with Notes, Glossary and Indices,* in Isidore Epstein (ed.), *The Babylonian Talmud* (London: 1948), 525, n. 4; Neusner, *Hullin,* 89. However, this raises the problems of an Israelite's purchasing foodstuffs from gentiles and the gentile's reselling the hip to an Israelite. The problem with an Israelite's purchasing meat from a gentile is obvious, and the issue of a gentile's reselling a prohibited item to an Israelite is not clearly stated in Mishnah-Tosefta; see Porton, "Forbidden Transactions," 328, especially ns. 47-48. The sinew of the hip is prohibited to Israelites by Gen. 32:32; therefore, the fact that the Israelite may send the hip with the sinew to a gentile indicates the different status of Israelites and gentiles.

slaughtered.[118]   Neusner states that mHul. 10:3-4 "deal with minor rules relevant to the shoulder, cheeks, and maw, with particular interest in the exemption to the liability to the priestly gifts . . .,"[119] so that our *sugya*, which mentions the gentile and these parts of the animal, fits into its context. MHul. 11:2 rules that if an Israelite bought the fleece of a gentile's sheep, he is exempt from the law of the first fleece. Chapter eleven deals with the first fleece, so that the reference to the gentile and the offering of the first fleece fits into the chapter. In both of these passages, the gentile is a non-Israelite, who is not obligated to support the religious professionals of the People Israel.

MBekh. 2:4 is based on the principle that only animals owned by Israelites are subject to the laws of the firstlings.[120] As Neusner notes, mBekh. 2:4 returns to the discussion of mBekh. 2:1,[121] and the reference to the gentile is appropriate to the discussion. As a non-Israelite, the gentile is not obligated to observe the Israelite rules which testify to YHWH's ownership of earthly creatures. According to mBekh. 5:2, the Hillelites ruled that an Israelite, and even a gentile,[122] could be counted with a priest for the consumption of a blemished[123] firstling. The Shammaites had forbidden the former and not mentioned the latter. In this context, the gentile represents that part of humankind not represented by Israelites. MBekh. 5:2 relates to the discussion in mBekh. 5:1 concerning a blemished or unconsecrated firstling.[124] MBekh. 5:3 raises an entirely new issue, the problem of a firstling which has been intentionally blemished. The text is relevant for us, for it contains a narrative which discusses a quaestor; however, it is unrelated to the reference to the gentile in mBekh. 5:2. From the end of mBekh. 5:2 to the opening of mBekh. 5:4, we do have a

----

[118]If an Israelite slaughtered a beast for a priest or for a gentile, he is exempt from bringing the priests' dues. If an Israelite jointly owned an animal with a gentile or a priest, he must bring proof of his partnership in order not to be liable for the priests' dues. Similarly, if priests or gentiles sell an animal to an Israelite, they may withhold the part due to the priest.

[119]Neusner, *Hullin*, 116.

[120]If an Israelite received a sheep or a goat from a gentile on "iron terms," the offspring is exempt from the law, but the latter's offspring is not. However, if the gentile stipulated that the offspring should stand in place of its mother, the former's offspring is exempt, while the offspring of its offspring is not. Simeon b. Gamliel claims that they are all exempt because the gentile still has a lien on them.

[121]Neusner, *Hullin*, 159.

[122]Neusner claims that the reference to the gentile is an "Aqiban" gloss; Neusner, *Rabbinic Traditions*, II, 245-246; Neusner, *Hullin*, 183.

[123]Albeck, *Qodashim*, 170.

[124]Neusner, *Hullin*, 180.

coherent unit; however, the gentile is not an issue, with the exception of the narrative in mBekh. 5:3.

In mArakh. 1:2, Meir states that an Israelite may pledge the valuation of a gentile, but a gentile may not pledge his, or another's, valuation. Judah states that a gentile may vow another's valuation, but his valuation may not be vowed by others. Both agree that gentiles may vow another's worth and that their worth may be vowed by others.[125] MArakh. 1:2, which discusses the gentile, relates to mArakh. 1:1, but is independent of mArakh. 1:3-4.[126] However, the contrast drawn between the gentiles and the Israelites seems appropriate at this point. The essential difference concerning the status of Israelites and gentiles is illustrated by this text.

MArakh. 8:4 classifies a gentile slave as the property of an Israelite, so that the same laws apply to the gentile slave as apply to other types of property. MArakh. 8:4 sets the issue of dedicating property which is carried forward in mArakh. 8:5-7,[127] so that the reference to the gentile slave is appropriate here. Although dealing with slaves, the difference in the classes of humanity represented by gentiles and Israelites underlies this passage.

MMid. 1:6 and mMid. 2:3 refer to parts of the Temple which were defiled, or breached, by the Greek kings. Each fits into its own context which discusses parts of the Temple and the Temple-mount. These pericopae serve to illustrate the point that the gentile government can be dangerous.

MKel. 1:8 states that the rampart which surrounds the inner courts of the Temple cannot be passed by gentiles "or any who have contracted corpse-uncleanness." The subject of mKel. 1:6-9 is the degrees of holiness,[128] and our text explains that "the rampart is still more holy" than the Temple Mount, while being less holy than the court of women. The reference to the gentiles serves to illustrate this point and fits into the context. The gentile *qua* gentile is seen as taboo with regard to the religious shrine of the People Israel.

MOhol. 17:3 opens by stating that a field plowed by a gentile cannot be counted as a grave-area if bones are found while he is plowing.[129] Chapter

----

[125]"According to Meir, the matter rests upon the action of the person who takes upon himself to pay the Valuation . . . . In Judah's view, the matter rests upon the status of that which is subject to Valuation;" Jacob Neusner, *A History of the Mishnaic Law of Holy Things Part Four Arakhin, Temurah. Translation and Explanation* (Leiden: 1979), 12.

[126]Neusner, *Arakhin*, 10.

[127]Neusner, *Arakhin*, 59.

[128]Jacob Neusner, *A History of the Mishnaic Law of Purities Part One Kelim. Chapters One Through Eleven* (Leiden: 1974), 16.

[129]The text presents a problem because the general rule with which the *sugya* ends states that the laws of the grave-area do not apply to Samaritans, and it does not mention gentiles.

seventeen discusses one who plows an area which may or may not be considered a grave-area, so that our discussion fits into the chapter. The laws of the grave-area apply to only Israelites, and gentiles are not Israelites.

According to mToh. 5:8, all spittle is unclean if it is found in a town in which there is a woman who is careless about her period, one who is a Samaritan, or one who is a gentile. The point is that the spittle of a woman during her period is unclean, and the three types of women who are mentioned are those who would not follow the purity-laws of the rabbis. Therefore, the reference to the gentile is appropriate. The chapter is a collection of rulings about purity in a public setting. The gentile is merely one of those groups of people who does not follow the strict purity-rules of the compilers of our texts.

MToh. 7:6 states that if tax-gatherers entered a house, everything within it becomes unclean. However, even if there is a gentile with them, they are believed if they said that they did not enter the house. They are not believed, however, if they claimed that they entered the house, but did not touch anything.[130] MToh. 7:2-6 discuss ways in which the items inside a house can become unclean, so that our passage fits into its context. If the commentators understand this text correctly, it testifies to the assumed power of the gentile government.

MToh. 8:6 opens with the general rule that clean food which is intended for a man is susceptible to uncleanness unless it is rendered unfit for dog-food, and it states that food given to a gentile counts as human food.[131] The chapter contains a list of rules concerning clean and unclean foodstuffs and vessels; therefore, our rule fits into its general context. The reference to the gentile is appropriate in this context, for even the gentile is considered human. Here the gentile symbolizes the non-Israelite sector of humanity.

----

[130]The exact reading of the text is uncertain; Danby, 726, n. 8; Hanokh Albeck, *The Six Orders of the Mishnah: Seder Tohorot*, (Tel Aviv: 1967), 322. Codex Parma has 'ynw written between the lines. Codex Kaufmann, Codex Paris, and Naples Edition do not have the negative. Codex Jerusalem Heb 4 has the negative. Cf., Jacob Epstein, II, 825, n. 3. If the negative belongs in the text, the assumption seems to be that if a gentile were with the collectors, he would have been certain that they faithfully inventoried the contents of the house; Albeck, *Tohorot*, 322. The point seems to stress the power of the gentile authorities, if Albeck's interpretation, following Bartinoro, *loc. cit.*, is correct.

[131]Thus, if a pigeon fell into a wine-press and one formed the intention to pick it out in order to give it to a gentile for food, it becomes susceptible to uncleanness. However, if an imbecile, a minor, or a deaf-mute intended to use the pigeon for food, it is unsusceptible to uncleanness because they cannot form a proper intention. But, if they picked it out to give it as food to a gentile, it is susceptible, for the act is important, even if they cannot form the proper intention. The gentile appears in order to indicate that the rule applies to the food of any human.

MMiq. 8:4 distinguishes between a gentile woman who discharges Israelite seed and an Israelite woman who discharges gentile seed. MMiq. 8:2-4 deal with those who suffer a genital emission; therefore, this text fits into its context. The Israelite purity taboos do not apply to gentiles.

MNid. 4:3=mEd. 5:1. The text fits here, for mNid. 4:1-3 discusses the blood of women who would not be expected to follow Israelite purity-rules.

According to mNid. 7:3, all blood stains that come from gentile women are clean, for the laws of cleanness do not apply to blood stains from gentiles, no matter where they are found. While chapter seven, with the exception of mNid. 7:2, deals with blood stains, the reference to the gentiles is only in our text. The mention of Samaritans in mNid. 7:3 is carried forward in mNid. 7:4-5. The appearance of the gentile is appropriate, for mNid. 7:2-5 discuss those who are not careful about the rabbinic laws of the cleanness of blood.

MNid. 9:3 states that if an Israelite woman lent a shift to a gentile woman or to a menstruant, she may claim that the blood stain on the garment came from the other woman, so that she need not be declared unclean. The mention of the gentile is appropriate, for like the menstruant woman, the former could possibly have left blood on the garment, especially because gentiles are not careful about matters of menstrual blood. MNid. 9:1-5 deal with the appearance of blood, so that our text fits.

MNid. 10:4 rules that a gentile corpse does not convey uncleanness by carrying. MNid. 10:4 deals with those who convey uncleanness by carrying, so that the reference to the gentile fits somewhat. While mNid. 10:4 deals with those who convey uncleanness by carrying, mNid. 10:5 discusses those who convey uncleanness by overshadowing; however, the problem of conveying uncleanness is, in an indirect manner, common to both texts. Again, the Israelite purity-taboos do not affect non-Israelites.

MYad. 4:4 refers to Deut. 23:9, which prohibits the Ammonites and Moabites from entering the Congregation of Israel.[132] This passage carries on the discussion of Ammon and Moab begun in mYad. 4:3. This text, which discusses biblical nations which were no longer in existence, testifies to the concept that Israelites and gentiles form different descent groups.

We have discovered that many of the references to the gentile in Mishnah fit into their contexts and serve to refine, or to illustrate, points of Israelite

----

[132]The text notes that there are no longer any pure Ammonites or Moabites. Gamliel does not accept this, while Joshua does; William S. Green, *The Traditions of Joshua Ben Hananiah Part One: The Early Legal Traditions* (Leiden: 1981), 309-310.

law. We also discovered that the picture of the gentile is far from uniform in these passages. Gentiles may symbolize that part of humanity not represented by Israelites, they may appear as a danger to the Israelites, and they may be similar, or dissimilar, to Israelite children. In general, however, we have seen that Israelite rules do not apply to gentiles, or, at best, there is disagreement among the sages on this point.

Sugyot in contexts with no thematic development

Some of the mishnaic chapters which contain discussions of the gentiles are a collection of texts on a variety of topics, so that the units do not exhibit any thematic development. MSheb. 4:3 states that an Israelite may lease from a gentile during the seventh year land which the latter recently plowed.[133] Also, an Israelite may help a gentile with his work[134] in his fields during the seventh year.[135] Chapter four deals with a variety of topics, cast in a number of literary frameworks,[136] and mSheb. 4:3 is only loosely connected thematically to what surrounds it, while it is unrelated formally. However, the passage does make the clear point that gentiles are not obligated to recognize the sacred nature of the Land of Israel through observing the Israelite Sabbatical year.

MErub. 8:5 takes up the issue of a person who restricts others living in a courtyard with regard to an *'erub*.[137] MErub. 8:3, 4, and 5 are independent of

----

[133]The reason that an Israelite may lease a newly plowed field from a gentile is that the gentile is not an Israelite; therefore, the laws concerning the seventh year do not apply to him or to his property.

[134]Exactly how an Israelite may aid a gentile while the latter is working in his field during the seventh year is ambiguous, but most feel that it is only through verbal support of his activities. Lehrman translates the Hebrew, wmhzyqyn ydy 'wbdy kwkbym bsby't, as "gentiles may be encouraged during the Seventh Year;" S. M. Lehrman, *Shebi'ith: Translated into English With Notes* in Isidore Epstein (ed.), *The Babylonian Talmud: Seder Zera'im* (London: Soncino Press, 1935), 161. Danby renders the phrase "and gentiles may be helped [when labouring in the fields] in the Seventh Year;" Danby, 43. Rashi, *loc. cit.*, states that if the Israelites found a gentile plowing his field, they may encourage him to do so. Cf., Hanokh Albeck, *The Six Orders of the Mishnah: Seder Zera'im* (Tel Aviv: reprint, 1959), 148. Newman translates, "and they assist;" Newman, 98.

[135]In an unrelated statement, the text adds that greetings may be offered to gentiles in the interests of peace. The last two statements in this mishnah, the reference to an Israelite's aiding a gentile and greeting him, also appear in mSheb. 5:9. The reason they are in the latter text is that it discusses things which are permitted "in the interests of peace."

[136]MSheb. 4:2 and mSheb. 4:4 contain Houses-debates, and our passage therefore intrudes into the Houses-section of this chapter. MSheb. 4:2 and mSheb. 4:4 discuss fields which have been prepared during the seventh year, or fields in which some type of work has been done.

[137]Meir states that if one, whether Israelite or gentile, has gone on a trip and left his house empty so that he cannot join in the establishment of the *'erub*, this restricts all of the houses in the courtyard, for he may return on the Sabbath to occupy his house. Judah argues that the empty house does not matter. Yosi rules that the gentile's empty house restricts the others, but not an Israelite's, for the Israelite is not likely to return home on the Sabbath. Simeon expands on Yosi's dis-

one another and of what precedes and follows them.[138] The relevant passage contains a disagreement over whether or not Israelites and gentiles are treated differently with regard to their empty houses on the Sabbath. The basic issue is whether the fact that the house is empty or the ethnic identification of the house's owner is more important. If the former is more important, than the gentile nature of the owner is insignificant from the point of view of the laws concerning the 'erub.

MPes. 4:3 lays down certain restrictions concerning the sale of animals to gentiles.[139] This passage has nothing to do with Passover,[140] and its original context is probably mA.Z. 1:6. The issues discussed here are obscure.[141] However, the mention of the gentile seems to be a central factor is this sugya.

MBes. 3:2 states that if traps for wild animals, birds, or fish are set out before a festival, the animals may not be removed from the trap on the festival. We are told that a gentile once brought a fish to Gamliel, who ruled that although the fish was permitted, he would not accept it from the gentile. MBes. 3:1-2 cover rules of hunting, so that our text fits into its context. However, there is nothing in the Gamliel-story which ties it to the festival, the setting of the trap before the festival, or the removal of the fish on the festival.[142] Furthermore, the reason for the reference to the gentile is unclear. But, the flow of the text suggests that Gamliel did not purchase the fish because the seller was a gentile; we assume that he would have purchased it from an Israelite or that an Israelite would not have offered it for sale.

----

cussion of the Israelite.

[138] According to Meir and Judah, there is no distinction between the Israelite and the gentile, while Yosi and Simeon do draw a distinction. Meir holds that if one member of a courtyard does not participate in the 'erub, it cannot be established, while Judah argues that an empty house need not be considered. Meir, Yosi and Simeon agree with the general principle behind mErub. 6:1 that everyone in a courtyard must participate in the 'erub. Judah seems unconcerned with this issue; Neusner, Erubin, 109.

[139] With regard to the sale of small animals to gentiles, one follows the local custom. However, an Israelite may not sell gentiles large domesticated animals, calves, or foals, "maimed or not." Judah permits the sale of maimed beasts, and Ben Bathyra permits the sale of horses.

[140] It is here because of its opening formula, mqwm šnhgw, which it shares with mPes. 4:1, mPes. 4:4, and mPes. 4:5. MPes. 4:2 is connected to mPes. 4:1 by kywsy' bw.

[141] Porton, "Forbidden Transactions," 323-324.

[142] Neusner, Besah, 37; Shamai Kanter, Rabban Gamaliel II: The Legal Traditions (Chico: 1980), 103-104.

MYeb. 2:5 distinguishes between males born of Israelite women and those whose mothers were slaves or gentiles.[143] Neusner divides the second chapter of Yebamot into three sections: MYeb. 2:1-2, 3-4, and the remainder which is "essentially miscellaneous."[144] The text again supports the Israelite practice of endogamy. MYeb. 8:3 explains that an Ammonite or a Moabite, Deut. 23:3, is forbidden from marring an Israelite; however, their women are permitted. An Egyptian or an Edomite, Deut. 23:7, may marry into the Congregation of Israel after the third generation. The references to these specific peoples are based on the Torah, and with the exception of the Egyptians, these people did not exist during the rabbinic period. While the *sugya* discusses a number of people who may join the congregation, mYeb. 8:3 stands alone in this chapter. The pericope reflects the rabbinic assumptions that Israelites represent a different descent group from non-Israelites and that this fact is accurately recorded in the Hebrew Bible.

MKet. 2:9 deals with a woman who has been held captive by gentiles.[145] Neusner describes mKet. 2:9 and mKet. 2:10 as singletons. The main issue of the chapter is conflicting testimony about the sexual activity of a woman;[146] therefore, the part of mKet. 2:9 with which we are concerned fits only loosely into the chapter. The *sugyot* presupposes that the only factor which will curb the gentiles' sexual appetite is greed. The gentiles appear as "uncivilized" human beings.

The idea of preventing the transfer of people to the control of gentiles is also found in mGit. 4:9, where we are told that if an Israelite sells himself or his children to gentiles in order to pay off a debt, he may not be redeemed, and his children may not be redeemed until after he dies. This would discourage one

----

[143]With respect to the laws of a levirate marriage, a valid Israelite brother or son is one whose mother was an Israelite woman, so that a valid brother or son with respect to Israelite law cannot have a gentile mother.

[144]Neusner, *Yebamot*, 35. Intercourse with a gentile woman is further discouraged in mYeb. 2:8, which states that if one is suspected of having intercourse with a gentile woman who converts, he should not marry her after she converts. Slotki suggests that such a marriage would confirm the rumor; Israel Slotki, *Yebamoth, Translated with Notes, Glossary and Indices*, in Isidore Epstein (ed.), *The Babylonian Talmud* (London: 1936), 147, n. 10.

[145]If the woman were imprisoned for a civil offense, she is permitted to return to her husband when she is freed. We assume that the gentiles wanted the husband to desire the return of his wife; therefore, it was important for the gentiles to ensure her sexual purity. However, if the woman were imprisoned for a capital offense, so that neither the Israelites nor the gentiles would expect her to be returned to husband, we infer that the gentiles would have sexually violated her.

[146]Jacob Neusner, *A History of the Mishnaic Law of Women Part Two Ketubot. Translation and Explanation* (Leiden: 1980), 22.

from paying off his debt to a gentile by placing himself or members of his family under a gentile's control. MGit. 4:9 also states that if an Israelite bought back a field he had sold to a gentile, he must still bring the first-fruits. This reflects the view that gentiles cannot validly hold property in the Land of Israel. Therefore, as soon as the Israelite buys the field, whatever crop is on it must be considered new produce. This text would discourage Israelites from selling fields to gentiles, for repurchasing them would not be economically feasible. MGit. 4:9 seems to be added onto the end of the chapter, perhaps because it ends with the phrase "for the good order of the world." While related in theme to mGit. 4:6, it is unrelated to mGit. 4:7-8.

The judgment of the Egyptians, mEd. 2:10, endures on the basis of biblical events.[147] Again we see an attempt to place the realities of the biblical period into the first centuries of the common era. Although mEd. 2:10 opens with the same phrase as does mEd. 2:9,[148] it is thematically unrelated to its context.

MEd. 7:7 indicates that Rabban Gamliel once went to the governor of Syria in order to have his authority as Patriarch confirmed.[149] Given the nature of mEduyot, one does not expect thematic development within a given chapter, as we find in the other mishnaic tractates.[150] The same can be said of tractate Abot. In mAbot 3:2, Haninah the Prefect of the Priests advises the Israelites to pray for the peace of the government. Like in the whole of mAbot, this saying stands by itself in its chapter from the point of view of its theme. These two passages testify to the facts that some sages took gentile political control of Palestine for granted and that some of them considered this reality to be an acceptable condition of life.

MHul. 8:5 states that the milk in the stomach of an animal which a gentile slaughters, or which is carrion, is forbidden.[151] The gentile is mentioned because his act of slaughtering determines the status of the beast, and the text equates a beast slaughtered by a gentile with carrion. Chapter eight focuses on the problem of milk and meat; however, Neusner sees mHul. 8:5 as "an ap-

----

[147]Danby, 426, n. 16; Albeck, *Neziqin*, 292.

[148]"He used to say . . . ."

[149]Cf., E. Mary Smallwood, *The Jews Under Roman Rule: From Pompey to Diocletian* (Leiden: 1976), 349, n. 70; Kanter, 172.

[150]Neusner, *Shebuot*, 79.

[151]The nature of the beast from which the milk came determines whether or not the milk is permitted, for the text also states that the milk found within the stomach of a *terefah*-animal which it had sucked from a valid beast is permitted, while the milk found within the stomach of a valid beast which it had sucked from a *terefah*-beast is not.

pendix . . . on the status of milk (not mixed with meat) in the belly of a beast . . . ."[152] Gentiles are not Israelites; therefore, they do not follow the Israelite rules concerning the proper preparation of meat. This passage would interfere with the normal social interaction between the two groups.

MToh. 1:4 rules that if an Israelite slaughtered an unclean beast for a gentile, it conveys food-uncleanness while it still jerks and carrion-uncleanness after it has died or had its head chopped off. The whole of mToh. 1:4 distinguishes between food- and carrion-uncleanness, so that our discussion fits in with the rest of mToh. 1:4. However, it stands by itself in relation to the other elements of this chapter. Here the text assumes that gentiles represent that part of humankind not symbolized by the term Israelite. However, both groups are human, and meat prepared for either group falls under the restrictions concerning human food.

Summary

We have seen that the references to the gentile in Mishnah appear in three ways. First, several of the texts introduce chapters. In these instances, the texts most frequently distinguish between the Israelite, to whom the issues in the chapter pertain, and the gentile, to whom the topics in the unit are irrelevant. Second, we discovered a number of references to the gentile which fit into the thematic development of the chapters. In these cases, the references to the gentile helped the editors to develop the chapter's theme in important ways. Third, there are a few examples where the references to the gentile do not fit easily into the thematic development of the units in which they occur; however, in most of these instances, there is no thematic development in the chapter. We can conclude, therefore, that for the most part, the references to the gentiles are integral to the thematic developments of the various units within Mishnah. The gentiles were important, for they served as a way in which to illustrate Mishnah's points and to develop the ideas important to the its editor(s). It does not appear that the gentiles were of interest merely because they were gentiles.

In general, the appearance of the gentile underscores the distinctive nature of the Israelite group: 1) Israelite purity and food taboos apply to them alone, so that these serve to differentiate between Israelites and non-Israelites;[153] 2) in the minds of many sages, Israelites alone are responsible for supporting their ethnic institutions--such as the Temple-cult and its priesthood--or the needy members of their group--such as the poor;[154] 3) the ethnic unity of

---

[152]Neusner, *Hullin*, 96.

[153]See below, Chapter Eleven.

[154]See below, Chapters Six and Eleven.

the People Israel is re-enforced by the prohibition against exogamy and the assumption that Israelites and gentiles represent different descent groups;[155] 4) because Israelites and gentiles represent two distinct groups, different rules concerning damages, financial matters, and judicial procedures apply to each unit.[156]

In some areas, however, the relationship between the gentile and the Israelites and the latter's ethnic institutions are much more complicated. 1) While gentiles do not separate the agricultural gifts which are assigned to the needy Israelites, there were sages who believed that the gentiles were required to separate the heave-offering, thus acknowledging YHWH's ownership of the Land of Israel. On the other hand, some rabbis believed that because Israelites had a special relationship to the Land of Israel, gentiles could not validly own property within the Land's borders.[157] 2) Although gentiles were not required to participate in the Temple-cult, they could bring some offerings; however, different regulations applied to gentile sacrifices from the ones which were applicable to Israelite offerings.[158] 3) Only Israelites were obligated to observe the periods of sacred time; however, when gentiles impinge on Israelite activity during these periods, the former's actions are also regulated.[159]

Although the relationship of the gentile to the Israelite institutions and practices was complex, the fact that many of the references to the non-Israelite fit naturally into their present contexts can be interpreted to mean that these *sugyot* were intended to set the parameters of permitted Israelite activity which serve to distinguish them from the peoples with whom they come into contact and among whom they live. In addition, a few of the pericopae seek to prevent commercial and social interaction between Israelites and non-Israelites simply on the basis of the different ethnic identities of the two groups. For example, an Israelite should not place himself in debt to a gentile, and the sale of certain items to non-Israelites and the purchase of some goods from them were severely restricted.[160]

These *sugyot* paint a number of different pictures of the gentile, some of them contradictory. Some passages suggest that gentiles *qua* gentiles are idolaters who must be avoided.[161] Others imply that gentiles *qua* gentiles are a

----

[155] See below, Chapter Eight.
[156] See below, Chapter Eight.
[157] See below, Chapter Six.
[158] See below, Chapter Ten.
[159] See below, Chapter Seven.
[160] Porton, "Forbidden Transactions."
[161] See below, Chapter Nine.

source of real or potential danger. Other texts indicate that gentiles exhibit un-controllable sexual urges or that they are greedy. In other *sugyot*, the gentiles symbolize the "other part of humankind," that group of people not described by the term Israelite, while yet in other passages, the gentile is mentioned as one of the several groups of people who inhabit the Land of Israel. A few pericopae describe the gentiles as simply being unconcerned with matters of importance to Israelites, so that scrupulous Israelites should beware lest by interacting with the non-Israelites they place themselves in awkward situations *vis-à-vis* their own ethnic traditions and values. In at least two passages, the gentiles' political con-trol of the Land of Israel is taken for granted and supported. We have also seen that at times gentiles are discussed in terms of biblical events and stories, even when the specific peoples mentioned in these biblical accounts were no longer identifiable in the rabbinic period.

For the most part, however, our texts picture the non-Israelite as some-one with whom the Israelite was likely to come into daily contact. The material suggests that they lived together, worked together, and at times, broke bread to-gether. They engaged in business dealings with one another, and Israelites and gentiles could jointly own property. While, from the point of view of the com-pilers of Mishnah, the proximity of the two groups could produce awkward and ambiguous situations, the texts take the daily interaction for granted. In fact, as we shall see below, as long as the gentile is not explicitly engaging in idolatrous activity, the sages do not attempt to separate the two groups. While some of our *sugyot* imply that it would be easier, perhaps even better, if Israelites did not have to interact continually with non-Israelites, only in the area of idolatry do our materials attempt to definitively separate the two groups. It is clear, how-ever, that there were a variety of views concerning the gentile and that exactly how Israelites should interact with gentiles was a matter of some uncertainty.

iii

Because Tosefta is edited according to different principles from Mish-nah, many of Tosefta's units do not exhibit the same thematic developments as are commonly found in Mishnah. Often the thematic units are confined to two or three passages within the present chapter divisions. At other times, two or three units on similar themes are separated by units on other issues. Thus, given the present state of Tosefta-scholarship and analysis, it seems useful to look at the *sugyot* in Tosefta in relationship to the material in Mishnah, as well as to their contexts in Tosefta. However, one cannot ignore the complex relationship which exists between Tosefta and Mishnah. In several of our texts, Tosefta supplements, complements or augments the discussion in Mishnah.[162] These passages can be divided into three types. In the first type, Mishnah mentions the gentiles and is the occasion for Tosefta's reference to them. In several of these texts, Tosefta does little more than quote Mishnah; however, we do find cases where Tosefta moves beyond Mishnah's reference to the gentile. In the second type of *sugya*, Mishnah does not mention the gentile, but Tosefta appears to add the gentile to Mishnah's discussion. In the third type, the relationship between Mishnah and Tosefta is so loose and general that one should treat Tosefta's discussion as virtually independent of Mishnah. When the passages in Tosefta alone mention the gentile, we again find two phenomena. In the first, the pericope fits into the context of Tosefta's larger discussion. In the second, Tosefta's reference to the gentile stands alone in its context.

Tosefta supplements Mishnah's reference to the gentile

TBer. 5:31 agrees with mBer. 8:6 that one does not recite a blessing over a gentile's lamp. Tosefta adds, however, that if a gentile lights his lamp from an Israelite's lamp, or if an Israelite lights his lamp from a gentile's lamp, the blessing must be recited. The context begins in tBer. 5:30 with the Houses-dispute concerning the order of the blessing for the elements of the *habddalah*-ritual. However, tBer. 5:31 concentrates on the blessing over the lamp, so that our discussion fits its context. The whole relates to mBer. 8:5-6, which introduce the gentile and his lamp. Tosefta expands Mishnah's point that one recites a blessing only over an Israelite's lamp, by requiring a blessing if an Israelite's lamp is involved in any way. The picture of the gentile remains the same in both texts.

Sarason notes that tDem. 5:21-24 "comprise a Toseftan essay on M[Dem]. 5:9, dealing primarily with the ambiguous status of Samaritan produce."[163] However, tDem. 5:21 opens with a citation of mDem. 5:9 and adds a dissenting opinion by Judah, Yosi, and Simeon. Thus, the gentile appears at the opening of the "essay" because of his occurrence in Mishnah, even though Tosefta's concern is with the Samaritan. While Mishnah records the opinion that one may take a tithe from an Israelite's produce for a gentile's produce, or vice versa, Tosefta includes the view that this is not allowed, so that Tosefta indicates that there were those who disagreed with the rule in Mishnah. The view

----

[162]On this issue see Jacob Neusner, *The Tosefta: Its Structure and Its Sources* (Atlanta: 1986), especially ix.

[163]Sarason, 194.

of the gentile is the same in both texts; however, Tosefta's version underscores more sharply that gentiles and Israelites represent two different segments of Israelite society.

TTer. 2:13 deals with the application of the laws of the fourth-year produce to a gentile's vineyard in Syria. The discussion belongs with mTer. 3:9 in which the gentile is mentioned; however, in its quotation of the dispute between Judah and sages in mTer. 3:9, Tosefta has added the reference to Syria. TTer. 2:13 thus makes the dispute in mTer. 3:9 fit into its context in Tosefta in a general way, for tTer. 2:9-13 speak about property outside the Land of Israel, and tTer. 2:10-11 focus on a gentile's property in Syria. Tosefta applies the same rules to a gentile's produce whether it is grown in the Land of Israel or in Syria, so that "even outside the Land of Israel, an Israelite may not without reservation eat produce grown in a gentile-owned orchard or vineyard."[164] Thus, the passage limits the social interaction between Israelites and gentiles.

TTer. 7:20, which speaks of Israelites' surrendering one of their number to gentiles, stands unrelated to its context, but it does pertain to mTer. 8:12, whose rule it cites and clarifies. Its placement here depends on the fact that the passages around it bear on the end of mTer. 8.[165] The picture of the dangerous gentile, found in mTer. 8:12, is expanded in Tosefta, for while the former speaks of gentiles who threatened to rape Israelite women, the latter speaks of gentiles who claimed they would kill Israelite males.

TShab. 1:22 quotes and expands upon the Shammaite opinion of mShab. 1:7, ignores the Hillelite statement, and adds a comment attributed to Aqiba. While mShab. 1:9 contains a statement by Simeon b. Gamliel in which he relates what occurred in his father's house with regard to giving clothes to a gentile launderer, tShab. 1:22 includes a statement attributed to Eleazar b. Sadoq in which he reports an expanded version of what occurred in Gamliel's house.[166] However, Tosefta's distinction between white and colored clothes does not add anything to Mishnah's discussion of the gentile.

While mPes. 2:1 states that an Israelite may sell *hames* to a gentile until the time that the former must stop eating it, tPis. 1:7 notes that before the time of Aqiba, Israelites would not sell, or give, leaven to a gentile, unless the latter

----

[164]Peck, 124.

[165]Cf., Peck, 248-249.

[166]Neusner, *Rabbinic Traditions*, II, 121-130. The context begins at tShab. 1:16 with the reference to the rules stated in the upper room of Hananiah b. Hezekiah b. Gurion (= mShab. 1:4). The issue of the preceding contiguous pericopae is what types of work may be done immediately before the Sabbath; Neusner, *Shabbat*, 28-31.

could use it up before Passover. Aqiba, however, ruled that one could give it to a gentile even until the very time of removal. Tosefta also contains a statement by Yosi in which he claims that Aqiba merely supported an earlier Hillelite ruling. Tosefta places Mishnah's ruling into "an historical context;" however, it does not add to our picture of the gentile.

TPis. 1:12 rephrases the statement of mPes. 2:2, but does not alter the picture of the gentile.

TSheq. 1:7 details what may be purchased from gentiles and which offerings may be accepted from them. TSheq. 1:7 may be loosely related to the mention of the gentile in mSheq. 1:5;[167] however, it does not seem intimately related to its context in Tosefta. Taken together, mSheq. 1:5 and tSheq. 1:7 indicate that the relationship between the gentile and the Temple-cult was a complex matter which produced some uncertainty and disagreement.

TSheq. 3:11 states that if a gentile brought his peace-offering and gave it to an Israelite or to a priest, either may eat it. Neusner suggests that this is related to the theme of mSheq. 7:6, which discusses the whole-offering which the gentile sent "from beyond the sea."[168] The point seems to be that although the gentile cannot eat holy things, he can give them to Israelites or to priests to eat,[169] so that one can read tSheq. 3:11 as an expansion of the statement in mSheq. 7:6. This passage implies that the relationship of the non-Israelite to the Temple-cult was extremely complex.

TTan. 2:12 expands upon mTan. 3:7's discussion of sounding the *shofar* when a town is besieged by gentiles; however, Tosefta does not alter or expand Mishnah's picture of the dangerous gentile.

TYeb. 14:7 expands upon the reference to the gentile's ability to give testimony concerning the death of an Israelite, mYeb. 16:5, by adding a narrative which illustrates Mishnah's general rule.[170] Both texts point to the fact that different judicial procedures apply to gentiles and to Israelites.

TKet. 3:2 cites Zechariah b. Haqassab's words concerning the gentiles' invasion of Jerusalem, found in mKet. 2:9, and the description of the dangerous gentile is not altered.

----

[167]Neusner, *Sheqalim*, 12.

[168]Cf., Neusner, *Sheqalim*, 51-52. Neusner cites a second tradition about a gentile who died; however, my text reads convert, gr, for Neusner's gentile, gwy.

[169]Saul Lieberman, *Tosefta Ki-fshutah: A Comprehensive Commentary on the Tosefta Part IV, Order Mo'ed* (New York: 1962), 703.

[170]Mishnah states that if a gentile intended to give such testimony, it is invalid. In Tosefta, Abba Yudan of Sidon recites a narrative, m'sh b, in which a gentile tells his Israelite companion that a certain Israelite had died where they were standing and that the gentile had buried and mourned for him there. Subsequently, sages permitted the dead Israelite's wife to remarry.

TSot. 9:1 cites and glosses mSot. 9:2 and its reference to a town in which there are gentiles. Both texts indicate that the presence of gentiles in the Land of Israel affected Israelite ritual activities. TSot. 15:8 cites mSot. 9:14's reference to the wars against Vespasian and Titus and glosses Mishnah's references;[171] both texts agree that during these wars with gentiles, normal Israelite customs were put into abeyance.

TGit. 1:4 cites and builds on mGit. 1:5 concerning documents which come from gentile registries with the signatures of gentile witnesses. Although Tosefta's version is quite different from that in Mishnah,[172] both texts recognize the gentiles' political control over the Land of Israel and explain what affect this has on Israelite legal documents.

TB.Q. 4:6 builds on mB.Q. 4:6's discussion concerning an ox which had intended to kill an Israelite but which killed a gentile instead. Tosefta focuses on the ox's owner, and it alone contains a dispute concerning the liability of the ox's owner. It also distinguishes between a dangerous ox and one not presumed to be harmful. However, these differences in Tosefta do not change Mishnah's point that the gentile represents a different sub-class of humankind from Israelites.

According to tB.Q. 9:10, if one injures his Canaanite slave, he is liable for all counts, except for compensation for loss of time, and this seems to be related to mB.Q. 8:3-5.[173] Tosefta does not add to our picture of the Canaanite slave's representing a different portion of humankind from a Hebrew slave.

----

[171]TSot. 15:8-15 form a unit which discusses the wars with Rome and complements mSot. 9:14.

[172]MGit. 1:5 states that any document drawn up in gentile registries, with the exception of writs of divorce and emancipation, are valid, even if they are signed by gentiles. Simeon remarks that even divorce documents and writs of emancipation are valid. TGit. 1:4 states that Aqiba declares all such documents valid, while sages do not accept writs of divorce or the emancipation of slaves, an opinion stated anonymously in Mishnah. Eleazar b. Yosi changes the issue which Aqiba and sages disputed to the case in which the documents were prepared by "unauthorized persons." Simeon b. Gamliel concludes that if there are no Israelites available to sign the documents, all documents are valid, no matter who signs them. This is an expansion of the opinion attributed to Simeon in Mishnah.

[173]In mB.Q. 8:3, we read that one is liable for everything but loss of time, if he injures a Hebrew slave, and subject to all counts, if he injures another Israelite's Canaanite slave. However, Judah responds that slaves are not compensated for indignity. In mB.Q. 8:5, we discover that if one injures his own Canaanite slave, he is exempt from all counts. Neusner places tB.Q. 9:10 in conjunction with mB.Q. 8:1-2; however, I am not sure why, for mB.Q. 8:3-5 deal with injury to slaves. If tB.Q. 9:10 belongs with mB.Q. 8:3-5, Mishnah is the occasion for the reference to the Canaanite slave in Tosefta. Neusner, *Baba Qamma*, 116.

Quoting mSanh. 9:2, tSanh. 12:4 attributes mSanh. 9:2 to Judah; however, the latter merely restates the former, so that both make the same point: Israelites and gentiles represent two different sectors of humankind.

TZeb. 5:6 opens with an anonymous quotation of Meir's comment in mZeb. 4:5, which is the occasion for the reference to the gentile in Tosefta, and expands upon Mishnah's concerns. However, Tosefta adds nothing to Mishnah's claim that the sacrifices offered by gentiles are not subject to the same ritual concerns as those brought by Israelites.

TMen. 10:13 merely repeats the rule in mMen. 9:8 that the laying on of the hands on an offering does not apply to gentiles, women, slaves, or minors.

THul. 7:3 builds on the reference to the gentile and the cut up hip in mHul. 7:2 and contains a rather long, complex discussion concerning meat and its sale to, and purchase from, gentiles.[174] Tosefta alone contains the statements that Israelites do not sell carrion to gentiles and that Israelites should not have a gentile purchase meat for them. Here, Tosefta's additions severely restrict the commercial, and perhaps social, interaction between Israelites and gentiles concerning meat, and they add a totally new dimension to Mishnah's *sugya*, which focused solely on the problem of sending a hip with the sinew to a gentile. Mishnah is concerned with only a specific edible item which was considered to be prohibited to Israelites in the Hebrew Bible. In Tosefta, however, the topic is expanded to cover meat in general.

THul. 8:12 states that one may curdle milk in the stomach of a beast slaughtered by a gentile, or in the stomach of an animal which is carrion (which amounts to the same thing). This is the opposite of the rule stated in mHul. 8:5, as Tosefta explicitly notes. Nevertheless, both texts equate an animal slaughtered by a gentile with carrion, so that the picture of the gentile is the same in both collections.

TBekh. 1:1 merely quotes the opening of mBekh. 1:1, while tBekh. 2:1 quotes and expands upon mBekh. 2:1.[175] The picture of the gentiles and the

----

[174]Porton, "Forbidden Transactions," 328. Cf., Saul Lieberman, *Tosefeth Rishonim: A Commentary Based on Manuscripts of the Tosefta and Works of the Rishonim and Midrashim in Manuscripts and Rare Editions. Part II: Seder Nashim Nezikin Kadashim* (Jerusalem: 1938), 237; Neusner, *Hullin*, 90.

[175]Tosefta and Mishnah both mention one who purchases a cow from a gentile, sells one to him, is a partner with him, receives or gives one to a gentile under contract and that these are exempt from the laws of the firstling. Tosefta adds Judah's comment that one who receives a cow from a gentile under contract to raise it and to share in the profits, gives half of its estimated price to the priest. If one gives a beast to a gentile under contract, he estimates its value, even up to ten times its price, and gives it all to the priest. Sages say that because "the finger of the gentile" is mixed up in it, it is free of the law of the firstling.

problem with the Israelite laws of firstling caused by an Israelite's purchasing an animal from them are the same in both texts.

TBekh. 2:5 quotes mBekh. 2:4's discussion of receiving an animal on "iron terms" from a gentile. The two *sugyot* present the same description of the gentiles and the problem caused by an Israelite's receiving a flock from them on "iron terms."

In tBekh. 3:15, Aqiba permits gentiles to be numbered with those who eat firstlings. The Shammaites had included only priests, while the Hillelites incorporated Israelites. This is a reformulation of mBekh. 5:2; Tosefta attributes the anonymous opinion in Mishnah to Aqiba, and cites Deut. 15:22 in support of his position.[176] Both texts, however, contain the same picture of the gentile.

TKer. 1:17 discusses the Canaanite slave, but it virtually repeats mKer. 2:5.[177]

TAhil. 18:16 discusses Qisri and an event concerning gentiles which once happened there. The context is a discussion of areas which are clean and unclean, and the reference to the gentiles is merely part of the story. Qisri and gentiles are juxtaposed in mOhol. 18:9, and this may have occasioned our text. The gentiles are pictured as not observing the Sabbatical year, exactly what we should expect. In any case, the focus of the story is the Israelites, not the gentiles.[178]

TNeg. 6:4 states that the walls of a house which is owned by a gentile and an Israelite cannot become unclean because of mildew. TNeg. 6:4 discusses houses which cannot become unclean by mildew, so that the jointly-owned house fits into the context. TNeg. 7:10 states that while an Israelite receives uncleanness and affords protection for clothing in a house afflicted with mildew, a gentile and an animal do not receive uncleanness and do not afford protection for clothing in such a house. TNeg. 7:7-12 discuss a house afflicted by mildew, and the contrast drawn in our *sugya* fits into the context. It is possible, however, that our text is an expansion of the reference to the gentile's house in mNeg. 12:1. In any event, here we do learn that with regard to the Israelite laws of mildew, gentiles are equated with animals and that any gentile association with the ownership of a house exempts the building from the Israelite laws of mildew.

----

[176]Neusner, *Rabbinic Traditions*, II, 245-246.

[177]Gary G. Porton, *The Traditions of Rabbi Ishmael Part Two: Exegetical Comments in Tannaitic Collections* (Leiden: 1977), 59-61.

[178]Jacob Neusner, *A History of the Mishnaic Law of Purities Part Four Ohalot. Commentary* (Leiden: 1974), 347-348.

TPar. 2:1 contains Eliezer's prohibition against purchasing a red heifer from gentiles. The comment is taken from mPar. 2:1.[179]

TMiq. 6:1 discusses immersion-pools of gentiles inside and outside the Land of Israel, and its agenda is derived from mMiq. 8:1, which mentions gentiles.

TMiq. 6:7 states that gentile semen is clean except for the urine in which it is located, and this agrees with, and is occasioned by, mMiq. 8:4; however, Tosefta alone refers to the urine.

TNid. 5:5, which relates to mNid. 4:3, deals with the blood of a gentile woman and the blood of purifying a woman with a skin disease. The Shammaites claim this is blood from the wound.[180]

In tNid. 9:14, Simeon rules that the corpse of a gentile does not impart uncleanness to one who carries it. This is anonymous in mNid. 10:4.[181]

The above examples illustrate that in some instances, Tosefta's mention of the gentiles derives from their appearance in a parallel *sugya* in Mishnah. Furthermore, Tosefta's discussions, while often different in specifics from those in Mishnah, do not usually alter the picture of the gentile derived from the latter text. In fact, only in tHul. 7:3, do we find that Tosefta's pericope significantly changes the issue from that encountered in Mishnah, for Tosefta's passage significantly affects the social and commercial interchange between Israelites and gentiles, while mHul. 7:2 does not. In general, the pictures of the gentile drawn in these pericopae from Tosefta differ from those in Mishnah, when they do differ, only in intensity. Israelites and gentiles represent two different categories of human beings, gentiles *qua* gentiles are dangerous, different judicial and commercial rules apply to Israelites and non-Israelites, gentiles do not have to observe Israelite sacred periods of time, and the like.

Tosefta complements Mishnah by mentioning gentiles

In tBer 2:13, Meir reports Aqiba's actions during the recitation of the *Shema'*, while a quaestor stood at the door. Although tBer. 2:13 opens with a discussion of one who suffered a nocturnal emission, the issue is whether or not one needs to recite the *Shema'* so that it can be heard; therefore, Meir's comment fits into this context, for Aqiba did not recite the prayer out loud while the quaestor stood at the door. This may be related to mBer. 2:3, which discusses

----

[179]Porton, "Forbidden Transactions," 325, n. 37. Neusner, *Eliezer*, I, 303-304.

[180]Neusner, *Rabbinic Traditions*, II, 308-309.

[181]The text in Tosefta appears here because it is one of the scribal rulings, as are two of the other rulings in this passage, it is attributed to Simeon, as is the ruling which immediately precedes it, and it deals with uncleanness by carrying, as do two other rulings in the *sugya*.

how loudly a person must recite the *Shema'*. The quaestor's presence is important to our *sugya*, and it seems to point out that the gentile authorities could be
hostile to Israelites; however, the central topic is the *Shema'*, not the gentile.

TPe. 3:1 falls into several parts, only two of which deal with the
gentile.[182] The first relevant section of tPe. 3:1 contains "two independent
rules . . . [which] take up a single topic, proper relations with gentiles:"[183] 1)
Gentile workers should not be hired for harvesting because they do not worry
about observing the laws of gleaning,[184] and 2) an Israelite may not designate
the poorman's tithe for a gentile. He may, however, give to the gentile-poor
common produce which has been properly tithed. The first rule was placed here
because it discusses gleanings.[185] The second rule was included because, like
the first, it focuses on the gentile. We have two separate issues concerning the
gentile. First, gentiles cannot be trusted to observe Israelite agricultural taboos
because they do not consider them important. Second, Israelite agricultural gifts
for the poor can be given to only Israelite poor; however, an Israelite may support the needy among the gentiles from other produce which has been properly
tithed. This reinforces the ethnic characteristics of the Israelite agricultural gifts
for the poor. In the second relevant section, the Shammaites and the Hillelites
agree that an Israelite may validly declare property ownerless for the benefit of
Israelites, but not for the benefit of gentiles. This relates to mPe. 6:1 in which
the Shammaites state that one may validly declare property ownerless for the
benefit of the poor, while the Hillelites rule that one may validly declare property ownerless even for the benefit of the rich. The juxtaposition of
gentiles/Israelites occurs only in Tosefta, and it serves to mark off the gentiles as
a distinct class of people from the Israelites. Mishnah, however, assumes that
both Houses discuss only Israelites.[186]

Part of tPe. 3:5 cites and explains mPe. 6:8's rule that forgotten standing corn in a field protects a nearby sheaf from being deemed forgotten and,
therefore, subject to the rules concerning forgotten sheaves. Although Mishnah

----

[182]Brooks, 96-104.

[183]Brooks, 97.

[184]Lqt.

[185]The Hebrew root lqṭ appears four times in the first six lines of the text; Saul
Lieberman, *The Tosefta According to Codex Vienna, with Variants from Codex Erfurt,
Genizah Mss. and Editio Princeps (Venice 1521) Together with References to Parallel
Passages in Talmudic Literature and a Brief Commentary: The Order of Zera'im*, (New
York: 1955), 50, ls. 1-6. Brooks, suggests that it supplements mPe. 4:10-5:6's "discussion of glean-
ings;" Brooks, 95.

[186]Brooks, 102-104. Neusner, *Rabbinic Traditions*, II, 55-58.

does not mention gentiles, in Tosefta, Meir states that the standing crop of a fellow Israelite protects the first person's crop, of wheat protects barley, and of a gentile protects that of an Israelite.[187] Again we see that gentiles are different from Israelites; in fact, these two groups are as different from each other as wheat is from barley.

TPe. 3:12 parallels tPe. 2:9,[188] for the former discusses a vineyard which a gentile sells to an Israelite, an Israelite sells to a gentile, or one which they own in partnership with relationship to the part of the vineyard left for the poor during the harvest. This continues the treatment of the vineyard declared ownerless in tPe. 3:11 and introduces the subject of the vineyard which has been dedicated, tPe. 3:13. The issue of the defective cluster, which is mentioned in our text, was first raised in mPe. 7:5 without reference to the gentile. Again we discover that Israelites alone are responsible for leaving the Israelite agricultural gifts for the poor among their people.

TPe. 4:1 talks about whether or not a poor person is believed when he declares that the produce in his possession belongs to the poor; however, the topic of believing the poor is raised in mPe. 8:2-4, which do not refer to the gentile.[189] The text in Tosefta claims that gentiles *qua* gentiles are usually un-

----

[187]Brooks, 113. Sages rule that only the same types and same species protect each other.

[188]TPe. 2:9 reads: gwy šmkr qmtw lyśr'l lqsw" hyyb bp'h yśr'l šmkr qmtw lgwy ptwr mn hp'h yśr'l wgwy šhyw šwtpym bqmh [hlqw šl yśr'l hyyb whlqw šl gwy ptwr r šm'" 'wmr yśr'l wgwy šhyw šwtpym bqmh ptwr mn hp'h; "A gentile who sold his standing corn to an Israelite for harvesting--[the produce that the Israelite harvests] is liable to [designation as] *peah*. An Israelite who sold his standing corn to a gentile [the produce that the gentile harvests] is exempt from [designation] as *peah*. An Israelite and a gentile who share [ownership] of standing corn--the portion that belongs to the Israelite is subject [to designation as] *peah*; but the portion that belongs to the gentile is exempt from [designation as] *peah*. R. Simeon says, 'An Israelite and a gentile who share [ownership] of standing corn, [the entire crop] is exempt from [designation] as *peah*.'" TPe. 3:12 substitutes vineyard for standing corn, so that it deals with the defective cluster, not with *peah*: gwy šmkr krmw lyśr'l lbswr hyyb b'wllwt wyśr'l šmkr krmw lgwy lbswr ptwr mn h'wllwt yśr'l wgwy šhyw šwtpym bkrm hlqw šl yśr'l hyyb šl gwy ptwr r šm'wn 'w" yśr'l wgwy šhyw šwtpym bkrm ptwr mn h'wllwt.

[189]Tosefta rules that one is not believed when he says that he bought a certain gleaning, lqt, from a gentile, for perhaps either he did not buy it from the gentile, or the produce cannot be considered a "gleaning" according to Israelite law. See Lieberman, *Zera'im*, 55. The text equates the Samaritan with the gentile, for neither knows anything about the rabbinic laws concerning gleaning. Our passage further maintains that gentile poor are not believed about anything. Lieberman argues that the intention may be that we do not believe that the gentile is poor; Saul Lieberman, *Tosefta Ki-fshutah: A Comprehensive Commentary on the Tosefta: Order Zera'im, Part I* (New York: 1955), 178. The *sugya* focuses on about what the poor can be believed. The reference to the gentile appears to make the point about what the Israelite poor cannot be believed. Throughout the passages, the gentile appears in conjunction with the Samaritan, a common occurrence in our documents. While the Samaritan and the gentile are parallel with regard to the poorman's claim of from whom he purchased the gleanings, the Samaritan poor and the gentile poor

trustworthy.

TKil. 5:19 rules that one should not sell to a gentile a piece of cloth which violates the laws of mixed-kinds, if the violation is not obvious.[190] Neither the gentile nor selling appears near this passage. The text may be related to mKil. 9:4, for both mention a pack saddle of an ass;[191] however, tKil. 5:18 quotes and expands on mKil. 9:4, and the gentile is mentioned only in Tosefta. Exactly why this concerned our authors is unclear. Perhaps they wished to make the point that Israelites should not derive any benefit at all from something which violated their taboos, and the gentile appears here as a symbol of the non-Israelite sector of humankind: Obviously one cannot sell such an object to an Israelite, and one cannot sell it to even a gentile.

TTer. 7:14 mentions that uncovered water may not be spilled out on the public road, may not be used to mix plaster, may not be given to a gentile, and may not be given to cattle owned by others to drink. As Peck notes, Tosefta augments mTer. 8:5's discussion of uncovered water by producing a list of things for which it cannot be used. The reference to the gentile, which occurs only in Tosefta, means that it cannot be given to any human to drink, only an *assumption* in mTer. 8:5,[192] so that the gentile here symbolizes that portion of humankind not covered by the term Israelites.

TSheb. 6:20 states that one may not sell seventh-year produce to, or buy it from, a gentile.[193] The topic of tSheb. 6:17-20 is the sale of seventh-year produce, first raised in mSheb. 8:3, so our passage fits into its context. The gentile appears only in Tosefta, along with references to others who are suspected of violating the laws of the seventh year. The observance of the restrictions of the seventh year marks off the true Israelites from gentiles, among others.

TMa. 3:8 opens with a citation of mMa. 5:1 and glosses it to include a reference to the gentile. Selling the shoots to a gentile is listed among acts which remove the shoots from the category of a crop which requires tithing. Thus, the reference to the gentile fits into the discussion of Tosefta's interpreta-

----

are not similar. The text reads: 'bl 'yn n'mn lwmr mplwny gwy lqhtyw m'yš plwny kwty lqhtyw 'nyy kwtym k'nyy yśr'l 'bl 'nyy gwym 'yn m'mynym lhm bkl dbr. "But he is not believed when saying, 'I purchased [this food] from so-and-so, a gentile,' [or] 'I purchased it from so-and-so, a Samaritan.' Poor Samaritans are deemed equivalent to poor Israelites; but poor gentiles, we do not believe about any thing."

[190]Porton, "Forbidden Transactions," 327.

[191]Mrd't hmwr.

[192]Peck, 235-236.

[193]Whether or not the prohibition also applies to Samaritans is disputed in the text.

tion of mMa. 5:1. Gentiles are not Israelites, so that they do not have to follow the Israelite agricultural regulations.

TM.S. 3:5 states that the value of second-tithe produce is set by three bidders, one of whom may be a gentile. Although the issue is raised by mM.S. 4:2, the reference to the gentile is Tosefta's example of a bidder. TM.S. 3:1-6 are related to mM.S. 4:2; therefore, in general, our passage relates to its context.[194] The point is that any knowledgeable farmer, even a gentile, may aid in setting the value of the second-tithe produce. The problem is how one determines the worth of the produce; it does not focus on the gentile.

TM.S. 4:1 states that an Israelite must pay the added fifth when he redeems the second tithe separated from his own produce, gathers untithed produce from his own crop, buys untithed produce, inherits it, receives it as a gift, or purchases it from a Samaritan or a gentile. Tosefta opens with a citation of mM.S. 4:3, which does not mention the gentile, and expands upon Mishnah's ruling. The Samaritan and the gentile are specified because their produce is likely to be untithed or tithed incorrectly, according to rabbinic law, so that the observance of the laws of tithing is a means of separating Israelites from other farmers who work the soil of the Land of Israel.

THal. 1:3 indicates that the liability for the dough-offering of the dough in a bakery depends on who owns the bakery.[195] Although related to mHal. 1:7, the *sugya* is unrelated to its context in Tosefta. Again we learn that the Israelite agricultural gifts are obligatory for only Israelites and that they serve a means of distinguishing between Israelites and non-Israelites.

TShab. 17:17 rules that one may not move an object which a gentile has brought from outside the Sabbath-limit. Neusner argues that the text relates to mShab. 23:4 and that this accounts for the "inclusion . . . in its present location."[196] However, tShab. 17:15 more directly parallels mShab. 23:4, for both deal with a coffin and a grave; therefore, the more general rule of tShab. 17:17 and its mention of the gentile may be Tosefta's creation.[197] The point seems to be that once it enters the Sabbath-limit, the object must be treated like any other object carried on the Sabbath across the Sabbath-limit, even though its owner

----

[194]Haas, 112-118.

[195]Dough produced in an Israelite bakery with gentile employees is liable for the offering, while dough produced in a gentile bakery with Israelite employees is not.

[196]Neusner, *Shabbat*, 202.

[197]While mShab. 24:1 states that an Israelite should give his purse to his gentile traveling companion if darkness falls on Friday evening, tShab. 17:20 claims that this is done only if the Israelite knows the gentile. If the former does not know the latter, he follows him to his house.

were a gentile. Tosefta implies that when a gentile's actions impinge on the Israelite's activity during the Sabbath, the gentile is treated *as if* he were an Israelite.

MErub. 7:11 states that one may prepare an *'erub* for a person only with his knowledge and consent, and tErub. 6:11 notes that one may prepare it for his Canaanite slave with or without his/her permission. The reference to the non-Israelite slave appears only in Tosefta.[198] The point is that Canaanite slaves are not considered independent adults.

TPis. 7:4 draws the familiar distinction between Hebrew slaves and Canaanite slaves;[199] the former are treated like independent adults, while the latter are not. The issue is related to mPes. 8:1; however, the Canaanite slave appears in only Tosefta.

TSuk. 4:28 discusses Bilgah's daughter, Miriam, who rejected her people and married an officer of the Greek royal house. The story is occasioned by the reference to Bilgah's wall niche which was blocked up, mSuk. 5:8; however, the reference to the gentile officer appears in only Tosefta. The text underscores the point that exogamous marriages are prohibited.

TR.H. 2:12 expands upon mR.H. 4:6. Yosi states that if the verses of remembrance[200] mention the punishment of the gentiles, each verse is read separately. The reference to gentiles is unique to Yosi's comment in this context. TR.H. 2:13 mentions verses of visitations, and tR.H. 2:14 returns to a discussion of the verses of remembrance. The text points to the negative feelings that some held concerning gentiles.

TTan. 3:10 explains that on the seventh of the month, the gentiles conquered the Temple and took the pillars, the sea, and the stalls. TTan. 3:9-10 discuss and expand upon the destruction of the Temple, mentioned in mTan. 4:6. These texts point to the hostile acts of past generations of gentiles.

TMo'ed 1:12 rules that on the intermediate days of a festival Israelites may purchase from gentiles fields, houses, vineyards, cattle and slaves because it is as if one rescues them from the gentiles. The occasion for the comment is mM.Q. 2:4, which states that one buys houses, slaves, and cattle only for the needs of the festival or the seller; the gentile appears in only Tosefta. The issue is the gentile *qua* gentile, for one may not purchase these things from Israelites.

----

[198]Neusner, *Erubin*, 108.

[199]One cannot slaughter the Passover-offering on behalf of the former without their permission; however, one can slaughter the offering for the latter with or without their consent.

[200]Now read as part of the *Mussaf Amidah* on Rosh HaShanah.

Interestingly, the business transactions are reclassified as "acts of redemption," so that the restrictions on *business* activities are still maintained.

TMeg. 2:16 discusses a gentile who dedicated a beam for a synagogue and wrote "for the Name" on it. If he vowed it to the Holy Name, it may not be used. If he vowed it for the synagogue, the Israelites remove the reference to the Name and store that piece away before using the rest of the beam. The reference to the gentile appears only here and has only a loose connection to its context, which deals with the way one treats consecrated objects.[201] The *sugya* points to the ambiguous relationship between the gentiles and Israelite sacred institutions. Neusner writes that this text supplements mMeg. 3:1, which is concerned with purposes for which one consecrates an object.[202]

TYeb. 8:1 states that if an Ammonite, a Moabite, an Egyptian, or an Edomite male nine years and one day old had intercourse with the daughter of a priest, a Levite, or an Israelite, the woman cannot marry into the priesthood.[203] The passage also applies the same conditions to a Samaritan, a *natin*, or a *mamzer*. Only the latter two are mentioned in mYeb. 6:2, whose list is quite different from what we find in tYeb. 8:1. Tosefta's list draws upon biblical people, who, with the exception of the Egyptians, were not part of the demography of the rabbinic period. Therefore, at least a portion of the text is "theoretical."

TKet. 1:6 expands on the discussion in mKet. 1:9 concerning a woman who claims that she was made pregnant by a priest. In Tosefta, Joshua states that a woman taken captive by gentiles is not believed when she says she is pure, and he uses this as a basis for an analogy to support his ruling in Mishnah.[204] The topic under discussion concerns proper witnesses, and this is discussed also in tKet. 1:5. The incidental reference to the gentile reflects the opinion that gentiles *qua* gentiles are sexually promiscuous.

MNed. 3:4 states that an Israelite may claim that his produce is heave-offering or belongs to the State, even if this is false, in order to avoid its confiscation by murderers, robbers or tax-collectors. TNed. 2:2 adds that to avoid paying the assessors or tax-collectors, an Israelite can falsely claim that the produce belongs to a gentile, the government, or that it is heave-offering. The gentiles are mentioned because the Israelite would not be responsible for paying

----

[201]Neusner, *Besah*, 159.

[202]Neusner, *Besah*, 159.

[203]There is a dispute between Simeon b. Gamliel and Yosi concerning these biblical nations. Yosi excludes the Egyptians, and Simeon excludes the Ammonites and Moabites; however, they do not mention them specifically in their comments; Neusner, *Yebamot*, 100-101.

[204]For an analysis of the passage see Green, *Joshua*, 141-142.

the former's taxes. In addition, the passage seems to imply that the gentile government treated gentiles differently from the way in which it acted towards Israelites.

TNed. 2:4 makes the point that the rest of the nations of the world are judged harshly because they are not circumcised; that is, they have not entered the covenant of Abraham. This parallels the point made in mNed. 3:11 that "uncircumcised" is a term for gentiles. The discussion of circumcision is continued in tNed. 2:5-6. Israelites and gentiles are different, and that fact is based on events recorded in the Israelite Scriptures.

TSot. 7:22 contains an exegesis of Deut. 20:7, *Lest another man take her.* In his exegesis, Simeon states that *another* refers to a gentile by analogy with *another* in Deut. 28:30, *If you speak for a woman in marriage, another man shall enjoy her.* The context is the rule that the priest before the battle should send home those who are newly married, for according to Deut. 20:7, they need not go into battle. The point of the text is that violating the Torah will lead to the gentiles' taking the absence groom's bride. The gentile is again seen as a source of potential danger to Israelites because of the former's uncontrollable sexual drives. The concern with one who need not enter into battle is found in mSot. 8:4-6.

TSot. 13:9 includes a statement by Yohanan[205] which refers to Israel's suffering while the rest of the nations of the world prosper. In this context, Israel's suffering, or the gentile nations' prospering, is a result of YHWH's "sleeping." The text attempts to underscore the special relationship which exists between YHWH and Israel, a relationship which might not always be evident in "the real world." TSot. 13:9-10 form a unit which relates to mSot. 9:10.

TGit. 6:4 points to the Israelites' use of gentile names, a practice which it accepts as a matter of fact. The text argues that one cannot tell whether a person is a gentile or an Israelite merely from his/her name.[206] While mGit. 8:5 mentions the changing of names, it does not mention the Israelites' use of gentile names. That issue is raised in only Tosefta.[207] The context in Tosefta is a discussion of names, for tGit. 6:5 deals with a man who has two names.

TQid. 4:16 stresses that marriages between Israelites and gentiles are invalid, for the male child of a gentile and an Israelite woman is a *mamzer.*

---

[205]Neusner, *Sotah,* 92.

[206]Writs of divorce which come from abroad are valid even if they contain gentile names because "Israelites overseas use names which are gentile names." Furthermore, converts may use gentile names, even changing an Israelite name for a gentile name.

[207]MGit. 8:5 does mention dating documents according to the era of the Medes or the Greeks, in which case, the documents are invalid.

MQid. 3:12 states that in a situation in which the woman has no right to betroth a man, the child is a *mamzer*, but Mishnah refers to only the forbidden relationships found in the Torah. Tosefta alone mentions the gentile male. The prohibition against exogamous marriages is familiar to us.

TB.Q. 9:33 rules that if a gentile forced an Israelite to take the possessions of another Israelite, the Israelite is exempt from punishment; however, if the Israelite took his fellow's possessions on his own accord and handed them over to a gentile, the former is liable for punishment. Although this seems to build on mB.Q. 8:7, the reference to the gentile appears in only Tosefta.[208] Gentiles can be dangerous.

According to tB.Q. 10:21, which relates to mB.Q. 10:1, if one steals in order to feed his dependents--his minor children or his Canaanite slave--he is exempt from paying restitution. The reference to the Canaanite slave appears in only Tosefta. MB.Q. 10:1 refers to children, with tB.Q. 10:21 adding the word "minor" and the reference to the Canaanite slave. The Canaanite slave is included because, like the child, the former is not an independent human being. TB.Q. 10:20-21 form a unit discussing robbery, so that our text fits here.

TB.M. 2:12 used the phrase "time of the Amorites" to indicate a time long since past, with reference to items found in an old pile or wall. The reference to "time of the Amorites" glosses the references to the pile and wall found in mB.M. 2:3. Unlike in other texts which mention the Amorites, here it is clear that they were present in the Land of Israel only a long time ago. TB.M. 2:11-14 take up the issues found in mB.M. 2:3-4, with tB.M. 2:12 and tB.M. 2:13 actually citing segments of the mishnaic text; therefore, this relationship to Mishnah provides the context for our *sugya*.

TB.M. 2:33 rules that one does not set a priority between gentiles and shepherds of large animals when seeking to retrieve lost objects. MB.M. 2:11 lists priorities with regard to seeking lost objects, and tB.M. 2:29-33 explain and expand Mishnah's list. The reference to gentiles appears in only Tosefta. It appears that the reference to gentiles is used to degrade the shepherds.[209]

TSanh. 13:2 opens with a citation and anonymous interpretation of *[Hew down the tree and destroy it], but leave the stump with its roots in the ground* (Dan. 4:3), which was first cited in tSanh. 13:1. The anonymous interpretation concludes that the wicked among the gentiles will not live in the world-to-come, nor will they be judged. Eliezer states, on the basis of Ps. 9:18,

----

[208]Neusner, *Baba Qamma*, 126.

[209]On the equation of shepherds and gentiles, see bA.Z. 26b.

Let the wicked be in Sheol, all the gentiles (gwym) who ignore God!, that none of the gentiles will have a portion in the world-to-come. Joshua, on the other hand, claims that because the verse mentions all the gentiles *who ignore God*, it implies that there are righteous ones among the rest of the nations of the world who do not ignore God and who will have a portion in the world-to-come. The concern with those who will not have a portion in the world-to-come is raised in mSanh. 10:2, and Mishnah mentions Balaam and Gahazi, both non-Israelites, who will not inherit the world-to-come. Tosefta indicates that the sages were divided concerning the fate of gentiles who died. TSanh. 13:4 equates gentiles and Israelites who sin with their bodies and states that they shall go down to Gehenna, where they are judged for twelve months, and after which their souls perish, their bodies are burned, Gehenna absorbs them, they are turned into dirt, and the wind scatters them under the feet of the righteous. Mal. 3:21--*And you shall trample the wicked to a pulp, for they shall be dust beneath your feet on the day that I am preparing*--is the basis of the comment. The references to the gentiles, which appear in only Tosefta, occur in tSanh. 13:2 and tSanh. 13:4. However, the concern with those who will not inherit the world-to-come runs throughout tSanh. 13:1-5 and mSanh. 10.

TSanh. 14:1 states that towns near the frontier cannot be declared apostate towns, for such towns must be destroyed, which would allow gentiles to invade the Land of Israel at those locations. The assumption that gentiles pose a threat to Israelites and the Land of Israel underlies this *sugya*. MSanh. 10:4-5 raise the issue of the apostate city and its destruction. Tosefta expands on Mishnah's discussion, and this is the reason for the reference to the gentiles.

TShebu. 2:5 states that if one imposes an oath on gentiles, women, children, relatives, and those invalid to give testimony, they are exempt from fulfilling the oath. This builds on mShebu. 4:1; however, the reference to the gentiles appears in only Tosefta.[210] Furthermore, the *sugya* in Tosefta seems to stand alone in its context. TShebu. 2:5 makes it clear that even adult gentiles may not function in the Israelite judicial system.

TShebu. 5:10 rules that one may impose an oath on, but in the case of claims may not accept an oath by, a deaf-mute, an imbecile, a minor, a gentile, and consecrated goods. The first three are listed in mShebu. 6:4, and it appears that the reference to the gentile was occasioned by this list of impaired individu-

---

[210]Mishnah mentions women, relatives, and those unfit to give testimony, but excludes the references to children and gentiles.

als.[211] In both of these *sugyot*, we see that adult gentiles stand outside the normal parameters of the Israelite legal system, like women, children and the ritually impaired individuals.

TZeb. 13:1, building on mZeb. 14:4, distinguishes between actions done before the tabernacle was erected and those which are done afterwards. According to Tosefta, gentiles[212] are now permitted to offer burnt-offerings which require flaying and chopping up on the high places which were outlawed for use by Israelites after the construction of the Tabernacle.[213] The point is that gentiles do not follow the same ritual procedures as Israelites, even when the former engage in ritual activities similar to the latter.

TMen. 10:17 notes that gentiles, women, slaves, and minors do not wave offerings before YHWH. While this builds on the reference to waving in mMen. 9:9, Mishnah does not contain a specific list of those who may or may not wave, as it does with reference to those who may or may not lay on hands. The rite of waving the offering is covered in tMen. 10:17-18. Gentiles are distinguished from Israelite males with regard to a specific sacrificial ritual, so that even if both Israelites and gentiles offer sacrifices at the Jerusalem Temple, they do so differently.

THul. 9:9 opens by citing mHul. 10:3's rule concerning purchasing something by weight from which the priestly dues must be taken. The text continues by stating that the priest may dispose of the gifts any way he wishes; he may even sell them to a gentile or throw them to the dogs. The pairing of gentiles and dogs is common in tHullin and seems to indicate the willful disposal of an object. The context is a discussion of the priestly gifts, tHul. 9:1-14.

TArakh. 5:9 states that one should not sell himself to an idolater, for he will become an apostate to idolatry. This text deals with hardships which can be caused by observing the prohibitions of the Sabbatical year.[214] MArakh. 9:2 sets the topics under discussion in Tosefta; however, the reference to the idolater, which here refers to a gentile, is found only in Tosefta. "Selling oneself" is the topic of tArakh. 5:8-9. The passage indicates that gentiles and Is-

----

[211]Why the consecrated goods were included is a mystery to me, and it presented a problem to the sages behind Tosefta who attempt to explain its meaning.

[212]Zuckermandel has hkwtym; Moses Zuckermandel, *Tosephta: Based on the Erfurt and Vienna Codices with Parallels and Variants* (Jerusalem: reprint, 1963), 498, l. 32. However, Lieberman, *Tosefeth Rishonim*, II, 216, prefers gentile, hgw".

[213]This same issue is raised in tZeb. 13:2-3.

[214]The prohibition is based on Lev. 25:47, *[and he sells himself to a sojourner,]* to *a member of the stranger's family*, which is cited in the text.

raelites regularly engaged in financial dealings; however, this could be dangerous for the Israelites. Furthermore, the *sugya* seems to argue that gentiles *qua* gentiles are idolaters.

TMe'. 1:18 states that the offerings of the gentiles are not available for use and are not subject to the laws of sacrilege. Although Tosefta parallels mMe'. 3:5, the reference to the gentile's offerings is unique to Tosefta. The two texts share in common only the reference to the eggs of turtledoves. TMe'. 1:17-19 discuss those items to which the laws of sacrilege apply, and this is the context for our passage. Again we see that with regard to sacrifices offered at the Temple in Jerusalem, gentiles are treated differently from Israelites.

In the previous section we saw that when Tosefta's discussion of the gentile was based on the appearance of the non-Israelite in Mishnah, the *sugyot* in the former collection changed little from those in the latter document. In fact, in only one instance did we notice that Tosefta moved in an entirely new direction. In the present section, however, the situation is different. Here, the sages behind the *sugyot* in Tosefta, although seemingly basing themselves on the material in Mishnah, have added references to the gentiles for what appear to be specific reasons. It seems that the rabbis who compiled and/or composed the pericopae in Tosefta wanted to put forth certain images of the gentiles for their own reasons; therefore, it is useful to summarize the pictures of the gentiles they chose to draw. If one argues that the editor(s) of Tosefta used different versions of *sugyot*, without any reference to Mishnah, the ones they consistenly employed produce a generally different impression of the gentile from those which occur in Mishnah.

Here, Tosefta presents us with several negative images of the gentile. First, the gentile is dangerous. Fear of the gentile caused Aqiba to alter the way in which he recited the *Shema'*. TTan. 3:10 emphasizes the hostile acts of gentiles towards Israelites which occurred in the past. Similarly, tB.Q. 9:33 suggests that gentiles can be dangerous, as does tSanh. 14:1. Second, the gentile cannot be trusted, tPe. 4:1, and in tPe. 3:1 we saw that the gentiles are not concerned with Israelite agricultural rules and cannot be trusted to observe them. Third, the point that gentiles are sexually uninhibited is made in tKet. 1:6 and tSot. 7:22. The above *sugyot* also provide the occasions for their creators to stress the differences between the Israelites and the non-Israelites. Gentiles do not observe the Israelite Sabbatical year, tSheb. 6:20. Because gentiles are not Israelites, the former may not support the needy among the latter, nor may the latter use their gifts designated for the poor to the aid the former, tPe. 3:1 and tPe. 3:12. One way in which the sages behind these passages in Tosefta stressed the differences between gentiles and Israelites was by noting that the former do not follow the latter's agricultural rules, tM.S. 4:1, tHal. 1:3, and tMa. 3:8. Another way in which the differences between the two groups were emphasized was by pointing to the different ways in which the elements of Israelite, and perhaps the non-Israelite, judicial system applied to the two groups, tNed. 2:2, tShebu. 2:5, and tShebu. 5:10. The distinctions between the gentiles and Israelites also applied in the context of the synagogue, tMeg. 2:16, and the Temple-cult, tZeb. 13:1, tMen. 10:17, and tMe'. 1:18. We have also seen that the sages behind our passages found occasions to state the prohibition against exogamous marriages, tSuk. 4:28, tYeb. 8:1, and tQid. 4:16. Another idea which occurs here is that Canaanite slaves are different from Hebrew slaves, for the former are not considered to be independent individuals, tErub. 6:11, tPis. 7:4, and tB.Q. 10:21. Lastly, we encounter the view, which we have seen elsewhere, that when gentiles impinge on Israelites during the latter's periods of sacred time, the gentiles fall under some of the Israelite restrictions, tShab. 17:17.

On the one hand, these passages from Tosefta leave the impression that tensions existed between the Israelites and the gentiles, that Israelites held negative views of the gentiles, and that Israelites believed that these tensions had been present from the very creation of the Israelite people, for in addition to the above cited texts which speak of the dangerous or sexually uninhibited gentile one can add tR.H. 2:12, tMo'ed 1:12, tNed. 2:4, tSot. 13:9, tSanh. 13:2, and tArakh. 5:9. THul. 9:9 even compares gentiles to dogs, and tPe. 3:5 indicates that gentiles are as different from Israelites as wheat is from barley. On the other hand, the two groups regularly interact: Israelites might even take on gentile names, tGit. 6:4, and legitimate gentile farmers can be trusted when they set a value to an Israelite's crop, tM.S. 3:5. Taken as a whole, these passages contain the same complex views concerning the non-Israelite that we have seen elsewhere; however, more of them present a negative image of the gentiles then present a positive description of them.

Other references to gentiles in Tosefta and their contexts

Above, we have paid attention to those *sugyot* in Tosefta which have some relationship to parallel or similar material in Mishnah. We saw that when Tosefta's mention of the gentile was derived from Mishnah, for the most part, the two texts treated the topic in the same way. On the other hand, when Tosefta appears to expand a portion of Mishnah to include a reference to the gentile, the former text generally seemed to present a negative view of the non-Israelite, although this was not true in all cases. Now we turn to those passages in Tosefta which have no relationship to Mishnah in an attempt to discover how Tosefta, on its own, deals with the gentile. In general, we shall see that the references to the gentile are generated by the topics and discussions integral to the contexts in which the pericopae are set.

TBer. 6:18 contains Judah's rule that one must thank YHWH for not creating him as a gentile. The whole chapter is a discussion of the blessings one must recite, so that this ruling fits generally into the chapter. Obviously, Judah points to the special relationship which exists between YHWH and the People Israel, and his comment implies a negative view of the gentiles.

TDem. 4:20 states that a traveling merchant's produce is *demai*, whether the merchant is a gentile, an Israelite, or a Samaritan, that is, no matter what type of human being he is. While tDem. 4:20-21 form a unit which discusses the traveling merchant, they are unrelated to their larger context.[215] The text focuses on the traveling merchant, not on the gentile, who merely appears as a portion of the population of the Land of Israel.

TDem. 5:2 discusses whether or not one believes the gentile when he makes a declaration about his produce. The discussion of the gentile forms an autonomous part of this *sugya*[216] which "contrast[s] the credibility of an Israelite *am haares* vendor with that of a gentile vendor."[217] This carries on the discussion, begun in tDem. 5:1, about the reliability of a vendor's claim. The gentile is not believed when his claims make his produce more desirable; however, he is believed when his comments make his saleable items less desirable to Israelites. Simeon b. Gamliel states that gentiles are never believed. The *sugya* points to a disagreement among the sages concerning the acceptability of statements by gentiles, in contrast to the reliability of statements made by Israelites or by an *am haares*.

TDem. 5:15 deals with a gentile dyer and the possibility that he might use libation-wine, or its byproduct, in the dying process. The Israelite does not need to worry that this has occurred if the gentile dyer provides him with an itemized bill, for the text assumes that one can trust the dyer to compose an honest accounting of his procedures and their costs. Although tDem. 5:15 alone mentions the gentile, Sarason treats tDem. 5:14-15 as "a redactional unit" "since they appear together a T.A.Z. 7[8]:10-11" and "thematically are broadly related to each other. Both deal with the same larger issue, namely, When is a man

----

[215]Sarason, 137-138. I suspect that the gentile is mentioned along with the Samaritan and Israelite in order to include all of the inhabitants of the Land of Israel.

[216]Sarason, 156-157.

[217]Sarason, 156-157.

deemed to act as the agent of another, such that the latter bears responsibility for the former's actions?"[218] Unlike in tDem. 5:1, here, in tDem. 5:15, gentiles can be trusted.

TDem. 7:11 discusses how one who allows a Samaritan or a gentile to sharecrop his field separates the tithes. TDem. 7:11-12 digress from the major theme of the surrounding *sugyot*. The context deals with the disposition of priestly dues under conditions of shared ownership.[219] The relevant pericope deals with an Israelite who allows a gentile to sharecrop his field, even though the passage states that an Israelite should not do this.[220] The passage equates the Samaritan and the gentile and differentiates them from the *am haareṣ*. Our text fits because it deals both with agricultural gifts and with produce which is owned by people of different status. However, tDem. 7:11 is the only text which treats the gentile.

TTer. 10:13 tells us that lees derived from a gentile's wine are forbidden, even if they are dried. The major subject of tTer. 10:12-13 is the lees of wine, and the text states that the lees of a gentile's wine are treated like the wine itself.[221] The gentile is mentioned so that the lees of all wine are covered, and the passage fits into this context. The text assumes that all gentile wine is libation-wine; therefore, it is forbidden to Israelites.[222]

TSheb. 4:7 states that the towns on the border of Israel must be protected, so that gentiles might not cross the border and desecrate the seventh-year produce. This is part of a larger unit, tSheb. 4:6-11, which defines the Land of Israel, discusses the area around specific cities, and deals with the border-areas, all with reference to the laws of the seventh year. Our pericope is the only one which mentions the border-areas and the concern with the gentiles' defiling the seventh-year produce, so that it is only loosely related to its context.[223] Again we see Tosefta's concern with the dangerous gentile.

TSheb. 5:9 rules that an Israelite may not sell, or hire out, village dogs, porcupines, cats or monkeys to gentiles. It continues by stating that one may sell to gentiles their brine, Bethenian cheese, bread, and oil. Discussions of selling items which are forbidden to Israelites appear in tSheb. 5:8 and tSheb. 5:10;

----

[218]Sarason, 185.

[219]Sarason, 223.

[220]Sarason writes that "the landowner therefore is penalized by being made to separate tithes for the sharecropper's portion, even when they divide the produce between them before it has reached the stage of liability to tithing;" Sarason, 224.

[221]Peck, 323-324.

[222]On libation-wine, see below, Chapter Nine.

[223]Newman, 123-124.

however, tSheb. 5:9 is the only passage which mentions gentiles. The prohibition against selling the animals to the gentiles presents several difficulties. It is possible, however, that it relates to the prohibition against raising small animals within the Land of Israel and that gentiles symbolize the non-Israelite segment of the Land's population. On the other hand, the text may relate to the concern of selling to gentiles animals which might cause harm to Israelites.[224]

TSheb. 5:21 prohibits the feeding of seventh-year produce to gentiles or to hired-hands. TSheb. 5:20-22 deal with the problem of using seventh-year produce for food. TSheb. 5:20 discusses food for animals, and tSheb. 5:21 treats human food, with tSheb. 5:22 stating that a court may decree that a woman can be supported with seventh-year produce. Although tSheb. 5:21 is the only text which refers to the gentile, the discussion fits into its context.[225] Newman appears correct, however, when he implies that this prohibition served as means of distinguishing Israelites from non-Israelites, for "[t]he yield of the Land during the seventh year has been designated by YHWH for the sustenance of Israelites alone."[226]

TKil. 5:24 prohibits the sale to gentiles of linen dyed with soot. The context is a discussion of wool, so that our *sugya* fits into its context; however, the reference to the gentile occurs only here. Soot was normally employed as a dye for wool, so that a piece of cloth dyed with soot might be mistaken for wool, when it was actually linen. While this might concern an Israelite, it seems unlikely that it would matter one way or another to a gentile. It is possible that the gentile here represents the non-Israelite portion of humanity and that the text means that the cloth should be destroyed instead of being sold to anyone.[227]

TShab. 8:5 refers to a convert who lives among the gentiles. Aqiba and Monobases debate whether or not the convert is liable for work he performed on the Sabbath. The issue of the convert's working inadvertently on the Sabbath is

---

[224]Cf., Porton, "Forbidden Transactions," 329-330. Newman, 143, suggests that tSheb. 5:9 somehow relates to mSheb. 7:3; however, he seems to base this comment on the fact that tSheb. 5:8 and tSheb. 5:10 clearly relate to mSheb. 7:3, which they quote. I do not see a clear relationship between our text and mSheb. 7:3.

[225]Newman suggests that our rule "exemplifies the rule of" mSheb. 8:4: "For they do not discharge a debt with money [received from the sale of produce] of the Sabbatical year;" however, this relationship seems rather tenuous; Newman, 162-165.

[226]Newman, 162-165. Newman states that the reason behind the ruling about the gentile is different from the logic behind the other statements in the text. This would strengthen the suggestion that tSheb. 5:21 is not related to mSheb. 8:4.

[227]See Porton, "Forbidden Transactions," 327-328 where the text is mislabeled tKil. 9:2, which is its designation in the Palestinian Talmud.

based on his living among gentiles, so that he did not have the benefit of an Israelite environment.[228] The context in Tosefta is a discussion of inadvertent violations of the Sabbath, so that our passage fits here. The gentiles are non-Israelites; therefore, they do not observe the Sabbath.

TShab. 15:15 rules that one may heat water for a sick person on the Sabbath, and it specifies that the work should be done by an adult Israelite and not by gentiles, children, or on the testimony of Samaritans or women. The context is a discussion of what one may do to save a life on the Sabbath, so that our text fits. The reference to the gentile underscores the fact that an *adult Israelite* is permitted to work on the Sabbath in order to save a life. The passage focuses on the permitted activity of the adult male Israelite, not on the gentile.

In tKip. 2:16, Eleazar b. Yosi states that in Rome he saw the veil from the Temple in Jerusalem and that it contained the blood stains from the ritual of the Day of Atonement. The context is a discussion of the priestly ritual on the Day of Atonement, which supplements mYoma 5:3-6. However, Eleazar's comment builds on an aside reference in Tosefta to the veil. The text points to the evil gentiles of the past, who had destroyed the Temple in Jerusalem.

TSuk. 2:6 discusses bad omens and specifies those which are bad for Israel and those which are bad for the other nations of the world.[229] The reference to the gentile nations parallels the reference to Israel. Neusner suggests that this text "complement[s] M[Suk]. 2:9 in a very general way, on the matter of bad omens;"[230] however, the relationship is tenuous. TSuk. 2:5-6 deal with eclipses and evil occurrences, and this provides the context for our passage. The underlying assumption is that the fate of all peoples can be read in the heavens. The *sugya* also points to the fact that the Israelites follow a lunar/solar calendar, while the gentiles mark their years by the sun alone.

TY.T. 2:6 states that one may not prepare food for gentiles or dogs on a festival. Tosefta also contains a narrative, introduced by m'sh b, which describes Simeon of Teman's preparing food for a gentile contingent which invaded his town on a festival. Judah b. Baba objects to Simeon's actions and quotes the opening rule in Tosefta. The context is an extended discussion on preparing food on the eve of a festival, food for the Sabbath, and food on a festival day. The discussion builds very loosely on mBes. 2:1, which deals with the problem of preparing food for the Sabbath, if Friday is a festival. The reference

----

[228]The text *may* be loosely related to mShab. 7:1; Neusner, *Shabbat*, 81.

[229]An eclipse of the sun is a bad omen for the other nations, for they mark their calendar by the sun.

[230]Neusner, *Sheqalim*, 147.

to the gentile and the dog serves to clarify the point that one prepares only food which is necessary for Israelites on the festival.

According to tYeb. 12:13, a gentile court cannot impose the rite of *halisah*;[231] however, the gentile court may tell an Israelite to do exactly what the rabbis had ordered him to do.[232] Chapter twelve discusses the rite of *halisah*, and mYeb. 12:6 sets forth the court procedure with regard to this ritual. Although the Toseftan pericope is set in the context of an extended treatment of the rite of *halisah*, tYeb. 12:13 and tYeb. 12:15 are the only texts which mention courts. Our passage deals with both types of judicial institutions present in Palestine; therefore, it refers to the gentile court. The text claims that gentile courts cannot act independently on cases involving Israelite matters. If they do rule in these matters, they must follow the decisions of the Israelite tribunals. The text attempts to vitiate the reality of the influence of the gentile judicial system over the Israelites in the Land of Israel.

TKet. 1:3 makes it clear that valid marriages cannot be contracted between Israelites and gentiles. If the gentile converted to Judaism after he had sexual contact with an Israelite woman, or if a non-Israelite woman converted to Judaism after she had intercourse with an Israelite, the two must enter into a marriage agreement because nothing legally occurred when they had previously engaged in intercourse. In neither case, however, is the woman considered a virgin. The reference to the gentile is included in a list of those with whom sexual contact does not effect a marriage, so it fits into this context.[233] The *sugya* fits into a larger context, which discusses a variety of marriage contracts, only in a loose way.

TKet. 5:1 states that one cannot acquire a Canaanite slave-girl through sex, but only through a written document. Sexual contact with a non-Israelite woman does not effect any legally acceptable arrangement, while sexual contact with an Israelite female does effectuate acquisition. The Canaanite slave is brought into an analogy with an Israelite girl in Judah b. Bathyra's *a fortiori* argument. Although the topic of this passage is whether or not a woman receives the heave-offering, first raised in mKet. 5:2-3, our portion of tKet. 5:1 is not closely related to mKet. 5:2-3. However, tKet. 5:1 is loosely related to

----

[231]Deut. 25:7-10.

[232]On whether or not a gentile court can rule on the matter of *halisah* see Saul Lieberman, *Tosefta Ki-fshutah: A Comprehensive Commentary on the Tosefta Part VI Order Nashim* (New York: 1967), 141-145.

[233]The reference may be occasioned by mKet. 1:2, which mentions a convert. However, the relationship is very general; Neusner, *Ketubot*, 17.

tKet. 5:2, which discusses how one provides food for his sister-in-law who is awaiting levirate marriage.

TKet. 12:5 ends by stating that one may force his wife to leave a town in which there is a gentile majority; however, he may not require her to move from a town in which there is an Israelite majority. The context is a discussion of whether or not a marriage contract is valid if a man wishes to remove the woman from one location to another. The reference to the towns in which there is a gentile or an Israelite majority fits into the context, but it is independent of the main "areas" mentioned in mKet. 13:10 and the rest of tKet. 12:5.[234] The passage evidences a negative view of the gentile environment.

TSot. 14:10 refers to a situation in which Israel was so beaten down that many were forced to accept charity from gentiles. The form, "when x . . . there was . . ." parallels mSot. 9:15; however, our text is unrelated to Mishnah. Clearly, being forced to rely on aid from those outside the ethnic group is an undesirable state of affairs.

TQid. 5:4 contains a long discussion of Egyptians, Edomites, and Ammonites, the status of their children, and whether or not they may eventually enter into the congregation of Israel. The section is tacked onto one which deals with the *natin* and *mamzer* and is unrelated to Mishnah. The passage reflects the importance of the biblical narrative in shaping the symbolic and mythological systems of the sages behind our documents.

TB.Q. 8:19 refers to the time of the Hittites, Amorites, Canaanites, Perizites, Hivites, and Jebusites, as the time before the Israelites took possession of the Land of Canaan. This is an aside in a text which fits into its context. Unlike tQid. 5:4, tB.Q. 8:19 does not view the biblical peoples as forming part of the contemporary population of the Near East.

TB.Q. 9:21 states that if one injures his Canaanite slave and there are no witnesses, he is exempt from paying damages, for the compensation is a fine, and a fine is not imposed without the testimony of witnesses. However, if he injured his Hebrew slave, the slave may take an oath and collect damages.[235] This text may build on mB.Q. 8:4, which states that one who injures a slave or a woman is liable. However, the discussion of the slave is found in tB.Q. 9:21-27, with only tB.Q. 9:21 mentioning the Canaanite slave, so that any relationship to

----

[234]MKet. 13:10 refers to the provinces of Judah, Transjordan, and Galilee, and tKet. 12:5 cites Mishnah and expands upon it. The relevant part of Tosefta occurs at the end of the discussion of the provinces mentioned in Mishnah.

[235]At issue are the fact that fines are not imposed only on the *testimony* of the injured party and the fact that Canaanite slaves cannot take oaths.

mB.Q. 8:4 is tenuous. The text agrees with those we have seen above which claim that the difference between Israelites and gentiles is expressed in the different judicial procedures applied to each set of people.

TB.Q. 10:15 states that if an Israelite robs a gentile, he must restore to the gentile what he has stolen, for "a more strict rule applies to robbing from a gentile than from an Israelite because of the profanation of the Divine name." Although tB.Q. 10:11-15 deal with various types of robbery and build on mB.Q. 9:5, tB.Q. 10:15 is the only reference to the gentile. The reference to the gentile completes the types of robbery, for tB.Q. 10:11-13, quoting mB.Q. 9:5, speak of one who steals from his fellow and one who steals from his fellow and takes a false oath. TB.Q. 10:14 talks about one who robs the public, not mentioned in Mishnah, and tB.Q. 10:15 completes the picture by mentioning one who steals from a gentile, thus covering all types of victims, Israelites and non-Israelites. Therefore, the relationship of tB.Q. 10:15 to mB.Q. 9:5 is weak. The *sugya* supports the claim we have seen elsewhere that one should strive to live at peace with the gentiles. In addition, the passage implies that Israelites should demonstrate the moral lessons of their culture in their activities with all peoples.

TB.M. 2:27 states that if an Israelite saw a gentile's ass bearing a heavy burden, he must take care of it just as if it were an ass belonging to an Israelite. However, if the ass were carrying libation-wine, he may not touch the wine. TB.M. 2:26, building on Ex. 23:4, states that one has a religious duty to unload the ass of his enemy among the Israelites. TB.M. 2:27 expands the biblical verse to include a gentile's ass. TB.M. 2:23-28 complement and supplement mB.M. 2:10; however, the issue of the enemy's ass appears only in tB.M. 2:26-27, with the former excluding the gentile enemy, and the latter treating the gentile. TB.M. 2:27 is only loosely connected to mB.M. 2:10. Again we see that the values of Israelite culture mandate that one treat non-Israelites with a certain amount of compassion.

TB.M. 8:11 argues that a gentile who treads out grain with the cow of an Israelite is not subject to transgressing the rule against muzzling an ox;[236] however, if an Israelite treads out grain with a gentile's cow, he is liable for the transgression. TB.M. 8:10-11 deal with some of those who do not transgress the rule of muzzling the ox. Tosefta builds loosely on mB.M. 7:4's reference to allowing an ass to nibble straw while it is being unloaded.[237] In this context, the difference between Israelites and gentiles is demonstrated in their following different rules concerning the treatment of their animals.

----

[236]Deut. 25:4.
[237]Neusner, *Baba Mesia*, 112-113.

THul. 1:6 states that if an Israelite holds an animal so that a gentile can slaughter it, the act of slaughtering is valid. This discussion interrupts the sustained citation and glossing of mHul. 1:2, which is carried out in tHul. 1:4-6. The opening of tHul. 1:6 relates back to tHul. 1:3. Concerning the proper slaughtering of an animal so that an Israelite can use it for food, it is necessary only for the Israelite to be present at the slaughtering and to take only a secondary role in the killing of the animal.

THul. 2:15 rules that if one slaughtered an animal for healing or for consumption by gentiles or by dogs, the meat cannot be used for any sort of gain. If one slaughters an animal which turns out to be carrion, kills it by stabbing, or tears loose the organs to be cut, if it were done for a gentile, the Israelite may benefit from the act. The issue of slaughtering for a gentile is raised in mHul. 2:7.[238] Tosefta's concerns and rulings are not found in Mishnah; however, the reference to the gentile in Mishnah may be the occasion for its appearance here. On the other hand, the list of three reasons for slaughtering is found in several places in tHullin, so the text may stand independently of Mishnah's reference. The point seems to be that an Israelite may not validly slaughter an animal for a gentile to eat; however, one may hand over to a gentile meat which was intended for Israelites, but which proved to be ritually unfit for them.

THul. 2:20 states that an Israelite may derive benefit from meat found in a gentile's possession; however, if the meat is coming out of a pagan temple, it is the same as meat from the sacrifices of corpses, and it is forbidden to Israelites. The context is a discussion of the *minim*, and the reference to gentiles is probably meant to indicate that *minim* are worse than gentiles. We further learn that an Israelite may benefit from, but not eat, gentile meat, as long as it is not associated with idolatry. As we shall see below,[239] our texts strive to separate the Israelites from any contact with gentile idolatrous practices. THul. 2:20, 2:15 and 1:6 illustrate that the type of meat the Israelites ate distinguished them from the gentiles.

THul. 3:24 explains that Israelites should not sell the eggs of prohibited birds, unless they are cracked in a dish, to gentiles, and that Israelites should not buy eggs which are cracked in a dish from gentiles. The context in which this passage is set focuses on the problem of how one determines if an animal is fit

----

[238]There, the anonymous text states that one may validly slaughter a gentile's beast for a gentile. Eliezer disagrees.

[239]See Chapter Nine.

for food or not. The discussion of eggs and gentiles, however, occurs only here.[240] Again, we see stress placed on the dietary laws as a means of distinguishing Israelites from non-Israelites.

THul. 6:4 centers on the requirement of covering the blood of a slaughtered animal and mentions one who slaughters for healing, for food for a gentile, for food for a dog, and the act of slaughter by a gentile. The first three references are separated from the last by a citation of mHul. 6:2. The references to the gentile, especially in the two stylized forms in which they appear here, fit with the style and concerns of tHullin. The context is a discussion of the need to cover the blood of a slaughtered animal, tHul. 6:4-10. An Israelite must cover the blood of a slaughtered animal, even if the animal was not intended to be used as food for Israelites, while a gentile need not cover the blood of animals he slaughters.

THul. 10:2 states that if a priest or a gentile gave a beast to an Israelite to sheer, he is free from the requirement of offering the first fleece because the animal belongs to the priest or the gentile. As Neusner notes, "T[Hul]. 10:2 reads M[Hul]. 10:3 into M[Hul]. 11:1,"[241] which mentions the requirement of giving the priest the first fleece. The context in Tosefta is a discussion of the first fleece, tHul. 10:1-8. Offerings to the priest are incumbent upon Israelites alone and should be taken from only items owned by Israelites.

TPar. 12:11 rules that if one dipped the hyssop for the sake of sprinkling something which is suitable for sprinkling but then sprinkled something not suitable for sprinkling, such as a gentile, the water which drips is clean, but unusable for sprinkling. This is loosely related to mPar. 12:3; however, Tosefta's specific formulation of the issue is its own, as is its reference to the gentile. The relevant *sugya* is set in the context of tPar. 12:1-12, which deals with the problem of sprinkling with the hyssop. We see that methods of purifying Israelites from ritual uncleanness were not applicable to gentiles. In fact, below we shall discover that for the most part, the Israelite rules of purity and impurity do not apply to gentiles.[242]

TToh. 5:2 notes that if a gentile's urine is mixed with other urine, the purity is decided according to the majority of the liquid. TToh. 5:1 discusses mixtures of blood and spit, while tToh. 5:2 deals with mixtures of urine. The gentile appears only in tToh. 5:2. TToh. 6:11=tAhil. 9:2.

---

[240]Porton, "Forbidden Transactions," 325, n. 38. MHul. 3:6 does raise the issue of the bird, but it does not mention eggs.

[241]Neusner, *Hullin*, 125.

[242]See Chapter Eleven.

TToh. 10:5 concerns a vat of olives purchased from gentiles and Is-raelites. Chapter nine of mTohorot discusses olives; but the gentiles appear in only Tosefta, and our text's relationship to Mishnah is tenuous. However, tToh. 10:2-12 deal with olives, so that the text fits into its context.

TToh. 11:6 states that if one presses grapes in a jug and the juice flows on his hand, it is not susceptible to uncleanness, and one does not worry lest a gentile make a libation with it.[243] TToh. 11:4-9 discuss grapes, but this issue is unique here. Again, Israelite strictures concerning purity and impurity do not apply to gentiles.

TNid. 2:5 allows an infant to suck from a gentile nurse, even on the Sabbath, as long as it has not been weaned. TNid. 2:1-5 treat nursing women, but tNid. 2:5 is the only reference to a gentile. It is difficult to know exactly what the problem is here. On the one hand, it could relate to the prohibition of having a non-Israelite perform a specific task for the benefit of an Israelite on the Sabbath. On the other hand, it may relate to the theory that gentiles pose a danger to Israelites, so that they should not be left alone with Israelite children.

TZab. 2:1 rules that gentiles are *not* susceptible to uncleanness through flux; however, a gentile is treated as one who suffers from flux. This may aug-ment mZab. 2:1, which mentions only those susceptible to uncleanness; how-ever, only Tosefta mentions the gentile. The issue of flux is raised in tZab. 2:1-4. This passage is interesting, for on the one hand it claims that the Israelite purity rules do not apply to gentiles, while on the other hand, it states that gentiles should be treated as unclean. This ambiguous relationship between the gentile and the Israelite system of purity and impurity will be further discussed below.[244]

TZab. 5:8 states that if one saw a gentile offer a libation from wine which is more than an olive's bulk, it imparts stringent uncleanness. If it were less than this, it imparts only liquid uncleanness. All other types of gentile wine, even though they are prohibited because of libations, only impart liquid unclean-ness. The issue is Tosefta's alone. The context is a discussion of idols in tZab. 5:5-8. This represents a refinement of the problem of libation-wine.[245]

When we analyzed the passages in Tosefta which were clearly related to parallel *sugyot* in Mishnah, we discovered that the treatment of the gentile depended upon the relationship between the pericopae in the two documents: 1)

----

[243]The same phrase appears in tToh. 11:9, which seems to quote our present text.
[244]See Chapter Eleven.
[245]See below, Chapter Eight.

If Tosefta's reference to the gentile were derived from Mishnah's mention of the non-Israelite, in all but one instance Tosefta merely follows Mishnah's description. 2) If Tosefta appeared to add the reference to the gentile to a parallel passage in Mishnah which did not refer to the non-Israelite, the compilers of the passages in the former document wanted to present a certain picture of the gentile, usually a negative one. In this section, we have looked at those passages in Tosefta which fit into their various contexts but which do not have a *clear* relationship to a parallel text in Mishnah. In these passages, we have seen the same phenomenon that we saw above when examining the singletons in Mishnah which also fit into their contexts: The issues around which the discussions are centered are of internal Israelite concern; the gentile is not usually the focal point of the *sugya*. Furthermore, it becomes evident that the gentile appears as a means of sharpening the applicability of the Israelite rules, regulations, prohibitions, concerns and the like to the Israelite community alone. This means that the gentile functions as a non-Israelite and that this fact is underscored by limiting the matter under discussion to Israelites.

In tBer. 6:18 Judah indicates that Israelites should be thankful that they are not gentiles, which implies that the former have a special relationship to YHWH, not shared by the latter. Of interest is the fact that the separation between Israelites and gentiles affects business transactions between the two groups, for Israelites are prohibited from selling to gentiles certain items, tSheb. 5:9, tKil. 5:24, and tHul. 3:24. Certain agricultural rules, purity rules, holiday restrictions, and dietary restrictions apply to Israelites alone, and their applications serve as a means of distinguishing between Israelites and non-Israelites: tSheb. 5:21, tY.T. 2:6, tB.M. 8:11, tHul. 1:6, tHul. 2:15, tHul. 2:20, tHul. 6:4, tHul. 10:2, tPar. 12:11, tToh. 5:2, tToh. 10:5, and tZab. 2:1. Two texts, tShab. 8:5 and tKet. 12:5, deal with the problems caused by Israelites' living among gentiles, and they either imply or explicitly indicate that this is not an ideal situation. However, Israelites should make the best of the situation, should strive to live at peace with the gentiles, and should act in ways which do not degrade Israelite culture in the eyes of the non-Israelites, tB.Q. 10:15 and tB.M. 2:27. While one text recognizes the authority of the gentile courts, it also claims that they may act only in accord with the Israelite tribunals, so that in effect, they are pictured as dependent, not independent, judicial institutions, tYeb. 12:13. In addition, it is a deplorable situation when Israelites must depend upon gentile public institutions for aid, tSot. 14:10.

Some of the issues discussed in this section have appeared elsewhere. For example, Israelites may not marry gentiles, tKet. 1:3, nor may one acquire a gentile slave through intercourse, even though one may acquire a Hebrew slave in this manner, tKet. 5:1. Israelites should not benefit from gentile wine or its by-products, tDem. 5:15 and tTer. 10:13. Gentiles and Israelites represent different sectors of humankind, and more specifically, the population of the Holy Land, and these differences are evidenced by the different ways in which the legal systems apply to each group, tB.Q. 9:21. In fact, this basic difference is seen in the very acts of nature, for each group has its own astrological signs which point to its good or bad fortune, tSuk. 2:6.

The images of the gentile presented here are complex, as they have been elsewhere. On the one hand, the gentile is dangerous, tKip. 2:16 and tSheb. 4:7, while on the other hand, Israelites may employ gentile nurses for their infants, tNid. 2:5. TDem. 5:2 contains a dispute on the trustworthiness of a gentile produce-vendor, while tDem. 5:15 assumes that gentile dyers will deal truthfully with Israelites. Furthermore, while appearing to deal with real non-Israelites, one text speaks of biblical peoples as if they were alive during the rabbinic era, tQid. 5:4, while tB.Q. 8:19 recognizes the fact that they lived only in the distant past.

Passages which stand alone in their contexts in Tosefta

In this present section we shall analyze those *sugyot* in Tosefta which mention the gentile and which appear to be unrelated to their contexts. Furthermore, these passage also do not evidence a relationship to a parallel pericope in Mishnah. TPe. 4:11 contains a story about the family of Navtalah who were related to Arnon the Jebusite.[246] Sages sent three hundred gold *sheqels* to the family, so that they would not have to leave Jerusalem because they were poor. The story appears in the context of whether one may sell his goods so that his level of poverty allows him to take the poorman's share from the fields. The narrative has little relation to its context, except that it shares the theme of poverty with the *sugyot* which surround it. The reference to the non-Israelite Jebusites is totally incidental to the story.

THal. 2:6 notes that Israelites should make known to a gentile that he is not obligated for the dough-offering in the Land of Israel or for the heave-offering outside of the Land and that the dough-offering is eaten by non-priests. The context is the discussion in tHal. 2:6 concerning produce from Syria and border areas, but the surrounding pericopae do not discuss either the gentile or the problems of tHal. 2:6.[247] The point of the *sugya* is that the agricultural gifts are obligatory for Israelites alone.

----

[246]Lieberman, *Tosefta Ki-fshutah Zera'im I*, 186.
[247]The text has some similarities with tTer. 4:13.

The opening of tOrl. 1:5 discusses when one begins counting the four years of a shade tree onto which a gentile has grafted a fruit tree. On the one hand, we learn that the laws of mixed-kinds do not apply to gentiles, for if an Israelite grafts a fruit tree onto a barren tree, it is a violation of the laws of "mixed-kinds", mKil. 1:7. On the other hand, we learn that all trees in the Land of Israel are subject to the laws of the fourth-year produce, for the pericope discusses how one counts the four years of this type of tree. In this one passage, which is unrelated to its context, we see the complex relationship of the gentile to the Israelite agricultural rules.[248]

TShab. 9:22 states that Israelite children do not suck from a gentile woman, or an unclean beast, unless it is a matter of life or death. The text is somewhat related to tShab. 9:21, which forbids drawing milk from a clean beast on a festival or the Sabbath. TShab. 9:22 opens by stating that a woman should not squeeze her breasts or force milk into a cup or plate on the Sabbath, and then the reference to the gentile occurs. The context is a treatment of forbidden labor on the Sabbath; however, our passage does not seem to fit into this category.[249] Rather, it compares the gentile nurse to an unclean animal and suggests that one should employ a gentile nurse only in extreme circumstances.

TKip. 3:20 reports that Simeon b. Qimhi was unable to serve as High Priest on the Day of Atonement because he was rendered unclean by the spittle of an Arab. Although Tosefta opens by quoting mYoma 7:4, the narrative, introduced by m'sh b, is basically unrelated. In fact, the narrative does not even refer to the Day of Atonement.[250] The point of the story is the last line--"the mother of these men witnessed two high priests [who were her sons serving] on the same day."[251] Therefore, its relation to its context is tenuous at best. The reference to the gentile supplies a source of unexpected impurity against which the High Priest had not guarded himself.

TMo'ed 1:2 states that a person may sell his spring of water to a gentile or make a trade with him on the Sabbath to take effect at the end of the Sabbath, without worrying that the spring runs dry and the person suffers a loss. This part of the pericope in Tosefta is unrelated to its context, except that the opening of

----

[248]See Essner, 119-120.

[249]Neusner, *Shabbat*, 83-84.

[250]Although the later versions, such as ARNA 35, do suggest that this event happened on Yom Kippur, these references may be based on the appearance of the story in its present context in Tosefta; Cf., Saul Lieberman, *Tosefta Ki-fshutah: A Comprehensive Commentary on the Tosefta, Part IV, Order Mo'ed* (New York: 1962), 805-806.

[251]Neusner, *Sheqalim*, 114.

the passage discusses watering a field on the intermediate days of a festival and the importance of attending to things on the intermediate days which might cause a loss to the owner. The gentile is mentioned, for the rules concerning the Sabbath are not applicable to him.

TShebu. 2:14 notes that one may take a false oath before gentiles, thugs, or tax-collectors, an issue we have encountered above,[252] and quotes Lev. 5:1 in support of its ruling.[253] The opening of tShebu. 2:14 stands alone in its context. Although elsewhere we have seen that an Israelite should be careful to uphold the correctness of the Israelite way of life before gentiles, here, non-Israelites are equated with the despicable elements of society, so that it is permissible for one to lie to them.

TShebu. 3:6 contains a debate between Reuben and "a certain philosopher" over the wording of the Ten Commandments; it stands alone in its context. Reuben demonstrates that the philosopher does not adequately understand the "philosophical" underpinnings of the Bible, so that he is defeated "at his own game."

THul. 8:16 points to the brutality of the foreign troops, for "there are no legions in which there are not scalps." This text seems to stand alone in its context.

TAhil. 1:4 rules that a utensil which touches a gentile who has touched a corpse is clean; however, the gentiles are not subject to the laws of uncleanness, so that they do not transmit second grade uncleanness. As Neusner notes, the items listed--the gentile, the beast, one who is eight years old, a clay utensil, and foods and liquids which touch a corpse--are not all of the same type, for the first three are not subject to the rules of uncleanness. Neusner also notes that the list "is an independent rule,"[254] so that the reference to the gentile is not closely tied to its context.

TAhil. 2:1 contains several rules: 1) If an Israelite slaughters an unclean animal for a gentile and slaughtered two organs or the greater part of two organs and the animal continues to jerk, it contaminates with the uncleanness of food, but not with that of carrion; 2) limbs and meat which are separated from it are considered as if they were separated from living creatures and are prohibited to gentiles; 3) if it were killed by stabbing, it does not contaminate through food-

----

[252]Cf., mNed. 3:4 and tNed. 2:2.

[253]Neusner argues that this supplements mShebu. 4:10-12; however, I do not see a clear relationship, for Mishnah centers on one's imposing an oath on another person; Neusner, *Shebuot*, 36.

[254]Neusner, *Ohalot*, 33-34.

uncleanness; 4) if the Israelite cut so much as to render it *terefah*, no unclean-ness pertains to it; 5) if a gentile slaughtered a clean beast for an Israelite and slaughtered in it two organs or the greater part of two organs and it is still jerk-ing, it renders unclean as food, and limbs and flesh separated from it are consid-ered to have been separated from a living creature, and it is prohibited to gentiles; 6) if he killed it by stabbing, it does not convey food-uncleanness; 7) if he slaughtered in it one organ or the greater part of one organ, there is no un-cleanness pertaining to it at all; 8) if a gentile cut only so much as does not render it *terefah*, and an Israelite completed the slaughtering, it is permitted for eating; 9) if an Israelite slaughtered in it two organs or the greater part of two organs--the same rule applies for gentiles and for Israelites; one chops flesh from it, waits until it dies, and then it can be used for food. This rather long dis-cussion relates to mOhol. 1:6's mention of a jerking beast, only in the most gen-eral terms. The extended essay belongs to Tosefta and does not really pertain to its context. The passage simply underscores the complexities surrounding the slaughtering of food for and by gentiles, and in one sense it attempts to define "food" in terms of the categories of uncleanness related to foodstuffs.

TAhil. 9:2 states that if one moved or stumbled against the millstones in the midst of which is a gentile or a menstruating woman, his clothes are rendered unclean with *midras*-uncleanness.[255] The reference to the millstones is found in mOhol. 8:3; however, the reference to gentiles and menstruating women is Tosefta's.[256] The passage stands alone in its context. Here the gentile is equated with the menstruating women, both of whom are sources of uncleanness.

TToh. 8:11 states that if one found a gentile near his wine-press or cistern when he re-entered the town, the wine is not considered libation-wine. The passage rules that the *am haareṣ* does not render the wine unclean, and the gentile does not render the wine unfit for use. This part of the *sugya* is not re-lated to its context.

In this section, we have collected those *sugyot* in Tosefta which men-tion the gentile and which are unrelated to their contexts. One imagines that these passages would supply us with texts which were interested in making specific points about the gentile; however, we discover that this does not appear

----

[255] Any object upon which a woman in childbirth, a man who has a genital discharge, or a woman who has suffered a discharge of blood sits, lies, rides, or leans suffers *midras*-uncleanness. Any object which is fit for one to sit, lie, or ride upon or upon which one normally sits, lies, or rides is considered to be susceptible to *midras*-uncleanness; Danby, 795.

[256] A gentile's moving something renders it unclean; Neusner, *Ohalot*, 194-195.

to be the case. In tPe. 4:11 the mention of the gentile is secondary to the issue at hand. The appearance of the gentile in tKip. 3:20 is also secondary, for he represents a source of uncleanness against which the High Priest did not, or could not, take any precautions, but any source of uncleanness would have sufficed to make the same point. THal. 2:6 tells us that gentiles are not obligated to separate the dough-offering, a point which fits into what we have seen elsewhere concerning the applicability of the agricultural gifts to the gentile's produce. This text applies a well-known principle specifically to the gentile, but there is nothing unique in this *sugya*. Given what we learned elsewhere, the same is true about tOrl. 1:5, for we already know that the laws of "mixed-kinds" are not applicable to gentiles and that the laws of fourth-year produce apply to any tree. This passage merely applies what is taught elsewhere to a specific case, which may be highly theoretical. TShab. 9:22 offers another opinion concerning the employment of gentile nurses by Israelites. While this text decries the practice, other texts support it, so that the present passage merely points up the complexity of the problem. The appearance of the gentile in tMo'ed 1:2 merely serves to illustrate the principle that one may engage in a business with a gentile which might cause the latter a loss. In tShebu. 2:14, we learn that one may take a false oath before gentiles, thugs, and tax-collectors, so that the issue is the permissibility of taking a false oath before certain segments of society, whether they are Israelites or not. In a sense, this serves to counter the view that one should strive to act so that a gentile does not have cause to challenge the values of Israelite culture. In tShebu. 3:6, we discover that gentile philosophers are unable to understand the value of the Hebrew Bible, *even on their own philosophical terms*. In this case, the appearance of the philosopher serves to underscore the fact that the Hebrew Bible is a valuable text, even when measured against the intellectual standards of the gentiles. The aside in tHul. 8:16 points to the cruelty of gentile troops, but this point is standard. TAhil. 1:4 makes the familiar point that the Israelites' rules of purity and impurity do not apply to gentiles. TAhil. 2:1 contains a detailed analysis of "food" in terms of slaughtering animals, and in this case the appearance of the gentiles is important, for without them there is no problem. TAhil. 9:2 equates gentiles with menstruating women, and this serves to illustrate the complexity involved with determining if gentiles *qua* gentiles are impure. TToh. 8:11 gives us one specific instance in which an Israelite need not worry about a gentile's using Israelite wine for a libation.

In brief, we learn virtually nothing new from these passages. Aside from the fact that the Hebrew Bible is pictured as philosophically consistent even in terms of gentile standards, we have a collection of specific cases which fit in with material we have seen elsewhere. As we now have Mishnah and Tosefta, the authors of these passages did not make new or important points concerning the gentile. At most they point to the inconsistency of the rabbinic images of the gentile, or to the complexities involved in relating the gentiles to the major Israelite symbols and issues. It is possible, of course, that as singletons originating in specific contexts, at particular times, and in unique situations, they did offer new and important information. However, in Tosefta as we have it today, this is not the case.

iv

The present chapter focuses on the *sugyot* in Mishnah and Tosefta which discuss the gentiles, but which are not elements of an essay on that topic, *primarily* in order to discover whether the discussions of the gentiles fit into their environments in Mishnah-Tosefta or whether they stand out from the pericopae which surrounded them. It is assumed that references to the gentile which fit into their various settings were included because they furthered the discussions of the larger topics of the contexts in which they appeared. On the other hand, if the passages stood out and appeared not to belong in their present environments, this would suggest that the mention of the gentile was more important for their being included than was their contribution to the development of the topic at hand in the unit. In brief, by focusing on the content of these passages and the ways in which they related to the pericopae which surrounded them, the present chapter seeks to answer the following questions: Did the topic of the gentile generate the passage, or did the mention of the gentile occur only in order to advance the discussion of the topic being developed in the surrounding pericopae?

In the overwhelming majority of cases, the references to the gentile appear to have been included in our texts in order to further the agenda of the documents. The gentiles appear so that they can set the parameters concerning the specific legal issues under discussion. In order to emphasize the ethnic nature of the laws, customs, and rituals, our *sugyot* indicate that the matters under discussion are relevant to only Israelites; gentiles are not obligated to follow the mandates of the laws being discussed. For example, gentiles do not join with Israelites to recite the grace after meals, gentiles need not distinguish the firstborn of their animals, neither gentiles nor their possessions contract uncleanness from skin diseases or mildew, gentiles may not validly slaughter an animal for an Israelite to eat unless an Israelite participates in the slaughtering, fields owned by gentiles are not liable for the gifts to the poor mandated by Israelite custom, gentiles are not trustworthy concerning the tithing of their produce, gentiles do not observe the restrictions of the seventh year, gentiles do not separate the dough-offering, gentiles may work on the Sabbath as long as they do not respond to the requests of Israelites, gentiles may not contribute the half-*sheqel* tax for the upkeep of the Temple in Jerusalem, gentiles may not marry Israelites, the presences of gentiles may affect the fulfillment of certain Israelite requirements such as the *'erub* or breaking the heifer's neck, the categories and rules concerning the offerings made by Israelites at the Temple did not apply to those brought by gentiles, and the like. In addition, several pericopae distinguish between Hebrew slaves, who may act as independent individuals, and Canaanite slaves, who have no independent status, so that their actions are considered to be those of their masters. Furthermore, numerous passages indicate that the gentiles and the Israelites participated differently in the Israelite legal system and that different laws of damages and torts applied to each group. By stating that the rules, customs, rituals, and laws did not apply to gentiles, our authors were able to demonstrate that these served as a means of defining the Israelites and of distinguishing them from everyone else, the gentiles.

Secondarily, the above analysis also uncovered a variety of images of the gentile, and these also serve to mark them off from Israelites. Often, the gentiles are assumed to be dangerous and threatening to Israelites. Frequently, this appears to be an inherent trait of the gentiles. Clearly, there were sages who believed that gentiles could not be trusted, although there were other rabbis who assumed that, at least in some circumstances, gentiles would be honest. In some passages, it is assume that all gentiles are sexually uninhibited, and at least one text implies that only greed prevents the gentiles from raping Israelite women whom they hold as prisoners. Frequently, the gentile appears as a symbol of that part of humankind not covered by the term Israelite, while in other cases the gentile represents a sub-set of the population of the Land of Israel. It is important to note that our texts rarely distinguish among different gentiles. In fact, the only times that specific gentile peoples are named--such as Amorites, Ammonites, Edomites, and the like--are in response to a biblical situation or statement, or with reference to the "Greeks," Titus, Vespasian, etc., who fought wars against the Israelites. In brief, all gentiles are grouped together as non-Israelites, and this also serves to divide the world and humanity between "us" and "them."

The present chapter also took up a third issue, for it looked at the ways in which the references to the gentiles functioned within their settings in Mishnah and Tosefta. Several pericopae which mention the gentile serve as introductions to chapters or units in Mishnah. A few, however, begin chapters, but do not introduce the chapters because they admit to no introductions. However, for the most part, the references to the gentile appear throughout the editorial units in Mishnah, but almost all of them are included in order to further the agenda of the unit. When the gentile is mentioned in Tosefta in a *sugya* which seems to parallel a reference in Mishnah, Tosefta rarely, changes anything. However, when Tosefta appears to add a reference to the gentile in its apparent reworking of a portion of Mishnah, it most often does so to paint a negative picture of the non-Israelite. We have seen that Tosefta contains more texts about the gentile than does Mishnah and that many of these paint a negative picture of the gentile, so that Tosefta has a much more unflattering image of the gentile than does Mishnah. It is almost as if the compiler(s) of Tosefta felt that Mishnah's more "neutral" image of the gentile had to be corrected, or that the editor(s) of Mishnah sought to compile, in distinction to Tosefta, a more "neutral" picture of the non-Israelite.

When we take all of the evidence into account, we are left with the impression that the non-Israelites were not a major topic of concern for the editor(s) of Mishnah, or for those who compiled Tosefta. The gentiles serve primarily as a means of stressing the point that Israelite law applies to only Israelites and that it provides a means of separating the Israelites from all other groups of peoples, collectively called "gentiles." Throughout, however, the texts assume that gentiles and Israelites come into contact with one another in virtually every sphere of life in the Land of Israel. For this reason, almost every major area of Israelite law, custom, and ritual must be set against the presence of the gentile. There is, on the other hand, little interest in or knowledge of what gentiles do *when they do not, or are not imagined to, impinge on Israelites*. The rabbis were not anthropologists, and the gentiles did not hold any inherent interest for them. One can assume that if gentiles and Israelites could have lived their lives in completely isolated spheres, the gentiles would have been dealt with, at least in part, in other ways than the ones we have encountered. By subsuming the discussions of the gentiles under the categories of mishnaic law and practices, they were treated as "normal" human beings. The point was not that the gentiles were not part of humanity; rather, our texts indicate that they were that part of humankind to whom rabbinic law did not apply. Like Israelites, gentiles were discussed in terms of those symbols and categories which applied to all human residents of the Land of Israel. Our texts tell us that gentiles were part of humanity, but they were of interest to our authors only a means through which the latter could better define the special nature of the People Israel. Furthermore, the different nature of these two groups appeared in every sphere of human activity in the Land of Israel, in the realms of agricultural activity, religious observances, civil law, and in daily social, cultural, judicial, and economic undertakings.

Chapter Four:

Literary Styles and Forms

i

The preceding two chapters focused on the content of the *sugyot* in Mishnah and Tosefta which mention the gentiles. They demonstrated that the passages which discuss the gentile seem to fit into their environments in ways which furthered the agenda at hand, and they argued that for the most part, the pericopae on the non-Israelites were generated by the internal Israelite matters debated within Mishnah-Tosefta, not by an inherent interest in the gentiles *qua* gentiles. The current chapter moves from emphasizing the content of the pericopae to an analysis of the literary structures in which they were cast, in order to ascertain if any particular literary patterns were created for our *sugyot*, or if any unexpected literary forms predominate. Given what we have seen above, we should not expect this to be the case, and indeed it is not.

Although recently the literary analysis of Tannaitic traditions has moved from the study of discrete *sugyot* to the examination of documents,[1] Mishnaic Orders,[2] tractates, chapters and their sub-units,[3] our materials do not

----

[1] Jacob Neusner, *Judaism: The Evidence of Mishnah* (Chicago and London: 1981); *The Talmud of the Land of Israel, Vol. 35: Introduction: Taxonomy* (Chicago and London: 1983); *Judaism in Society: The Evidence of the Yerushalmi, Toward the Natural History of a Religion* (Chicago and London: 1983); *Judaism: The Classical Statement. The Evidence of the Bavli* (Chicago: 1986); *The Bavli and Its Sources: The Question of Tradition in the Case of Tractate Sukkah* (Atlanta: 1987).

[2] Alan Avery-Peck, *Mishnah's Division of Agriculture: A History and Theology of Seder Zeraim* (Chico: 1985). Jacob Neusner, *A History of the Mishnaic Law of Appointed Times Part Five. The Mishnaic System of Appointed Times* (Leiden: 1983); *A History of the Mishnaic Law of Women Part Five. The Mishnaic System of Women* (Leiden: 1980); *A History of the Mishnaic Law of Damages Part Five. The Mishnaic System of Damages* (Leiden: 1985); *A History of the Mishnaic Law of Holy Things Part Six. The Mishnaic System of Sacrifice and Sanctuary* (Leiden: 1980).

[3] Jacob Neusner, *A History of the Mishnaic Law of Appointed Times* (Leiden: 1981-1982), *A History of the Mishnaic Law of Women* (Leiden: 1979-1980), *A History of the Mishnaic Law of Damages* (Leiden: 1982), *A History of the Mishnaic Law of Holy Things* (Leiden: 1978-1979), *A History of the Mishnaic Law of Purities* (Leiden: 1974-77). Richard Sarason, *A History of the Mishnaic Law of Agriculture Section Three: A Study of Tractate*

allow us to undertake this type of investigation. Our pericopae are distributed throughout the entire corpus of Mishnah-Tosefta, and few are grouped together in chapters or other units. Thus, we must return to type of analysis with which the contemporary literary study of Tannaitic traditions began,[4] an examination of the individual *sugya*, not its larger literary context.

Investigations of the literary features of the Tannaitic *sugyot* have demonstrated that the materials appear in a limited number of forms: Disputes, debates, narratives, testimonies, and the like. While there are variations on the "pure" forms--such as the disputes and debates[5]--there is *not* an unlimited selection of literary structures.[6] In addition, the various forms are distributed unevenly among the several Tannaitic documents, for the editors/authors of specific collections often preferred the use of particular forms, even recasting the literary style of a pericope which appeared in one document, so that it "fit" better into its "new" setting.[7] In addition, at least some forms were created by

----

Demai Part One, Commentary (Leiden: 1979). Peter Haas, *A History of the Mishnaic Law of Agriculture: Tractate Maaser Sheni* (Chico: 1980). Louis Newman, *The Sanctity of the Seventh Year: A Study of Mishnah Tractate Shebiit* (Chico: 1983). Martin Jaffe, *Mishnah's Theology of Tithing: A Study of Tractate Maaserot* (Chico: 1981). Irving Mandelbaum, *A History of the Mishnaic Law of Agriculture: Kilayim* (Chico: 1982). Alan Peck, *The Priestly Gift in Mishnah: A Study of Tractate Terumot* (Chico: 1981). Roger Brooks, *Support for the Poor in the Mishnaic Law of Agriculture: Tractate Peah* (Chico: 1983). Margaret Wenig Rubenstein, "A Commentary on Mishnah-Tosefta Bikkurim Chapters One and Two," in William Green (ed.), *Approaches to Ancient Judaism Volume III: Texts as Context in Early Rabbinic Literature* (Chico: 1981), 47-88. David Weiner, "A Study of Mishnah Tractate Bikkurim Chapter Three," in Green, *Ibid.*, 89-104. Howard Essner, "The Mishnah Tractate *'Orlah*: Translation and Commentary," in Green, *Ibid.*, 105-148. Abraham Havivi, "Mishnah Hallah Chapter One: Translation and Commentary," in Green, *Ibid.*, 149-184.

[4]Jacob Neusner, *Development of a Legend: Studies on the Traditions Concerning Yohanan ben Zakkai* (Leiden: 1970), Jacob Neusner, *Rabbinic Traditions About the Pharisees Before 70*, 3 Volumes (Leiden: 1971); *Eliezer Ben Hyrcanus: The Tradition and the Man*, 2 Volumes (Leiden: 1973). Gary G. Porton, *The Traditions of Rabbi Ishmael*, 4 Volumes (Leiden: 1976-1982). William S. Green, *The Traditions of Joshua Ben Hananiah Part One: The Early Legal Traditions* (Leiden: 1981). Robert Goldenberg, *The Sabbath-Law of Rabbi Meir* (Missoula: 1979). Shamai Kanter, *Rabban Gamaliel II: The Legal Traditions* (Chico: 1980). Jack Lightstone, *Yose the Galilean: I. Traditions in Mishnah-Tosefta* (Leiden: 1979). Charles Primus, *Aqiva's Contribution to the Law of Zeraim* (Leiden: 1977).

[5]Porton, *Ishmael*, IV, 29-49.

[6]Neusner, *Rabbinic Traditions*, III, 5-68. Porton, *Ishmael*, IV, 53-54.

[7]Porton, *Ishmael*, IV, 17-56.

different schools, for specific purposes.[8] Given these facts, the creators of our documents could have produced one or more literary patterns to use for their treatment of the gentile. Alternatively, the compilers of our passages could have limited themselves to one or two specific forms, or variations of accepted patterns. In brief, the references to the gentiles could have been cast in such a way that they would have stood out within the editorial units of Mishnah-Tosefta. That none of these options was taken underscores the point that the gentiles were treated like any other topic in Mishnah-Tosefta. In the context of Mishnah-Tosefta, the individual treatments of the non-Israelites are neither unique nor memorable from the point of view of their literary formulations.

ii

Anonymous Statements

Many of the previously cited statements are anonymous, and they are cast in complex and compound sentences, like the rest of the anonymous comments and attributed sayings throughout the Tannaitic collections.[9] Three hundred forty-six *sugyot* contain anonymous comments about the gentile.[10] This is

----

[8]For example, the "According to Rabbi Y"-form probably was invented by Yohanan's school in Tiberias as a means of juxtaposing the sayings of Ishmael with those of Aqiba in the Palestinian *gemara*. And, when the form is broken, the pericope frequently becomes incomprehensible; Gary G. Porton, "According to Rabbi Y: A Palestinian Amoraic Form," in William S. Green (ed.), *Approaches to Ancient Judaism I: Theory and Practice* (Missoula: 1978), 173-188. Neusner suggests that the dispute form was created specifically for the Houses-materials; Neusner, *Rabbinic Traditions*, III, 14; 89-100.

[9]Jacob Neusner, *From Mishnah to Scripture: The Problem of the Unattributed Saying* (Chico: 1984). Neusner states, 1, that "unattributed sayings form no distinct group, exhibiting characteristics different from attributed ones."

[10]MBer. 7:1, mBer. 8:6, mPe. 2:7, mPe. 4:9, mDem. 3:4, mDem. 6:1, mDem. 6:2, mDem. 6:10, mSheb. 4:3, mSheb. 5:7, mSheb. 5:9, mTer. 1:1, mTer. 3:9, mTer. 8:12, mTer. 9:7, mM.S. 4:4, mHal. 3:5, mOrl. 1:2, mShab. 16:6, mShab. 16:8, mShab. 23:4, mShab. 24:1, mErub. 3:5, mErub. 4:1, mErub. 7:6, mPes. 2:1, mPes. 2:2, mPes. 2:3, mSheq. 1:5, mYoma 8:7, mBes. 3:2, mTan. 4:6, mYeb. 2:5, mYeb. 7:5, mKet. 2:9, mNed. 3:11, mSot. 9:2, mGit. 2:5, mGit. 4:6, mGit. 4:9, mGit. 5:9 (=mSheb. 5:9), mGit. 9:2, mGit. 9:8, mQid. 3:12, mB.Q. 4:3, mB.Q. 4:6, mB.Q. 8:5, mB.M. 1:5, mB.M. 5:6, mSanh. 9:2, mSanh. 9:6, mSanh. 10:2, mA.Z. 1:3, mA.Z. 1:4, mA.Z. 1:7, mA.Z. 1:9, mA.Z. 2:1, mA.Z. 2:3, mA.Z. 2:6, mA.Z. 4:4, mA.Z. 4:8, mA.Z. 4:9, mA.Z. 4:12, mA.Z. 5:1, mA.Z. 5:5, mA.Z. 5:6, mA.Z. 5:7, mA.Z. 5:12, mMen. 9:8, mHul. 1:1, mHul. 7:2, mHul. 8:5, mHul. 9:1, mHul. 10:3, mHul. 11:2, mBekh. 1:1, mBekh. 2:1, mMid. 1:6, mMid. 2:3, mKel. 1:8, mOhol. 17:3, mOhol. 18:7, mOhol. 18:10, mNeg. 11:1, mNeg. 12:1, mToh. 1:4, mToh. 5:8, mToh. 7:6, mMiq. 8:1, mMiq. 8:4, mNid. 7:3, mNid. 9:3, mNid. 10:4, mMakh. 2:3, mMakh. 2:6, mMakh.2:8, mMakh. 2:9, tBer. 5:31, tPe. 2:9, tPe. 2:10, tPe. 2:11, tPe. 3:1, tPe. 3:12, tPe. 4:1, tPe. 4:11, tDem. 1:15, tDem. 1:16, tDem. 1:17, tDem. 1:18, tDem. 1:20, tDem. 1:21, tDem. 1:22, tDem. 1:23, tDem. 4:20, tDem. 4:26, tDem. 4:27, tDem. 5:15, tDem. 6:2, tDem. 6:4, tDem. 6:12, tDem. 6:13, tDem. 6:14, tDem. 7:11, tTer. 1:15, tTer. 2:11, tTer. 4:12, tTer. 4:13, tTer. 7:14, tTer. 7:20,

unexpected, for as Neusner writes, "in the average, something like 10% of the whole of the Mishnah's and Tosefta's tractates in the division of Purities may be constituted by unattributed sayings. But in some tractates the percentage is 1% or 2%. For the Mishnah alone, separate from the Tosefta, the proportion is still smaller."[11] However, Neusner did not study the collections of *sugyot* on specific topics; rather, he focused on tractates. Therefore, his results may be less significant for our purposes than they first appear to be. It is possible that anonymous comments are much more evident on certain topics than on others.

The anonymous comments function in several different ways and occur in a number of different settings and configurations. In many of the passages from Mishnah, the anonymous sentence is the only part of the pericope which refers to the gentile. In some cases, the gentile is the primary subject of the passage, while in other pericopae, the gentile is not the major topic under discussion. In these latter examples, the non-Israelite appears only to illustrate fully the unit's rule or point. This latter phenomenon is often encountered when the gentile appears in lists of "impaired" persons, unqualified individuals, or other items which serve to make the *sugya's* point or to illustrate its law.[12]

----

tTer. 10:13, tSheb. 3:12, tSheb. 3:13, tSheb. 4:7, tSheb. 5:9, tSheb. 5:21, tKil. 2:15, tKil. 2:16, tKil. 5:24, tMa. 3:8, tM.S. 3:5, tM.S. 4:1, tHal. 1:3, tHal. 2:6, tOrl. 1:5, tShab. 6:1-14, tShab. 6:19, tShab. 7:4, tShab. 7:6, tShab. 7:7-8, tShab. 7:10, tShab. 7:12, tShab. 7:15-16, tShab. 7:18, tShab. 7:19, tShab. 7:21, tShab. 9:22, tShab. 13:9, tShab. 13:10, tShab. 13:12, tShab. 13:13, tShab. 15:15, tShab. 17:14, tShab. 17:15, tShab. 17:20, tErub. 3:5, tErub. 3:7, tErub. 3:8, tErub. 5:18, tErub. 5:19, tErub. 6:11, tPis. 1:7, tPis. 1:12, tPis. 2:5-14, tPis. 7:4, tSheq. 3:11, tSuk. 2:6, tY.T. 2:6, tTan. 2:12, tTan. 3:7-8, tMeg. 2:16, tMo'ed 1:2, tMo'ed 1:12, tMo'ed 2:14, tYeb. 4:6, tYeb. 12:13, tYeb. 14:7, tKet. 1:3, tKet. 12:5, tNed. 2:2, tSot. 9:1, tSot. 14:10, tSot. 15:8, tGit. 3:13, tGit. 3:14, tB.Q. 1:1, tB.Q. 1:2, tB.Q. 4:1, tB.Q. 4:2, tB.Q. 4:6, tB.Q. 8:19, tB.Q. 9:10, tB.Q. 9:21, tB.Q. 9:33, tB.Q. 10:15, tB.Q. 10:21, tB.M. 2:12, tB.M. 2:27, tB.M. 2:33, tB.M. 5:14-20, tB.M. 8:11, tSanh. 13:4, tSanh. 14:1, tShebu. 2:5, tShebu. 2:14, tShebu. 5:10, tA.Z. 1:2, tA.Z. 1:3, tA.Z. 1:8, tA.Z. 1:13, tA.Z. 1:15-16, tA.Z. 2:1, tA.Z. 2:4, tA.Z. 2:7, tA.Z. 2:8, tA.Z. 2:9, tA.Z. 3:2, tA.Z. 3:3, tA.Z. 3:4, tA.Z. 3:5, tA.Z. 3:6, tA.Z. 3:11, tA.Z. 3:14-15, tA.Z. 3:16, tA.Z. 3:17, tA.Z. 3:19, tA.Z. 4:3, tA.Z. 4:8, tA.Z. 4:9, tA.Z. 4:11, tA.Z. 4:12, tA.Z. 5:3, tA.Z. 5:5-6, tA.Z. 6:2, tA.Z. 6:8, tA.Z. 6:9, tA.Z. 7:1, tA.Z. 7:3, tA.Z. 7:4, tA.Z. 7:5-12, tA.Z. 7:13, tA.Z. 7:14, tA.Z. 7:16-17, tA.Z. 8:2, tA.Z. 8:4, tA.Z. 8:5, tA.Z. 8:6, tHul. 1:1-3, tHul. 1:6, tHul. 2:15, tHul. 2:20, tHul. 3:24, tHul. 5:2-3, tHul. 6:4, tHul. 7:3, tHul. 8:12, tHul. 8:16, tHul. 9:2-3, tHul. 9:9, tHul. 10:2, tMen. 10:13, tMen. 10:17, tBekh. 1:1, tBekh. 2:1, tBekh. 2:5, tBekh. 2:11, tMe'. 1:18, tAhil. 1:4, tAhil. 2:1, tAhil. 9:2, tAhil. 18:6, tAhil. 18:8-11, tAhil. 18:12, tNeg. 6:4, tNeg. 7:10, tNeg. 7:14-15, tNid. 2:5, tMiq. 6:4, tMiq. 6:7, tToh. 6:11 (=tAhil. 9:2), tToh. 8:8, tToh. 8:9, tToh. 8:11, tToh. 10:5, tToh. 11:6, tToh. 11:8, tToh. 11:9, tZab. 2:1, and tZab. 5:8.

[11]Neusner, *From Mishnah to Scripture*, 119.

[12]The Samaritan and the gentile appear in the following anonymous statements: MBer. 7:1, mDem. 3:4, mDem. 6:1, mSheq. 1:5, tPe. 4:1, tDem. 4:26, tDem. 4:27, tDem. 6:4, tDem. 7:11, tSheb. 3:12, tSheb. 3:13, tM.S. 4:1, tShab. 15:15, tA.Z. 2:4, tA.Z. 3:5, tHul. 1:1, tHul. 2:20, tAhil. 18:6. Gentiles and robbers are mentioned together in mPe. 2:7, tShebu. 2:14, and tA.Z. 1:16. The gentile occurs with other "impaired" individuals in mTer. 1:1, mGit. 2:5, tShebu. 5:10, and mMen. 9:8. In the following passages feeding or giving something to a gentile is juxtaposed with feeding or

A review of the pericopae before us demonstrates that several of these anonymous statements appear in complex *sugyot* which contain a variety of forms and that some unattributed sayings appear in the same contexts with attributed comments. MDem. 3:4 contains two anonymous statements concerning the gentile. The second one is placed in a dispute with Simeon.[13] MDem. 6:2 has two comments concerning the gentile. The first is unattributed, while the second one is assigned to Judah.[14] MTer. 3:9 includes an anonymous statement, a debate between Judah and sages, and Simeon in dispute with an anonymous statement.[15] The unattributed statement in mTer. 8:12 is attached to the Eliezer/Joshua-dispute in mTer. 8:11 by wkn.[16]

In mShab. 16:8, a narrative is attached to the last anonymous statement, which illustrates the latter's point.[17] In mErub. 3:5, Judah glosses the last part of the unassigned comment. However, his statement has nothing to do with the gentiles mentioned in the opening of the *sugya*.[18] MErub. 4:1 opens with an anonymous sentence. This is followed by two unattributed conditional statements, which assume the opening comment. The second one serves as a superscription for a dispute between Gamliel/Eleazar b. Azariah and Joshua/Aqiba. The attached narrative seems unrelated to the issue of the gentile.[19] The dispute between Judah and sages in mPes. 2:1 is unrelated to the anonymous comment which mentions the gentile, with which the passage opens.[20] Gamliel's comment in mPes. 2:3 is unrelated to the unassigned statement about the gentile which precedes it.[21] In mSheq. 1:5, the anonymous statement is attributed to "they."[22] MBes. 3:2 contains an anonymous conditional sentence and a narra-

----

giving something to dogs: TT.Y. 2:6, tHul. 2:15, tHul. 5:2, tHul. 6:4, tHul. 9:2, and tHul. 9:4.

[13]Sarason, 140-141.

[14]Sarason, 204-206.

[15]Peck, 121-123.

[16]Peck, 243-245 and Jacob N. Epstein, *Introduction to the Text of the Mishnah*, Second Edition (Tel Aviv: 1964), II, 1049.

[17]Kanter, 51-52.

[18]Jacob Neusner, *A History of the Mishnaic Law of Appointed Times Part Two Erubin, Pesahim. Translation and Explanation* (Leiden: 1981), 45-46.

[19]Neusner, *Erubin*, 55-56.

[20]Neusner, *Erubin*, 162.

[21]Neusner, *Erubin*, 163.

[22]Jacob Neusner, *A History of the Mishnaic Law of Appointed Times Part Three Sheqalim, Yoma, Sukkah. Translation and Explanation* (Leiden: 1982), 12.

tive about Gamliel and a gentile, which need not relate to the unattributed sentence.[23]

MKet. 2:9 opens with an anonymous rule. The point of a second unattributed rule, which *may* involve gentiles, is illustrated by a debate between Zechariah b. HaQassab and "they" in which the gentile is specifically mentioned.[24] MSot. 9:2 is a complex *sugya*; however, Eliezer's statement, as it is now formulated, does not respond to the anonymous comment, which mentions the gentiles. However, Neusner suggests that the unassigned statement may be defective, and he offers a suggested reading which brings it into conjunction with Eliezer's remark.[25] MNed. 3:11 is a complex pericope with several parts. The first section contains a series of anonymous conditional statements dealing with a variety of vows and contrasting Israel with the Nations of the World. There is an interpolation in this segment, which discusses business dealings covered by the oaths.[26] The second part contains a number of biblical quotations, introduced by "for it is said"[27] or "and it says,"[28] which illustrate that the term "uncircumcised" applies to gentiles. The third section contains a statement by Eleazar b. Azariah, and the fourth unit is a collection of statements attributed to variety of sages which opens with "great is circumcision." MGit. 4:6 begins with an unattributed sentence which mentions the gentile. The anonymous text then turns to the prisoner, and we find a lemma attributed to Simeon b. Gamliel which takes up this subject. The gentile is again mentioned in the anonymous sentence with which the passage ends.[29]

----

[23]Jacob Neusner, *A History of the Mishnaic Law of Appointed Times Part Four Besah, Rosh Hashshanah, Taanit, Megillah, Moed Qatan, Hagigah. Translation and Explanation* (Leiden: 1983), 37; Kanter, 103-104.

[24]The perfect 'mr appears; therefore, I have called this a report instead of a lemma. Jacob Neusner, *A History of the Mishnaic Law of Women Part Two Ketubot. Translation and Explanation* (Leiden: 1980), 30-31.

[25]Neusner, *Eliezer*, I, 202-203; Jacob Neusner, *A History of the Mishnaic Law of Women Part Four Sotah, Gittin, Qiddushin. Translation and Explanation* (Leiden: 1980), 84-85. In the latter volume Neusner does not attempt to bring the two statements together.

[26]The literary patterns in this passage are complex, and the pericope breaks form and uses a variety of stylistic patterns which do not always conform to the topics discussed, so that it is difficult to establish a relationship between form and content; Jacob Neusner, *A History of the Mishnaic Law of Women Part Three Nedarim, Nazir. Translation and Explanation* (Leiden: 1980), 35-36.

[27]Šn'mr.

[28]W'wmr.

[29]Neusner, *Sotah*, 153-154.

MSanh. 9:2 includes a series of unassigned sentences. Simeon disputes the last comment, which does not mention the gentile.[30] MSanh. 10:2 is also a complex *sugya*. It opens with an anonymous declarative sentence, and this is followed by a gloss with which Judah disagrees. This turns into a debate, for "they said to him." The last unassigned statement returns to the topic of the opening sentence and contains a list of named individuals, as did the anonymous superscription with which Judah disputed, which refers to non-Israelites.[31] The unassigned comment with which mA.Z. 1:3 concludes is independent of the dispute between Meir and sages which precedes it.[32] Although mA.Z. 1:4 does not specifically mention the gentile, the context suggests that the topic under discussion is whether or not one can engage in business with gentiles under the conditions mentioned in the text. Although mA.Z. 2:3 contains two disputes, it ends with an anonymous statement.[33] MA.Z. 2:6 contains an unattributed list of gentile items which are forbidden, but from which an Israelite may derive benefit; however, in the middle of the passage, there is an aside which mentions that Rabbi and his court permitted oil.[34]

MHul. 7:2 begins with an anonymous comment. The dispute between Judah and a second unattributed saying is unrelated to the opening reference to the gentile.[35] Judah's comment in mHul. 9:1 is unrelated to the anonymous statement, which mentions the gentile.[36] MHul. 11:2 is a complex pericope in which Neusner finds five autonomous units. The unassigned comment, which mentions the gentile, is unrelated to the attributed sayings in the passage.[37] Although the reference to the gentile appears in an anonymous declarative sentence towards the end of the passage, the *sugya* also contains two debates, a proof-text and its interpretation, and other anonymous sentences which do not refer to the gentile.

MMiq. 8:1 opens with an anonymous statement about immersion-pools within the Land of Israel and another one concerning the immersion-pools of

----

[30] Jacob Neusner, *A History of the Mishnaic Law of Damages Part Three Baba Batra, Sanhedrin, Makkot. Translation and Explanation* (Leiden: 1984), 210-211.

[31] Neusner, *Baba Batra*, 216.

[32] Jacob Neusner, *A History of the Mishnaic Law of Damages Part Four Shebuot, Eduyot, Abodah Zarah, Abot, Horayot. Translation and Explanation* (Leiden: 1985), 144.

[33] Neusner, *Shebuot*, 157.

[34] Epstein, II, 949.

[35] Jacob Neusner, *A History of the Mishnaic Law of Holy Things Part Three Hullin, Bekhorot. Translation and Explanation* (Leiden: 1979), 89.

[36] Neusner, *Hullin*, 106-108.

[37] Neusner, *Hullin*, 125-126.

gentiles. This is followed by an unassigned statement about the immersion-pools within the Land of Israel, with which Eliezer disputes. Eliezer's comment need not refer to gentiles.[38] MMiq. 8:4 opens with two conditional anonymous sentences, constructed in parallel form, which mention the gentile. Two un-attributed conditional sentences follow, with Yosi in dispute with the latter of the two; however, none of these statements refers to a gentile. MNid. 7:3 contains a dispute between Judah and an anonymous sentence, followed by an un-assigned sentence which refers to gentiles. This latter sentence is dependent for its sense on the opening of the anonymous superscription of the dispute. A dispute between Meir and sages concerning Israelites and Samaritans concludes this pericope. MNid. 10:4 opens with a conditional anonymous sentence, followed by an unattributed declarative sentence which mentions the gentile. The passage closes with a Houses-dispute, which does not refer to the gentile. In mMakh. 2:8, an anonymous statement concerning a town in which there are Is-raelites and gentiles is followed by a dispute between Judah and an unassigned comment. Although the gentiles are not specifically mentioned in mMakh. 2:9, the passage's context suggests that a town in which gentiles and Israelites reside is under discussion.

Tosefta is edited differently from Mishnah so that the former's *sugyot* tend to be more eclectic with regard to their literary forms. For this reason, it is not unusual to find a variety of literary patterns in one pericope. TPe. 2:9 and its parallel, tPe. 3:12, open with three anonymous sentences constructed in parallel form. These are followed by a statement attributed to Simeon. It is possible that Simeon's comment is in dispute with the last unassigned statement. On the other hand, one could argue that Simeon's comments form a complete unit by themselves, especially if the question, "under what circumstances does this app-ly," and the answer are also attributed to him.[39] Thus, there are either three un-attributed sentences and an independent comment attributed to Simeon, or two anonymous sentences and Simeon in dispute with an unassigned superscription. TPe. 4:1 begins with a lemma attributed to Judah; this is followed by an anonymous complex sentence. TDem. 6:2 opens with Simeon in dispute with an unattributed superscription. This is followed by an anonymous section which includes an unassigned conditional sentence, an unattributed question with an answer in two short clauses, and an anonymous citation from mDem. 6:2 to which is attached an unassigned clause opening with "therefore."[40] TTer. 1:15

----

[38]Neusner, *Eliezer*, I, 391.
[39]Brooks, 78-79.
[40]Lpykk. Sarason, 207-212.

commences with an anonymous citation from mTer. 1:1. This is followed by a narrative which tells of an incident between an Israelite and a gentile which occurred in Pegah and concerning which Simeon b. Gamliel offered an opinion. Then, Isaac's statement disputes the opening anonymous citation from Mishnah. If one were to remove the narrative, there would be a dispute between Isaac and the unassigned opening comment; however, as it stands, Isaac's comment could stand on its own.[41] TTer. 4:12 begins with an extended anonymous section, containing a variety of syntactical structures. It ends with a words-of dispute between Rabbi and Simeon b. Gamliel on the status of the Samaritan, with the former claiming that the Samaritan is treated like a gentile.[42] TTer. 4:13 starts with an extended anonymous section and finishes with three words-of disputes between Rabbi and Simeon b. Gamliel.[43] TTer. 7:20 opens with an extended unassigned section. Judah glosses the discussion,[44] and a proof-text and two interpretations, the latter of which is attributed to Simeon, follow the gloss. TTer. 10:13 commences with an unattributed declarative sentence which is followed by an anonymous statement, a question and answer, an unassigned comment, and a response by Leazar b. Jacob; however, nothing after the opening sentence deals with the gentile.[45] Similarly, tMa. 3:8 begins with an anonymous complex conditional sentence, followed by a dispute which does not deal with the gentile.[46]

TShab. 6:14 starts with an unassigned statement which is followed by a dispute between sages and an unattributed superscription. TShab. 7:6 contains an anonymous statement and a lemma attributed to Judah on the same topic; however, Judah's statement could stand by itself and need not refer to "the ways of the Amorites." TShab. 7:16 includes an unassigned comment and a narrative which illustrates the point of the anonymous statement. The unattributed comment, which mentions "the ways of the Amorites" and opens tShab. 7:18, is followed by another anonymous comment which glosses the opening statement. The *sugya* closes with a narrative which serves to illustrate the point of the gloss. TShab. 13:9 has a narrative which illustrates the point of the unattributed comment. TShab. 13:13 begins with an anonymous section which need not deal with a gentile; however, in the words-of dispute between Rabbi and Simeon b.

----

[41]Peck, 46-47.
[42]Peck, 125-126.
[43]Peck, 126-129.
[44]The form is 'mr R. Judah.
[45]Peck, 322-324.
[46]Jaffe, 146.

Gamliel which follows, a gentile captain of the ship is assumed.[47] Simeon's statement in tShab. 17:20 pertains to the second anonymous comment, which does not mention the gentile, in the *sugya*. TErub. 3:7 opens with an un-attributed section, to which is attached an exegetical comment on Deut. 20:20 at-tributed to Shammai. Shammai's comment could stand by itself.[48] TPis. 1:7 commences with an anonymous compound-complex sentence. This is followed by a report about Aqiba's ruling which altered previous practice. Yosi then reports[49] on the relationship of Aqiba's ruling to the opinions of the Houses.[50] In tPis. 1:12, Simeon b. Gamliel and Ishmael b. Yohanan b. Beroqa gloss the un-attributed rule and extend its application to holy things; however, they do not mention the gentile. TY.T. 2:6 begins with an anonymous statement which is followed by a narrative containing a debate between Simeon of Teman and Judah b. Baba in which Judah repeats the opening unattributed rule. TTan. 2:12 starts by citing mTan. 3:7. This is followed by an anonymous gloss which ex-pands Mishnah's ruling. A statement by Yosi, which offers an alternative expla-nation of the unassigned gloss, follows.[51] TMo'ed 2:14 contains an anonymous comment and an unassigned report of Aqiba's changing the accepted practice. In TTan. 2:12, Yosi glosses the anonymous statement and explains why its ruling is stated; however, he does not mention the gentiles.

TYeb. 14:7 opens with a citation of an unassigned rule from mYeb. 16:5. This is followed by a narrative, attributed to Abba Yudan of Sidon, which deals with a gentile. The following narrative, attributed to Simeon b. Gamliel, does not specifically mention the gentile; however, it does refer to "a band of prisoners" who went to Antioch, so that the reference to the gentile is implied.[52]

In tB.Q. 4:6, the dispute between Judah and Simeon glosses and builds upon the anonymous reference to the gentile, which is cited from mB.Q. 4:6.[53]

----

[47]Neusner supplies the reference to "the gentile ship-master" in brackets as the antece-dent of "him" in Rabbi's comment; Jacob Neusner, *The Tosefta. Translated from the Hebrew Second Division Moed (Appointed Times)* (New York: 1981), 52.

[48]The exegetical comment is introduced by wkk hyh . . . dwrš.

[49]The perfect, 'mr, appears.

[50]TPis. 1:12 can be divided into two unrelated sections, the first of which is anonymous and irrelevant. The second part contains an anonymous comment which mentions the gentile. It is followed by a statement attributed to Simeon b. Gamliel and Ishmael b. Yohanan b. Beroqa which glosses the anonymous statement, but which does not refer to the gentile.

[51]Yosi's comment is introduced by wkn hyh . . . 'wmr; Porton, *Ishmael*, IV, 24-25.

[52]Jacob Neusner, *History of the Mishnaic Law of Women Part One Yebamot. Translation and Explanation* (Leiden: 1980), 210-212.

[53]Jacob Neusner, *A History of the Mishnaic Law of Damages Part One Baba Qamma. Tranlsation and Explanantion* (Leiden: 1983), 59-62.

TA.Z. 1:1 begins with a lemma attributed to Nahum the Mede. This is followed by an unassigned question and answer which relates to mA.Z. 1:1. Next there is a long lemma attributed to Joshua b. Qorha which relates to the same pericope of Mishnah.[54] TA.Z. 1:3 starts with an anonymous comment. This is followed by a dispute between Simeon b. Eleazar and a second unattributed statement. TA.Z. 2:4 commences with an extended unassigned section, and Judah disputes the last anonymous sentence. In the middle of the unattributed comments in tA.Z. 2:7, we find a dispute between Nathan and one of the anonymous rulings. The unassigned opening statement of tA.Z. 2:8 is followed by a dispute between Meir and Yosi. TA.Z. 2:9 is similar; however, the dispute is between Simeon b. Gamliel, who cites mA.Z. 1:9 and glosses it, and Simeon. While this appears to be a dispute, both statements could stand on their own. The anonymous section of tA.Z. 3:3 is a glossed citation of mA.Z. 2:1. The words-of dispute at the end is between Meir and sages. The unassigned section of tA.Z. 3:4 opens with a citation of mA.Z. 2:2. Ishmael b. Yohanan b. Beroqa disputes the last anonymous ruling. This is followed by another unattributed section, which contains a proof-text. TA.Z. 3:11 includes a long anonymous section, which is followed by an extended lemma attributed to Yosi. TA.Z. 3:16 has a short unattributed section which is glossed by Simeon b. Gamliel. This is followed by an extended anonymous section. The beginning of tA.Z. 3:19 is unattributed. A debate between Judah and "they" deals with an item not discussed before. This is followed by a debate between Yosi and "they." TA.Z. 4:8 contains an anonymous ruling which relates to mA.Z. 2:3 and mA.Z. 2:6. Yosi disputes the unassigned comment which follows the opening sentence.[55] TA.Z. 4:9 starts with an anonymous comment. This is followed by a testimony of Simeon b. Gode'a, in the name of Gamliel the Elder, before Gamliel's son. Next comes an unattributed comment stating that "they" rejected the ruling. TA.Z. 4:10 opens with a dispute between Simeon b. Gamliel, in Joshua b. Qopesai's name, and an anonymous superscription. This is followed by an extended unassigned section. TA.Z. 4:11 is a long anonymous passage in which is inserted a report that Judah and his court permitted oil produced by gentiles. The passage also contains some material focusing on the *am haares*. TA.Z. 4:12 begins with an extended unassigned section and ends with a words-of dispute between Meir, Judah and Judah b. Gamliel in the name of Hanania b. Gamliel. In the middle of the anonymous statements in tA.Z. 6:8, we find a comment attributed to Simeon b.

---

[54]Neusner, *Shebuot*, 143.
[55]Neusner, *Shebuot*, 158.

Eleazar and a dispute between Simeon b. Eleazar and an unattributed comment, which is derived from mA.Z. 3:8. TA.Z. 7:1 commences with an anonymous section. This is followed by a dispute between Meir and an unattributed comment. TA.Z. 7:4,[56] tA.Z. 7:6, and tA.Z. 7:7 contain an anonymous section followed by a case[57] which came before sages, in the first two pericopae, or before Simeon b. Eleazar, in the last *sugya*. The unassigned beginning section of tA.Z. 7:13 assumes the presence of a gentile. This is followed by a debate between Simeon b. Eleazar and Judah. TA.Z. 8:4 starts with an extended anonymous section which includes a declarative sentence followed by glosses in the form of questions and answers. To this is appended a words-of dispute between Meir and sages. Similarly, tA.Z. 8:6 begins with an unattributed question and answer which gloss part of tA.Z. 8:4. There follows a dispute between Rabbi and Eleazar b. Simeon.[58] Next Eleazar explains his opinion,[59] and then comes an anonymous statement. The passage ends with lemmas attributed to Hananiah b. Gamliel, Hidqa, Simeon, and Yosi, with the latter providing a proof-text.

THul. 3:24 ends with a statement attributed to "they." The disputes which occur in tHul. 5:2 and tHul. 5:3 do not deal with the rules as they apply to the gentiles. THul. 8:12 ends with a ruling which "they returned to say," hzrw lwmr. TBekh. 2:1 opens with an anonymous citation from mBekh. 2:1 and adds a minor gloss. It closes with a dispute between Judah and sages. TBekh. 2:5 starts with a citation of mBekh. 2:4 and finishes with a comment attributed to Simeon b. Gamliel. Simeon's comment disputes part of the preceding unassigned section.[60] The anonymous citation of mBekh. 3:1 in tBekh. 2:11 is followed by a statement attributed to Yosi b. Judah. However, something is clearly wrong with the *sugya*.[61]

In the middle of the collection of unassigned rules in tAhil. 18:12, we find a dispute between Rabbi and sages, along with a dispute between Judah and Yosi. Abba Saul's dispute with the unattributed comment in tNid. 2:5 does not deal with the gentile. Yosi b. Judah glosses the last anonymous statement in tToh. 8:8. TToh. 11:8 opens with an unattributed sentence which is followed by an unassigned superscription with which Yosi b. Judah disputes.

---

[56] A statement attributed to "they" appears at the end of tA.Z. 7:4.

[57] M'sh.

[58] Rabbi pṭwr, and Eleazar mḥyyb.

[59] The perfect 'mr appears.

[60] I cannot tell exactly which part is relevant to Gamliel's comment, for the antecedents of his pronouns are unclear; Cf., Neusner, *Hullin*, 160.

[61] Porton, *Ishmael*, I, 173-176.

We have seen that anonymous statements concerning the gentile can appear in a totally anonymous *sugya*, or in a complex pericope which also includes disputes, debates, narratives, and/or lemmas attributed to named sages. However, this phenomenon is not unique to our material. Throughout Mishnah-Tosefta, one can easily find numerous other examples of the same pattern. On the one hand, therefore, our material does not appear to be unique or different from the other materials in Mishnah-Tosefta. On the other hand, however, we do find an unusually high number of unattributed sayings which treat the gentile. This means that the compilers of our texts and their sub-units could not, or chose not to, place much of the discussion of the gentile into a chronological framework, or, to assign them to particular circles of rabbinic masters. In the next chapter we shall directly address the problem of the chronology of the discussions of the gentile and the rabbis to whom the attributed comments are assigned. At present, suffice it to say that a good deal of the material we have before us will be unassignable to any specific generation, chronological period, or rabbinic circle. Furthermore, the sayings are cast in the usual variety of literary forms, so that attention to the literary characteristics of these *sugyot* does not tell us anything specific about their location in time or space.

Lemmas and Glosses[62]

Just as the anonymous *sugyot* are cast in the literary forms we expect to find in Mishnah-Tosefta, so too the attributed sayings are set in the usual literary patterns. A lemma is an independent comment attributed to a named master. For our purposes, the central characteristic of the lemma is that it can stand by itself. It may be of any length; but, it should be a self-contained comment or combination of statements.[63] Normally, the lemma is preceded by the participle "says;"[64] however, other verbal forms may appear.[65] In our corpus, the participle "says" introduces the following lemmas: MAbot 3:2, mBekh. 3:2, tBer. 6:18, tPe. 2:9,[66] tPe. 3:12,[67] tPe. 4:1, tTer. 1:15,[68] tShab. 1:22, tShab.

----

[62]In examining the literary forms in which statements attributed to named sages appear, we shall concentrate only on those comments which discuss the gentile.

[63]In the traditions attributed to Ishmael, one of the Tannaim, the independent lemma is a rare occurrence in the non-exegetical Tannaitic collections; Porton, *Ishmael*, IV, 18-21.

[64]'wmr.

[65]Porton, *Ishmael*, IV, 18-28.

[66]Although Simeon's comment disputes the anonymous superscription, it could stand alone; therefore, I have classified it as a lemma; Cf., Brooks, 78-79.

[67]This parallels tPe. 2:9.

[68]The passage opens with an anonymous declarative sentence from mTer. 1:1. A narrative follows. Isaac's comment follows. Even though Isaac disagrees with the opening sentence, his comment is formulated so that it could stand on its own as an independent statement; Peck, 46-47.

7:24, tShab. 7:25, tSot. 7:22, tB.Q. 4:3, tA.Z. 1:1, tA.Z. 2:3,[69] tA.Z. 3:11, tA.Z. 4:6, tA.Z. 8:8, and tBekh. 2:11,[70] mOhol. 18:9.

The perfect, "said,"[71] appears in place of "says" in mShab. 1:9,[72] mSheq. 7:6, mA.Z. 2:5,[73] tShab. 6:14,[74] tKip. 2:16, and tKet. 3:2. In addition, tPe. 4:11 contains an anonymous lemma with the plural perfect attributed to "they."

MA.Z. 2:3 contains a statement attributed to Aqiba which is cast in the words-of form.[75] The pattern R. X "used to say,"[76] appears in tShab. 7:23, tQid. 5:11, and tBekh. 2:16, while R. X "used to expound"[77] is found in tErub. 3:7.

In contrast to a lemma, a gloss is statement which cannot stand by itself, but relates to what precedes it. A gloss does not disagree with the statement upon which it relies. The following pericopae contain comments which serve as glosses: MDem. 6:2,[78] tTer. 7:20,[79] tKil. 5:19,[80] tSanh. 12:4,[81] tA.Z. 1:21,[82] tA.Z. 3:16,[83] tA.Z. 4:10,[84] tBekh. 3:15,[85] and tNid. 5:5.[86]

----

[69]This is a complex *sugya*; however, Simeon b. Eleazar's lemma does stand alone; Neusner, *Shebuot*, 150.

[70]Yosi b. Judah's lemma could stand alone, for it seems to interrupt the flow of the *sugya*; Porton, *Ishmael*, I, 176.

[71]'mr.

[72]Epstein, II, 1199-1200.

[73]Judah reports a debate between Ishmael and Joshua; Porton, *Ishmael*, I, 159-161.

[74]The statement is attributed to sages: "But sages said."

[75]Epstein, II, 1161.

[76]Hyh ... 'wmr.

[77]Hyh ... dwrš.

[78]Judah's comment opens with 'p; therefore, it is a gloss. Epstein, II, 1007ff. See especially 1007.

[79]Judah's comment, which opens with "about what things did they speak," clearly glosses what precedes it.

[80]Simeon b. Eleazar does not disagree with the opening anonymous comment; he merely builds on it.

[81]Judah's second comment is introduced by "an he concedes," wmwdh. The sentence depends on the dispute between Judah and Simeon, and Judah's comment comes from mSanh. 9:2.

[82]This pericope contains two glosses. There is an anonymous sentence and a question and answer, attributed to Judah b. Peterah, and an anonymous sentence, a citation of mA.Z. 1:5, and an interpretation of Mishnah in the form of a question and answer attributed to Judah.

[83]The antecedents of the pronouns within Simeon b. Gamliel's ruling appear in the anonymous opening sentence of the pericope.

[84]Simeon b. Gamliel's comment, which he states in the name of Joshua b. Qopesai, builds on the opening words of the *sugya*.

[85]Aqiba's comment assumes the Houses-dispute and builds on it.

[86]The comment of the House of Shammai builds on the anonymous opening words of the pericope.

Disputes

A common form in which attributed Tannaitic statements appear is the dispute. Usually, the participle "says," occurs in the dispute. We may find an anonymous superscription with R. X says, or, more often, an anonymous superscription with R. X says . . . R. Y says . . . .[87] The next most common form of the dispute is the words-of dispute, in which the superscription is usually contained in the saying of the first master.[88] A third form of the dispute is one in which the Hebrew root 'mr, "says," does not appear. Rather, the sages permit,[89] prohibit,[90] declare clean,[91] declare unclean[92] or employ a similar verb. We shall call these disputes "indirect discourse disputes."[93] There are, in addition, numerous variations of the dispute form,[94] most of which do not appear in our corpus. The remarks set in the dispute form *should* deal with the problem set forth in the superscription, and they should respond to each other.[95]

1) Anonymous superscription + R. X says: ". . . ": MDem. 3:4, mGit. 1:5, mB.Q. 8:3,[96] mA.Z. 1:8,[97] mA.Z. 2:3, mA.Z. 2:7, mA.Z. 4:11, mA.Z. 5:3, mA.Z. 5:4,[98] mBekh. 2:4, mMakh. 2:7, mMakh. 2:8, tDem. 4:25,[99] tDem. 6:2, tSheb. 6:20,[100] tShab. 1:22, tShab. 7:1, tShab. 7:2, tShab. 7:3, tShab. 7:5, tR.H. 2:12, tQid. 4:16, tA.Z. 1:3, tA.Z. 2:4, tA.Z. 3:4, tA.Z. 5:4, tBekh. 2:5, tBekh. 2:14, tAhil. 18:7, tToh. 11:8.

2) R. X says: ". . . ." + R. Y says: ". . .": MTer. 3:9, mTer. 8:11,

----

[87]Neusner, *Rabbinic Traditions*, III, 5-14. Porton, *Ishmael*, IV, 28-30.

[88]Porton, *Ishmael*, IV, 34-39.

[89]Mtyr or mtr.

[90]'wsr or 'swr.

[91]Mthr.

[92]Mtm'.

[93]Neusner, *Rabbinic Traditions*, III, 7.

[94]Porton, *Ishmael*, IV, 28-41.

[95]Gary G. Porton, "The Artificial Dispute: Ishmael and 'Aqiba," in Jacob Neusner, (ed.), *Christianity, Judaism and Other Greco-Roman Cults: Studies for Morton Smith at Sixty* (Leiden: 1975), IV, 18-29.

[96]Judah's comment could stand by itself, and it could appear in any number of contexts. However, here Judah's comment is meant to dispute the anonymous ruling which precedes it.

[97]The passage contains two relevant disputes.

[98]This *sugya* contains two relevant disputes.

[99]The statement in dispute with the anonymous rule is attributed to two sages, Simeon b. Gamliel and Simeon.

[100]The sentence which disagrees with the opening rule is attributed to "others."

mErub. 4:1,[101] mTan 3:7,[102] mYeb. 16:5, mA.Z. 1:2, mA.Z. 1:5, mA.Z. 5:11, mArakh. 1:2, tTer. 1:14, tTer. 2:13, tShab. 7:11, tYeb. 8:1, tA.Z. 2:9, tA.Z. 5:7, tBekh. 2:1, tKer. 1:17.[103]

3) Indirect discourse disputes with one sage: MTer. 3:9, mHul. 2:7, mToh. 8:6, tA.Z. 4:8.

4) Indirect discourse disputes with more than one sage: MHal. 4:7, mPes. 4:3, mA.Z. 1:6, tShab. 8:5, tGit. 1:4, tA.Z. 8:1, tAhil. 18:12.

5) Words-of disputes: MShab. 6:10,[104] mErub. 6:1, mErub. 8:5,[105] mQid. 1:3, mA.Z. 1:3, mA.Z. 1:8, mA.Z. 2:2, mA.Z. 2:4,[106] mZeb. 4:5,[107] mMakh. 2:10, tPe. 3:5, tDem. 1:12, tDem. 5:2, tDem. 5:21,[108] tTer. 4:12, tTer. 4:13,[109] tTer. 4:14, tShab. 13:13, tA.Z. 2:5, tA.Z. 2:8, tA.Z. 3:3, tA.Z. 3:12, tA.Z. 4:12,[110] tA.Z. 8:4, tZeb. 5:6.[111]

6) Mixed and broken forms: MShab. 1:7,[112] mShab. 1:8,[113] mEd. 5:1,[114] mA.Z. 3:5,[115] mBekh. 5:2,[116] mArakh. 8:4,[117] mPar. 2:1,[118] mNid.

----

[101]Four sages appear in the *sugya*; however, each of the two opinions is attributed to two sages.

[102]Sages, "But sages did not agree with him," are added to the dispute after Simeon of Teman's comment.

[103]Porton, *Ishmael*, II, 60-62.

[104]The dispute is either between Meir and sages or Yosi and Meir; Robert Goldenberg, *The Sabbath Law of Rabbi Meir* (Ann Arbor: 1978), 23-24.

[105]There is a "words-of" opinion by Meir. Then, Judah "says." This is followed by Yosi "says" and Simeon "says."

[106]This *sugya* contains three relevant disputes.

[107]The opening statement is in the "words-of" form; however, Yosi "declares liable."

[108]The first statement is in the "words-of" form; however, the responding statement is attributed to Judah, Yosi and Simeon.

[109]This *sugya* contains three relevant disputes.

[110]Although the first statement of the dispute is in the "words-of" form, two responses with "says" follow it.

[111]Although the opening statement is in the "words-of" form, the responding statement opens with "said," *'mr.*

[112]The House of Shammai "says," and the House of Hillel "permits."

[113]The Shammaite opinion employs the plural participle "say," *'wmryn*, while the Hillelite opinion uses the indirect discourse, "permit," *mtyryn*.

[114]The House of Shammai "declare clean," while the House of Hillel "say."

[115]The text opens with an anonymous statement and a proof-text. Yosi, whose comment is introduced by the participle "says," interprets the text. An anonymous aside about the *Asherah* follows. Aqiba seems to dispute Yosi's comment; however, Aqiba's comment is preceded by the perfect, "said;" Neusner, *Shebuot*, 173.

[116]The Shammaite opinion employs the plural participle "say," *'wmryn*, while the Hillelite opinion uses the indirect discourse, "permit," *mtyryn*.

[117]Eleazar's comment is in the "words-of" form, while Eleazar b. Azariah's comment is introduced by the perfect, said. In addition, Eleazar b. Azariah's remark glosses Eleazar's comment

4:3,[119] tDem. 6:1,[120] tSheq. 1:7.[121]

Debates

In the debate-form, we usually find the perfect, "said," in place of the participle, "says." After the appearance of the first comment, the following statements are introduced by "said to him," or "said to them." In the earliest material, the debate-form seems to have been created for the Houses-material, and Neusner suggests that the debate-form's purpose was "to spell out the reasons assigned to each House as the basis of its legal ruling." Neusner further recognized that "the debate is clearly artificial. It does not represent the transcription of a conversation that actually took place on a given day or in a given place."[122] The importance of the debate-form is that it allows for a complex elaboration of the dispute or lemma.[123] In the major variation of this form, the participle "says" introduces the statement of the first master, while the perfect "said" appears in the rest of the passage.[124] The following pericopae which deal with the gentile contain debates: MYeb. 8:3, mKet. 2:9, mNed. 4:3, mSanh. 7:3, mA.Z. 1:1,[125] mA.Z. 3:4,[126] mHul. 2:7,[127] mBekh. 3:1,[128] tBer. 2:13, tDem. 1:13, tTer. 2:13, tKet. 1:6, tKet. 5:1, tSanh. 13:2,[129] tShebu. 3:6, tA.Z. 2:3, tA.Z. 6:7, tA.Z. 7:13,[130] tHul. 2:24, tPar. 2:1.

----

instead of disputing it; Neusner, *Arakhin*, 63.

[118]Eliezer "says," while sages "declare fit."

[119]The Shammaites employ the indirect discourse, mthrym, while the Hillelite opinion is introduced by the plural participle, "say;" Neusner, *Rabbinic Traditions*, II, 299-300.

[120]The text opens with a citation of mDem. 6:1, which is then expanded. Simeon b. Gamliel, who disputes the anonymous opening statement, opens with a question and responds with a citation of mDem. 6:1. This is introduced by the perfect, "said;" Sarason, 207, 209.

[121]The first statement is in the "words-of" form; however, Aqiba "said to him."

[122]Neusner, *Rabbinic Traditions*, III, 17.

[123]Porton, *Ishmael*, IV, 41.

[124]Porton, *Ishmael*, IV, 43.

[125]Contains both participle and perfect for the verbs.

[126]Perfect, "asked," s'l appears.

[127]The passage opens with an anonymous sentence, which gives Eliezer's ruling in the form of indirect discourse. We find a second statement attributed to Eliezer, which employs the perfect, said. Yosi responds, also introduced by the perfect, with an *a fortiori* argument, which responds to the opening statement and not Eliezer's second comment. Neusner calls this passage "a complex debate;" Neusner, *Hullin*, 38. Cf., Neusner, *Eliezer*, I, 383.

[128]The stylistic forms of this *sugya* present a number of problems; however, Aqiba's response is formulated as a debate. Cf., Porton, *Ishmael*, I, 174.

[129]Participle and perfect appear.

[130]Participle and perfect occur.

Narratives

Most Tannaitic statements, whether lemmas, glosses, disputes, or debates, lack a descriptive setting. Normally we find comments without any "historical" framework or context. However, there are some instances in which the sages' remarks are placed in an "historical" situation, or in which an event is described which serves as a legal precedence or example.[131] Neusner states, "What separates the legal narratives from conventional, testimonial, and debate-sayings is their historical focus, the reference in the past tense to a one-time action, ruling, setting, or event."[132] Narratives are introduced by "it once happened."[133] Often, the narratives contain debates. The narrative seems to have been frequently used for transmitting sayings of the Patriarch Gamliel and his family,[134] and many of our narratives do discuss the Patriarchs. The following passages contain narratives: MShab. 16:8, mErub. 4:1, mEd. 7:7, mBekh. 5:3, tTer. 1:15, tTer. 2:13, tShab. 7:16, tShab. 7:18, tShab. 13:9, tShab. 13:14, tPis. 2:15, tKip. 3:20, tY.T. 2:6, tMo'ed 2:15, tYeb. 14:7, tA.Z. 3:7, tPar. 2:1, tMiq. 6:3.

Testimonies

We find two examples of the testimony-form in our corpus, tA.Z. 4:9 and tAhil. 18:7. The testimony-form substitutes the verb "testified,"[135] for the participle, "says." Neusner writes, "Unlike *says* which represents a timeless present, *testified* may be qualified as to place, time, and setting, and may suggest a one-time historical occasion."[136] The appearance of this form outside of Tractate Eduyot is rare.

Summary: A review of the literary patterns in which the sayings about the gentile are cast reveals one important fact: There are no unusual literary patterns created for use with the topic of the gentile. All of the literary patterns and syntactical structures are common throughout Mishnah-Tosefta, are distributed among the tractates and orders, and are employed with the full range of topics discussed in these documents. However, it is difficult to assess the importance of the distribution of forms or the appearance of so many anonymous comments. We do not have any other studies like the present one which examine a topic throughout the entire corpus of Mishnah-Tosefta. The monographs on the

----

[131]Neusner, *Rabbinic Traditions*, III, 23.
[132]Neusner, *Rabbinic Traditions*, III, 24.
[133]M'śh š or m'śh b.
[134]Kanter, 246-251.
[135]H'yd.
[136]Neusner, *Rabbinic Traditions*, III, 14-15.

sayings attributed to particular sages skew the evidence, for they contain, by definition, few anonymous statements. Similarly, the study of the literary forms by tractates or orders may also lead to conclusions which are not helpful to us. What is important for our purposes is that there is nothing in the literary structures of the passages under consideration here which points to a particular school, setting, or source. The sayings about the gentile exhibit the same limited variety of patterns as do the other corpora which have been studied from this point of view.

We know that certain forms were created for particular purposes,[137] and that particular themes were treated in specific literary patterns in a given tractate;[138] therefore, it would have been possible for our editors/authors to have created a particular form for the topic of the gentile. However, the subject of the gentile did not engender the creation of special literary constructions. The materials which deal with the non-Israelite were *not* cast overwhelmingly in a particular pattern. The *sugyot* before us do not point to anything outside of the ordinary. We are left to conclude that the discussions of the gentile in Mishnah-Tosefta were dealt with in the same ways as all other topics. In fact, it is the normalcy of the material before us which is the most striking. The discussions of the non-Israelite are carried on and transmitted in exactly the same ways as the treatments of sacrifices, the holidays, the family, the matters of civil law, and the purity laws. The topic of the gentile fits into the literary scheme of the Mishnah-Tosefta as if it were any other subject of concern.

One could argue that the authors of Mishnah-Tosefta had no other choice, for the very nature of the documents forced them to deal with all matters in the same way. Of course, this is true only in a general sense. First, many important topics and discussions were omitted from Mishnah-Tosefta altogether, so that the inclusion of material on the non-Israelite in the context of the earliest rabbinic text is significant. Second, different topics are treated differently, various matters are cast in a specific forms, and the like, so that treating the gentile in this fashion appropriates the topic as an internal rabbinic concern. The matter of the gentile has been fully incorporated into the program of Mishnah-Tosefta, and it has been fully "rabbinized," and this is the point: The gentiles were discussed in styles appropriate to Mishnah-Tosefta. The topic was approached from a purely rabbinic point of view.

----

[137]For example the "according to Rabbi Y"-form; Porton, "According to Rabbi Y."

[138]For example, Tractate Middot is constructed in the form of a "descriptive-narrative;" Neusner *A History of the Mishnaic Law of Holy Things Part Six*, 207.

iii

Above we have investigated the external literary forms of the *sugyot* in which the discussions about the gentile are cast. We concluded that the topic of the gentile did not cause the creation of any unusual or unexpected literary patterns, nor did the appearance of specific forms lead us to expect a reference to the non-Israelite. Now we turn to an internal literary feature of our *sugyot*: The juxtaposition of the gentile with other phenomena. Our question here is the following: Do references to certain types of individuals, animals or other phenomena generate the appearance of the gentile? For example, does a reference to a Samaritan mean that we shall usually find the non-Israelite mentioned in the same passage? If we find the phrase "feed to dogs," should we also expect to discover a reference to the gentile? Our goal is to discover whether or not the gentile is mentioned in a particular passage for reasons other than a concern with the non-Israelite. The previous two chapters presented arguments which concluded that the discussions of the gentiles were incorporated into Mishnah and Tosefta in order to further the discussions on other topics in these documents. Above, in the present chapter, it was noted that the treatment of the gentile was fully "rabbinized" in its literary characteristics. The following discussions approach the problem of the gentile from a third point of view, for they ask if there are some contexts in which the references to the gentiles are a result of their being placed in specific contexts, or of their being included in certain categories: Are there pericopae in which the mention of the gentile is generated by the other items included in the text? Are their certain lists, concepts, symbols, or phrases which more often than not lead us to expect the appearance of the gentile? This offers us one more tool for determining why the gentiles appear in our texts, and how they function in their settings.

The Samaritan

The Samaritan and the gentile are juxtaposed in several *sugyot*: MBer. 7:1, tPe. 4:1, mDem. 3:4, tDem 4:26-27, mDem. 5:9, tDem. 5:21, mDem. 6:1, tDem. 1:2, tDem. 4:20, tDem. 6:4, tDem. 7:11, tTer. 1:14, tTer. 3:9, tTer. 4:12, tSheb. 3:13, tSheb. 6:20, tM.S. 4:1, tShab. 15:15, mSheq. 1:5, tYeb. 8:1, tA.Z. 2:4, tA.Z. 3:5, tHul. 1:1, tHul. 2:20, mOhol. 17:3, tAhil. 18:6, mToh. 5:8, tMiq. 6:1. According to Kasovsky[139] the Samaritan appears in thirty-five *sugyot* in

----

[139]Chayim Y. Kasovsky, *Thesaurus Mishnae Concordantiae Verborum quae in Sex Mishnae ordinibus Reperiuntur* (Tel Aviv: nd), III, 930.

Mishnah. In seven of those texts, or 20%, the Samaritan and the gentile appear in the same passage. There are approximately forty-one pericopae in Tosefta which mention the Samaritan.[140] Twenty-two of these passages, slightly over 53%, also mention the gentile. In all, over 38% of the passages in Mishnah-Tosefta which deal with the Samaritan also treat the gentile.

In several texts, the gentile is contrasted with the Samaritan, while in other passages the two are treated the same. In the rabbinic texts, the Samaritans occupied a middle ground between the gentiles and the Israelites. At times the Samaritans were treated as if they were Israelites, while in other instances they were seen as non-Israelites.[141] Also, the Israelites, Samaritans, and gentiles were, from the point of view of the authors of our texts, the three major classes of people who dwelt in the Land of Israel, held property within its borders, and were the actors in the events which occurred there. Thus, on a number of issues, the Samaritans would be important people with whom our texts should deal, and they could serve as the "intermediate group" between the Israelites and the non-Israelites.

In the first set of texts, the gentile and the Samaritan are treated differently. MBer. 7:1 considers the Samaritan an Israelite in its discussion of those who may recite the grace after meals, while the gentile is excluded from those who may recite the blessing after eating. The *sugya* contains two balanced lists,

----

[140]This number is approximate, for I arrived at it by skimming the texts of Zuckermandel and Lieberman and looking for the word kwty; Moses Zuckermandel, *Tosephta: Based on the Erfurt and Vienna Codices with Parallels and Variants* (Jerusalem, reprint 1963); Saul Lieberman, *The Tosefta According to Codex Vienna, With Variants from Codex Erfurt, Genizah Mss. and Editio Princeps (Venice 1521) Together with References to Parallel Passages in Talmudic Literature and a Brief Commentary* (New York: 1955-1973), 4 Vols.

[141]This ambiguity is seen on bQid. 75a-76a, where the Samaritans are called "lion-converts," whose conversion was forced upon them because they feared the lions sent against them, IIKgs. 1:25. In the *gemara* we also find the statement attributed to Simeon b. Gamliel which claims that every Israelite precept which the Samaritans adopted, they observe with minute care, "[even] more than the Israelites," Cf., tPis. 2:3. See also, bBer. 47b, bGit. 10a, bHul. 4a, bNed. 31a, bSot. 33b, and bSanh. 90b. It is important to note that these are Amoraic texts which were composed in Babylonia a good deal of time after the closure of the documents with which we are concerned here. However, the *sugyot* which deal with the Samaritans in Mishnah-Tosefta reflect the same ambiguity with regard to the status of the Samaritans. The bibliography on the Samaritans is extensive and growing yearly. For example, see James D. Purvis, "The Samaritans and Judaism," in Robert A. Kraft and George W.E. Nickelsburg (eds.), *Judaism and its Modern Interpreters* (Atlanta: 1986), 81-98.

with the Samaritan and the gentile occupying corresponding places.[142] TPe. 4:1 both equates and contrasts the gentile and the Samaritan. A poor Israelite is not believed if he stated that he had purchased gleanings from a gentile or a Samaritan.[143] The two probably are equated because both were suspect with regard to the fine points of the Tannaitic laws concerning gleanings. In contrast to this statement, the *sugya* also claims that with regard to any matter about which a poor Israelite is believed, a poor Samaritan is also presumed to have spoken the truth. On the other hand, a poor gentile is not believed about anything.[144] The assumption that the Samaritan, but not the gentile, will respect the observant Israelite's concerns with regard to tithes and seventh-year produce stands behind mDem. 3:4 and its complement, tDem. 4:26-27.[145] These passages pair the Samaritan with the *am haares* and assume that they can be trusted with Israelite produce. This is in contrast to the gentile, who is not trustworthy.[146]

----

[142]The lists are as follows: 1a) One who ate *demai*-produce, 1b) one who ate first tithe from which the heave-offering had been removed, 1c) one who ate second tithe or dedicated produce which had been redeemed, 1d) a servant who ate an olive's bulk of food, and 1e) a Samaritan; 2a) one who ate untithed produce, 2b) one who ate first tithe from which the heave-offering had not been separated, 2c) one who ate second tithe or dedicated produce which had not been redeemed, 2d) a servant who ate less than an olive's bulk, 2e) a gentile.

[143]Lieberman suggests that the person is believed when he states that he purchased the gleanings from a poor Israelite; however, he is not certain about this. He further claims that the gentile is not believed on two counts: 1) That he purchased the gleanings from the Samaritan or gentile poor, and 2) that the gentile or Samaritan sold the Israelite produce from the gifts to the poor; Saul Lieberman, *Tosefta Ki-fshutah: A Comprehensive Commentary on the Tosefta Order Zera'im, Part I* (New York: 1955), 178.

[144]The exact issue over which they are believed or not is unclear. Lieberman notes that in *Masseket Kutim*, we read that the Samaritan are trusted about the claims they make with regard to the laws of gleaning, forgotten sheaf, *pe'ah* and second tithe which they observe and that Israelites give these gifts to them. However, I am not sure that this is the issue here, for it does not seem to parallel the claim that the gentile poor are not believed about anything. Lieberman notes that this may indicate that we do not even accept their claims of poverty; Lieberman, *Toseftah Ki-fshutah Zera'im I*, 178.

[145]Sarason, 140-143.

[146]MDem. 3:4 rules that an Israelite's grain milled by a Samaritan or *am haares* or grain given to a Samaritan or an *am haares* to keep for the Israelite does not change status with regard to tithes and seventh-year produce; however, grain given to a gentile miller is considered *demai*-produce after it is ground, and grain given to a gentile to keep takes on the status of the gentile's produce. TDem. 4:26 discusses one who sends his produce by an *am haares*, Samaritan, or gentile, and tDem. 4:27 worries about the miller's whetting down the grain, so that it becomes susceptible to uncleanness. Both texts agree that the Samaritan and the *am haares* do not give cause for concern, while the gentile does.

Although tDem. 1:12-13 form a unit, only Judah's comment in the latter text is relevant for the present discussion.[147] Judah[148] contrasts a storehouse into which Israelites and gentiles place their grain with one in which Israelites and Samaritans deposit produce. Sages' ruling, that even one Israelite depositor places all of the grain into the status of *demai*, applies to only the former storehouse. With regard to the latter storehouse, the grain takes on the status of the produce of the majority of the depositors. Thus, Judah assumes a distinction between Israelites and Samaritans, as well as a distinction between gentiles and Samaritans.[149] However, the passage simply may be corrupt,[150] for there is no natural reason for the Samaritans to be mentioned in this context. Neither sages, nor Meir, nor Yosi speaks of them, and Yosi's gloss on sages' comment makes sense, while Judah statement, which does not appear in all of the early versions of Tosefta, causes a good deal of difficulty.

TA.Z. 3:5[151] states that an Israelite should watch in a mirror when he gets a haircut from a gentile; however, he need not worry about doing this if his barber were a Samaritan.[152] Explaining the ruling in mHul. 1:1, tHul. 1:1 states that an act of slaughtering by a Samaritan, an uncircumcised male, and an Israelite apostate are valid, while an act of slaughtering by a gentile is invalid,[153]

----

[147]TDem. 1:12 contains a dispute between Meir and sages concerning a storehouse into which gentiles and Israelites deposit grain. Meir holds that if the majority of those who place grain in the storehouse are Israelites, all the produce is *demai*; however, if the majority are gentiles, or if there is an even division between Israelites and non-Israelites, the grain is considered untithed. Sages claim that even if just one Israelite deposits his grain in the storehouse, all of the grain is considered *demai*. In tDem. 1:13, Yosi and Judah discuss the type of storehouse the sages referred to in tDem. 1:12, ignoring the substance of the dispute. Yosi's comment is irrelevant for us, for he draws a distinction between public and private storehouses.

[148]Judah's opinion does not appear in all versions of the passage; Sarason, 48; Lieberman, *Tosefta Ki-fshutah Zera'im I*, 200.

[149]Sarason, 50, accepts Lieberman's assumption that the grain in the storehouse is intended for sale; otherwise, Judah's comment does not make any sense. However, the text itself does not mention that the grain is being held for sale.

[150]"They" object to Judah's teaching. Their claim that he taught that grain in a storehouse near Yavneh in which the majority of the population were Samaritans was *demai* suggests that "they" believed that Judah would equate the gentile's grain with that of the Samaritan. Lieberman's suggestion that Judah had changed his mind and thus could hold two seemingly contradictory opinions need not trouble us here; Lieberman, *Tosefta Ki-fshutah Zera'im I*, 200.

[151]This expands upon mA.Z. 2:2, which does not mention the Samaritans.

[152]Gamliel, however, permitted the members of his household to take this precaution in the presence of a Samaritan because the former were governmental officials.

[153]The text also states that a *min* slaughters for idols.

thus distinguishing between a gentile and a Samaritan.[154] The gentile is discussed in tHul. 1:1-1:3+1:6; the Samaritan appears only in the opening of tHul. 1:1, as an explanation of Mishnah's "all." Although gentiles and Samaritans are both mentioned in tHul. 2:20-21, the term "Samaritan" appears as an adjective modifying the bread of the *minim* ("their bread is deemed the bread of a Samaritan"), while the gentile appears in an unrelated context. TMiq. 6:1 opens by stating that the land, immersion-pools, gutters, and paths of the Samaritans are clean. The text continues with a detailed discussion of the gentiles' immersion-pools inside and outside of the Land of Israel, so that the immersion-pools of the two classes are different.[155]

In the second set of passages, the Samaritan and the gentile are considered similar. TDem. 4:20 opens by stating that the possessions of all traveling merchants, whether they are gentiles, Israelites, or Samaritans, are *demai*. The text is then refined: This is the case only when Israelite farmers bring produce to the merchant; however, if the produce came from gentiles or Samaritans, it is considered to be untithed. Although the text opens by equating Israelite, gentile, and Samaritan merchants, when it discusses the farmers who supply produce to the merchants, it distinguishes between Israelite and gentile/Samaritan farmers.

MDem. 5:9 and tDem. 5:21 deal with tithing one type of produce from another type of produce; they mention the Israelite, the gentile, and the Samaritan, and they treat the latter two groups in the same way.[156] The Samaritan and gentile are comparable because gentiles do not tithe their produce, and Samaritans do not tithe produce which they sell in the market.[157]

----

[154]Neusner states that "T[Hul]. 1:1 opens with attention to M[Hul]. 1:1A, adding to M[ishnah]'s interest in deaf-mutes, imbeciles, and minors, the matter of intermediate categories: Samaritans, apostates;" Neusner, *Hullin*, 17.

[155]The discussion is built on mMiq. 8:1, which mentions gentiles but not Samaritans.

[156]Tithe may be given from what is bought from an Israelite for what is bought from a gentile or Samaritan, and from what is bought from a gentile or Samaritan from what is bought from an Israelite. Eliezer forbids the tithing of what is bought from certain Samaritans for what is bought from other Samaritans. TDem. 5:21 contains a different version of the opinion in mDem. 5:9; however, the rulings amount to the same thing. TDem. 5:21 does contain a dissenting opinion; however, it too treats the Samaritan and the gentiles in the same way, for it forbids separating tithes from one group's produce for the crop of another group.

[157]Sarason, 192. In Tosefta, Meir holds that one may tithe from an Israelite's produce for that of a gentile, from a gentile's produce for that of an Israelite, from an Israelite's produce for a Samaritan's produce, from a Samaritan's produce for that of an Israelite, "and from everything for everything." Judah, Yosi, and Simeon say that one may tithe for one Israelite from another Israelite's produce, for one Samaritan from another Samaritan's produce, and for one gentile from another gentile's produce, but not from an Israelite's produce for a gentile's or a Samaritan's produce and not from either of these for an Israelite's produce. Meir holds that the produce of both gentiles and Samaritans must be tithed and that neither would have tithed produce they were going to sell. Judah, Yosi, and Simeon hold that gentile and Samaritan produce is exempt from the requirement of

MDem. 6:1 deals with an Israelite who sharecrops a field for an Israelite, a gentile, or a Samaritan.[158] The three classes are equated because the passage centers on how the one who sharecropped the field separates his tithe, so that the status of the actual owner of the field is irrelevant.[159] TDem. 6:4 equates the gentile, the Samaritan, and "one who is not trustworthy in the matter of tithing," for we cannot *assume* they all correctly have tithed their produce.[160] TDem. 7:11 discusses an Israelite who has a field which is sharecropped by a gentile, a Samaritan, or "one who is not trustworthy in the matter of tithing."[161] In these cases, the Israelite is obligated to separate the tithes for the sharecropper.[162]

In tTer. 1:14, we find that the gentile and the Samaritan are equated and viewed as sources of possible contamination for an Israelite's heave-offering.[163] TTer. 3:9 equates gentiles and Samaritans and gives them the same power to sanctify produce as it assigns to Israelites.[164] TTer. 4:12 discusses a gentile who separates heave-offering and opens by citing and qualifying the rule of mTer. 3:9, according to which a gentile may validly separate heave-offering.[165] The passage ends with a dispute between Rabbi and Simeon b. Gamliel on the status of a Samaritan. Rabbi treats the Samaritan like a gentile, while Simeon treats him like an Israelite. The same dispute is repeated in tTer.

----

tithes; therefore, their produce cannot be tithed for an Israelite's produce, nor can an Israelite's produce be tithed for their produce; Sarason, 195.

[158]No matter who owns the field, the sharecropper must divide the produce in their presence--giving the owner of the field his percentage of the yield--and then separate the tithes from his own percentage.

[159]Sarason, 205.

[160]An Israelite may not tell these people to pay his taxes for him in kind, for it will appear that he approves of their payment with untithed produce and that they are acting as his agent. The Israelite may, however, give them less specific instructions to discharge his obligation with whatever produce they choose; Sarason, 210-211.

[161]The text includes an aside which states that the Israelite is not permitted to do this.

[162]See Sarason, 224, for an explanation of how the Israelite separates the tithes.

[163]Eleazar states that if an Israelite carrying food in the status of heave-offering were passing among gentiles and Samaritans and he could not reach the city before the food spoiled, he should place it on a rock. Yosi says he should place it in his sack until the food rots, and then he may give it to non-Israelites. The text is related to mTer. 8:11, which contains a dispute between Joshua and Eliezer concerning an Israelite who is confronted by a gentile who demands part of his heave-offering. The Samaritan does not appear in Mishnah; Peck, 242-246.

[164]The text opens by stating that gentiles and Samaritans may give heave-offering, tithes, or hallowed things. It then ignores the Samaritan and focuses on the gentile. After moving to a discussion of the fourth-year vineyard, the text returns to the gentile's heave-offering; Peck, 122.

[165]Peck, 125.

4:14, where it serves as an introduction to a discussion of the Samaritan.[166]

TSheb. 3:13 rules that the laws of grave-areas do not apply to gentiles and Samaritans,[167] and mOhol. 17:3 makes the same point; however, the latter text is less than clear, for it states that an area plowed by a *gentile* cannot constitute a grave-area because the laws of a grave-area do not apply to a *Samaritan*.[168] The anonymous statement in tSheb. 6:20 rules that Israelites may not sell seventh-year produce to, or purchase it from, gentiles or Samaritans. "Others"[169] disagree and teach that Israelites may sell Samaritans four *issars* worth of produce.[170] TM.S. 4:1 equates the Samaritan and the gentile with regard to the payment of the added fifth by an Israelite when he redeems the second tithe from the produce he purchased from them.[171]

----

[166]The Samaritan does not appear in tTer. 4:13, which discusses the gentile who sets apart the firstling of a clean animal or of an ass, or the dough-offering. TTer. 4:13 also contains three disputes between Rabbi and Simeon cast in the same "words-of" form as are the disputes in tTer. 4:12 and tTer. 4:14; Peck, 126-127.

[167]If a gentile or a Samaritan plowed a field and in the process unearthed a grave, the field is not treated as a "grave-area, for they [the rabbis] decreed only rules which they could enforce." Newman offers two explanations of the text: 1) The number of fields rendered unclean would increase, so that it would be impossible for the Israelites to live in the Land of Israel, and 2) attributed to Lieberman, the sages recognized that they had no authority over the Samaritans and the gentiles; Newman, 99, and 99, n. 11.

[168]Albeck reads: wkn nkry shrs--'ynw 'wsh 'wth byt prs; sy'n byt prs lkwtyym; "and thus a gentile who plows--he does not make it a grave-area, for there are no grave-area[s] for the Samaritans." Kaufman reads : wkn nwkry shrs 'ynw 'wsh byt prs lkwtym. Parma reads: wkn n" nkry shrs 'yn 'wsyn 'wtw byt prs w'yn byt prs lkwtym. Naples reads wkn nkry shrs 'ynw 'wsh byt prs s'yn byt prs lkwtyym. Paris reads: wkn nkry shrs 'yn 'wsyn 'wtw byt prs w'yn byt prs lkwtym. Albeck states that we are suppose to see an *a fortiori* argument: If the laws of the grave-area do not apply to the Samaritan, how much the more do they not apply to the gentile; but, this explanation clearly moves beyond the sense of the text which in no way implies the existence of such an argument; Hanokh Albeck, *The Six Orders of the Mishnah: Order Tohorot* (Tel Aviv: 1957), 181; Neusner, *Ohalot*, 323. Parma's version of the passage makes the most sense, but I have no idea if it is original or a scribal solution to a difficult textual problem.

[169]Erfurt reads "sages;" Saul Lieberman, *Tosefta Ki-fshutah A Comprehensive Commentary on the Tosefta Order Zera'im, Part II* (New York: 1955), 565.

[170]The passage opens by stating that an Israelite may sell only enough seventh-year produce for three meals to another Israelite "who is suspected of violating the seventh year." The *sugya* refines this rule and then moves on to our section. In this passage, "others" equate the Samaritan with the Israelite, for one may sell him a small amount of food. Lieberman notes that the various versions of this passage disagree on the amount one may sell (or buy) from a Samaritan. The texts mention enough food for one meal, two meals, or three meals; Lieberman, *Zera'im Part II*, 565.

[171]The *sugya* opens by quoting mM.S. 4:3, which does not mention either the gentile or the Samaritan. The passage contains a list of five types of produce for which the Israelite must pay the added fifth, and the Samaritan and the gentile are equated as one item in the list; Haas, 127.

TShab. 15:15 refers to both the Samaritan and the gentile and makes the point that neither can be classified as an adult Israelite male.[172] MSheq. 1:5 equates the gentile and the Samaritan and contrasts them to women, slaves, and minors.[173]

TYeb. 8:1 notes that an Ammonite, Moabite, Egyptian, Edomite, Samaritan, *natin* or *mamzer* who is nine years old and one day and who has sexual relations with the daughter of a priest, a Levite, or an Israelite disqualifies the woman from entering the priestly clan.

TA.Z. 2:4 prohibits the sale of swords, stocks, neck-chains, ropes, iron chains, scrolls, *tefillin*, *mezuzot*, fodder, grain, and trees which have been detached from the ground to gentiles or to Samaritans.[174]

TAhil. 18:6 states that the same rules apply to the dwellings of gentiles and Samaritans with regard to the need to examine the dwellings for sources of uncleanness.[175] MToh. 5:8 equates women who are imbeciles, gentiles, or Samaritans, for spittle found in a town in which these women live is unclean.[176]

While the gentile and Samaritan do appear together in a number of *sugyot*, and a significant number of Samaritan-pericopae also refer to the gentile, it does not appear that the mention of one group necessarily generated the reference to the other. The reference to the two segments of Palestinian society can be seen as deriving from the topics dealt with and the concerns of

----

[172]The two are treated similarly, but not placed in the same category. Gentiles are equated with children with regard to not performing the act of providing hot water for an ill Israelite on the Sabbath, while Samaritans are equated with women with regard to not providing testimony that the Israelite should prepare the heated water on the Sabbath.

[173]If a woman, a slave, or a minor paid the *sheqel*-tax, it is accepted from them; however, it is not accepted from Samaritans and gentiles. Similarly, Samaritans and gentiles cannot give the bird-offerings of one with flux or a woman after childbirth, sin-offerings, or guilt-offerings. On the other hand, they may make vow-offerings and freewill-offerings. The text contains a general rule, supported by Ezra 4:3, *It is not for you and us to build a House to our God*: What is vowed or freely offered is accepted from them; what is not vowed or freely offered is not accepted.

[174]Gary G. Porton, "Forbidden Transactions: Prohibited Commerce with Gentiles in Earliest Rabbinism," in Jacob Neusner and Ernest Frerichs (eds.), *"To See Ourselves as Others See Us" Christians, Jews, "Others" in Late Antiquity* (Chico: 1985), 320.

[175]The text lists marriages and slaves of the two groups as if they were not considered the same: A gentile married to a Samaritan woman, a Samaritan married to a gentile woman, a gentile with Samaritan slaves and a Samaritan with gentile slaves make their dwellings suspect with regard to the burying of abortions within the house or its precinct. Cf., Neusner, *Ohalot*, 346.

[176]Although the spittle of each is declared unclean for a different reason, the final results are the same. The imbeciles do not know to watch their spittle during their periods, gentile women are considered to be like a person with flux, and all Samaritan women are considered menstruants from birth; Albeck, *Tohorot*, 317.

the pericopae. The fact that the Samaritan was considered by some Tannaim to be similar to a gentile in some cases and like an Israelite in other matters led to his appearance with the gentile in discussions of some specific topics, especially with regard to matters of agricultural rules. Juxtaposing Samaritans with gentiles served as a means of defining both groups with regard to themselves, each other, and the Israelites.

Robbers

Gentiles and robbers[177] appear together in four passages: MPe. 2:7, mShab. 2:5, tShebu. 2:14, tA.Z. 1:16. In the latter three *sugyot*, gentiles and robbers pose a threat to the Israelite, while in the first, they, along with ants, cattle, and wind, are not the proper harvesters of a field's produce. Robbers appears in eight other passages in Mishnah,[178] so that their juxtaposition with gentiles occurs in about 20% of the *sugyot* in which they appear in Mishnah.

In the Interest of Peace

In seven passages, Israelites act in specific ways towards gentiles "in the interests of peace:"[179] MSheb. 4:3, mSheb. 5:9, mGit. 5:8, mGit. 5:9, tGit. 3:13, tGit. 3:14, and tA.Z. 1:3. This phrase appears in chapter four of mShebi'it only with reference to greeting a gentile, and the exact same phrase appears in mSheb. 5:9 and mGit. 5:9. However, in the latter context, the phrase appears to be appended to a *sugya* in which "in the interests of peace" occurs with reference to what an Israelite woman may lend to her neighbor who is suspected of not observing the Sabbatical year.[180] MGit. 5:8-9 form a unit which opens with "and these are the things they said [one must do] in the interests of peace," and the phrase appears nine times. Three times the phrase concerns the gentile; however, the last reference, to greeting the gentile, is a stock phrase, which we have encountered in two other contexts. TGit. 3:13-14 complement mGit. 5:8's closing reference to the gentile.[181] TA.Z. 1:3 tells Israelites to seek the welfare of the gentiles on their festivals "in the interests of peace." The phrase appears only one other time in Mishnah, mSheq. 1:3, and there it is used with reference to priests. In Tosefta the phrase is attached to only gentiles.

There is probably some editorial link between the phrase "in the interests of peace" and the gentiles. MSheq. 1:3 is the only passage in Mishnah in

---

[177]Lstym.
[178]Kasovsky, III, 1073.
[179]Mpny drky šlwm.
[180]Newman, 120. This also appears in the opening of mGit. 5:9.
[181]Neusner, *Sotah*, 164-165.

which the gentile does not appear in the same context as the phrase "in the interests of peace," and it is always associated with the gentile in Tosefta.

Ritually Impaired Individuals

The gentile is listed along with the ritually "impaired" individuals--the deaf-mute, the blind person, the imbecile, and/or a minor--in seven passages; however, the *sugyot* are quite different. MTer. 1:1 opens by stating that there are five types of people who may not separate the heave-offering; it then lists the five types in two different formulary patterns.[182] The deaf-mute,[183] imbecile, and minor appear in one form, and two different types, including the gentile, are cast in the other literary pattern. All five probably were not originally set in this context, for the latter two, including the gentile, do not respond to the superscription.[184] The juxtaposition of the gentile and the impaired individuals has occurred during the editorial process.

MGit. 2:5 contains two lists of the impaired individuals, and the gentile appears only in the second list.[185] The first list enumerates those who can write a divorce document, while the second catalogue deals with those who may not deliver the writ of divorce. MGit. 2:6 builds on the second rule in mGit. 2:5 and explains that even if after they received the writ of divorce from the husband, the deaf-mute was able to speak, the blind man was able to see, the imbecile regained his senses, or the gentile converted, the document still is invalid.

MSanh. 3:3 excludes as witnesses the usurer, those who race pigeons and those who trade in seventh-year produce, and tSanh. 5:4 excludes testimony given while one was a trader in seventh-year produce who later reformed himself, while one was a deaf-mute who later gained the power of hearing and speech, while one was a blind person who later gained his sight, while one was an imbecile who later gained his senses, and while one was a gentile who later converted. Although Tosefta begins with *one* of the persons specified in Mishnah, the former text includes the stylized catalogue of the impaired individuals and the gentile.

MShebu. 6:4 mentions the deaf-mute, imbecile, and minor. TShebu. 5:10 quotes the list in Mishnah and adds the reference to the gentile. MMen. 9:8 refers to the impaired individuals, the gentile, the slave, the agent, and the

---

[182]Peck, 31.

[183]For convenience I employ this translation of hrš, although mTer. 1:2 gives two different interpretations of the term.

[184]Peck, 32.

[185]The first list contains the deaf-mute, imbecile, and minor; the second list adds the blind man and the gentile to the items mentioned in the first list.

woman. In mToh. 8:6 the gentile appears as the object of the activity of the deaf-mute, imbecile, and minor.

The deaf-mute, imbecile, and minor are juxtaposed nineteen times in Mishnah.[186] The number of *sugyot* in which the gentile is mentioned is probably statistically insignificant, about 30%; however, when we add Tosefta's references to the list, we see that the gentile has been added in several instances, for what appear to be editorial considerations. Thus, to some of our authors, the gentile was a natural addition to the standard list of ritually impaired individuals.

Evil spirits

There are only two references to evil spirit[187] in Mishnah,[188] and in both cases the "dangerous" gentile appears. MShab. 2:5 juxtaposes gentiles, robbers, and evil spirits, while mErub. 4:1 speaks of an Israelite who has been taken across the Sabbath-limit by a gentile or evil spirit. TA.Z. 1:16 also mentions fear of gentiles, robbers, or an evil spirit.

Dogs

Although mNed. 4:3 places a reference to gentiles in the same context as feeding something to dogs, the juxtaposition occurs most often in Tosefta, especially, tHullin. In mNed. 4:3 Eliezer states that unclean cattle can be sold to gentiles or fed to dogs. TY.T. 2:6 prohibits preparing food for gentiles or dogs on a holiday.

THul. 2:15, tHul. 5:2, tHul. 6:4, and tHul. 9:2 speak of one who slaughters an animal for the purposes of healing, for consumption by gentiles, or for consumption by dogs.[189] THul. 9:9 mentions one who sells something to a gentile or places it before his dog, and this may be somewhat related to the others. At best, we can see that this was a stock phrase to the editor(s) of tHullin.

Summary

We have seen that there are certain complexes of words in which we would expect to find a reference to the gentile. In tHullin, the stock phrase "slaughtering an animal for healing, for consumption by gentiles, or for consumption by dogs" occurs five times. In two other texts, one in Mishnah and one in Tosefta, feeding dogs and gentiles are juxtaposed. Furthermore, we discovered that the phrase "evil spirit" occurs twice in Mishnah, and in both cases it is joined with a reference to the gentile. While the list of those who are ritually

----

[186]Kasovsky, II, 735.

[187]Rwḥ r'h.

[188]Kasovsky, IV, 1660.

[189]MB.Q. 7:2 contains this phrase without the reference to the gentile.

impaired often appears without including a reference to the gentile, we found several places, especially in Tosefta, in which a mention of the gentile was included at some phase of the editorial process among the references to the impaired individuals. Clearly, some believed that gentiles should be included among the stylized list of the ritually impaired Israelites. This makes sense, for the gentile could not participate in the ritual life of the Israelites any more than could those who were ritually impaired. We also discovered that frequently the gentile is included in discussions of the Samaritan; this is probably a result of the ambiguous status of the Samaritan, who stood somewhere between the Israelite and the non-Israelite. Furthermore, doing acts "in the interest of peace," easily led to the inclusion of the gentile.

In brief, when Mishnah-Tosefta include references to Samaritans, to feeding dogs, to evil spirits, to the ritually impaired, and to things done to create a peaceful environment, they may speak about the gentile for stylistic reasons as much as for reasons of substance. This last point is important, for it suggests that at least in some cases gentiles could appear in our texts not as a result of their non-Israelite status, but because the literary style of Mishnah-Tosefta engendered a mention of them, or because they were believed to really belong in the listed categories. Again, this points to the fact that references to gentiles in Mishnah-Tosefta have been "rabbinized," for their inclusion in at least some of the *sugyot* is a result of the rabbinic style of phrasing issues and categorizing people and concerns. The gentiles composed part of the rabbis' world of thought, and the former were treated in the same way as the other constructs of the "rabbinic mind." The social reality to which our texts point is that the gentiles were "real" to our sages and that the former needed to be dealt with in Mishnah-Tosefta. When the non-Israelites were discussed, however, they were fully incorporated into the styles and concerns of Mishnah-Tosefta. If the gentiles were believed to fall into the category of "ritually impaired individuals," they were "ritually impaired" from the rabbinic point of view. If non-Israelites stood further away from Israelite culture than did Samaritans, it was according to the rabbinic definition of Israelite culture. If gentiles are juxtaposed to dogs or evil spirits, this conformed to the rabbinic system of metaphors.

Throughout, we have seen that the style and agenda of Mishnah-Tosefta determined when, how, and why the gentiles were mentioned, and this is what we would expect. For this reason, it is difficult to move from the material we have to the "real world," or to distinguish practical from theoretical discussions. References to gentiles in Mishnah-Tosefta have been "rabbinized," so that they tell us more about the minds and thoughts of the rabbinic masters than they do about the gentiles.

Chapter Five:

Rabbinic Masters

i

Our final analysis of the formal traits of the *sugyot* concerning the gentiles focuses on the sages to whom these sayings are attributed in Mishnah-Tosefta. Specifically, we want to know to whom the comments about the non-Israelite are assigned in order to determine which generations appear to have been most concerned with the issue of the gentile. However, before we turn to our investigation, a few words about the limits of our inquiry and its conclusion are in order.

Although we have a number of sayings assigned to specific Tannaim, and we have stated, and shall continue to state, that "Rabbi X said" something, we do not mean to imply that we have Rabbi X's actual words. An array of recent studies on the sayings of specific Tannaim[1] has demonstrated the impossibility of unearthing the actual teachings of the Tannaim in Mishnah-Tosefta. Nor can we use the material before us, as Green notes, to produce

----

[1]Gary G. Porton, *The Traditions of Rabbi Ishmael* (Leiden: 1976-1982), 4 Vols. Gary G. Porton, "The Artificial Dispute: Ishmael and Aqiba," in Jacob Neusner (ed.), *Christianity, Judaism, and Other Greco-Roman Cults: Studies for Morton Smith at Sixty* (Leiden: 1975), IV, 18-29. Jacob Neusner, *The Rabbinic Traditions About the Pharisees Before 70* (Leiden: 1973), 3 Vols. Jacob Neusner, *Development of a Legend: Studies in the Traditions Concerning Yohanan ben Zakkai* (Leiden: 1970). Jacob Neusner, *Eliezer ben Hyrcanus: The Tradition and the Man* (Leiden: 1973), 2 Vols. Joel D. Gereboff, *Rabbi Tarfon: The Tradition, the Man, and Early Rabbinic Judaism* (Missoula: 1979). Robert Goldenberg, *The Sabbath Law of Rabbi Meir* (Missoula: 1979). William S. Green, *The Traditions of Joshua Ben Hananiah. Part I: The Early Traditions* (Leiden: 1981). Shamai Kanter, *Rabban Gamaliel II: The Legal Traditions* (Chico: 1980). Jack N. Lightstone, "Yose the Galilean in Mishnah-Tosefta and the History of Early Rabbinic Judaism," *Journal of Jewish Studies*, 1979. Jack N. Lightstone, "R. Sadoq," in William S. Green, *Persons and Institutions in Early Rabbinic Judaism* (Missoula: 1977), 49-148. Jack N. Lightstone, *Yose the Galilean: I. Traditions in Mishnah-Tosefta* (Leiden: 1979). Charles Primus, *Aqiva's Contribution to Law of Zera'im* (Leiden: 1977). Tzvee Zahavy, *The Traditions of Eleazar ben Azariah* (Missoula: 1978).

biographies of the important sages of the first centuries of our era.[2] Because each Tannaitic collection is organized according to its own agenda, and the materials it contains were selected and formulated in terms of its own scheme, "the teachings of the individuals have been made subservient to the goals of the documents."[3] In addition, the sayings of all of the masters have been cast in a surprisingly limited number of literary patterns. In Green's words,

> "In the process of transmission and redaction the discrete sayings and rulings have been cast into rhetorical patterns, many of them stereotyped . . . . [And these] forms by nature remove us from a historical figure because they 'package' or epitomize his thought, obscure idiosyncrasy and unique modes of expression, and thereby conceal distinctive elements of personality, character, and intellect. The very presence of forms means at the outset that we cannot claim to have the exact words"

spoken by the named sages.[4] Furthermore, Green argues that we cannot even be certain that we have accurate representations of the sages' ideas and positions:

> ". . . [W]e cannot be certain of the extent to which a master's views on a given matter have been revised in the tradental and redactional processes, and we therefore cannot automatically suppose that the superscriptions in disputes involving him accurately depict his perceptions and definitions of the issues and problems they represent."[5]

Finally, Green warns us that

> "[t]he continued reduction of a master's thoughts on a variety of issues to stereotypic language and rigid formal structures can create an illusion of consistency and thereby transform a distinctive, individual intellect into the personification of a single posture or position."[6]

If we cannot hope to ascertain a sage's words or even gain certainty that we have an accurate picture of his ideas, why concern ourselves with the attributions? Neusner has argued that we have

----

[2]William S. Green, "What's in a Name--The Problematic of Rabbinic 'Biography,'" in William S. Green (ed.), *Approaches to Ancient Judaism: Theory and Practice* (Missoula: 1978), 77-96.

[3]Green, "Biography," 80.

[4]Green, "Biography," 81.

[5]Green, "Biography," 82.

[6]Green, "Biography," 82.

"no suitable method for distinguishing reliable from unreliable attributions of sayings to a *particular* named authority . . . . When we take attributions seriously, it is to the very limited extent that we assign what is attributed to the *period* in which the person to whom the saying is assigned is assumed to have lived."[7]

By collecting together the sayings assigned to the masters of a specific generation or period, Neusner has been able to write his histories of Mishnah's laws on a variety of topics. While I do not believe that we can construct a similar history of the statements concerning the gentile,[8] it does seem important to determine to which generations the editors/authors of Mishnah-Tosefta assigned the discussions of the gentile. At the most, we shall be able to determine which sages were concerned with the gentile and what issues occupied their minds.[9] At the least, this will tell us when our writers *thought* the topic of the non-Israelite exercised the minds of the Tannaim.

----

[7]Jacob Neusner, *From Mishnah to Scripture: The Problem of the Unattributed Saying* (Chico: 1984), 17. Neusner first worked this out in his *History of the Mishnaic Law of Purities* (Leiden: 1974-1977), 22 Vols; see Neusner, *From Mishnah*, 3.

[8]Neusner's project works because his analysis proceeds tractate by tractate and because he has developed a system of verification which allows him to determine if specific statements within a tractate build upon, or assume the existence of, other rulings. We cannot do this with our material because it has been gathered from a number of tractates throughout Mishnah-Tosefta. Our *sugyot* deal sporadically with a wide number of topics, and they do not build on one another, as do the sayings in individual chapters and tractates. On Neusner's method of verification, see *From Mishnah*, 17-19 and Jacob Neusner, *Judaism: The Evidence of Mishnah* (Chicago: 1981), 15-22. For a summary of his conclusions concerning the history of Mishnah's laws, see *Judaism*, 45-166.

[9]Neusner and Avery-Peck have argued that Mishnah's various tractates do exhibit a development of ideas and laws. While not claiming that we possess the actual teachings of the sages, these two scholars have shown that frequently one can demonstrate that the ideas from the generation of Usha are later than those from the period between the Great Revolt and the Bar Kokhba War and that the latter are developed from concepts expressed in the period of Yavneh. See Alan Avery-Peck, *Mishnah's Division of Agriculture: A History and Theology of Seder Zeraim* (Chico: 1985), 35-389. Neusner, *Judaism*, 45-229. Jacob Neusner, *A History of the Mishnaic Law of Holy Things Part Six. The Mishnaic System of Sacrifice and Sanctuary* (Leiden: 1980), 223-272. Jacob Neusner, *A History of the Mishnaic Law of Damages Part Five. The Mishnaic System of Damages* (Leiden: 1985), 147-178. Jacob Neusner, *A History of the Mishnaic Law of Women Part Five. The Mishnaic System of Women* (Leiden: 1980), 179-238. Jacob Neusner, *A History of the Mishnaic Law of Appointed Times Part Five. The Mishnaic System of Appointed Times* (Leiden: 1983), 195-242.

We saw in the previous chapter that we have a large number of un-attributed traditions which discuss the non-Israelite. We can conclude, perhaps, that our editors/authors wanted us to see those unassigned statements which are juxtaposed with assigned comments as coming from the same generation as the named master.[10] With regard to those anonymous remarks which are not set into the same context as a comment attributed to a named sage, however, the matter is more complicated. While many have claimed that the anonymous sayings pre-date Mishnah and represent the "pre-history" of the Mishnaic text,[11] Neusner's work leads us to reject this generalization, for the unattributed sayings can be placed in a variety of periods within the unfolding of Mishnah's laws. What is clear, however, according to Neusner, is that ". . . as a group un-attributed ideas do not form a bridge from the Mishnah back to Scripture (let alone from Tosefta anywhere). When we contemplate the unattributed sayings, in no way need we call to mind the myth of the dual Torah and explain that at hand is that missing link between the written and Oral Torah."[12] Thus, because I do not believe that we can write a "history" of the Mishnaic law of the gentile in the same way that Neusner has been able to write the history of the laws of Mishnah's individual tractates--for his method of verification cannot be applied to our material--we shall have to forego an attempt to assign the independent anonymous traditions to any specific generation or period.

To summarize: The purpose of the present chapter is to discover to which generations our editors/authors assigned specific comments concerning the non-Israelite, so that we can discover when they thought the topic of the gentile was of major concern to the Tannaim. To this end, below, we shall set out to divide the specific issues concerning the gentiles by the generations to which they are assigned, and we shall categorize the images of the gentiles along these same lines.

ii

We shall begin with those Tannaim to whom comments about the gentiles have been attributed which appear in Mishnah.

---

[10]Neusner, *From Mishnah*, 7.

[11]Neusner, *From Mishnah*, 8-11.

[12]Neusner, *From Mishnah*, 119.

Pre-70[13]

Houses (7): MShab. 1:7, MShab. 1:8, mEd. 5:1=mNid. 4:3, mBekh. 5:2,[14] mOhol. 18:7-8.

Zechariah b. HaQassab (1): MKet. 2:9.

Hanina the Prefect of the priests (1): MAbot 3:2.[15]

70-135

Gamliel (5): MHal. 4:7,[16] mShab. 16:8, mErub. 4:1,[17] mBes. 3:2, mA.Z. 3:4.[18]

Joshua (3): MTer. 8:11,[19] mErub. 4:1,[20] mA.Z. 2:5.[21]

Eliezer (7): MTer. 8:11,[22] mHal. 4:7,[23] mNed. 4:3, mHul. 2:7,[24] mArakh. 8:4,[25] mPar. 2:1,[26] mMiq. 8:1.

Eleazar b. Azariah (2): MErub. 4:1,[27] mArakh. 8:4.[28]

Ishmael (3): MA.Z. 1:2, mA.Z. 2:5,[29] mA.Z. 4:1.

Aqiba (3): MErub. 4:1,[30] mA.Z. 3:5,[31] mA.Z. 2:3.[32]

Yohanan b. Nuri (1): MToh. 8:6.

Judah b. Baba (1): MYeb. 16:5.

----

[13]The dates assigned to the generations are only approximations.

[14]House of Shammai does not mention the gentile; however, the Houses' opinions form a dispute.

[15]Speaks about ruling power, supposedly the Roman government.

[16]Eliezer also appears.

[17]Eleazar b. Azariah, Joshua, and Aqiba also appear.

[18]Gamliel discusses with Prokolos the bath of Aphrodite in Acre.

[19]Eliezer also appears.

[20]Gamliel, Eleazar b. Azariah, and Aqiba also appear.

[21]Judah reports a debate between Joshua and Ishmael.

[22]Joshua also appears.

[23]Gamliel also appears.

[24]Yosi also appears.

[25]Eleazar b. Azariah also appears.

[26]Sages also appear.

[27]Joshua, Aqiba, and Gamliel also appear.

[28]Eliezer also appears.

[29]Judah reports a debate between Joshua and Ishmael.

[30]Gamliel, Eleazar b. Azariah, and Joshua also appear.

[31]Yosi the Galilean also appears, and Yosi and Aqiba discuss hills and mountains which gentiles worship.

[32]Simeon b. Gamliel also appears.

Yosi the Galilean (1): MA.Z. 3:5.[33]
Ben Bathyra (2): MPes. 4:3=mA.Z. 1:6.

135-160

Judah (17): MPe. 4:6,[34] mDem. 6:2, mTer. 3:9, mErub. 8:5,[35] mPes. 4:3=mA.Z. 1:6,[36] mQid. 4:3, mB.Q. 8:3, mSanh. 7:3, mA.Z. 1:1, mA.Z. 1:5,[37] mA.Z. 1:8,[38] mA.Z. 2:5,[39] mArakh. 1:2,[40] mMakh. 2:5, mMakh. 2:7, mMakh. 2:8.

Meir (11): MErub. 8:5,[41] mQid. 1:3,[42] mA.Z. 1:3,[43] mA.Z. 1:5, mA.Z. 1:8,[44] mA.Z. 2:2,[45] mA.Z. 2:4,[46] mA.Z. 3:1,[47] mZeb. 4:5,[48] mArakh. 1:2,[49] mMakh. 2:10.[50]

Simeon (6): MTer. 3:9,[51] mErub. 8:5,[52] mSheq. 7:6, mYeb. 8:3, mGit. 1:5, mA.Z. 4:10.[53]

Eliezer b. Jacob (1): MErub. 6:1.

Yosi (5): MErub. 8:5,[54] mA.Z. 1:8,[55] mA.Z. 2:7, mA.Z. 3:3,[56]

---

[33]Aqiba also appears.

[34]Although Judah does not employ the term gentile, it is the antecedent of the masculine singular pronoun in his comment. The term gentile appears in the anonymous comment to which Judah responds.

[35]Meir, Yosi, and Simeon also appear.

[36]Ben Bathyra also appears.

[37]Meir also appears.

[38]Meir and Yosi also appear.

[39]Judah reports a debate between Ishmael and Joshua.

[40]Meir also appears.

[41]Judah and Simeon also appear.

[42]Sages also appear.

[43]Sages also appear.

[44]Yosi and Judah also appear.

[45]Sages also appear.

[46]Sages also appear.

[47]Sages and Simeon b. Gamliel also appear. While gentiles are not mentioned, the masters appear to discuss gentile images.

[48]Sages also appear.

[49]Judah also appears.

[50]Sages also appear.

[51]Although Simeon does not mention the gentile, his comment is dependent on the anonymous comment in which the gentile does appear.

[52]Meir, Judah, and Yosi also appear.

[53]Sages also appear.

[54]Meir, Judah, and Simeon also appear.

[55]Meir and Judah also appear.

[56]Simeon b. Gamliel also appears, and the rabbis seem to discuss gentile images.

mHul. 2:7.[57]

Simeon b. Gamliel (10): MShab. 1:9, mA.Z. 2:3, mA.Z. 3:1,[58] mA.Z. 3:3,[59] mA.Z. 5:3, mA.Z. 5:4, mA.Z. 5:10, mBekh. 2:4, mBekh. 3:2, mOhol. 18:9.

160-220

Simeon b. Eleazar (1): MA.Z. 4:11.
Rabbi (1): MA.Z. 5:11[60]

No specific date can be assigned

Sages (15): MShab. 6:10,[61] mQid. 1:3,[62] mA.Z. 1:3,[63] mA.Z. 1:4,[64] mA.Z. 2:2,[65] mA.Z. 2:4,[66] mA.Z. 3:1,[67] mA.Z. 4:10,[68] mA.Z. 4:12, mA.Z. 5:2,[69] mA.Z. 5:11,[70] mZeb. 4:5,[71] mBekh. 5:3,[72] mPar. 2:1,[73] mMakh. 2:10.[74]

Elders in Rome (1): MA.Z. 4:6.

The most frequently quoted authorities are Judah b. Ilai, Meir and Simeon b. Gamliel. These three sages appear in thirty-two different *sugyot*. These masters lived immediately following the Bar Kokhba revolt, when the

----

[57]Eliezer also appears. Yosi glosses Eliezer's comment, but does not deal with gentile.

[58]Meir and sages also appear. Although the rabbis discuss images and not gentiles, these are clearly images made by gentiles.

[59]Yosi also appears. Although the gentile is not mentioned, the rabbis seem to be discussing gentile images.

[60]Sages also appear.

[61]Meir also appears.

[62]Meir also appears.

[63]Meir also appears.

[64]Sages deal with images on a gentile's festival.

[65]Meir also appears.

[66]Meir also appears.

[67]Meir and Simeon b. Gamliel also appear. The masters seem to discuss gentile images.

[68]Simeon also appears.

[69]Sages discuss libation-wine.

[70]Rabbi also appears.

[71]Meir also appears.

[72]Sages discuss rams which a quaestor blemished.

[73]Eliezer also appears.

[74]Meir also appears.

Roman presence in the Land of Israel reached a peak.[75] In fact, there are a total of thirty-nine pericopae in which six different masters from this generation appear. Eliezer b. Hyrcanus is the next most quoted sage, and he appears with nine other rabbis from the generation between the destruction of the Second Temple and the outbreak of the revolt lead by Simeon bar Kokhba. However, only seventeen different passages contain sayings attributed to rabbis who lived at this time. The period before the destruction of the Temple has nine, with seven assigned to the Houses. Two passages are assigned to the generation of the editing of Mishnah. The breakdown of the pericopae assigned to named sages in Mishnah follows the contours of the history of gentile involvement and presence in the Land of Israel. The editor(s) of Mishnah presented the statements in an historically plausible manner. Even if the statements are not the actual words of the sages, or do not reflect the individual rabbis' thoughts, the distribution of attributed sayings corresponds to what we would expect from our knowledge of the political and social history of Palestine in the first two centuries of the common era.

The following chart divides the issues raised and the images of the gentile found in Mishnah's attributed *sugyot* by generation, in an attempt to ascertain if certain images or topics cluster around one another during specific periods of times.

Pre-70

Source	Topic	Image[76]
Shab. 1:7	Work begun before Sabbath	N
Shab. 1:8	Work begun before Sabbath	N
Ed. 5:1	Blood of gentile women	N
Nid. 4:3	" " "	"
Bekh. 5:2	Consumption of firstling	N
Ohol. 18:7	Unclean dwelling-places	U
Ohol. 18:8	" " "	U
Ket. 2:9	Invasion of Jerusalem	S
Abot. 3:2	Pray for government	P

----

[75]Michael Avi-Yonah, *The Jews of Palestine: A Political History from the Bar Kokhba War to the Arab Conquest* (New York: 1976), 15-83. E. Mary Smallwood, *The Jews Under Roman Rule: From Pompey to Diocletian* (Leiden: 1976), 428-506.

[76]N=Non-Israelite; U=Uncivilized; I=Idolatry; B=Biblical Image; Ph=Part of humanity; S=Sexually uninhibited; P=Powerful rulers; D=Dangerous; Sm=Samaritan; L=Libation; Df=Defilement; M=Magician; Ut=Untrustworthy.

70-135

Hal. 4:7	Agricultural gifts in Syria	N
Shab. 16:8	Sabbath work benefit Israelite	N
Erub. 4:1	Causes violation of 'erub	D
Bes. 3:2	Gentile's fish for food	N
A.Z. 3:4	Philosopher/Aphrodite	N
Ter. 8:11	Defile heave-offering	D/Df
A.Z. 2:5	Gentile cheese	I
Ned. 4:3	Feed them unclean cattle	N/dogs
Hul. 2:7	Slaughter for gentile	N
Arakh. 8:4	Canaanite slave is property	N
Par. 2:1	Buy Red Heifer from them	N
Miq. 8:1	Gentile immersion-pools	N
A.Z. 1:2	Business around their festivals	I
A.Z. 4:1	Stones and Mercury	I
A.Z. 3:5	Sacred mountains	I
Toh. 8:6	Food Item given to them	N/Ph
Yeb. 16:5	Evidence concerning death	N
Pes. 4:3	Sale of animals to them	N/Ph
A.Z. 1:6	" " " " " " "	
A.Z. 2:3	Meat entering into idol	I

135-160

Pe. 4:6	Agricultural gifts for poor	N
Dem. 6:2	Tithes/heave-offering/ tenant	N
Ter. 3:9	Tithes/heave-offering	N/Sm
Erub. 8:5	Empty house in courtyard	N
Qid. 4:3	Intermarriage among those forbidden in congregation	B

B.Q. 8:3	Wound Canaanite slave	N
Sanh. 7:3	Gentiles behead people	D/U/P
A.Z. 1:1	Repay loans on their festivals	N
A.Z. 1:5	Can't sell items for idolatry	I
A.Z. 1:8	Sale/make items for idolatry	I
A.Z. 2:5	Gentile cheese	I
Arakh. 1:2	Valuation of gentiles	N
Makh. 2:5	Heating bath-house	N/Ph
Makh. 2:7	Abandoned child	" "
Makh. 2:8	Found bread	" "
Qid. 1:3	Acquire Canaanite slave	N
A.Z. 1:3	Gentile festivals	I
A.Z. 2:2	Gentile doctors/barbers	D
A.Z. 2:4	Jars/skin-bottles of wine	I/L
A.Z. 3:1	Gentile images	I
Zeb. 4:5	Gentile offerings	N
Makh. 2:10	Store-house/demai	N/Ph
Sheq. 7:6	Whole-offering/ drink-offering	N
Yeb. 8:3	Marriage to Israelites	B
Git. 1:5	Writs in gentile registries signed by gentiles	N/P
A.Z. 4:10	Gentile contact with wine in vat	I/L
Erub. 6:1	'Erub in courtyard with gentile	N
A.Z. 2:7	Gentile foodstuffs	N/I
A.Z. 3:3	Figures on objects	I
Shab. 1:9	Work completed before Sabbath	N
A.Z. 2:3	Hides pierced at the heart	I
A.Z. 3:1	Idols which hold object	I
A.Z. 5:3	Gentile helps move wine	I/L

A.Z. 5:4	Israelite left wine	I/L
A.Z. 5:10	Sale mixture of wine and libation wine to them	N
Bekh. 2:4	Firstling/offsprings of animals purchased from them	N
Bekh. 3:2	Firstling/animal purchased from them	N
Ohol. 18:9	Gentile-dwelling place/ ruins	U

160-220

A.Z. 4:11	Left wine prepared for gentile	I/Ph
A.Z. 5:11	Coated winepress of gentile	I/L

The above chart reveals some interesting information. The earliest generation of sages commented upon problems related to the Sabbath, the blood of gentile women, the consumption of firstlings, the impurity of gentiles' dwelling-places, the gentiles as an invading army, and the gentiles as rulers of Palestine. The agenda is extremely limited, so that a number of topics-- agricultural rules, temple-cult, idols, social interaction, and the like--are not topics of interest. Furthermore, while we find a neutral image of the gentile in most of the *sugyot*, the picture of the non-Israelite as a sexually uninhibited, un-civilized, but powerful, force finds expression in this generation.

The agenda for the sages of the next period, 70-135, is considerably different from that of the rabbis who lived before 70. The previous generation had concerned itself with aiding a gentile to commence work before the Sab-bath, while this generation moves the discussion to the prohibition of a gentile's working on the Sabbath for an Israelite's benefit, and the possibility that a gentile will cause an Israelite to violate the established Sabbath-limit. There is some concern with food provided by, or produced by, gentiles, but the issue is severely circumscribed, and it is limited to fish and cheese. Similarly, the con-cern with agricultural matters is limited to gentiles in Syria. The problem of the gentile as idolater appears during this period for the first time; however, it is limited to a concern with the stones around a statue of Mercury, sacred mountains, meat being brought to an idol, and doing business with them near their festivals. The impact of gentiles on Israelite practices is expressed in the concern over whether or not the Red Heifer may be purchased from them, and whether or not an Israelite may use their immersion-pools. Three *sugyot* deal with an Israelite's providing a gentile with meat, and from these we learn that a gentile is treated differently from an Israelite. Similarly, rules of evidence are different for gentiles than they are for Israelites. In addition, certain prohibitions are set forth concerning the sale of animals to non-Israelites. The issue of the Canaanite slave first appears at this time. Gentiles are pictured as dangerous, and as a source of defilement with regard to the heave-offering. In addition, they may pose an intellectual challenge to Israelites.

Although the gentile as idolater first appears in the generation of 70-135, the focus is mainly on their objects of worship. On the other hand, several pericopae from this period assume that gentiles and Israelites regularly engage in economic activity, even involving foodstuffs. What is most striking about the passages attributed to masters of this period is that they do not seem to build upon the materials of the previous generation. Furthermore, while the gentile as idolater first appears at this time, the scope of this concern is limited.

Because we possess relatively more *sugyot* concerning the gentile from the period 135-160 than from the other periods, we would expect the comments from this generation to cover a large variety of topics. The relationship of the gentile to the Israelite agricultural gifts first finds full expression in this period, and this parallels the fact that the system of land ownership in Palestine underwent severe changes after the Bar Kokhba War.[77] Similarly, the increased number of gentiles and the changing demographic conditions of Palestine are reflected in the issue of establishing an 'erub in a courtyard in which Israelites and gentiles dwell, and in the problem of determining the ownership or status of items encountered in cities with a mixed Israelite/non-Israelite population. There is a deeper concern with the gentiles as idolaters expressed in the *sugyot* from this generation than in the previous periods. We find passages which deal with the problems related to gentiles' repaying loans on their festivals, and purchasing items which they might use in their idolatrous practices. Furthermore, we find discussions on which of their images/idols or objects of worship are forbidden, and which of the festivals require a cessation of business transaction with them. The concern with libation-wine also arises at this time. The matter of libation-wine is the only item from this generation which is taken up by the

----

[77]Avi-Yonah, 15-25.

sages who lived between 160 and 220. During the period of 160-220 we first encounter the gentiles' relationship to the Israelite cult. The problem of determining whether or not an animal purchased from a gentile has produced a firstling appears in the period of 135-160. The problem of a gentile's valuation is also raised in the generation of 135-160 and reflects a similar concern with Israelite cultic practices. Although the pre-70 generation knew that the gentiles ruled Palestine, in this period we find a specific reference to their governmental activities and registries, so that their rule is expressed in much more concrete terms. This is also expressed in the statement concerning the government's practice of beheading people. There is some social interaction between the groups, which is seen in two specific discussions of the acquiring and reimbursement of "Canaanite" slaves, the danger posed by using gentile barbers or doctors, and the concern with intermarriage. However, it is interesting that problems of marriage to or among gentiles are expressed only in terms of biblical paradigms and peoples, so that the sages' ideas appear guarded in these passages. Finally, the problem of the gentiles' dwelling-places occupied this generation, as it did the pre-70 generation. The predominant image of the gentile during this period is of a non-Israelite; however, the gentile as idolater also becomes important at this time. Similarly, the gentiles as rulers of Palestine are most forcefully encounter in the sayings of this generation.

Although Mishnah contains only sixty-nine pericopae which contained statements about the gentiles which are attributed to named sages, they offer us an interesting picture. First, their range of concerns is rather limited. While, many issues found in these passages will be fully explored in anonymous comments, the unassigned sayings will also mention a large number of matters not covered in the assigned sayings. Second, it does not appear that the concerns of one generation generated the discussions of following generations. While we have a few instances in which a generation takes up an issue discussed during a previous period, there is no clear development of laws concerning the gentile or the treatment of them. Third, the matters discussed by the various generations seem to reflect what we know about the presence and the activity of the gentiles in Palestine, for it is only after the Bar Kokhba war and the subsequent shifts in population, demography, land-tenure, and economic activity which occurred in its aftermath that the statements about the gentile become more specific and the issues more vivid.

iii

We now turn to a discussion of the assigned comments which occur in Tosefta.

Pre-70

Zechariah b. Haqassab (1): TKet. 3:2.
Nahum the Mede (1): TA.Z. 1:1.[78]
Houses (4): TShab. 1:22,[79] tPis. 1:7,[80] tBekh. 3:15,[81] tNid. 5:5.

70-135

Gamliel (8): TTer. 2:13,[82] tShab. 7:11,[83] tShab. 7:25, tShab. 13:14,[84] tPis. 2:15, tMo'ed 2:15, tKet. 1:6,[85] tA.Z. 4:9.[86]
Eliezer (6): TTer. 1:14,[87] tKet. 1:6,[88] tSanh. 13:2,[89] tHul. 2:24,[90] tAhil. 18:7,[91] tPar. 2:1.[92]
Joshua (2): TKet. 1:6,[93] tSanh. 13:2.[94]
Aqiba (8): TBer. 2:13,[95] tShab. 1:22,[96] tShab. 8:5,[97] tPis. 1:7,[98]

----

[78]Joshua b. Qorha also appears.
[79]Aqiba and Eleazar b. R. Sadoq also appear. House of Hillel does not appear. Gamliel also is mentioned.
[80]Aqiba and Yosi also appear.
[81]Aqiba also appears.
[82]Judah and sages also appear.
[83]Eleazar b. R. Sadoq also appears.
[84]Elders also appear.
[85]Gamliel and Joshua also appear; however, Joshua is the only one who specifically mentions gentiles.
[86]Simeon b. Gamliel also appears.
[87]Yosi also appears.
[88]Joshua and Gamliel also appear.
[89]Joshua also appears.
[90]Eliezer appears before Hegmon.
[91]Yosi b. Judah appears, and Abba Yudan of Sidon quotes Eliezer.
[92]Judah also appears.
[93]Eliezer and Gamliel also appear.
[94]Eliezer also appears.
[95]Meir and quaestor also appear.
[96]House of Shammai, Eleazar b. R. Sadoq, and Gamliel also appear.
[97]Monobases also appears.
[98]Yosi and Houses appear.

tMoʻed 2:14, tSheq. 1:7,[99] tGit. 1:4,[100] tBekh. 3:15.[101]

Ishmael (2): TA.Z. 6:14, tKer. 1:17.

Hananiah b. Tardiyon (1): TMiq. 6:3.

Yosi the Galilean (1): TSheq. 1:7.[102]

Judah b. Baba (1): TY.T. 2:6.[103]

Simeon of Teman (1): TY.T. 2:6.[104]

Monobases (1): TShab. 8:5.[105]

Hananiah b. Gamliel (2): TA.Z. 5:2,[106] tA.Z. 8:4-8:8.[107]

Hidqa (1): TA.Z. 8:4-8:8.[108]

135-160

Meir (12): TBer. 2:13,[109] tPe. 3:5,[110] tDem. 1:12,[111] tDem. 5:21,[112] tQid. 5:11, tB.Q. 4:3, tA.Z. 1:4, tA.Z. 1:5,[113] tA.Z. 2:5,[114] tA.Z. 2:8,[115] tA.Z. 3:3,[116] tA.Z. 3:12.[117]

Joshua b. Qorha (1): TA.Z. 1:1.[118]

Judah (24): TBer. 6:18, tPe. 4:1, tPe. 4:20,[119] tDem. 1:13,[120] tDem. 5:21,[121] tTer. 2:13,[122] tTer. 7:20, tShab. 7:1, tShab. 7:2, tShab. 7:3, tShab. 7:6,

----

[99] Yosi the Galilean also appears.

[100] Leazar b. Yosi also appears.

[101] House of Shammai and House of Hillel also appear.

[102] Aqiba also appears.

[103] Simeon of Teman also appears.

[104] Judah b. Baba also appears.

[105] Aqiba also appears.

[106] Judah and Simeon b. Eleazar also appear.

[107] Hidqa, Eleazar b. Simeon, Rabbi, Yosi, and Eleazar also appear.

[108] Rabbi, Yosi, Eleazar, Eleazar b. Simeon, and Hananiah b. Gamliel also appear.

[109] Aqiba also appears.

[110] Sages also appear.

[111] Sages also appear.

[112] Judah, Yosi, and Simeon also appear.

[113] Sages also appear.

[114] Sages also appear.

[115] Yosi also appears.

[116] Sages also appear.

[117] Sages also appear.

[118] Nahum the Mede also appears.

[119] Meir and sages also appear.

[120] Yosi also appears.

[121] Meir, Yosi, and Simeon also appear.

[122] Sages and Gamliel also appear.

tB.Q.4:6,[123] tSanh. 12:4,[124] tA.Z. 1:21, tA.Z. 2:3,[125] tA.Z. 2:4, tA.Z. 3:19,[126] tA.Z. 4:11, tA.Z. 5:2,[127] tA.Z. 7:13,[128] tBekh. 2:1,[129] tAhil. 18:12,[130] tPar. 2:1,[131] tToh. 5:2.

Simeon (12): TPe. 2:9, tPe. 3:12, tDem. 4:25,[132] tDem. 5:21,[133] tDem. 6:2, tSot. 7:22, tB.Q.4:6,[134] tSanh. 12:4,[135] tA.Z. 2:9, tA.Z. 8:4-8:8,[136] tZeb. 5:6,[137] tNid. 9:14.

Eliezer b. Jacob (1): TNeg. 2:15.

Yosi (14): TDem. 1:13,[138] tDem. 5:21,[139] tTer. 1:14,[140] tShab. 7:23,[141] tPis. 1:7,[142] tR.H. 2:12, tYeb. 8:1,[143] tA.Z. 2:8,[144] tA.Z. 3:11, tA.Z. 3:19,[145] tA.Z. 4:8, tA.Z. 8:4-8:8,[146] tZeb. 5:6,[147] tAhil. 18:12.[148]

Eleazar b. R. Sadoq (3): TShab. 7:5, tShab. 7:11,[149] tShab. 1:22.[150]

Simeon b. Gamliel (14): TDem. 4:25,[151] tDem. 5:2,[152] tDem. 6:1,

---

[123] Simeon also appears.

[124] Simeon also appears.

[125] Simeon b. Eleazar, Ben Petra, and Rabbi also appear.

[126] Yosi also appears.

[127] Hananiah b. Gamliel and Simeon b. Eleazar also appear.

[128] Simeon b. Eleazar also appears.

[129] Sages also appear.

[130] Rabbi, Yosi, and sages also appear.

[131] Eliezer also appears.

[132] Simeon b. Gamliel also appears.

[133] Meir, Judah, and Yosi also appear.

[134] Judah also appears.

[135] Judah also appears.

[136] Rabbi, Eleazar b. Simeon, Hidqa, Yosi, Eleazar, and Hananiah b. Gamliel also appear.

[137] Yosi also appears.

[138] Judah also appears.

[139] Meir, Judah, and Simeon also appear.

[140] Eliezer also appears.

[141] Nehori also appears.

[142] Aqiba and Houses also appear.

[143] Simeon b. Gamliel also appears.

[144] Meir also appears.

[145] Judah also appears.

[146] Rabbi, Eleazar b. Simeon, Hidqa, Eleazar, Hananiah b. Gamliel and Simeon also appear.

[147] Simeon also appears.

[148] Rabbi, Judah, and sages also appear.

[149] Gamliel also appears.

[150] House of Shammai, Aqiba, and Gamliel also appear.

[151] Simeon also appears.

[152] Rabbi also appears.

tTer. 1:15,[153] tTer. 4:12,[154] tTer. 4:13,[155] tTer. 4:14,[156] tShab. 13:13,[157] tYeb. 8:1,[158] tA.Z. 2:9, tA.Z. 3:16, A.Z. 4:10,[159] tBekh. 2:5, tBekh. 2:14.

Nehori (1): TShab. 7:24.[160]

Ishmael b. Yohanan b. Beroqa (1): TA.Z. 3:4.

Judah b. Petera (1): TA.Z. 1:21.

Ben Petera (1): TA.Z. 2:3.[161]

160-220

Rabbi (10): TDem. 5:2,[162] tTer. 4:12,[163] tTer. 4:13,[164] tTer. 4:14,[165] tShab. 13:13,[166] tA.Z. 2:3,[167] tA.Z. 5:4,[168] tA.Z. 8:1,[169] tA.Z. 8:4-8:8,[170] tAhil. 18:12.[171]

Yosi b. HaMeshullan (1): TDem. 6:7.[172]

Simeon b. Eleazar (6): TA.Z. 1:3, tA.Z. 2:3,[173] tA.Z. 4:6, tA.Z. 5:2,[174] tA.Z. 7:8, tA.Z. 7:13.[175]

Isaac (1): TTer. 1:15.[176]

Yosi b. Judah (2): TAhil. 18:7,[177] tToh. 11:8.

----

[153]Isaac also appears.

[154]Rabbi also appears.

[155]Rabbi also appears.

[156]Rabbi also appears.

[157]Rabbi also appears.

[158]Yosi also appears.

[159]Simeon quotes Joshua b. Qopesai.

[160]Yosi also appears.

[161]Judah, Simeon b. Eleazar, and Rabbi also appear.

[162]Simeon b. Gamliel also appears.

[163]Simeon b. Gamliel also appears.

[164]Simeon b. Gamliel also appears.

[165]Simeon b. Gamliel also appears.

[166]Simeon b. Gamliel also appears.

[167]Simeon b. Eleazar, Judah, and Ben Petera also appear.

[168]Jacob is quoted by Rabbi.

[169]Sages also appear.

[170]Eleazar b. Simeon, Hidqa, Yosi, Eleazar, Hananiah b. Gamliel and Simeon also appear.

[171]Judah, Yosi, and sages also appear.

[172]Nathan and Eliezer Hisma also appear.

[173]Judah, Ben Petera, and Rabbi also appear.

[174]Judah and Hananiah b. Gamliel also appear. The rabbis discuss gentile images.

[175]Judah also appears.

[176]Rabbi also appears.

[177]Eliezer and Abba Yudan of Sidon also appear.

Eleazar b. Simeon (2): T.A.Z. 8:4-8:8.[178]
Jacob (1): T.A.Z. 5:4.[179]
Joseph b. Simai of Sihin (1): TShab. 13:9.
Eleazar b. Yosi (2): TKip. 2:16, tGit. 1:4.[180]
Abba Yudan of Sidon (2): TYeb. 14:7, tAhil. 18:7.[181]
Joshua b. Qopesai (1): T.A.Z. 4:10.[182]
Nathan (2): TDem. 6:7,[183] tA.Z. 2:7.
Eleazar (1): T.A.Z. 8:4-8:8.[184]

No specific date can be assigned

Sages (16): TPe. 3:5,[185] tPe. 4:20,[186] tDem. 1:12,[187] tTer. 2:13,[188] tShab. 6:14, tA.Z. 1:5,[189] tA.Z. 2:5,[190] tA.Z. 3:3,[191] tA.Z. 3:12,[192] tA.Z. 5:1, tA.Z. 6:7,[193] tA.Z. 7:4, tA.Z. 7:6, tA.Z. 8:1,[194] tBekh. 2:1,[195] tAhil. 18:12.[196]
Joseph the Priest (1): TShab. 13:11.
Reuben (1): TShebu. 3:6.
Hanin (1): TAhil. 18:16.

The following chart divides the issues raised and the images of the gentile found in Tosefta's attributed *sugyot* by generation in an attempt to ascertain if certain images or topics cluster around one another in specific periods of times.

---

[178]Hidqa, Rabbi, Yosi, Eleazar, and Hananiah b. Gamliel also appear.
[179]Rabbi also appears.
[180]Aqiba also appears.
[181]Eliezer and Yosi b. Judah also appear.
[182]Simeon b. Gamliel also appears.
[183]Eliezer Hisma and Simeon b. Gamliel also appear.
[184]Hidqa, Eleazar b. Simeon, Rabbi, Yosi, and Hananiah b. Gamliel also appear.
[185]Meir also appears.
[186]Meir and Judah also appear.
[187]Meir also appears.
[188]Judah and Gamliel also appear.
[189]Meir also appears.
[190]Meir also appears.
[191]Meir also appears.
[192]Meir also appears.
[193]Philosopher questions sages in Rome.
[194]Rabbi also appears.
[195]Judah also appears.
[196]Rabbi, Judah, and Yosi also appear.

Pre-70

Source	Topic	Image
Ket. 3:2	Invasion of Jerusalem	S
A.Z. 1:1	Business in exilic community near their festivals	I
Shab. 1:22	Work begun before Sabbath	N
Pis. 1:7	Sale of leaven to gentiles	N
Bekh. 3:15	Consumption of firstling	N
Nid. 5:5	Blood of gentile women	N

70-135

Ter. 2:13	'Orlah in Syria	N
Shab. 7:11	Ways of Amorites	M/B
Shab. 7:25	Amorites are considerate	B
Shab. 13:14	Sabbath work benefit Israelite	N
Pis. 2:15	Give leaven to gentiles	N
Mo'ed 2:14	Seat by gentile shop on Sabbath	N
Mo'ed 2:15	" " " " " "	
A.Z. 4:9	Israelite wine in gentile containers	I/L
Ter. 1:14	Defile heave-offering	D/Df
Ket. 1:6	Defilement of captive women	S
Sanh. 13:2	Gentiles in world to come	N/Ph
Hul. 2:24	Gentile ruler/hegmon	P
Ahil. 18:7	Gentile dwelling-places	U
Par. 2:1	Purchase of Red Heifer	N
Ber. 2:13	Quaestor	P/D
Shab. 1:22	Work begun before Sabbath	N
Shab. 8:5	Living among gentiles	N
Pis. 1:7	Sell leaven to gentiles	N

Sheq. 1:7	Offerings given by gentiles	N
Git. 1:4	Writs in gentile registries/signed by gentiles	N/P
Bekh. 3:15	Consumption of firstling	N
A.Z. 6:14	Stones near Mercury	I
Ker. 1:17	Canaanite slave	N
Miq. 6:3	Immersion-pool in Rome	N/Df
Y.T. 2:6	Prohibition against preparing food for gentiles on holidays	N/dogs
A.Z. 5:2	Rings and seals with images	I
A.Z. 8:4	Noachite laws	N
A.Z. 8:5	" "	"
A.Z. 8:6	" "	"
A.Z. 8:7	" "	"
A.Z. 8:8	" "	"

135-160

Ber. 2:13	Quaestor	P/D
Pe. 3:5	Forgotten sheaves	N
Dem. 1:12	Demai/untithed	N
Dem. 5:21	Tithes	N
Qid. 5:11	Social status	N
B.Q. 4:3	Damages	N
A.Z. 1:4	Festivals/their definition	I
A.Z. 1:5	Business at fairs	I
A.Z. 2:5	Gentile amphitheater	I
A.Z. 2:8	Property in Syria	N
A.Z. 3:3	Midwives	I/D
A.Z. 3:12	Circumcision	D
A.Z. 1:1	Their repayment of loans on their festivals	I
Ber. 6:18	Blessing for not being	

	gentile	N
Pe. 4:1	Do not believe their poor	N/Ut
Pe. 4:20	Idolatry=not being just	I
Ter. 2:13	*'Orlah* in Syria	N
Ter. 7:20	Threaten Israelites	N/D
Shab. 7:1	Ways of Amorites	M/B
Shab. 7:2	" " "	" "
Shab. 7:3	" " "	" "
Shab. 7:6	" " "	" "
B.Q. 4:6	Ox kills gentile	N
Sanh. 12:4	Person kills gentile	N
A.Z. 1:21	Sell items related to idolatry	N/I
A.Z. 2:3	Sale of specific animals	N
A.Z. 2:4	Sale of fodder/grain/tree	N
A.Z. 3:19	Business at fair	I
A.Z. 4:11	Foodstuffs	N
A.Z. 5:2	Rings and seals with images	I
A.Z. 7:13	Leave wine on boat	I/L
Bekh. 2:1	Firstling	N
Ahil. 18:12	Gentiles' dwelling-places	U
Par. 2:1	Purchase of Red Heifer	N
Toh. 5:2	Urine	N
Pe. 2:9	*Pe'ah*	N
Pe. 3:12	Poor's gleaning	N
Dem. 4:25	Tithes/seventh year	N
Dem. 5:21	Tithes	N
Dem. 6:2	Tithes/heave-offering	N
Sot. 7:22	Take Israelite women	D
A.Z. 2:9	Rent fields to them	N
Zeb. 5:6	Gentiles' sacrifices at Temple	N
Nid. 9:14	Their corpses	N
Neg. 2:15	Bright spot on skin	N
Dem. 1:13	Storehouse/*demai*	N
Ter. 1:14	Defile heave-offering	D/Df
Shab. 7:23	Amorites are harshest	B

Pis. 1:7	Sell leaven to them	N
R.H. 2:12	Verse about their punishment	N
Yeb. 8:1	Marriage into priesthood	N/B
A.Z. 2:8	Sale and rental of property within Land of Israel	N
A.Z. 3:11	Circumcised slaves	N
A.Z. 3:19	Idols bought at fair	I
A.Z. 4:8	Food containing vinegar	I/L
Shab. 7:5	Saying "healing" not ways of Amorites	M/B
Shab. 7:11	Ways of Amorites	" "
Shab. 1:22	Work begun before Sabbath	N
Dem. 5:2	Do not believe gentiles	Ut
Dem. 6:1	Tithe	N
Ter. 1:15	Heave-offering	N
Ter. 4:12	Heave-offering	N
Ter. 4:13	Heave-offering	N
Shab. 13:13	Sea voyage on Sabbath	N
A.Z. 2:9	Do not rent bath-house to them	N
A.Z. 3:16	Sale of slaves to them	N
A.Z. 4:10	Skins belonging to them	N
Bekh. 2:5	Firstling	N
Bekh. 2:14	"	"
Shab. 7:24	Sodomites were considerate	B
A.Z. 3:4	Carrying weapons when walking with them	D
A.Z. 1:21	Sale of items for idolatry	I
A.Z. 2:3	Sale of horses to them	N

160-220

Dem. 5:2	Believing gentile produce-vendor	N/Ut

Ter. 4:12	Heave-offering	N
Ter. 4:13	Heave-offering	N
Ter. 4:14	Tithes/second tithes	N/Sm
Shab. 13:13	Sea-voyage on Sabbath	N
A.Z. 2:3	Sale of horses to them	N/D
A.Z. 5:4	Nullify their idols	I
A.Z. 8:1	Implements for use with wine	I/L
A.Z. 8:4	Noachite laws	N
A.Z. 8:5	" "	"
A.Z. 8:6	" "	"
A.Z. 8:7	" "	"
A.Z. 8:8	" "	"
Ahil. 18:12	Gentiles' dwellings	U
Dem. 6:7	Father's field from them	N/D
A.Z. 1:3	Working on their festivals	I
A.Z. 2:3	Sale of specific animals	N
A.Z. 4:6	Living abroad and eating at gentiles' banquet	I
A.Z. 5:2	Rings and seals with images	I
A.Z. 7:8	Preparing their wine	I/L
A.Z. 7:13	Leave wine on boat	I/L
Ter. 1:15	Heave-offering	N
Ahil. 18:7	Gentiles' dwelling-places/heave-offering	U/Df
Toh. 11:8	Grapes spread on ground	N
Shab. 13:9	Working for Israelite on Sabbath	N
Kip. 2:16	Saw blood on Temple-curtain	D
Git. 1:4	Writs in gentile registries signed by gentiles	N/P
Yeb. 14:7	Testimony concerning death	N
A.Z. 4:10	Skins belonging to them	N

| Dem. 6:7 | Father's field from them | N/D |
| A.Z. 2:7 | Their amphitheater | D |

Similar to the distribution of named *sugyot* we discovered in Mishnah, the most often named sages in Tosefta come from the generation immediately following the Bar Kokhba Revolt. Judah (24), Simeon b. Gamliel (14), Yosi (14), Meir (12), and Simeon (12) are the most frequently mentioned sages in pericopae in Tosefta which discuss the gentile. These five masters appear in fifty-five different passages. The generation immediately preceding the Bar Kokhba revolt is cited with about the same frequency as the generation which flourished at the time the Mishnah was edited. Gamliel (8), Aqiba (8), and Eliezer (6) are the most commonly cited of the twelve sages mentioned from the generation which ended with the fall of Bethar in 135ce. Rabbi (10) and Simeon b. Eleazar (6) are the two most frequently cited masters of the thirteen sages quoted from the generation which ended with the completion of the Mishnah. We find twenty-five *sugyot* from Rabbi's generation, and twenty-six from the generation preceding the Bar Kokhba uprising. Thus, both Mishnah and Tosefta agree that the masters most interested in dealing with problems relating to gentiles flourished immediately after the Bar Kokhba Revolt, 135-160ce.

Unlike Mishnah, however, Tosefta does contain some passages in which masters from different generations appear. The significance of this phenomenon is unclear. Furthermore, Tosefta, more than Mishnah, suggests that the concern with the gentile continued until the closure of Mishnah-Tosefta by the middle of the third century of the common era. However, both documents agree that the generation which flourished after the destruction of the Second Temple also had reason to deal with gentiles. Thus, the *sugyot* which contain traditions assigned to a rabbinic master conform to the pattern we would expect, for the frequency of these passages follows the contours of the influence and presence of gentiles in the Land of Israel.

Because Tosefta contains more assigned *sugyot* than Mishnah, we would expect a wider range of issues addressed in specific generations in the former than in the latter. For the most part, however, the pre-70 generation appears the same in both texts. Tosefta does contain one reference to the gentile as idolater, which does not appear in Mishnah during this generation, and the former alone contains a discussion of the sale of leaven to gentiles during Passover. However, the matter of the gentiles' dwelling-places is addressed in Mishnah during this generation, but not in Tosefta. Similarly, Tosefta does not contain the admonition that Israelites should pray for the welfare of the gentile government.

In Tosefta, there are thirty-one statements assigned to sages who lived during the period of 70-135, while there are only twenty such comments in Mishnah. Tosefta discusses the *'orlah* from gentile crops in Syria, while Mishnah discusses the dough-offering. The "ways of the Amorites" are first addressed in this generation in Tosefta, and Mishnah does not speak of the gentile in terms of biblical peoples until the next generation. In this generation, both texts first speak of gentiles working on the Sabbath for Israelites; but, Tosefta alone contains the narrative about sitting near a gentile's shop on the Sabbath. The issue of the gentiles' offering wine-libations to their gods is mentioned first during this generation in Tosefta; however, it is not raised until the next generation in Mishnah. Gentiles as defilers of heave-offering appears during this generation in both texts, while gentiles who defile their captive women appears only in Tosefta at this time. Similarly, the gentiles as rulers of the Land of Israel is first raised in Tosefta at this time, as is the problem of whether or not gentiles might inherit the world-to-come. As we saw above, the discussion of the uncleanness of the gentiles' dwelling-places first appears here in Tosefta, while it was raised in the previous generation in Mishnah. The problem of work begun before the Sabbath is assigned to this generation in Tosefta, although it is stated that it agreed with opinions of the Houses from the previous generation, and it is again mentioned by sages of the next generation, in this text. The sale of leaven to gentiles is again raised in this generation, as well as in the next period, while the issue is not assigned to any specific generation in Mishnah. Offerings given by gentiles are first raised during this generation in Tosefta, while it does not appear until the following generation in Mishnah. Tosefta continues the discussion of the consumption of firstlings in this generation, although Mishnah places it in only the previous one. The discussion of the stones near Mercury is assigned to this generation in both texts. During this period, Tosefta first raises the issue of rings and seals with images, and Mishnah deals with another aspect of this problem. Discussions of gentiles and immersion-pools occur in both collections during this time. The discussion of the Noachite rules first is assigned to this generation; however, it will be continued by those who lived 160-220. Tosefta alone contains the rule that an Israelite may not prepare food for a gentile on the former's holy days. Canaanite slaves are first mentioned in this generation in both texts. Both collections raise the issue of purchasing the Red Heifer; however, Tosefta continues the discussion in the next generation.

The gentile government is specifically mentioned again in the period from 135-160 in Tosefta, while it only seems to be implied in Mishnah during this time. Although Mishnah and Tosefta concentrate on different aspects of Israelite agricultural law, both contain most of their discussions of this issue during this period. Similarly, both collections assigned to this generation detailed discussions of gentile festivals, their definition, and the activity in which an Israelite may engage during the festivals. However, Tosefta alone includes references to the gentiles' fairs and amphitheaters. Although Tosefta discusses the problem of the wine-libations of the gentiles, this is a much more important topic for Mishnah during this period. During this generation, both texts raise the problem of seeking a gentile's medical help, but they do so in different ways. Gentiles' offerings are discussed during this generation in both texts. Tosefta alone spends time on the problem of selling real estate to gentiles at this time; however, both collections deal with the problem of selling other items to them during this period. However, the latter topic is more fully discussed in Tosefta. The problem of intermarriage appears only in Mishnah; however, Tosefta does know that for purposes of marriage gentiles have a different status from Israelites. In fact, Tosefta twice makes it clear that gentiles and Israelites represent two different segments of humankind. Firstlings are discussed in both texts during this generation. The untrustworthiness of the gentiles appears during this time in Tosefta alone. Similarly, Tosefta alone assumes that one should be careful when walking on a road with non-Israelites, and Tosefta also pictures the gentiles as posing a threat to Israelites. Problems of the purity laws with regard to gentiles are discussed with regard to several specific issues during this generation in Tosefta, while it does not appear in Mishnah at this time. Furthermore, Tosefta alone contains the prayer for not being a gentile, and it alone calls one who acts unjustly an idolater. Mishnah's concern with items found in towns with a mixed-population does not appear in Tosefta.

Mishnah assigns only two comments to the period 160-220, and both center on the issue of wine. Tosefta contains thirty-two statements attributed to masters from this period, so that we find a larger variety of topics under discussion. The issue of the agricultural gifts and the gentile is carried forward, as are discussions of the trustworthiness of gentiles, of selling horses and other animals to gentiles, of the Noachite laws, of the gentiles' dwellings, of the images on rings and seals, of wine and gentiles, of their working for the benefit of Israelites on the Sabbath, of Israelites' attending gentile amphitheaters, and of real estate transactions. The reference to gentile registries, which is attributed in Mishnah to the period of 135-160, is found in this generation in Tosefta. Similarly, the concern with a gentile's ability to testify to the death of an Israelite appears here in Tosefta, but in the period of 70-135 in Mishnah. The comments about working on gentile festivals, about living abroad being equated with idolatry, about seeing the blood on the Temple-curtain, and about the use of animal skins belonging to gentiles are attributed in Tosefta to sages of this period.

Several points become clear. First, there is a good deal of similarity between the agenda of any given generation recorded in Mishnah and that found in Tosefta. This is especially true of the pre-70 generation. Second, in contrast to the similarity between the texts, there is also some divergence, and the divergence increases as we move closer to the period in which the texts were finalized. Third, issues which may be assigned to only one period in Mishnah, appear in several generations in Tosefta. Fourth, when the two collection deal with similar issues, they may, but they need not, address the issue in the same way or with the same comments. Fifth, it appears to be impossible to demonstrate that issues which arose in one generation generated further discussions or formed the basis for comments on similar issues found in later periods. However, issues are discussed by more than one generation more often in Tosefta than in Mishnah. Sixth, because we have more *sugyot* in Tosefta than in Mishnah, the former collection contains a discussion of a broader range of issues than the latter.

While in general terms, the appearance of specific issues in Mishnah seemed to correspond to what we know of the social, political, and economic situation in Palestine during the first three centuries of the common era, when we examine the materials from Tosefta, this relationship becomes less clear, for several issues seem to be have been raised in Tosefta "earlier" than they were discussed in Mishnah. This means that if we review all of the material before us, it is difficult to learn much from analyzing the material by generations, for the two texts often do not assign their agenda to the same generations. Both texts exhibit an interest in the gentile, and both express this interest through a limit range of issues. However, it is not exactly the same range of issues, and even common matters are not always dealt in a similar manner. Each document had its own agenda, and that agenda determined what aspects of the Israelite-gentile interaction were covered and how they would be examined.

A note of caution is appropriate at this point. The distribution of the attributed sayings among the generations may not be significant, for it seems to correspond to the general distribution of sages which is found throughout Mishnah-Tosefta. That is, in general Mishnah-Tosefta contain more sayings attributed to the generation of 135-160 than to any other generation, so that the fact that the most of the discussions of the gentile are assigned to sages of this period may not have any relationship to the increased presence of the gentile in Palestine at that time. Rather, it simply may be the result of the general characteristics of these texts. Furthermore, Tosefta contains more comments assigned to sages of the period of 160-220 than does Mishnah, so that the increased references to the gentile in this period in Tosefta again may be the result of the nature of the text, and not of any relationship to the realities of the world at that time.[197]

----

[197]See Abraham Goldberg, "The Mishna--A Study Book of Halakha," in Shmuel Safrai (ed.), *The Literature of the Sages First Part: Oral Tora, Halakha, Mishna, Tosefta, Talmud, External Tractates* (Philadelphia: 1987), 215-222. Abraham Goldberg, "The Tosefta--Companion to the Mishna," in Safrai, 293-298.

Chapter Six:

The Land of Israel and the Gentiles

i

The preceding chapters examined the corpus of passages on the gentile *sugya* by *sugya*, and document by document. Until the present chapter, the individual pericopae were the focus of our attention. Information was collected and analyzed concerning the contents/contexts of the various pericopae, the literary forms in which the individual references were cast, and the generations to which the comments were attributed. The goal was to explain how each discussion of the gentile was included in Mishnah-Tosefta. It soon became evident that the pericopae which mention the non-Israelite were much like those which dealt with virtually any other topic. Like the discussions of the agricultural rules, the holy days, the cult, and the like, the sections on the gentile have been fully "rabbinized." For the most part, the pericopae which refer to the gentiles fit well into their contexts, contribute to the larger issues under consideration, are set in literary forms which commonly appeared with any number of other themes, and are attributed to the same variety of rabbis to whom comments on any number of other topics are also assigned. While the topics connected with the gentile in Mishnah evidence a correlation with what we know about the political, social, and economic conditions of Palestine in the first two centuries of the common era, the correlation became weaker when we moved to the *sugyot* in Tosefta, so that we could not claim that the "realities" of the world provide the reasons for the inclusion of the pericopae which discuss the non-Israelite. Furthermore, it is also possible that the distribution among the various generations is a result merely of the general characteristics of these texts, so that it has no relationship to the actual presence of the gentiles in the Land of Israel.

Our attention now moves from the questions about "how" these pericopae were created and included in Mishnah-Tosefta to the problem of "why" they appear in these documents. The obvious answer to this inquiry is that the Israelites confronted the gentiles in their daily life, so that the creators of Mishnah-Tosefta could not ignore them. While this is no doubt partially true, it does not completely answer our question. There are any number of issues with which the Israelites were confronted that were ignored by the compilers of Mishnah-Tosefta. These texts are not collections of statements on *every* relevant issue which confronted the rabbis or the common Israelite; rather, they are carefully constructed compilations with set agenda constructed for their own purposes. For example, given the fact that Palestine was ruled by the Romans, there is surprisingly little in Mishnah-Tosefta about Rome, her governmental agencies, or their procedures.[1] In addition, one need but review any of the topical outlines of Mishnah to conclude that only a few of the possible issues are addressed in this document, and even many of those which are addressed are done so in a circumscribed fashion.[2] Exactly why Mishnah was finally set in its present form remains an open question, for scholars have not been able to agree on reasons for its compilation. To the many plausible explanation set forth by scholars, for Mishnah's compilation,[3] one more should be added: It will be argued below, in Chapter Twelve, that Mishnah-Tosefta can be viewed as an attempt to establish the identity of the Israelite people as an ethnic group whose identity was derived mainly from its religious foundations.

In order to support the claim that the discussions of the gentiles serve to create a definition of the People Israel as an ethnic unit, we shall now look at Mishnah-Tosefta as whole documents organized around a finite number of ideas, and we shall analyze the pericopae which deal with the non-Israelite in terms of these symbols. The major symbols, concepts, or ideas around which this ethnic identity was formulated gave raise to the major divisions of Mishnah-Tosefta: The Land, the Periods of Holy Time, the People Israel, the Israelite Legal System, the Temple and its cult, and the Purity rules. When the *sugyot* which refer to the gentiles are examined in relationship to these major concepts, it becomes clear that not only the descriptions of the Israelites, but also the images of the non-Israelites, were constructed in terms of these concepts. The present chapter and those that follow demonstrate that the pericopae which deal with the gentile were designed with an eye to differentiating between the Is-

---

[1]Gunter Stemberger, "Die Beurteilung Roms in der rabbinischen Literatur," in Hildegard Temporini and Wolfgang Haase (eds.), *Aufstieg und Niedergang der römischen Welt* (New York: 1979), II.19.2, 338-396.

[2]Jacob Neusner, *Judaism: The Evidence of Mishnah* (Chicago: 1981), 352-379. Adin Steinsaltz, *The Essential Talmud*, translated by Chaya Galai (New York: 1976), 279-283. Alan J. Avery-Peck, *Mishnah's Division of Agriculture: A History and Theology of Seder Zeraim* (Chico: 1985).

[3]Jacob Neusner, *The Modern Study of the Mishnah* (Leiden: 1973).

raelites and the non-Israelites in terms of these basic ideas. The definition of the People Israel was partially designed in terms of these symbols by distinguishing between the ways in which Israelites and gentiles relate to them.

ii

A major issue addressed by Mishnah-Tosefta is the relationship of the People Israel to the Land of Israel. Our understanding of this matter is sharpened by the discussions of the manner in which gentiles relate to the Land and its holiness. The theme of the special relationship of the People Israel to the Land of Israel runs throughout the Hebrew Bible and the texts of rabbinic Judaism.[4] This unique association between the Israelites and the Land was established from the outset of the Patriarchal history, when God told Abram to *"go forth from your native Land and from your father's house to the land that I will show you."*[5]

Orlinsky views the Land as "the cornerstone, the essence of the exclusive contract into which God and each of Israel's three progenitors voluntarily entered. . . . Were it not for the Land that God promised on oath to Abraham and to Isaac and to Jacob and to their heirs forever, there would be no contract."[6] However, as Davies notes, the borders of the Land of Israel are never precisely defined. He concludes from this that "it [the Land of Israel] is an idea as well as a territory. It seems always to have carried ideal overtones without geographical and political precision."[7] Furthermore, because the territory which

----

[4]On the latter, see the collection of rabbinic sayings on the Land of Israel in "Aretz-Israel" in Shlomo J. Zevin (ed.), *Encyclopedia Talmudica: A Digest of Halachic Literature and Jews law from the Tannaitic Period to the Present Time Alphabetically Arranged* David B. Klein (trans.), Harry Freedman (ed.) (Jerusalem: 1978), III, 1-68.

[5]Gen. 12:1.

[6]Harry M. Orlinsky, "The Biblical Concept of the Land of Israel" in Lawrence A. Hoffman (ed.), *The Land of Israel: Jewish Perspectives* (Notre Dame: 1986), 34. Orlinsky notes that the blessings of Isaac and Jacob "are marked by one major and most significant fact, namely, that Isaac and Jacob are to receive the land of Canaan whereas Ishmael and Esau must be content with another region;" 34. Further the changes of the names of two of the Patriarch "[are] associated with the Land;" 36. In addition, Orlinsky suggests that "the transaction involving the burial place of the patriarchs and matriarchs too presupposes the special status of the Land;" 37. With the death of Jacob, Orlinsky claims, "the covenant with God ceases to be individual, and becomes national;" 37. Orlinsky also states that the biblical laws, "from the Exodus on," are structured so as to emphasize "getting to and into the Promised Land and on the kind of society to be set up there;" 38f.

[7]William D. Davies, *The Gospel and the Land: Early Christianity and Jewish Territorial Doctrine* (Berkeley and Los Angeles: 1974), 17, n. 13.

God gave to Abram and his descendants originally belonged to other people, "the land they [Abram's descendants] are to possess is to be theirs by divine authority."[8]

Although the Bible knows that the Land of Israel belonged to other peoples, such as the Canaanites, it also contains the belief that ultimately the Land belonged to YHWH and that it was his to dispose of.[9] In order to acknowledge YHWH's ownership of the Land and their stewardship of his property, specific obligations were laid upon the People Israel when they finally took possession of their gift. They had to give from their crops, especially from the first-fruits,[10] to YHWH or his representatives,[11] they had to support the poor from their crops,[12] they had to keep the various crops of the Land separate,[13] they had to allow the Land to rest,[14] and they could use certain fruits only after the trees or vines had matured.[15]

In addition, the People Israel's successful occupation of the Land was dependent upon their adhering to YHWH's requirements concerning their activity, which were set forth in his Revelation.[16] Biblical statements concerning the necessity that the People Israel adhere to YHWH's Revelation in order to

----

[8]Davies, 17.

[9]Davies, 27ff. Davies lists several different biblical ideas which point to YHWH's ownership of the Land of Israel: 1) "The earth of Israel was not tribal property, but was given by Yahweh for cultivation by lot," 27-28; 2) "The cultic statements about the harvest are to be understood in the light of Yahweh's ownership of the land," 28; 3) "Yahweh's possession of the land is acknowledged in the commandment that the land should keep a Sabbath to the Lord," 28-29; 4) "Yahweh's possession of the land was expressed in terms of 'holiness,' a conception which in its origin had little, if anything, to do with morality, but rather denoted a relationship of separation for or consecration to a god;" 29.

[10]Ex. 23:19, Ex. 34:26, Deut. 26:1-11.

[11]Lev. 19: 23-25, Lev. 22:10-14, Lev. 27:30-31, Num. 15:17-21, Num. 18:8, Num. 18:11-12, Num. 18:21-32, Deut. 12:6, Deut. 14:22-27, Deut. 18:4, Deut. 26:12-15.

[12]Lev. 19:9-10, Lev. 23:22, Deut. 24:19-22, Deut. 14:28-29, Deut. 26:12.

[13]Lev. 19:19, Deut. 22:9-11.

[14]Ex. 23:10-11, Lev. 25:1-7, Deut. 15:1-3, Deut. 15:9-10.

[15]Lev. 19:23. These were dietary rules, for if the proper regulations were not followed, the crops of the Land belonged to God and could not be used by human beings. Scripture assumes that these rules applied to all humans who properly occupied the Land, and even Mishnah assumes that some of these rules should be followed by all people.

[16]Davies states: "Deuteronomy . . . fused together the promise of the land made to the early patriarchs and the tradition of the giving of the Law at Sinai. The relationship of the commandments to the land is regarded in Deuteronomy as twofold. On the one hand, the commandments are regulatory, that is, they are intended to provide guidance for the government of the land, for the conduct of the cultus, and for the arrangements demanded by the settlement. On the other hand, the commandments are conditional; that is, only if they are observed can the land be received and possessed;" 20.

reside, successfully and peacefully, on the Land[17] were included in the rabbis' liturgy, recited twice daily as part of the *Shema'*.[18] Thus, Israel's living on the Land became the visible expression that she was fulfilling her duty to YHWH.[19]

In Mishnah-Tosefta,[20] as in Scripture, the People Israel's duties to YHWH which resulted from their living on the Land find concrete expression in the ways the People must deal with the crops which grow in the holy soil. In Mishnah-Tosefta and the Bible, three entities are important for these regulations: YHWH, the Land of Israel, and the People Israel. In Mishnah-Tosefta, however, we witness a major shift from the centrality of YHWH, found in the Torah, to the centrality of the Israelites themselves.

In Mishnah-Tosefta, the process of designating gifts for the poor begins when the *landowner* indicates his desire for the produce, or it comes into play when the *poor* person makes known his wishes and need for sustenance.[21]

----

[17]Deut. 11:13-21.

[18]MBer. 1:1-3 assume that the *Shema'* was to be recited twice daily. MBer. 2:2 assumes that Deut. 11:13f was part of the *Shema'*.

[19]Cf., Davies, 31; Orlinsky, 38-40. Orlinsky goes on to show that the importance of living in the Land according to YHWH's law was central to the Prophets, as well as to the author of Deuteronomy; Orlinsky, 40-55.

[20]The relationship between Mishnah and Tosefta is complex. Neusner argues that Tosefta is composed of three different types of material: 1) Those passages which serve as a commentary to Mishnah and which cite it *verbatim*, 2) those statements which appear autonomous of Mishnah but which respond to comments in Mishnah, and 3) those *sugyot* which are completely autonomous of Mishnah and which "constitute statements independent of the base-document;" Jacob Neusner, *The Tosefta* (Atlanta: 1986), ix. However, Tosefta's agenda is similar to that of Mishnah, which it complements. For this reason, at this point, I have juxtaposed comments from both texts.

[21]Alan Avery-Peck, *Mishnah's Division of Agriculture: A History and Theology of Seder Zeraim* (Chico: 1985), 35-36. The Torah maintains that the Israelite poor have a right to part of the produce grown within the Land of Israel. Lev. 19:9 and Lev. 23:22 discuss the *peah*, the corners of the field, and the gleanings. The forgotten sheaf appears in Deut. 24:19, the separated grapes in Lev. 19:10, the defective clusters in Lev. 19:10 and Deut. 24:21, and the poorman's tithe in Deut. 26:12. No one else except the poor may eat this produce; Roger Brooks, *Support for the Poor in the Mishnaic Law of Agriculture: Tractate Peah* (Chico: 1983), 17. Brooks argues that Mishnah's discussion of these gifts is based on an analogy between the priests and the poor: "God owns the entire Land of Israel . . . and a portion of each crop must be paid to him . . . . God claims that which is owed him and then gives it to those under his special care, the poor and the priests;" Brooks, 18. Because the poor have no claim on the landowner for support, the householder does not take as active a part in the separation of the gifts for the poor as he does in the separation of the priestly gifts; Brooks, 19. The landowner must designate what he intends for the poor; however, his obligations are not fulfilled until the poor takes possession of what is due him; Avery-Peck, 25, 36. Whether it is the poor person or the landowner, humans remain the primary actors.

Mishnah assumes that the tithes were a tax which the Israelites had to pay YHWH for the privilege of using the crops grown on his land,[22] and it seeks "to determine, and then regulate, the respective claims of man and God to the produce of the Land of Israel."[23]   It concludes that the *Israelite* is the key actor in determining when a crop needs to be tithed.[24] The second tithe is a Mishnaic creation, based, to be sure, on a particular reading of Scripture, and Mishnah's major concern is to regulate the *farmer's* activity with regard to the sacred produce which must be taken to the Holy City, Jerusalem.[25] Although the heave-offering was given to the priests for their maintenance, Mishnah is little interested in the priests. Rather, it focuses on what the *Israelite* must know to fulfill properly his obligation to give heave-offering.[26] Mishnah concludes that the

----

[22]Lev. 27:30 states: *All tithes from the land, whether seed from the ground or fruit from the tree, belong to YHWH.*

[23]Mishnah's questions revolve around the issues of when a crop is sufficiently grown to be able to be used as a tithe and when the tithes must actually be paid. Mishnah takes the position that crops are suitable for use as tithes as soon as they become ripe, for this is when they assume value to the grower; however, the tithes need not be paid until the farmer actually claims the crop as his own personal property. A considerable amount of time may elapse between the time that a crop ripens and the moment that the farmer actually claims possession of the crop, and during this period the crop's status is ambiguous: The crop is not yet sacred food, for it has not been given to the priests, nor can it be used as common food, for God's portion has not been removed. Mishnah solves this problem by ruling that crops in this ambiguous status may not be eaten in meals. Mishnah spends the bulk of its time dealing with the specifics of this solution. See Martin S. Jaffee, *Mishnah's Theology of Tithing: A Study of Tractate Maaserot* (Chico: 1981), 1-4.

[24]"God himself plays no active role in establishing when the produce must be tithed. . . . Human actions and intentions . . . move God to affect the world. God's claims against the Land's produce . . . are only reflexes of those very claims on the part of Israelite farmers. . . . God's interest in his share of the harvest . . . is first provoked by the desire of the farmer for the ripened fruit of his labor;" Jaffee, 4-5.

[25]Deut. 14:22-26 speak of a tithe which the Israelite farmer must set aside and take to Jerusalem to eat, and this is the basis of Mishnah's discussion of the second tithe. Because this tithe may be eaten only in Jerusalem, the holy city, Mishnah's sages assume that the tithe itself is holy; therefore, Mishnah is concerned with describing the special restrictions which concern the use of this sacred produce. "Mishnah's authorities want to insure [sic] that the farmer who designates produce as second tithe does not lose or destroy any part of it through carelessness. The full amount of what he sets aside must be eaten in Jerusalem." Mishnah defines "the specific uses the farmer may make of the produce" and rules that "the farmer [must] receive the full value of his consecrated produce when he sells it;" Peter J. Haas, *A History of the Mishnaic Law of Agriculture: Tractate Maaser Sheni* (Chico: 1980), 2.

[26]"The tractate prescribes how Israelites are to designate a portion of their produce to be heave-offering, and outlines their responsibility to protect it from common use until they convey it to the priests;" Alan J. Peck, *The Priestly Gift in Mishnah: A Study of Tractate Terumot* (Chico: 1981), 1. From Num. 18:8-13, Mishnah derives the facts that the heave-offering is holy and must be eaten in a state of cultic purity only by priests and members of their household. Thus, Mishnah's discussions of how the Israelite must separate and protect the heave-offering complete and complement the Torah's description. However, Mishnah achieves its goal of making it possible for an Israelite to fulfill his Scriptural obligation of giving the heave-offering to the priest by focusing on two

produce is not inherently holy, for it is the common *Israelite* who "has the power to cause produce to be deemed holy" and to transform common produce into sanctified produce through his intentions.[27] The *Israelite farmer* is also the one who determines whether or not crops planted together violate the biblical prohibition against planting "mixed-kinds" in a single field.[28]

Mishnah's discussions of the Sabbatical year derive from the biblical passages on the topic, to the extent that the order of topics in Mishnah follows the order of their presentation in the Bible; however, Mishnah's theory of the Sabbatical year is different from that of Scripture. For Mishnah, *Israelite farmers* play the major role in determining how the specific restrictions concerning the Sabbatical year are to be applied.[29] Finally, Mishnah's concern for doubt-

----

related issues: The process of sanctification and the effect which this sanctified produce has on un-sanctified produce with which it may be mixed; Peck, 2.

[27]Peck, 3. Mishnah's second major issue is derived from the fact that the heave-offering becomes holy, not when it is handed over to the priest, but when the farmer makes his intentions known. Therefore, sanctified produce remains in the possession of the commoner who must now protect it, so that it is not used for any purpose other than the maintenance of the priesthood; Peck, 4-5.

[28]"[M]an . . . both defines what constitutes a class [of produce] and determines how to keep the different classes distinct from one another. Man thus imposes upon an otherwise disorderly world limits and boundaries which accord with human perception [sic] of order and regularity;" Irving Mandelbaum, *A History of the Mishnaic Law of Agriculture: Kilayim, Translation and Exegesis* (Chico: 1982), 1. The commingling of different types crops "is prohibited only if the resultant mixture appears to man to contain a confusion of kinds, but not if the different kinds are arranged in an orderly manner." While it is concerned with keeping different types of plants from commingling, Mishnah focuses on ways in which one can keep separate distinct classes of plants which grow together; Mandelbaum, 3. See Samuel Cooper, "The Laws of Mixture: An Anthropological Study in Halakhah," in Harvey E. Goldberg (ed.), *Judaism Viewed From Within and From Without: Anthropological Studies* (Albany: 1987), 55-74.

[29]"Mishnah focuses its attention on the impact of Israelites' actions upon the restrictions of the Sabbatical year;" Louis E. Newman, *The Sanctity of the Seventh Year: A Study of Mishnah Tractate Shebiit* (Chico: 1983), 17. When farmers work their land during the sixth year, they set in motion the restrictions pertaining to the seventh year. "By taking into account the deeds of Israelite farmers and their long-term impact upon the land Mishnah moves beyond the strictly calendrical conception of the Sabbatical year presented in Leviticus. . . . [I]n Mishnah's view Israelites . . . play a role in determining when the restrictions of the Sabbatical year begin to take effect;" Newman, 18. Mishnah assigns to the farmer "an important role in determining what farmers may not do during the seventh year . . ." and "claim[s] that Israelites . . . play an active part in sanctifying their land;" Newman, 18-19. In the Torah, God is the sole arbitrator of these issues. While not denying that the Land is God's and holy because He willed it to be holy, Mishnah maintains that "the sanctity of the seventh year is activated and regulated by the thoughts and deeds of the community of Israel;" Newman, 19. Cf., Zvi Zohar, "The Consumption of Sabbatical Year Produce in Biblical and Rabbinic Literature," in Goldberg, 75-106.

fully tithed produce, *demai*-produce, which is not found in the Bible, revolves solely around *human* activity.[30]

The centrality of the Israelites is important in Mishnah-Tosefta's treatment of the agricultural gifts, for these documents seem to understand themselves as a guide for Israelites who wish to be true inheritors of the Torah's teachings. The Torah was given to the Israelites at Sinai, and the obligation to fulfill its precepts devolves upon those who received it. Therefore, Mishnah-Tosefta explain, in detail, how Israelites are to fulfill what their authors understand to be the precepts of the Torah. However, the framers of Mishnah-Tosefta also know that non-Israelites inhabit YHWH's Holy Land, till her soil, and enjoy the benefits of her fertility. For this reason, Mishnah-Tosefta cannot totally ignore the gentile, and they must wrestle with the problem of the holiness inherent in the Land, even when she is inhabited by and worked by those who do not fall under the Torah's dicta or recognize her teachings about the Land's sanctity. Mishnah-Tosefta's point seems to be that because the Land is sacred independently of who lives on her or works her, all of her inhabitants should respond to her holiness in some way. However, because the Israelites enjoy a special relationship to YHWH, and therefore to the Land of Israel which YHWH

---

[30]Produce of the Land cannot be properly consumed during a meal until one knows for sure that it has been tithed. A question arises with regard to produce about which one does not have certain knowledge that it has been tithed. One of the major factors which gives rise to this problem is that the framers of Mishnah assume that those who would eat only properly tithed crops live among and do business with those who do not share their concerns and who may not have followed properly the regulations concerning tithing; Richard S. Sarason, *A History of the Mishnaic Law of Agricultural Section Three: A Study of Tractate Demai, Part One* (Leiden: 1979), 1-2. While acknowledging Mishnah's interpretation of Scripture's rules concerning the removal of God's portion from the produce of the Land, tractate *Demai* establishes its own procedures for removing God's gifts from the produce about which one is uncertain that it has been properly tithed. Sarason, 9, outlines Mishnah's requirements concerning how much must be given for each gift: heave-offering, first tithe, heave-offering of the tithe, second tithe, poorman's tithe, and dough-offering. Mishnah assumes that all Israelites separate the heave-offering at the threshing-floor and also remove the first tithe. These, therefore, need not be separated from *demai*-produce. However, one does need to "designate" the first tithe within the produce. If the Levite wishes to make a claim on the *demai*-produce, he must demonstrate that he has not received his share. The heave-offering of the tithe must be removed from *demai*-produce, as must the dough-offering. The second tithe must at least be "designated," and in the third and sixth year of the Sabbatical cycle, the poorman's tithe must also be "designated." "Taken as a whole, only those tithes which a non-priest is forbidden to eat . . . must be separated from *dema'i*-produce and given to their rightful recipient. The preeminent concern expressed in this tithing procedure, then, is not to violate the taboo against eating a priestly offering;" Sarason, 10. Notably, then, contrary to Scripture's interest, Mishnah does not focus on whether or not the priests and Levites actually get their share. The offerings must be designated and separated, not delivered.

has given them, they react to the Land's holiness in ways different from those who do not share in this covenant with YHWH. In brief, the difference between those who accept YHWH and His Torah and those who do not is evidenced in the unique ways each group responds to the Land's sacred nature. And, in turn, the distinction between the two groups is reinforced by the different ways in which they take the Land's sacred nature into account in their daily activity.

On the one hand, Mishnah-Tosefta find it easy to distinguish between Israelites and non-Israelites with reference to *some* of the agricultural gifts, as well as for the laws of the Sabbatical year and for the produce set aside for the poor. Israelites are responsible for taking these matters into account and acting properly in relation to them, while the gentile is not. On the other hand, the problem is more complex with regard to other agricultural issues. For example, the requirement to allow a tree to mature for four years applies to all trees, those which were planted by Israelites, and those which were planted by gentiles. Similarly, some sages held that gentiles could separate a valid heave-offering from their crops, just like Israelites.

Summary: Mishnah-Tosefta, following the Bible, accept the sacred quality of the Land of Israel and believe that this is a result of YHWH's special relationship to the it. Furthermore, the covenant between the People Israel and YHWH is concretized in the rules which regulate the ways in which the former deal with the Land and her crops. For these reasons, the Land becomes one of the central elements in the definition of the People Israel in Mishnah-Tosefta. However, non-Israelites also live on the Land and work her soil. Because the Land is holy no matter who works her, Mishnah-Tosefta had to regulate how the non-Israelite should respond to the Land's holiness. Because Israelites stood in a different relationship to YHWH and his Land from the gentiles, Mishnah-Tosefta sought to mark this difference through their discussions of the gentiles and the Israelite agricultural rules. These discourses resulted from the different relationship which the gentiles and the Israelites had with YHWH, and the regulations stated in these documents served to reinforce these distinct relationships. Mishnah-Tosefta could not ignore the gentiles when the former discussed the Israelite agricultural rules, but they dealt with the gentiles from the points of view of their non-Israelite nature and the inherent holiness of the Land of Israel.

iii

In order to illustrate the claims made above, let us turn to an analysis of the discussions of the agricultural rules and the gentiles. Several of our passages assume that gentiles are distinguished from Israelites by the fact that only the latter are obligated to carry out the Torah's demands with regard to its agricultural rules. In general, gentiles need not separate the required gifts for the poor, observe the laws which prohibit the growing of "mixed-kinds," or separate the dough-offering. These categories are similar in that the rabbis' teachings on these subjects were not based solely on the idea that the Land is inherently holy. The gifts for the poor are considered to be an internal communal affair, according to which Israelites are required to provide sustenance and support for one another. The rules of "mixed-kinds" derived from the rabbis' conception of an ideal, well-ordered world, and not only from the holiness of the soil. And, the dough-offering was required only during the production of the dough, after the grain had been removed from the holy soil.[31] Therefore, rules connected to these issues were irrelevant to the gentile, for the regulations partially reflected ideas to which gentiles did not have to respond. From the point of view of these matters, the gentile was a non-Israelite, and these topics were applied to only members of the Israelite group.

The requirement to leave the corners of a field for the Israelite poor[32] falls upon only Israelites,[33] who must perform an intentional act of designating

----

[31]One key factor in determining that dough is subject to the requirement to separate the dough-offering is that the grain from which the dough is made is subject to leavening; Avery-Peck, 305. The dough becomes liable for the offering when the grain is made into dough, and it remains subject to this requirement even if the dough is not baked into bread, as long as the amount of dough is equal to that which is normally made into bread; Avery-Peck, 306.

[32]TPe. 3:1 rules that Israelites should not designate the agricultural gifts for the gentile poor.

[33]If a gentile harvested his field and then converted, he is not required to leave the produce for the poor, for he was not an Israelite when he harvested the crop, mPe. 4:6. TPe. 2:10 makes the same point in a different way. If a gentile dies and Israelites divide his property, the Israelite who takes possession of the crops attached to the ground must make all of the agricultural gifts. On the other hand, the Israelite who takes possession of produced which had already been harvested is not liable for the offerings. This much of the text is clear; however, the rest of the *sugya* presents a problem. The passage continues by ruling that if an Israelite takes possession of standing corn, he is liable for tithing the produce, but not for the gifts to the poor. Exactly how the standing corn differs from the crops "attached to the ground" is unclear. Lieberman attempts to harmonize the texts by explaining the anonymous opinion in Tosefta in terms of R. Hisda's view in yMa. 1:1; Venice 48c. Hisda rules that if one declared the standing corn ownerless and then purchased it and separated the heave-offering, it is a valid heave-offering. Similarly, if one separated the heave-offering from the standing corn before it was declared ownerless, it is a valid heave-offering. Lieberman argues that in Hisda's view if one declared a field ownerless and then purchased the crop while it was attached to

the field's unharvested corners for the poor. The gentile could not designate gifts for the poor *in fulfillment of the Torah's demands.*[34] This does not mean, of course, that gentiles could not leave gifts for the poor. Rather, while a gentile may allow poor Israelites to gather the gleanings, the forgotten sheaves, or the produce from the corners of his fields, he does so for reasons other than those of Israelites. In any event, the crops do not become "special;" they are considered to be common produce, and the Israelite must remove the tithes from them before they can be used for food,[35] unless the gentile has declared the field owner-less property.[36] Because a farmer's employees have the responsibility to leave the gifts for the poor on his behalf, as agents, gentile workers were not to be hired to harvest an Israelite's field.[37] For some,[38] produce grown by gentiles is different from crops owned and grown by Israelites, because the crops' status is

----

the ground, the tithes must be separated from the crop; Saul Lieberman, *Tosefta Ki-fshutah: A Comprehensive Commentary on the Tosefta Order Zera'im, Part I* (New York: 1955), 150-151. Brooks argues that Lieberman's distinction between "attached to the ground" and "standing corn" should be rejected, for elsewhere, e.g. tPe. 2:9, "standing corn" is treated the same as "attached to the ground" in the present *sugya*; Brooks, 79. Both Brooks and Lieberman agree that the *halakhah* does not follow the last anonymous ruling in this text, a ruling which Lieberman claims agrees with Hisda's view.

[34]If a gentile harvests an Israelite's field without the latter's knowledge or permission, the corners need not be left unharvested for the poor, MPe. 2:7. Lowe, Paris, Naples, Kaufman, and Parma have gentile, as does Solomon Adeni. The Rom text, Bartinoro, Akiba Iggar, Tosafot Anshei Sham, and Tosafot Hadashim read Kutim, which is likely a scribal correction. Although Albeck argues that the text discusses a gentile's field, Bartinoro, Israel Lipschuetz, Sholom Igger, Maimonides and Samson b. Abraham of Sens seem correct in their claim that the issue is a gentile who harvests an Israelite's field on his own accord. Albeck's interpretation does not make sense in this context; Hanokh Albeck, *The Six Orders of the Mishnah: Order Zeraim* (Tel Aviv: 1957), 45. Similarly, if an Israelite sold his field or vineyard to a gentile to harvest, the gifts for the poor need not be set aside, tPe. 2:9 and tPe. 3:12. These texts closely parallel each other. On the other hand, if the gentile sold his field to an Israelite to harvest, the gifts must be given. If a field is jointly owned by a gentile and an Israelite, the anonymous text in Tosefta rules that only the Israelite's share is liable for the gifts to the poor. In both texts, Simeon rules that the field is exempt from the requirement of the gifts for the poor. In tPe. 2:9, the anonymous text explains that this is the case only if the gentile objects to the Israelite's giving the gifts.

[35]MMa. 1:1 states that whatever is used for food, no matter who grows it, must be tithed before it can be eaten.

[36]MPe. 4:9 and tPe. 2:11 have similar rulings. MPe. 1:6 states that produce from owner-less property does not need to be tithed.

[37]TPe. 3:1. There may be several reasons for this statement. First, gentiles cannot be expected to fulfill a requirement about which they are unconcerned or ignorant. Second, even if they do fulfill requirement, we have no guarantee that they will do it properly. Third, a gentile cannot serve as an Israelite's agent, mTer. 1:1.

[38]Designated as "sages" in this text.

related to the owner's obligation to give the gifts to the poor. Therefore, one sheaf of grain may remove another sheaf from the category of "forgotten sheaves"[39] only if they are the same type of grain and only if both grains were grown by an Israelite. Meir, on the other hand, allows different types of grains to affect each other, and he believes a gentile's sheaf can "protect" one grown by an Israelite.[40] In brief, the *obligation* to leave the gifts for the poor fell upon Israelites alone, who had to support the members of their group; it was not required of gentiles, who were under no obligation to help out needy Israelites.[41] Although in the Torah these gifts probably were related to YHWH's ownership of the Land and his concern for the poor,[42] to the authors of Mishnah-Tosefta, this has become a community obligation which relates to the nature of the group, independently of the holy status of the soil and the crops that grow in it. Furthermore, it becomes a means of building group solidarity and interdependence, and this probably explains why the gentiles are not obligated to separate these gifts.

The laws of "mixed-kinds" can be approached from two different points of departure: If the *sugya* focuses on the *gentile*, the laws of "mixed-kinds"[43] do not apply, because gentiles are not obligated to adhere to Israelite law. Therefore, if a gentile produces a hybrid tree or plant, an Israelite may take a shoot or a seed from the tree and plant it, even though the Israelite himself was forbidden from creating the hybrid.[44] The laws of "mixed-kinds" have not been violated, because a gentile, not an Israelite, produced the hybrid. As if to underscore the ruling that an Israelite may in no way violate the laws of "mixed-kinds," we read that an Israelite may not aid another person in violating the agricultural rules, so that one Israelite may not help another Israelite grow "mixed-

----

[39]MPe. 6:6-8.

[40]Sages ignore the issue of the gentile; however, one can deduce that only "like affects like," so that a sheaf of a gentile's crop has no affect on a sheaf of an Israelite's produce; Brooks, 110-114.

[41]Requiring Israelites alone to leave these gifts for the poor would not have been difficult based on the biblical text. The Torah consistently speaks of leaving the gifts for the poor during *your* harvesting of *your* field: Lev. 19:9-10, Lev. 23:22, Deut. 24:19-22.

[42]Lev. 19:10 and Lev. 23:22 explain that the gifts should be left for the people because *I am YHWH your God.* Deut. 24:19 and Deut. 14:29 state that the crops should be left in the field *so that YHWH your God will bless all of the works of your hands.* Deut. 24:22 states that *you shall remember that you were a slave in the Land of Egypt; therefore, I commanded you to do this thing.*

[43]Lev. 19:19 and Deut. 22:9-11.

[44]TKil. 2:15.

kinds" in the latter's field, nor may an Israelite aid a gentile's growing of "mixed kinds" in the latter's field.[45]

By contrast, if the pericope begins from the point of view of the *holiness of the Land*, even gentiles should not violate the laws of "mixed-kinds,"[46] for from this perspective, the restrictions pertain to the Land, independently of the individuals who work her. This is underscored by the ruling that if a gentile's field is not considered part of the Land of Israel, an Israelite may aid him in planting "mixed-kinds."[47]

The concern with "mixing of kinds," according to Cooper, is "an indigenous category, which appears often in the cultural repertoire of the Jews. . . ."[48] Cooper writes that the Jewish "legal system recognizes that certain mixtures are a problem *for Jews* [italics mine] and need to be addressed formally."[49] From the point of view of the category of "mixed kind," the discussions in Mishnah-Tosefta present the topic as a category of concern to only the Israelites. The gentile, in general, need not be concerned with "mixed-kinds" because that concern is based on the Israelites' view of the world and their "well-defined system of classification [in which] the combination of opposites may be perceived as threatening the stability of the whole system,"[50] a problem of no import to the non-Israelite.

Because the dough-offering is taken from the product produced from the grain which has been *removed* from the holy soil, the obligation to separate the dough-offering is incumbent upon Israelites alone. The determination of whether or not the dough or its leavening agent[51] is subject to the removal of the dough-offering depends on who owns the dough at the point that offering

----

[45]Lieberman argues that because a gentile cannot own property within the Land of Israel, an Israelite cannot assist him in growing diverse-kinds; Lieberman, *Zera'im II*, 620.

[46]This issue comes up in the context of a discussion of whether or not Syria is considered part of the Holy Land; therefore, it is clear that the issue is the sacred nature of the Land, not the status of the gentile, tTer. 2:13.

[47]TKil. 2:16. The *sugya* refers to two towns, Bet Anah and Emah, which Lieberman places to the north on the east side of the Jordan river; Lieberman, *Zera'im, II*, 620-621. Mandelbaum, 143-144; Peck, 124. Cf., mQid. 1:9.

[48]Cooper, 56.

[49]Cooper, 57-58.

[50]Cooper, 59.

[51]If an Israelite owns a bakery, the dough-offering must be removed, even if the workers are gentiles. On the other hand, if the gentile owns the bakery, the dough-offering need not be removed, even if the workers are Israelites; tHal. 1:3.

must be removed.[52] Even if a gentile separates a dough-offering, it is eaten by non-priests, for it is not considered to have attained the sacred status of a dough-offering.[53]

It would not have been difficult for our authors to see in the biblical text a connection between the dough-offering and the People Israel, for YHWH tells Moses *to speak to the Children of Israel. . . .: When* you *come into the Land into which I shall bring* you, *and when* you *eat from the bread of the land . . . . The first of* your *dough* you *shall separate . . . .*[54] Because the Bible explicitly states that this rule applies to the Israelites and their dough and because the offering is taken from dough and not from something which grows in the holy soil, it is understandable why the gentile is not obligated to bring the dough-offering. In addition, the fact that the offering has been removed from Israelites' dough marks their dough products as distinct from those made by gentiles. However, this latter fact would have been evident to only Israelites.

Although the laws concerning the Sabbatical year[55] are related to the holiness of the Land,[56] the gentile is not required to observe these regulations,[57] perhaps because the Sabbatical year parallels the Sabbath, which the gentile also does not observe.[58] If a gentile worked his field during the seventh

----

[52]If a gentile gave an Israelite dough to prepare for him, the dough-offering need not be separated, for the dough belongs to the gentile. If a gentile gave the dough to an Israelite as a gift, the Israelite is responsible for separating the offering only if he received the dough before it was rolled out, thus becoming liable for the offering. Finally, if a gentile and an Israelite prepared their dough together, the Israelite must separate the dough-offering only if his portion is the amount from which the dough-offering must be taken; mHal. 3:5. MHal. 3:6 makes the same point by speaking about a convert. If the dough were already rolled out before the gentile converted, he need not remove the offering after he converted; however, if he rolled out the dough after he converted, he must separate the offering. Cf., tHal. 2:12.

[53]THal. 2:6, tTer. 4:13.
[54]Num. 15:17-21.
[55]Lev. 25:1-7.
[56]There are discussions concerning a gentile's relationship to the Sabbatical year in Syria, but these revolve around the issue of whether or not Syria is part of the Land of Israel, or whether or not a gentile may actually own a parcel of the Holy Land.
[57]The assumption that gentiles do not need to observe the restrictions of the seventh year is carried forward in the ruling that a potter may sell a limited number of vessels to Israelites during the Sabbatical year because each Israelite can process only a small number of grapes and olives which he may gather from ownerless property. If the potter sells him more containers, he encourages him to gather more than he is permitted. On the other hand, the potter may sell as many containers as he wishes to gentiles or to Israelites living outside the Land of Israel, for neither of these groups is required to observe the rules of the seventh year; mSheb. 5:7; Newman, 118.
[58]As Zohar notes, the biblical phrase *a sabbath of solemn rest* occurs only with reference to the weekly Sabbath, the Day of Atonement, and the Sabbatical year; Zohar, 89.

year, an Israelite may lease it from him for use in the eighth year.[59] And, Israelites may assist[60] gentiles while the latter work in the their fields during the sabbatical year.[61] If an Israelite regularly rents a field from a gentile, the latter must agree to work the field during the seventh year and not require the Israelite to pay rent on field he cannot sow.[62] The limited amount of produce available during the seventh year and the fact that YHWH had appointed the available produce for the sustenance of the Israelites[63] precluded an Israelite's feeding it to gentiles, or selling it to them.[64] Furthermore, an Israelite cannot buy seventh-year produce from a gentile, but the reason behind this ruling is unclear.[65]

Zohar argues that in Mishnah, laws concerning the seventh year "acquired some limiting properties . . .: restrictions to an in-group which included Jews alone. . . . [S]abbatical produce now was characterized as holy, a description which, while the Bible may have hinted at it, became explicit only in the Oral Torah."[66] In brief, the laws of the Sabbatical year became a way for the

---

[59]Newman, 98.

[60]Mhzyqyn ydy. The exact meaning of this term is unclear. Bartinoro, followed by Israel Lipschuetz, Albeck, and Lehrman suggests that the Israelite may give verbal support and encouragement while the gentile is working in his field; Albeck, *Zeraim*, 148; S.M. Lehrman, *Shebi'ith: Translated into English with Notes* in Isidore Epstein, *The Babylonian Talmud* (London: 1948), 161. Danby translates, "and gentiles may be helped [when labouring in the fields] . . . ; Herbert Danby, *The Mishnah: Translated from the Hebrew with Introduction and Brief Explanatory Notes* (London: 1933), 43. Cf., Newman, 98, 299, n. 7.

[61]MSheb. 4:3, 5:9.

[62]TSheb. 3:12.

[63]TSheb. 5:22; Newman, 165.

[64]TSheb. 6:20. An Israelite may sell enough seventh-year produce for three meals to an Israelite suspected of violating the laws of the Sabbatical year. Cf., Zohar, 84.

[65]TSheb. 6:20. Newman suggests that non-Israelites cannot derive benefit from the seventh-year produce, or from the money received from its sale; Newman, 163. Lieberman cites some commentators who held that there was concern that the gentile was selling forbidden Israelite produce and that the payment for seventh-year produce would be handed over to the gentiles. Lieberman also suggests that the prohibition may relate to the principle of 'bq šb't, an occupation indirectly related to those prohibited in the Sabbatical year; Saul Lieberman, *Tosefta Ki-fshutah: A Comprehensive Commentary on the Tosefta: Order Zera'im, Part II* (New York: 1955), 565. Marcus Jastrow, *A Dictionary of the Targumim, the Talmud Babli and Yerushalmi, and the Midrashic Literature* (New York, reprint 1971), 8a. Jacob Levy, *Worterbuch uber die Talmudim und Midraschim* (Darmstadt: Reprint, 1963), I, 14. Alexander Kohut, *Aruch Completum sive Lexicon vocabula et res, quae in libris Targumicis, Talmudicis et Midraschicis continetur, explicans auctore Nathane filio Jechielis* (New York, nd), I, 16.

[66]Zohar, 100.

Israelites to express their unity[67] and their relationship to the Land of Israel and YHWH, thus emphasizing their distinctness from the gentile.

From the point of view of Mishnah-Tosefta, the requirement that one must wait several years before enjoying a tree's fruit derives solely from the holiness of the Land and is applied to any tree which grows in the holy soil.[68] Unlike the discussions of "mixed-kinds," these rules don't derive from a "categorization scheme" constructed to make the world comprehensible, and in opposition to the tithes or other agricultural-offerings, the produce is not given to YHWH[69] or to his representatives. Furthermore, in contrast to the gifts to the poor, the rules of fourth-year produce are not designed to create a support system for a segment of the ethnic unit. Therefore, the gentile is obligated to observe these restrictions.[70] If a gentile grafts a food tree onto a shade tree, so that he creates a "new" tree by violating the rules of "mixed-kinds," he begins counting the four years from the time that he "planted"[71] the new tree.[72] Elsewhere,[73] sages declare gentile vineyards subject to these laws. However, there was opposition to this view, for in the latter two *sugyot*, Judah disagrees and exempts the gentile's vineyard from the rules of the fourth year.[74]

That the focus of the concern with the fourth-year produce is on the holy status of the Land of Israel is emphasized by the fact that similar to the rules concerning the gifts to the poor, the Torah speaks directly to the Israelites, in the second person: *When you enter the land and you plant any tree for food, you shall regard its fruit as forbidden. Three years it shall be forbidden for you, not to be eaten. In the fourth year all its fruit shall be set aside for jubilation before YHWH; and only in the fifth year may you use its fruit that its yield to you*

----

[67]Cf., Zohar, 102.

[68]MTer. 3:9, tTer. 2:13.

[69]Like the second tithe, the fourth-year produce was taken to Jerusalem and eaten there.

[70]MOrl. 1:2.

[71]Essner notes that this is awkward. He suggests that perhaps the correct reading is "grafted" for planted; Howard Essner, "The Mishnah Tractate *'Orlah*: Translation and Commentary," in William S. Green, *Approaches to Ancient Judaism Volume III: Text as Context in Early Rabbinic Literature* (Chico: 1981), 120. Lieberman suggests that it might mean that one begins counting from the time that the tree bears fruit, for the laws of *'orlah* apply to only fruit trees; Lieberman, *Zera'im II*, 819.

[72]TOrl. 1:5.

[73]MTer. 3:9, tTer. 2:13.

[74]I assume that Judah's ruling derives from the fact that in Lev. 19:23 the rules concerning the fourth year are directed to the Israelites and are to be followed after they enter the Land and plant the trees.

may be increased: I am YHWH your God.[75] It appears that Mishnah's authors chose to emphasize the fact that it was set aside *for a jubilation before YHWH,* instead of the fact that the Torah directed these laws to the Israelites alone, for with regard to this agricultural rule, Mishnah-Tosefta chose to play down the emphasis on the People Israel.

The rules concerning the tithes and the heave-offerings derive from the holy status of the Land of Israel and are in some ways independent of the farmer. For this reason, the gentile's relationship to these rules is complex. Even though a gentile is not *required* to separate tithes, he *may* separate valid tithes[76] at the threshing floor.[77] Because the obligation to separate the tithe derives from the holy status of the Land, some completely disregarded the farmer's status and argued that one can separate the tithe from an Israelite's produce for a gentile's produce and from a gentile's produce for an Israelite's produce.[78] However, others challenged this assumption and held that whether or not produce should be tithed depended on where it was grown, in the Land of Israel, *and* by whom it was grown, an Israelite.[79] If an Israelite were weeding with a gentile in the latter's field of leeks which were planted from untithed seed, the Israelite may make a chance meal from the crop, even though it is untithed.[80] If a gentile and an Israelite jointly owned a field,[81] the Israelite must remove the tithes from all of the grain before the gentile takes his portion of the field because one cannot designate before the harvest which part of the crop belongs to which partner.[82] Simeon, on the other hand, rules that the Israelite separates

----

[75]Lev. 19:23.

[76]He may offer also other agricultural gifts.

[77]MTer. 3:9. However, if he took the produce into his house, Israelites must separate the tithes from the produce before they may eat it; tTer. 4:12. However, this becomes the subject of a dispute in tTer. 4:13. If a gentile took first tithe from within his house, Rabbi says it is treated like tithed produce mixed with untithed produce, while Simeon b. Gamliel states it is treated liked tithed produce.

[78]MDem. 5:9; Cf., tDem. 5:21. The text also discusses a Samaritan's produce, but this issue does not concern us. The determining factor is *where* the produce to be eaten was grown, not *who* grew it; Sarason, 191-192.

[79]So, against Meir, to whom Tosefta assigns Mishnah's anonymous rule, Judah, Yosi and Simeon argue that one cannot separate the tithe for a gentile's produce from an Israelite's produce or *vice versa;* tDem. 5:21.

[80]MTer. 9:7; Peck, 263. The assumption here is that a gentile's produce is not liable for tithes; therefore, the Israelite may make a chance meal from the crop.

[81]TDem. 6:2. Sarason notes that some versions read "leases" for "divides." This reading solves many of the problems in interpreting this text; Sarason, 210.

[82]Sarason suggests that alternatively, the text "does not recognize gentile ownership rights to render produce exempt from tithing;" Sarason, 210.

only the heave-offering before the harvest is divided.[83] If a gentile sold his produce to an Israelite, the latter must separate the tithes.[84] While Israelites are obligated to separate tithes and heave-offering, gentiles may also validly perform these rites, although they do not seem to have been required to do so.

One who is concerned about tithing should not encourage anyone to eat or to use untithed produce. But a sharecropper[85] needs to tithe only his own produce, no matter if the field is owned by an Israelite or a gentile.[86] However, elsewhere we read that if a gentile owns the field, the sharecropper separates the tithe from all of the produce because the gentile will not tithe what he is given.[87] According to this view, all produce grown in the holy soil must be tithed, and it is the Israelite's obligation to see that this is done properly. Simeon b. Gamliel, however, believes that the gentile need not tithe the produce, so that if the gentile objects to the sharecropper's removing the tithe before he gives the landowner his share, the sharecropper removes the gifts from his own portion.[88] If an Israelite had a gentile[89] sharecropper on his property, the Israelite must tithe from his produce for the gentile.[90] If one leased[91] a field from an Israelite, he separates the heave-offering, but not the tithe, before he gives the share to the landowner.[92] But, if he leased the field from a gentile, the tenant removes the heave-offering and the tithes before he pays his rent.[93] Yosi

----

[83]Sarason notes that this is a difficult text, for it is unclear why Simeon requires the Israelite to separate the heave-offering before the harvest is divided; Sarason, 210.

[84]TDem. 6:1.

[85]A sharecropper works someone else's field in exchange for a certain percentage of the yield, while the field remains in the possession of the landowner.

[86]MDem. 6:1, Sarason, 205.

[87]TDem. 6:1.

[88]In agreement with Mishnah.

[89]The text also mentions a Samaritan or an Israelite who is untrustworthy with regards to tithes.

[90]TDem. 7:11. This practice is forbidden because it could result in part of the crop not being tithed; therefore, the landowner is penalized by having to remove the tithe for the sharecropper from his own produce; Sarason, 224.

[91]One who leases a field pays the landowner a set amount of the produce regardless of the yield. Because the one leasing the field takes all of the risk, he is treated as if he owned the land.

[92]MDem. 6:1. Judah disagrees and argues that this procedure is followed only when the tenant farmer gives the landowner produce from the same field from which he had agreed to pay him. If he gives him produce from another field, the tenant removes the tithes first.

[93]MDem. 6:2. Sarason argues that the text distinguishes between a field rented from an Israelite and one rented from a gentile because this *sugya* does "not recognize the right of a gentile to own property in the Land of Israel. When the gentile leases a field to an Israelite, all of the produce is deemed to belong to the Israelite, including the portion which the gentile receives back in rent;" Sarason, 206. In the same text, Judah agrees with this theory and rules that an Israelite who sharecrops a field from a gentile which once belonged to the Israelite's father separates the tithes and then pays his rent. However, Sarason notes that Judah's ruling is based on his belief that gentiles cannot own a portion of the Holy Land: "[Judah] holds that Israelite landholdings can never be

b. HaMeshullam[94] makes the obvious point that if the Israelite sharecrops his father's field from a gentile but had agreed to pay his rent from produce which was not ready to be tithed, he may pay it without separating the tithes. An Israelite may purchase a sown field from a gentile, before or after it has sprouted,[95] without worrying that the gentile has planted the field with seed that needed to be tithed.[96] However, an Israelite may not sow or bury untithed seed, and he may not aid a gentile in sowing or burying such seed.[97]

An Israelite may not use untithed produce in any way, nor may he indirectly allow others, even gentiles, to use untithed produce on his behalf. Therefore, an Israelite cannot give a gentile[98] money with which to purchase the grain needed to pay the former's taxes and tell him specifically to pay his taxes in kind, for the gentile might pay the Israelite's taxes with untithed produce, so that it would appear that the Israelite approves of the use of untithed produce. The Israelite may, however, express a general desire that the gentile find a way to release him from his obligations, without specifying that the he pay the taxes with produce.[99] Similarly, an Israelite may not tether his animal next to a gentile's animal which is feeding, for placing an Israelite's animal in a situation where it is likely to eat untithed produce is like feeding the animal untithed grain.[100] However, if the animal eats the untithed produce on its own accord, the Israelite need not worry about it. An Israelite may hire out his animal to a gentile and specify that the gentile should feed it, as long as he does not specify the amount or type of feed to be used.[101] If an Israelite uproots the

----

alienated by a gentile. The field which once belonged to the family of the Israelite sharecropper is still deemed to belong to him, and for this reason he must tithe the gentile owner's share of the total yield;" Sarason, 206.

[94]TDem. 6:7; Yosi cites other authorities.

[95]TDem. 1:18 rules that if an Israelite forgot and planted a field with untithed produce, he must uproot it before it sprouts. If it has already sprouted, he need not worry about it. This distinction does not apply to a gentile's field.

[96]TDem. 1:17.

[97]TDem. 1:18. This assumes that the gentile's produce grown in the Land of Israel must be tithed; Sarason, 53.

[98]Or anyone else who is not careful about tithing produce.

[99]TDem. 6:4; Sarason, 210-211.

[100]TDem. 1:20. This assumes that the gentile must tithe his grain which grows in the Land of Israel; Sarason, 54.

[101]If the Israelite is specific in his instructions, the gentile can be considered to be his agent, so that the Israelite would be responsible for the gentile's feeding untithed produce to the animal.

shoots from his field[102] and sells them to a gentile,[103] he must remove the tithe from the uprooted shoots.[104] If the poor Israelite maintains that his relatives gathered the poor-offerings, one need not remove the tithes from the produce; however, if the Israelite claims that he purchased the grain from a gentile[105] who told him that the produce had the status of a poor-offering, the tithes must be separated.[106]

A gentile may separate the heave-offering from his own produce, within the Land of Israel,[107] but not in Syria.[108] Some[109] argue that this applies only if the gentile separated the heave-offering on the threshing floor and immediately gave it to a priest. If he brought the produce into his house, some argued that it became invalid.[110] A gentile may separate the heave-offering, tithes, and poor-man's gifts from his produce at the threshing floor and give them to the Israelites to eat; however, if the gentile takes the produce into his house, the Israelite must separate the tithes before eating the produce.[111] A gentile cannot separate heave-offering on behalf of an Israelite, even with the latter's consent;[112] but this parallels the rule that one Israelite cannot separate

----

[102]An issue raised in MMa. 5:1.

[103]The text lists a number of other acts which have the same result of removing the yield from the category of produce which must be tithed.

[104]TMa. 3:8. The principle is that once produce comes under the category of requiring that tithes be taken, the Israelite must remove the tithes. He cannot perform an act which would remove the crop from its previous status. The same principle is operative in tTer. 2:11.

[105]Or a Samaritan.

[106]TPe. 4:1. The issue is framed in terms of "believing" the Israelite. However, I am not sure why one would not believe his statement that he purchased the grain from a gentile, or Samaritan, who claimed it was one of the poor-offerings. Because it was assumed that neither the Samaritans nor the gentiles properly tithed their produce, and because neither were obligated to give or receive the poor-offerings, the poor Israelite had little to gain by making a *false* claim concerning his purchasing the grain from them. It seems to me that one could believe the claim of the Israelite, but not believe what the Samaritan and gentile had told him, so that the tithe would have to be separated from the produce. Lieberman states that he is not believed when he claims the purchased the grain from the poor gentile or Samaritan or that the gentile or Samaritan sold him one of the poor-offerings; Lieberman, Zera'im, II, 178. Brooks apparently reads the text in the same way that I do; Brooks, 142.

[107]MTer. 3:9.

[108]TTer. 4:12 and tHal. 2:6.

[109]TTer. 4:12.

[110]TTer. 4:13. Rabbi rules that if the gentile took the heave-offering which had been removed into his domicile, it is treated like heave-offering mixed with untithed produce. Simeon b. Gamliel says it is considered to be valid heave-offering. Simeon, therefore, believes that we can trust the gentile to keep the sanctified grain separate from his common produce.

[111]TTer. 4:12.

[112]MTer. 1:1.

the heave-offering from the produce of another Israelite, for one person cannot sanctify another individual's produce.[113] However, if a gentile can separate a valid heave-offering, he, like an Israelite, has the power to sanctify common produce.[114] This is unexpected, for we would expect that only Israelites have the power to render common produce sanctified.

The gentile may tithe his crops and separate a valid heave-offering because the rabbis saw these rules as essentially derived from the holiness of the Land of Israel. In the Bible, the tithe is separated for YHWH, who then gives it to the Levites as an inheritance because he has not allowed them to own real estate within the Land.[115] Similarly, the heave-offering was given by YHWH to Aaron and his descendants.[116] Thus, the tithe and the heave-offering belonged to YHWH because the Land of Israel was his possession; therefore, non-Israelites who tilled the soil could choose to separate these gifts and to give them to the Land's true owner.[117] One aspect of the Israelite laws of tithing, which will find expression in other areas of rabbinic concern, is the requirement that one obey the regulations in ways which do not allow them to go unfulfilled by gentiles. Thus, the Israelite must tithe his grain, even if the grain will eventually end up in a gentile's possession. Although the gentile *need not* tithe

----

[113]The text also prohibits an imbecile, a minor, and a *haresh*, defined in mTer. 1:2, from separating heave-offering; however, as Peck notes, the reasons that these cannot separate valid heave-offering are different from the reason that a gentile cannot separate heave-offering; Peck, 31-32. We find a narrative in tTer. 1:15 which relates events which occurred in Pegah. An Israelite asked a gentile to separate heave-offering for him at the threshing floor; however, some of the sanctified produce fell back on the floor. Simeon b. Gamliel ruled that the separation was not valid because the gentile acted as the Israelite's agent, and this was not proper. Isaac ruled, however, that if the owner stood by the gentile's side and validated the separation, the heave-offering is acceptable. For Isaac, the validity of the heave-offering depended on the one who designated it, not on the one who actually separated it; Peck, 47.

[114]MTer. 3:9 states that a gentile's heave-offering renders produce with which is mixed subject to the rules of heave-offering, so that if it is eaten in error by a non-priest, it is subject to the law of the added fifth. Simeon argues that it is not subject to the law of the added fifth. The anonymous rule in Mishnah states that a gentile, like an Israelite, may dedicate produce to the Temple. Simeon, however, claims that while a gentile may give produce to a priest, the produce does not become holy; therefore, it is not subject to the same laws as the holy things separated and dedicate by Israelites. Simeon treats the gentile's offering as produce about which there is a doubt concerning whether or not it is properly separated heave-offering. Simeon believes that only Israelites have the ability to separate properly the gifts from produce grown in the Land of Israel, for God gave the Land to the Israelites alone, and he made the Israelites alone responsible for the agricultural gifts he outlined in the Torah; Peck, 122-123.

[115]Num. 18:21-24.

[116]Num. 18:8, Num. 18:11-12, Num. 18:25-32, Deut. 18:4. Lev. 22:10-14, Deut. 12:6.

[117]On the heave-offering, see Zohar, 87-88, 99-102.

his grain, any grain which he receives from an Israelite must be tithed. The mere fact that the grain will leave the Israelite's possession does not free him from his obligations. The holiness of the Land is the issue, so that no matter who ultimately will eat the produce, it must be "set right" through the separation of tithes. In addition, from the point of view of the Israelites, these rules also are designed to mark the grain as distinctly Israelite before it comes into the gentile's possession. Whether or not the gentile realizes that the grain he has received from the Israelite has been specifically "marked" as Israelite is not important, for I assume that the gentile would not be able to distinguish between tithed and untithed grain. The whole matter is framed with only the Israelite in mind, for he alone surely would know that the tithes have been removed from the grain.

If one rents a field from a gentile and is required to pay his rent with coins instead of produce, but decides to settle his debt with produce, he separates the heave-offering and the tithes and pays his rent from the tithed produce.[118] Paying taxes is comparable to repaying a debt; therefore, one separates the tithes and the heave-offering before he pays his taxes to the gentile government.[119] Again, only from the Israelites' perspective would this make a difference. They, and YHWH, would know that this grain was different from the grain used by others to pay their taxes, and from the point of view of Mishnah-Tosefta, the former are the only parties who matter.

With regard to the agricultural laws, crops grown in Syria presented a problem to the rabbis. Some considered Syria to be part of the Land of Israel and to share in latter's holiness, while others did not.[120] If an Israelite purchased a field in Syria and then sold it to a gentile, the field remains subject to the requirements of tithes. It continues to be treated as Israelite land. However, in the case of sharecroppers, tenant farmers, hereditary land-tenants, or a gentile who mortgaged his property to an Israelite, the crops are not subject to tithes, because the Israelite never actually owned the property.[121] According to Eliezer,[122] if an Israelite leases a Syrian field from a gentile, he must separate the tithes, for Eliezer considers Syria to be part of the Land of Israel. Gamliel

----

[118]TDem. 6:2. He tithes before he pays the gentile because in this case he is repaying a debt and not returning to the gentile his own produce; Sarason, 210.

[119]TDem. 6:3.

[120]See Richard S. Sarason, "The Significance of the Land of Israel in the Mishnah," in Hoffman, 121-123.

[121]TTer. 2:11. It is probable that the authority behind this ruling believed that gentiles could not own parcels of the Holy Land.

[122]MHal. 4:7.

does not consider Syria to be part of the Land of Israel and rules that the Israelite does not have to separate tithes, unless the land belongs to the Israelite.[123] Again, Israelite land and the crops grown on it are different from gentile fields and their yields. If the soil is part of the Holy Land, the Israelite must take note of that fact and distinguish the crops he grows, accordingly.

The concern with *demai*-produce results from the authors of Mishnah-Tosefta realizing that *only they and their followers* would remove the tithes, so that even some Israelites could not be trusted in these matters. If one could not trust all Israelites to have properly removed the tithes from their produce, it is obvious that one cannot assume that gentiles would have been concerned about the rabbis' agricultural rules. The concept of *demai* pertains only if there is *uncertainty* whether or not the produce has been tithed, or if there is possibility that untithed produce has been intermingled with tithed produce.[124] Therefore, if an Israelite brings his grain to a gentile miller, the grain becomes *demai* because the gentile miller will not take care to prevent the mixing of the tithed produce with untithed produce.[125] If one leaves his tithed produce with a gentile, Simeon argued that it became *demai*, while others ruled that it was considered to be untithed.[126] If an Israelite sends his grain to market with a gentile, he must worry about the gentile's mixing the tithed produce with some untithed grain.[127] However, if one employs a gentile ass-driver to carry the tithed grain from a threshing-floor, he need not worry, for the ass-driver assumes that he is being

----

[123]Bartinoro, *loc. cit.*

[124]Only if gentiles are *required* to tithe their produce, therefore, do the laws of *demai* apply to them. However, if gentiles need not separate the tithes from their crops, their produce is *certainly* untithed, and the rules of *demai* are not relevant.

[125]MDem. 3:4. If the miller were a Samaritan or an *am haares*, we assume that he will be careful with the Israelite's grain, so that its status with regard to tithes and seventh-year produce does not change. Furthermore, a gentile miller cannot be trusted to keep the grain dry, so that it does not become susceptible to uncleanness; tDem. 4:27. The Samaritan and the *am haares*, unlike the gentile, will be concerned with the Israelite's rules. This is a stereotypic section which consistently juxtaposes the gentile with the Samaritan and *am haares*. The gentile is pictured as unconcerned with matters important to the Israelites, while the Samaritan and the *am haares* do take the Israelites' matters seriously. Of course, these rules would discourage and Israelite from using a gentile miller, a gentile-owned grain storage facility, or a gentile teamster. On the other hand, if the gentile hoped to gain business from an Israelite, the former would have to take the Israelite's issues under consideration.

[126]MDem. 3:4. Simeon rules that the grain becomes *demai* because the gentile's grain does not need to be tithed, and any amount of an Israelite's grain mixed with a gentile's grain makes the whole *demai*. The rule is the same in tDem. 4:25; however, it is formulated according to the style of tDem. 4:24. In Tosefta, Simeon and Simeon b. Gamliel claim the produce is *demai*.

[127]He need not worry if he sends his grain with a Samaritan or an *am haares*.

observed, so that he will not mix the tithed grain with untithed produce.[128] If an Israelite tenant farmer who paid his rent to the gentile from tithed produce repurchased the produce from the gentile, or if another Israelite purchased it from the gentile, it is considered *demai*-produce, for the gentile might have mixed some untithed produce with the tithed produce.[129] According to Meir, grain found in a storehouse used by gentiles and Israelites is *demai* if the majority of those who used the storehouse were Israelites.[130] Sages, however, rule that even if there is just one Israelite who stores his grain in the silo, all of the grain is considered *demai*, for they do not require a gentile to tithe his grain.[131] *Demai*-produce needs to be tithed only if it is used for food.[132] Therefore, if an Israelite purchased or inherited produce with the intention of using it for *his* food, but afterwards changed his mind and decided to dispose of it by feeding it to cattle or selling it to gentiles, it still must be tithed.[133] These rules assume that gentiles do not tithe their produce and will not be careful about keeping their untithed grain separate from the Israelites' tithed produce.

An Israelite may not put untithed oil on a gentile's wound, for no one may derive any sort of benefit from certainly untithed produce.[134] However, he may use *demai*-oil.[135] If a gentile spread out his untithed oil on a marble table in a bath-house and greased himself with it, an Israelite may sit on the table because the oil is no longer fit for tithing.[136] By using his untithed oil, the gentile renders it unfit for tithing, so that the Israelite may come into contact with it. The produce which a traveling merchant sells is considered to be *demai*, whether he is a gentile, an Israelite, or a Samaritan, unless the produce comes from

----

[128]TDem. 4:26.

[129]Sarason, *History*, 210.

[130]If the majority are gentiles, the grain is considered untithed; if there are an equal number of Israelites and gentiles, the produce is considered untithed.

[131]TDem. 1:12; tDem. 1:12 appears also at mMakh. 2:10. In tDem. 1:13, Yosi limits the sages' ruling to a private storehouse; if it is a government controlled storehouse, one "follows the majority" because Yosi assumes that Israelites pay their taxes with untithed grain. However, Sarason notes that Yosi's ruling does not make sense; Sarason, *History*, 49. Judah claims that sages' ruling applies if gentiles and Israelites share the storehouse, but not if Samaritans and Israelites share the storage facility.

[132]MDem. 1:3.

[133]TDem. 1:15-16. Sarason argues that even though it is not specified that the produce is *demai*, this is certainly the subject of the pericopae; Sarason, *History*, 51-52.

[134]Sarason, *History*, 54.

[135]TDem. 1:22.

[136]TDem. 1:23; Sarason, *History*, 55.

gentiles or Samaritans, in which case it is assumed to be untithed.[137] One cannot trust a traveling merchant to know the status of the grain he sells, no matter his own status. However, if the Israelite knows for sure that the grain comes from those who do not tithe, such as gentiles, the grain is assumed to be untithed.

For the most part, the discussions of *demai*-produce assume that gentiles are not required to tithe their produce. Furthermore, Mishnah's laws of *demai* assume that the gentile will not care about the Israelite laws and will not be concerned about keeping an Israelite's produce, which is tithed, separate from the non-Israelite grain. In fact, it is this assumption about the gentile's general disregard for Israelite rules and sensibilities which generates the above discussions. Also, there would be nothing distinctive about the tithed grain which would allow the gentile to distinguish between tithed and untithed grain. The indication that grain is tithed would be that it came from an Israelite who practiced tithing; therefore, the person who supplied the grain is the crucial factor.

There is some debate concerning a gentile's reliability with regard to the second tithe. If a gentile took the second tithe from within his house and stated that it has been redeemed by coins, he is ignored; however, if he tells the Israelite to redeem it himself, Rabbi states that it is considered to be second tithe produce mixed with untithed produce, while Simeon b. Gamliel states that it is considered second tithe produce. According to Rabbi, we do not believe a gentile's claim that he has valid second tithe produce or that he has redeemed the produce. Simeon, however, assumes that the gentile's claim is valid and that he has kept the second tithe separate from the rest of his untithed produce.[138] Some consider gentiles to be legitimate farmers who know their business and can be trusted. For purposes of redeeming the second tithe, the value of the produce can be set by three bidders,[139] and the bidders may include the prospective buyer, the one who owns the produce, or a gentile.[140] An Israelite need not pay a penalty if someone else buys his second tithe grain and then resells it to him. However, non-Israelite servants, "Canaanite servants," are considered their master's property and do not have the legal status of individuals. An Israelite may give his adult child or his Hebrew slave coins and have him redeem his sec-

---

[137]TDem. 4:20. This assumes that most of his produce was grown by Israelites who properly tithed their produce.

[138]TTer. 4:13.

[139]MM.S. 4:2.

[140]TM.S. 3:5.

ond tithe, so that he need not pay the added fifth. However, he may not do this with his child who is a minor or his Canaanite slave because "their deed is considered his deed."[141] The name "second tithe" is not given in the Bible. This is the term the rabbis apply to the tithe which could be sold and the money spent in the place which YHWH chose.[142] The key issue is that the grain is consumed in YHWH's presence, so again it relates to the holiness of the Land, which is derived from its stewardship by YHWH. Zohar notes that in the Torah, this tithe is an internal Israelite institution which "brings together all levels and classes of [Israelite] society."[143] In other words, it is a boundary-maintaining agricultural rule.[144] While the situation in Mishnah-Tosefta is, in general, similar to that in the Bible, Simeon, at least, believes that non-Israelites could be trusted with regard to their claims about the second tithe.

iv

The reasons behind the rulings in tTer. 2:11 and tDem. 6:2 may be related to the question of whether or not a gentile may own a parcel of the Holy Land. For these *sugyot*, however, the problem is whether or not the fact that gentiles own part of the Holy Land affects its sacred status, so that it still produces foods subject to tithes or to the other agricultural gifts. Elsewhere, this matter is addressed from different points of view, without reference to the implications of gentile ownership with regard to the agricultural rules, but with an eye to the problem of idolatry.[145] Meir forbids the rental to gentiles of houses or fields in the Land of Israel, while Yosi permits the rental of houses, but not fields.[146] Citing Deut. 7:26, an anonymous authority states that permission to rent to gentiles could not apply to dwelling-places because they bring idols into

----

[141]MM.S. 4:3-4:4, tM.S. 4:1; Haas, 129-130.

[142]Deut. 14:22-27, Deut. 26:12-15, Lev. 27:30-31. See Haas, 1-2.

[143]Zohar, 88.

[144]Zohar, 99-100. Even though Zohar's interpretation seems plausible, one should not ignore the possibility that this tithe is a thinly disguised means of supporting the economy of Jerusalem.

[145]These texts, mA.Z. 1:8-9 and tA.Z. 2:8-9, also deal with the question of whether or not Syria is part of the Land of Israel; however, this is not important for our present purposes.

[146]MA.Z. 1:8. In tA.Z. 2:8, the anonymous author forbids the rental of houses, fields, or vineyards. Meir forbids the rental of fields in Syria and Israel, while Yosi permits the rental of both fields and houses. TA.Z. 2:9 forbids the rental of houses to gentiles because they bring idols into them; however, it permits the rental of stables, storehouses, and inns. Simeon b. Gamliel prohibits the rental of bath-houses to gentiles because they will be used on the Sabbath, and Simeon forbids the rental of fields to gentiles because they will work them on the Holy Days.

them, and the buildings in which the idols were placed would be known as Israelite property.[147] We discover that in our texts, the issue of a gentile's owning a parcel of the Holy Land was not settled--some of our texts assume that gentiles could own property in the Land of Israel, while other texts prohibit their owning such property--and that the problem could be approached from at least two points of view, idolatry and agricultural rules.

V

From an early period, the special relationship between the People Israel and YHWH finds expression in the connection between the Israelites and the Land of Israel. Hoffman even suggests that in some contexts the Land is more essential to the identity of the People Israel than is the Torah. He argues that Deut. 26:1-10 set forth "early Israel's Sacred Myth," which

"presents Israel first as wanderers, seeking a place to settle; they end up as settlers in the Promised land.... They began history independently . . . but finished their tale as YHWH's people, for it is YHWH who 'heard our plea and saw our plight' (v. 7), 'freed us from Egypt' (v. 8) and 'brought us to this place and gave us this land. . . . [T]he essential problematic of Israel's history (according to this myth) is not the dichotomy between Israel without, and then Israel with, the divine gift of Torah. No, the dominant theme to which the biblical pilgrim gave voice was the role of landedness. Israel began its career unlanded; it ended with land. Land, not Torah, is the essential gift from YHWH that our pilgrim remembers."[148]

Although the issue is much more complex from the point of view of Mishnah-Tosefta, the special nature of the Land still finds expression. Hoffman argues that from the fact that the rabbis in their blessings "differentiated food. . . on the basis of whether it grew in the Land [of Israel] or outside of it," we can deduce that for the rabbis, "the Land of Israel was no mere human-made demar-

----

[147]The Babylonian *gemara* argues that Yosi distinguished between fields and houses because a "twofold objection" applied to the former; bA.Z. 21a. Elmslie states that the fields fall under the prohibition of "allowing foreigners to a acquire property in Palestine, and . . . the law exacting tithes and first-fruits;" W.A.L. Elmslie, *The Mishna on Idolatry 'Aboda Zara: Edited with Translation, Vocabulary, and notes* (Cambridge: 1911), 15. The Palestinian Talmud states that it was common to profit from a house, but not common to profit from a field, but this does not tell us much.

[148]Lawrence A. Hoffman, "Introduction: Land of Blessing and 'Blessings of the Land,'" in Hoffman, 8.

cation of a segment of the earth's surface. It was a natural geographic phenomenon, equally as inherent to the earth's structure as tress and vines. . . ."[149]

Although Primus argues that mQid. 1:10 offers us "a neutral" image of the Land,[150] he notes that in mHal. 2:1 we find Aqiba and Eliezer holding different views concerning the sanctity of the Land of Israel.[151] Primus states that for Eliezer, the holiness of the Land adheres to the land's products, while for Aqiba, the holiness attaches to the products *only within the borders of the Land.*[152] For Aqiba, the space inhabited by the Land is sacred. Primus concludes that "[i]n Judaic idiom these thoughts [about the sacred] can be expressed in terms of living in the Land of Israel, the promised home of the people, Israel."[153] In short, Primus too admits to the sacred nature of the Land of Israel and to the People Israel's special relationship to this sacredness, which reaches a peak when the Holy People live within the borders of the Holy Land.

The discussions of the gentiles and the agricultural rules are a result of the Israelites' conception of their relationship to YHWH, which found concrete expression in the way they treated the crops which grew in his holy soil. When concentrating on *gentiles*, our texts consistently agree that they are not obligated to act like Israelites, for the latter are the *only* inhabitants of the Land who must offer the proper gifts to YHWH as an expression of their special relationship to the Land and its Possessor. However, when *the holy nature* of the Land becomes the focus of attention, the gentiles too *may* respect the Land's sacred nature. Thus, in the area of agricultural regulations, gentiles may act like Israelites, because like Israelites, gentiles live on YHWH's holy soil.

While admitting the potential similarity between gentiles and Israelites, the general tendency of the discussions in Mishnah-Tosefta is to focus on the differences between them. Although the Land of Israel is holy no matter who dwells on it, so that gentiles may validly offer tithes and heave-offering, one does not expect them to do so because they do not have the same relationship to

----

[149]Hoffman, 16.

[150]Charles Primus, "The Borders of Judaism," in Hoffman, 100-102. On 102 Primus states, "[I]t [mQid. 1:10] illustrates the relatively neutral quality of the image of the Land. This neutrality, not to say passivity, is characteristic of most sources of the Land in Mishnah." While this *might* be the case, there are clearly passages, such as many of those which we have discussed above, which point to the sacred nature of the Land of Israel and the special relationship which exists between the People Israel and the Land of Israel.

[151]Primus, 103-105, especially 104-105.

[152]Primus, 105.

[153]Primus, 106.

the Land or to YHWH, its Possessor, as do the Israelites. This is made most clear with regard to the laws which require the Israelite to tithe produce *before* he pays his rent to the gentile, regulations concerning *demai*-produce, which assume that the gentile does not care about the Israelites' agricultural rites, and statutes which turn the gifts to the poor into an internal communal affair. In fact, much of our material makes the point that Israelite produce is, and should be, distinguished from gentile produce by having the required agricultural gifts to YHWH removed from it. Thus, through the agricultural laws, the rabbis attempted to draw boundaries between themselves and the non-Israelites who lived on the Land with them, planted crops in her holy soil, and benefited from her fertility.

While the crops grown, harvested, sold, and eaten by Israelites and non-Israelites were the same, they were also different, and this seems to be the point of much of the agricultural legislation in Mishnah-Tosefta which deals with the gentiles. However, the distinctive nature of the Israelites' produce would be evident to only Israelites through their actions, for grain from which the agricultural gifts had been removed would not look any different from grain from which the gifts had not been separated. Thus, it is doubtful that gentiles or Israelites would be able to discern whether any specific grain was tithed or untithed, unless they knew who had grown the crop and the farmer's opinion on the agricultural rules. The only person who certainly would know the status of any produce was the farmer who had grown the crop, for only he knew if he had followed the proper Israelite agricultural rules. The boundaries were formulated in the Israelite farmer's mind and concretized in his actions; however, they did not leave a mark on the produce. The only way in which gentiles would know that their grain was treated differently from Israelite grain was by witnessing the Israelites' actions when the latter harvested their crops, separated the agricultural gifts, or consumed their produce only in specific locations. Unless the specific gentile, or for that matter, Israelite, had seen the farmer separate the tithes or heave-offering from a particular amount of produce, the boundary would be uncertain. If gentiles jointly owned property with Israelites, rented fields from them, or leased land to them, they would be made aware that Israelites separated a certain amount of produce from what they harvested, or that they had left some of the grain unharvested in the field. Also, when the Israelite purchased grain from a gentile vendor, the issue of tithes could arise. The boundaries were created for the sake of the Israelites, and they provided a means for them to separate themselves from gentiles. It seems to have made no difference to the authors of Mishnah-Tosefta whether or not the gentile understood that they were different from Israelites. The important thing was that Israelites knew that they were different from gentiles.

Sarason has written "that virtually every Mishnaic case involving the Land of Israel deals with issues of boundaries and confusion of boundaries, both spatial and social."[154] As Sarason notes, Mishnah's problematic is that gentiles inhabit the Holy Land and till its soil, while the Bible suggests that only Israelites would enjoy these privileges. The realities of the period after the Bar Kokhba Revolt were such that the theory of the Holy Land belonging exclusively to Israelites would have been difficult to maintain,[155] so that the problematic which Sarason sees in Mishnah's rulings probably resulted from the dissonance between the biblical view of reality and the social situation which confronted the authors of Mishnah-Tosefta. Sarason also states that

> "the prevailing tendency in Mishnah's rulings is to exempt gentiles living in the Land from the observance of these laws; the divinely ordained economy of the Land is not absolute but relative to the presence and agricultural activity of its Jewish inhabitants. Still, Mishnah records the position that gentile offerings of raw produce are deemed valid after the fact, perhaps indicating a wish that all of the Land's produce be subject to Scripture's requirements."[156]

To repeat, the reason behind the inconsistency in Mishnah and Tosefta, which Sarason notes, reflects their ambiguity concerning the primary category of the Israelite group's relationship to the Land. From the point of view of those who started from the holiness of the Land, no borders should be drawn, or the borders were drawn in subtle ways because everyone who lived on the Land or who worked her soil had to take her holiness into account, albeit, in somewhat different ways. This finds in expression in the idea that Israelites *must* separate the agricultural gifts, while gentiles *may* do so. Furthermore, some sages held that even if the gentiles separated the tithes, they were not really to be considered proper priestly gifts. But, from the point of view of the Israelite group's identity which is partially manifest through its unique relationship to the Land and its Possessor, YHWH, the gentile does not, and should not, offer these gifts.

----

[154]Sarason, "Significance," 112.

[155]Michael Avi-Yonah, *The Jews of Palestine: A Political History from the Bar Kokhba War to the Arab Conquest* (New York: 1976), 15-31. On the situation in the Third Century, see Daniel Sperber, *Roman Palestine 200-400: The Land* (Ramat-Gan: 1978), 160-186.

[156]Sarason, "Significance," 118.

In fact, because the Land was occupied by "outsiders," Mishnah-Tosefta seek to establish the unification of the People Israel and the Land of Israel through their discussions of the agricultural gifts.

Above we saw that Mishnah-Tosefta have moved the focus from the Bible's emphasis on YHWH to an emphasis on humankind. This was necessary because Mishnah-Tosefta made the creation of the borders between Israelites and gentiles the responsibility of the individual Israelites. The point of Mishnah-Tosefta's agricultural laws in the context of their discussions of the gentile is to state explicitly that the individual Israelites must maintain the border between themselves and the gentiles, by following the agricultural rules that YHWH had set forth in the Torah. And, as we have argued above, these borders were firstly evident to only the Israelites, for it was their actions *before* the grain came to the market which created the borders. However, Israelites could also draw the borders in the market-place or in their social interactions with non-Israelites, for the former would not purchase untithed grain, or at least would not make use of untithed or *demai*-produce until the tithes had been removed. Furthermore, in the view of Mishnah-Tosefta, Israelites presumably would not eat produce, unless they were certain that the required agricultural gifts had been removed.

To conclude, the Bible had stated that the People Israel had a special relationship to the Land of Israel, and Mishnah-Tosefta constructed ways in which this unique relationship could be expressed and maintained. In fact, the existence of this relationship became one of the major ways through which the identity and uniqueness of Israel were created. And this unique relationship was made clear by differentiating between the Israelites and gentiles with regard to the agricultural gifts discussed in Mishnah-Tosefta.

Chapter Seven:

Israelite Sacred Time and the Gentiles

i

The determination whether or not the gentiles must observe the agricultural rites of the Israelites depended upon the point of departure taken by particular rabbis. Many sages viewed the obligation to separate the required gifts from the produce grown in the Land of Israel as a means of distinguishing between Israelites and gentiles. They therefore held that only Israelites were required to separate the agricultural gifts, such as the tithes. But others began with the principle that YHWH's land was holy, no matter who enjoyed her benefits. In their view, accordingly, gentiles could separate the gifts such as the tithes and heave-offering, if they wished to do so. A similar issue, although debated to a lesser degree, is found in the discussions of the gentiles' relationship to Israelite sacred time. While the texts are consistent in their position that gentiles cannot participate in the Passover rites, the question of a gentile's Sabbath-observance is subject to dispute. The differences between the way the texts picture the Israelite-gentile interaction on these two holidays reflect not only the underlying biblical ideologies, but also their relative importance in establishing the unique identity of the Israelites. As before, we also see here that the gentile functioned as a foil, a mode of defining who and what an Israelite is, by distinguishing the activities of the members of the two groups with regard to a major set of symbols, in this case, the periods of Israelite sacred time.

The marking out of sacred time thus becomes a way of distinguishing between Israelites and gentiles. Israelites observe the restrictions connected with the sacred days, while gentiles do not. However, each period of time is dealt with in terms of a unique set of categories, through which it, in particular, is defined. Two categories--Time and Space--are important for setting forth the relationship of the gentile to the sacredness of Sabbath. The special nature of Passover is marked, however, through food-stuffs, specifically leaven. The intermediate days of Passover and Sukkot are differentiated from other days of the year by a reduction of "normal" activity, and this is expressed in the different ways one deals with Israelites and non-Israelites. There is no single concept that runs throughout the description of the gentile *vis-a-vis* the holy periods in Mishnah-Tosefta, other than the fact that they are not Israelites. Again, the gentiles do not form an independent category which is dealt with from only one perspective. Rather, they are treated in terms of the essential elements of the various holidays, so that the texts which deal with the non-Israelite may be used as a source for discerning the essence of each particular period of Israelite sacred time.

ii

The holiness of the Sabbath finds expression in two categories, Time and Space. The temporal Sabbath is marked off from the rest of the temporal week by altered activity; certain things may not be done on the Sabbath, while other things may be done only in unique ways. The spatial Sabbath relates to the temporal Sabbath by the curious fact that within the demarcated space, certain Sabbath-restrictions do not apply. In a sense, the sacredness of the Space neutralizes the sacredness of the Time, so that one may perform activities within the specified Space on the Sabbath which one may not perform outside that area. For example, one may not carry an item between a public and a private domain on the Sabbath. However, one may combine public and private realms into a single private area for purposes of carrying, or walking, on the Sabbath. The designation of space, like that of time, is artificial; it must be made before the onset of the sacred period, it alters the definitions and dimensions of profane space, and it ends with the completion of the period of the sacred time.

Mishnah-Tosefta discuss the gentile and the Sabbath in terms of both Time and Space. Because the sacredness of time is characterized by altered activity, the gentiles, who do not recognize the sacred character of the Sabbath, do not necessarily need to change their patterns of behavior. Left on their own, gentiles engage in normal activity throughout the Sabbath. However, as we shall see below, the gentiles' activity may be altered by an Israelite's interaction with them on the Sabbath. It is, however, the Israelites who alter their actions *vis-a-vis* the gentile, and who, therefore, may cause the gentile to respond by acting in other than "normal" ways.

Similarly, the sacredness of the Space is defined by altering the borders of profane space. Here, the issue becomes complex, but again it is viewed entirely from an Israelite perspective. For some, the continuity of the sacred area is broken by the presence of gentiles, while for others, the gentile's presence is of no import.

The Sabbath is a uniquely Israelite period of time,[1] concerning which the Torah offers two explanations for the requirement that Israelites must limit their activity. In Genesis[2] and Exodus[3], one rests on the Sabbath because YHWH rested on that day upon his completing the work of creation. In this view, the Sabbath has cosmic significance, which is built into the very structure of the universe. From this perspective, one *could* argue that even gentiles are obligated to rest on the Sabbath.

Mishnah-Tosefta, however, chose to follow Deuteronomy's[4] view of the Sabbath. According to the fifth book of the Torah, Israelites rest on the Sabbath because they were once slaves in Egypt. In this view, the Sabbath is a uniquely Israelite period of time, which is related to the founding of the People Israel and the establishment of their special relationship with YHWH.[5] From

---

[1]Most recently Hallo has demonstrated that the seven-day week was an Israelite creation. William W. Hallo, "New Moons and Sabbaths: A Case-study in the Contrastive Approach," *Hebrew Union College Annual*, XLVIII (1977), 1-18.

[2]Gen. 2:1-4: *The heaven and the earth were finished, and all their array. And on the seventh day God finished the work which He had been doing and He ceased on the seventh day from all the work which He had done. And God blessed the seventh day and declared it holy, because on it God ceased from all the work of creation which He had done. Such is the story of heaven and earth as they were created.*

[3]Ex. 20:8-12: *Remember the sabbath day and keep it holy. . . . For in six days YHWH made heaven and earth and sea, and all that is in them, and He rested on the seventh day; therefore YHWH blessed the sabbath day and hallowed it.* Cf., Ex. 31:14-17, especially 34:17.

[4]Deut. 5:12-15. *Observe the sabbath day and keep it holy . . . . Remember that you were a slave in the land of Egypt and that YHWH, your God, freed you from there with a mighty hand and an outstretched arm; therefore, YHWH, your God has commanded you to observe the sabbath day.*

[5]It is significant that the rabbinic myth of the Oral Torah, which begins shortly after the Bar Kokhba Revolt and finds its first expression in Mishnah-Tosefta, centers on the Revelation at Sinai as the foundation-event of the People Israel and that the Sabbath is the only period of sacred time mentioned in the so-called Ten Commandments. On the topic of the Oral Torah and the rabbinic myth, see Jacob Neusner, *The Rabbinic Traditions About the Pharisees before 70* (Leiden: 1971), III, 143-179. Jacob Neusner, *There We Sat Down: Talmudic Judaism in the Making* (New York: 1978). Jacob Neusner, *Torah: From Scroll to Symbol in Formative Judaism* (Philadelphia: 1985). Lawrence A. Hoffman, "Introduction: Land of Blessing and 'Blessing of the Land'" in Lawrence A. Hoffman, *The Land of Israel: Jewish Perspectives* (Notre Dame: 1986), 8: "Rabbinic society transferred the emphasis [of Judaism] to Torah. . . ."

this outlook, the Sabbath easily could become a means of distinguishing between those who shared the Exodus experience and those who did not.[6]

In temporal terms, the Sabbath is a period of time during which Israelites must restrict their normal activity, while the gentiles' patterns of work and play exhibit no abnormalities, *unless* they interact with Israelites. Even then, the altered activities are the result of the limitations placed on Israelites. Not only must Israelites not engage in the prohibited tasks on the Sabbath, but also they must not be responsible, in any way, for gentile activity on the Sabbath.[7] An Israelite could benefit from the activity of gentiles *only* if the latter performed the task for their own advantage and not for the sake of the Israelite. Therefore, an Israelite may use a lamp which the gentile lit for himself,[8] water his animals in a trough which the gentile has filled for his own animals,[9] feed his animal from hay remaining from grain which a gentile brought to feed his animal,[10] walk down a gangplank the gentile erected for himself,[11] use a coffin a gentile constructed for another gentile or a grave one gentile dug for another gentile,[12] and even play dirges on flutes brought from a nearb-by place by

----

[6]As is well-known, Juvenal, *Satire* 14:96-106, saw the Jews' laziness on the Sabbath as one of their essential characteristics. On the views of the non-Israelites concerning the Sabbath, see Robert Goldenberg, "The Jewish Sabbath in the Roman World up to the Time of Constantine the Great," in Hildegard Temporini and Wolfgang Haase, *Aufstieg und Niedergang der römischen Welt* (Berlin and New York: 1979), II.19.1, 414-447, especially, 430-442, and the literature cited there. Add to Goldenberg's references John G. Gager, *The Origins of Anti-Semitism: Attitudes Toward Judaism in Pagan and Christian Antiquity* (New York and Oxford: 1985), "Sabbath," *passim*.

[7]This is already found in the Torah's statement that a person's servants, and *the strangers within your gates*, should also rest on the Sabbath; however, in our context it is extended to include all non-Israelites.

[8]MShab. 16:8.

[9]MShab. 16:8.

[10]TShab. 13:12. Tosefta refines the discussion and states that the Israelite may benefit from the water and hay which the gentile brought, only if the gentile does not know the Israelite. If the gentile knows the Israelite and knows that he will feed his animals, the gentile will perform the task in order to benefit the Israelite.

[11]MShab. 16:8. The text includes a narrative which states that Gamliel and the elders disembarked on a gangplank erected by a gentile. TShab. 13:14 contains a parallel passage. In Tosefta, part of the discussion centers around the question of whether or not the ship had entered the port's Sabbath-limit before the Sabbath began; this issue does not concern Mishnah.

[12]TShab. 17:15 changes the issue. Tosefta states that if on the Sabbath the gentile made a coffin or dug a grave for an Israelite, *that* Israelite may not be buried in the coffin or the grave; however, *another* Israelite may be buried in them.

gentiles.[13] However, if the gentile performed any of these activities for an Israelite, the Israelite may not benefit from them.

The point at issue here, however, is the Israelite's not working or causing work to be done. Therefore, there is no distinction between Israelites' having gentiles work for them, or one Israelite working for another Israelite. The issue is not the Israelite or gentile status of the individuals, or an attitude toward the non-Israelite. The prohibition against work on the Sabbath is so important that Israelites did not draw distinctions between Israelites and non-Israelites as providers of labor on the Sabbath. This idea follows easily from the Torah, for the prohibition against working on the Sabbath applies to *you, your son or your daughter, your male or female slave, your ox or your ass, or any of your cattle, or the stranger in your settlements* (Deut. 5:14). This command to let others rest and the rabbinic prohibition against allowing even gentiles to labor for Israelites on the Sabbath become the topic of much of the material in Mishnah-Tosefta which connects the gentile to the concerns of the Sabbath.

The principle that an Israelite may not cause a gentile to engage in activity which is prohibited on the Sabbath finds expression in a classic disagreement between the Hillelites and the Shammaites, which revolves around the question of whether or not an Israelite is permitted to begin work before the Sabbath which will not be completed until after the Sabbath has begun. Both Houses apply the same standards to work done by Israelites and to labor undertaken by gentiles in which Israelites play a direct role.[14] A somewhat related

----

[13]MShab. 23:4. TShab. 17:14 changes the issue. If a gentile brought the flutes to play a dirge for a *particular* Israelite, they cannot be used for *that* Israelite; however, they may be used for *another* Israelite.

[14]MShab. 1:7. The Shammaites hold that one may *not* begin such work, while the Hillelites rule that one *may* engage in such activity. The Shammaites rule that on Friday, an Israelite may not sell anything to a gentile, help a gentile load his pack-animal, or help him load something on his shoulders, unless the gentile has time to reach "a near-by place," defined in tShab. 1:22, before the Sabbath begins. Similarly, they rule that an Israelite may not give hides to a gentile tanner or clothes to a gentile launderer, unless the work he intends to do can be completed before the commencement of the Sabbath. In MShab. 1:9, Simeon b. Gamliel tells us that his father would give clothes to a gentile launderer only before Thursday. The Hillelites permit an Israelite to engage in these activities. Similarly, one should not rent utensils to a gentile on Friday, but he may do so on Wednesday or Thursday, tShab. 13:10, and an Israelite should not send mail with the gentile post on Friday, but he may on Wednesday or Thursday, TShab. 13:11. The *sugyot* assume that not only should the Israelite not violate the Sabbath, but also he should not be responsible for anyone else's violating the Sabbath, even if his contribution is merely helping a gentile place a load on the latter's shoulder or animal. I assume that the Houses would claim that the Israelite's helping the gentile makes it appear as if the gentile is working for the Israelite. However, the primary issue is whether or not one can complete work on the Sabbath which was begun before sun-down on Friday; the reference to the gentile is a secondary matter, which serves to emphasize the point that the Israelite cannot engage, or appear to engage, in any work on the Sabbath nor may he be *responsible* for any-

text states that if a gentile comes to put out a fire on the Sabbath, the Israelite may neither tell him to put it out, nor not to put it out.[15] If the Israelite speaks to the gentile, one might conclude that the gentile is following the Israelite's instructions, no matter what they were.

While in the above *sugyot* we see a distinct line of argument againt an Israelite's indirectly violating the Sabbath by acting through a gentile, we do find passages which take a different stance. If an Israelite is carrying a purse when the Sabbath begins, he should give the purse to a gentile to carry.[16] Although the Israelite has caused the gentile to do something for the Israelite which the Israelite himself may not do, this does not present a problem here. The point in this context seems to be that the Israelite not carry the money, so that he may take any measures to achieve that end.[17] Similarly, within a *sugya* which discusses whether or not one may embark on a long sea-voyage less than three days before the Sabbath, Rabbi and Simeon b. Gamliel disagree as to whether or not the Israelite must make the captain, presumably a gentile,[18] agree not to sail on the Sabbath.[19] Elsewhere,[20] we read that on the Sabbath,

----

one else's working on the Sabbath. For a detailed discussion of the literary style of these passages, see Jacob Neusner, *The Rabbinic Traditions About the Pharisees Before 70* (Leiden: 1971), II, 121-125.

[15]MShab. 16:6. I find the text's stated reason, that an Israelite is not responsible for a gentile's keeping the Sabbath, to be awkward, for it should have been obvious that the Israelite is not responsible for the gentile's working on the Sabbath, unless it is for the Israelite's benefit. However, the text also states that an Israelite must prevent his minor child from extinguishing the fire because he is responsible for the minor's observing the Sabbath. Thus, one of the *sugya*'s goals is to explain that an adult is responsible for a minor's actions on the Sabbath, and this might explain why the passage is phrased in the way it is. TShab. 13:9 contains a narrative about Joseph b. Simai of Sihin who had a fire in his courtyard. When a detachment of soldiers came from Sepphoris, he prevented them from putting out the fire. However, after the Sabbath, he sent a payment to each soldier. Sages ruled that he did not need to have prevented the soldiers from putting out the fire.

[16]MShab. 24:1. TShab. 17:20 states that the Israelite does this if he knows the gentile. The text continues that if he does not know the gentile, he follows him to his house. However, the text presents some difficulties; Cf., Saul Lieberman, *Tosefta Ki-fshutah: A Comprehensive Commentary on the Tosefta Part III: Order Mo'ed* (New York: 1962), 296.

[17]Cf., Bartinoro, *loc. cit*, who suggests that the Israelite gives his purse to the gentile while it is still light. One could argue that the only benefit the Israelite derives from the gentile's action is that the Israelite will not have to violate the Sabbath. If there is no gentile accompanying him, the Israelite may place his purse on his pack-animal; this is an act of last resort, for the Torah states that an Israelite's animals must also rest on the Sabbath.

[18]TShab. 13:13-13:14. Jacob Neusner, *A History of the Mishnaic Law of Appointed Times Part One Shabbat. Translation and Explanation* (Leiden: 1981), 154.

[19]In which case the Israelite may undertake the voyage less than three days before the Sabbath; Lieberman, *Tosefta Ki-fshutah III: Mo'ed*, 218. Simeon b. Gamliel states that the Israelite does not need to make a deal with the captain, while Rabbi holds that the Israelite must seek such an agreement. Lieberman cites the Gaon Mar Jacob b. Mordecai who implies that according to Simeon, the Israelite may embark on the voyage even on Friday without making a deal with the

Israelites may sit on chairs near a gentile's business, even if they are the chairs in which the gentile's customers normally sit or on which he normally displays his wares. The text further states that this rule was enacted by Aqiba, for before his time "they" would not allow Israelites to occupy these chairs on the Sabbath. TMoʻed 2:15 includes a narrative about Gamliel who sat in one of these chairs in Akko. However, when he was challenged, he left instead of arguing for the correctness of his action.[21] But the main point seems to be giving the appearance that one is violating the Sabbath. The gentile status of the vendor is important only because non-Israelites could work in their shops on the Sabbath, while Israelites could not engage in business on that day. What is curious to my mind is that the passage seems not to care that the Israelite here gives the appearance of doing business with the gentile, for at least "since the time of Aqiba," Israelites could sit near the gentile's shop on the Sabbath.

In general, then, our texts not only emphasize that an Israelite may not engage in normal activity on the Sabbath,[22] but they also make it clear that whatever Israelites may or may not do should be done, or not done, especially when they come into contact with a gentile. By their activity on the Sabbath in the presence of non-Israelites, the Israelites underscore their uniqueness with regard to this period of sacred time.

Just as the Sabbath is discussed in terms of a cessation of labor, its essential feature in Mishnah-Tosefta, so also Passover is treated from the perspective of one of its most distinctive characteristics, the Israelite taboo with respect to leaven. In fact, as Bokser notes, one of the features of Mishnah's Passover is its transforming the eating of unleavened bread, and by implication the abstention from leaven, to a practice of equal importance to the offering of the

----

ship's captain; Lieberman, *Tosefta Ki-fshutah III: Moʻed*, 218.

[20]TMoʻed 2:14-15.

[21]For a discussion of this passage, see Shamai Kanter, *Rabban Gamaliel II: The Legal Traditions* (Chico: 1980), 119-120.

[22]Goldenberg writes that the list of thirty-nine categories of forbidden activity on the Sabbath, mShab. 7:2 "is an artificial list. Certain activities which represent the essence of forbidden activity (e.g. buying and selling) do not appear, while others which do appear can hardly have been part of the average person's round of activities. On closer examination, the list can be seen to revolve around the basic concerns of human civilization: preparing bread and clothing, preparing skins and writing on them, building homes and lighting fires. It is less an index to Sabbath-law than a general systemization of the full range of human endeavor. Its purpose is to suggest that all these areas of life were to be suffused with that foretaste of heaven which the Sabbath was said to bring;" Goldenberg, 423-424.

Passover-sacrifice, the central feature of the biblical Passover.[23] In this regard, it is significant that the first three chapters of mPesahim deal with the laws regarding leaven and its removal, while the Passover-sacrifice does not appear until the fifth chapter of the tractate.

Israelites may neither consume nor possess leaven during the seven days of Passover,[24] and all but one of the Passover-texts which discuss the gentile focus on issues related to leaven.[25] In the view of these passages, an Israelite is one who does not possess or eat leaven during Passover, while a gentile is one who does not adhere to these prohibitions. While an Israelite cannot cause a gentile to violate the Sabbath, the former may cause the latter to do something which is prohibited to the former during Passover, for an Israelite may give leaven to a gentile to hold during Passover, and the former may use that leaven as soon as Passover ends.[26] Clearly, the leaven is not the issue;

----

[23]Baruch M. Bokser, *The Origins of the Seder: The Passover Rite and Early Rabbinic Judaism* (Berkeley and Los Angeles: 1984), especially 9, 39-44. Bokser writes: "It [the Mishnah] elevates the unleavened bread and the bitter herbs to equal status with the Passover-offering and makes all features of the celebration independent of the offering;" 77. "The unleavened bread, rather than sacrifice, symbolizes redemption. . .;" 79.

[24]Ex. 12:14-15, Ex. 12:17-20, and Ex. 13:6-7 are the major sources for these restrictions.

[25]TPis. 7:4 is the only Passover-*sugya* which discusses the gentile without focusing on leaven. The text equates the "Canaanite" slave with a child and indicates that neither may act independently. The text states that an Israelite may slaughter the Passover-offering on behalf of his Canaanite slave with or without his consent, for the latter does not have the right to act on his own behalf.

[26]An Israelite may derive benefit from the leaven within his house, sell it to gentiles, or feed it to cattle, wild animals or birds up until the time designated for its removal. After that time, one may not derive benefit from it, mPes. 2:1. An anonymous comment in tPis. 1:7 claims that before Aqiba, Israelites did not sell leaven to gentiles; however, Aqiba ruled that Israelites could sell their leaven to gentiles, even at the very time the former were required to remove it from their possession. Yosi claims that all Aqiba did was to lend his support to the Hillelite view of the matter. Employing Ex. 13:7 as a proof-text, *[Throughout the seven days unleavened bread shall be eaten; no leavened bread shall be found with you] no leaven shall be found with you [within all your borders]*, mPes. 2:2 rules that after Passover, it is forbidden to derive benefit from leaven which is in an Israelite's possession during Passover; however, after Passover, an Israelite may derive benefit from leaven which was in the possession of a gentile over the holiday. TPis. 1:12 states that the gentile's leaven may be used immediately after Passover. TPis. 2:15 contains a story about Rabban Gamliel, and we are told that one of the things we learn from the narrative is that the leaven of a gentile is permitted immediately after Passover. TPis. 2:6 and 2:8 expand upon this principle: If leaven is found in the goods within a gentile's shop in which there are Israelite workers or within the shop itself, the leaven may be eaten after Passover, for it is considered to be the property of the shop's owner. TPis. 2:5 and tPis. 2:7 reverse the roles of the Israelite and the gentile in tPis. 2:6 and 2:8, respectively, and hold that the leaven cannot be used. MPes. 2:3 states that if a gentile lent money to an Israelite who used leaven as security for the loan, the leaven may be used by an Israelite after Passover. However, if an Israelite loans money to a gentile who deposited leaven as security for the loan, the Israelite may not derive benefit from the leaven after Passover. The text in Lowe states that the leaven the Israelite left as security for his loan is

rather, it is who possessed/owned the leaven which causes it to be usable or unusable after Passover.

We see that the Sabbath and Passover are approached from two different points of view. With regard to the Sabbath, the Israelite is forbidden from working by either engaging in labor, or by causing another to work. In the latter instance, there is no distinction drawn between Israelites and non-Israelites, for an Israelite may not cause members from either group to work on the Sabbath. Passover, however, is addressed in terms of leaven, which an Israelite may neither own, nor eat, during the holiday. However, the restriction applies to only Israelites, so that they may dispose of their leaven by giving it to gentiles.

On a festival, an Israelite may prepare only the food he needs to eat; he

----

prohibited, while that which the gentile left is permitted. Kaufman reads the same as Lowe; however, the text has been corrected to read as the printed Mishnah. With regard to the leaven which the Israelite deposited, the word "prohibited" has been erased and "permitted" is written above the line. With reference to the leaven which the gentile used a security, the word "permitted" appears in the text, with "prohibited" written above it. Paris and Naples read as the printed text. TPis. 2:9 states that if a gentile lent money to an Israelite who deposited leaven as security and said, "If I have not come back to you before Passover, lo, this is sold to you," then an Israelite may derive benefit from the leaven. Similarly, if the Israelite lent money to a gentile who deposited his leaven as security and recited the same phrase, the Israelite cannot derive benefit from the leaven, tPis. 2:10. Epstein suggests that Tosefta either represents an interpretation of Mishnah or a new ruling by "other Tannaim;" Jacob N. Epstein, *Introduction to the Text of Mishnah*, Second Edition (Jerusalem: 1954), II, 714-715. Cf., Saul Lieberman, *Tosefta Ki-fshutah: A Comprehensive Commentary on the Tosefta Part IV: Mo'ed* (New York: 1962), 491-493. Lieberman offers several later authorities who read the text in different ways. However, he does not really solve the problem. There are two possible issues: 1) A gentile's leaven is prohibited after Passover, or 2) the person with whom the security is deposited after the phrase is recited is considered the owner of the leaven. I favor the second possibility. If a gentile came to an Israelite's house carrying leaven, the leaven need not be burnt. However, if the gentile deposited the leaven with the Israelite, the latter must dispose of it, unless he places it in a location set aside for holding the gentile's leaven, for then he can claim that it was not really in his possession, tPis. 2:11. If an Israelite and a gentile were traveling on a boat, and the Israelite gave his leaven to the gentile as a unrestricted gift, without stipulations, the former may buy back his leaven after Passover, tPis. 2:12. Furthermore, an Israelite may encourage a gentile to buy more leaven than he intended, with the assurance that the Israelite will purchase it from him after Passover, tPis. 2:13. An Israelite may hire his ass to a gentile to carry leaven from one place to another during Passover, tPis. 2:14. However, see Lieberman, *Tosefta Ki-fshutah IV: Mo'ed*, 497-498 for a collection of commentators who are concerned with this ruling. If after Passover the Israelite found a large quantity of leaven on the road, he may benefit from it; however, he is not permitted a small amount of leaven, tPis. 2:14. Lieberman states that this refers to a location in which the majority of the population are Israelites. The small amount of leaven is not permitted, according to Lieberman, because the Israelite cannot be sure that it was ownerless leaven during Passover; Lieberman, *Tosefta Ki-fshutah IV Mo'ed*, 498.

may not prepare food for gentiles or for dogs.[27] The text makes the point that gentiles are not Israelites, and the latter may not engage in permitted activity for the former's benefit. This ruling re-enforces the ethnicity of the holidays. The Israelites' activity is limited during this period, for each may prepare food only for him/herself, and this specifically excludes the gentiles. Furthermore, the transposition of gentiles with dogs implies that the former are "less than human," at least when compared to Israelites. If Israelites are to work on the festival, they may do so only for those who are celebrating the festival.

Passover and Sukkot extend over a period of seven-days, and this period is marked by somewhat altered activity. On the intermediate days of these festivals, Israelites may purchase from gentiles fields, houses, vineyards, cattle, and slaves, for such purchases fall under the category of redeeming these items from the control of the gentiles. In order to finalize such purchases during the week of the festival, one may write and register deeds in the gentile archives.[28] Again, we discover a distinction between those activities which one Israelite may do vis-a-vis another Israelite and activities in which an Israelite may engage with a gentile, for an Israelite may purchase items from a gentile during a festival which he may not procure from another Israelite. Interestingly, although the sugya permits an Israelite to buy items from a gentile which he may not procure from another Israelite, it adds a justification for these purchases which moves them out of the category of simple business transactions into the theological category of redemption. The Israelite may engage in business with the gentile because his actions are not normal business transactions; rather, they take on the aura of sacred acts, acts of redemption, for through his acquiring these items, the Israelite removes them from the gentile's possession. In this way, the text upholds the limitation on business activity, while at the same time permitting the Israelite to purchase these items from gentiles.

----

[27]TY.T. 2:6. When Simeon of Teman absented himself from the school house on the eve of a festival, Judah b. Baba questioned his actions. Simeon responded that he had to perform a religious duty, for his town had been invaded by gentile soldiers. In order to prevent the troops from causing trouble, Simeon prepared food and drink for them. Judah responded that Simeon had acted incorrectly, for one does not prepare food for gentiles on the holiday.

[28]TMo'ed 1:12. MM.Q. 2:4 prohibits an Israelite from purchasing houses, slaves, or cattle from another Israelite during the festival week, unless these items are needed for the Feast, or the seller needs the money for food. Cf., tA.Z. 1:8 where in the context of a discussion of gentile fairs, we find the same passage, only with the inclusion of the negative, "may not purchase," which does not make sense; Saul Lieberman, *Tosefeth Rishonim: A Commentary based on Manuscripts of the Tosefta and Works of the Rishonim and Midrashim in Manuscripts and rare Editions Part II Seder Nashim Nezikin Kadashim* (Jerusalem: 1938), 186.

Even though one may not sell an item during the festival-week, unless not doing so will cause a loss to the Israelite, an Israelite may sell a spring of water to, or make a trade with, a gentile during this time, if it involves something which may bring a loss to the Israelite if it is not done at this time; however, the Israelite need not worry that the gentile will suffer a loss through the purchase. Again, in this case an Israelite may engage in a business transaction with a gentile, as long as it is a special type of transaction.[29]

To sum up: With regard to activities which mark off the sacred times of the Sabbath, Passover, and the Festival-week, we find a concern with the Israelite's actions *vis-à-vis* the gentile's activity. In general, the gentiles act as they normally do. However, with regard to the Sabbath, all of the gentile's activity must be done *independently* of the Israelite. As we saw, this has nothing to do with the gentile's being a gentile; rather, it is a result of the prohibition against the Israelites' engaging in any work, either directly or indirectly. With regard to Passover and the Festival-week, this is not the case. During Passover, the gentile may serve as a repository for the *Israelite's* leaven, as long as this is not explicitly stated. Here, an Israelite is defined as one who neither eats nor possesses leaven, while a gentile is one who consumes or owns *hames*. During the Festival-week, business in some items between the Israelite and the gentile goes on as normal, but it is not referred to as a business transaction, or it falls into a unique category of such activity. Thus, in all cases, the sacred period of time causes Israelites to alter their activity, especially with regard to gentiles, and this would have resulted also in the gentile's altering their normal activity *vis-à-vis* the Israelite. The celebration of the Israelite periods of sacred time occurred in public, and the observance of these holidays was manifested in the cessation, or altering, of normal daily activity. Because the authors of Mishnah-

----

[29]TMo'ed 1:2; Jacob Neusner, *A History of the Mishnaic Law of Appointed Times Part Four Besah, Rosh Hashshanah, Taanit, Megillah, Moed Qatan, Hagigah. Translation and Explanation*(Leiden: 1983), 184. Saul Lieberman, *The Tosefta According to Codex Vienna, with Variants from Codices Erfurt, London, Genizah Mss. and Editio Princeps (Venice 1521) Together with References to Parallel Passages in Talmudic Literature and A Brief Commentary* (New York: 1962), 366. Saul Lieberman, *Tosefta Ki-fshutah: A Comprehensive Commentary on the Tosefta Part V Order Mo'ed* (New York: 1962), 1228-1229. The text refers to the sale occurring on the Sabbath to take effect after the Sabbath has ended; however, this does not really make sense. Hasde David reads the text as referring to a sale before the Sabbath, even though the Israelite knows that the gentile will use the spring during the Sabbath; however, the text does not really allow for this reading. Probably here "Sabbath" refers to the festival week; if not, I do not see how this part of the *sugya* relates to the rest of the passage, which clearly refers to the festival-week.

Tosefta assume that gentiles and Israelites interacted socially, economically, and politically, the former had to be dealt with in the context of the latter's sacred periods of time.

The fact that the gentiles themselves are not the major issue under discussion runs throughout the treatments of the holidays: The passages on the Sabbath focus on the problem of work, the *sugyot* on Passover center on the matter of leaven, the texts on the holidays focus on the redemption of specific items. While in the latter two instances the non-Israelite nature of the gentile is important for the formulation of the rulings, everything is designed from the point of view of Israelite concerns and points of view.

iii

To this point, we have focused on the temporal aspect of the Israelite sacred periods of time; however, the Sabbath also has spatial ramifications, and these affected the gentiles. On the Sabbath, travel was limited to a confined area near one's private domain, and transporting objects between private and public areas was forbidden. However, the authors of Mishnah-Tosefta created two means by which Israelites could transform a public area into a temporary private space, so that they might freely move beyond the severely limited confines allowed by the strictures of Sabbath-law. Both of these "transformed areas," the *'erub* and the *shittuf*,[30] could be established by only adult Israelites.[31] In general terms, the transformation occurs by extending an Israelite's domicile, which is defined in terms of a person's eating: The place where one plans to spend the Sabbath is the place in which he plans to eat the meal he has prepared for the Sabbath.[32]

Only space controlled by, or inhabited by, Israelites needs to be, or can be, transformed on the Sabbath,[33] and, ideally, all of the residents around a

----

[30]A *shittuf* joins together the residences along an alley way. One person living on the alley sets down a jar of food or drink and declares that it belongs to everyone living on the alley way, and those living on the alley accept possession of the food.

[31]In creating a *shittuf*, it is possible for a person to set down a jar and to have his adult children, his wife, or his Hebrew slaves stand in for the other members of the alley; however, he may not have his minor children or his gentile slaves serve this function, for they cannot act independently of the master of the house, mErub. 7.6. Similarly, one may prepare an *'erub* for his minor son or daughter or his non-Israelite slave with or without their consent, for they cannot act independently, tErub. 6:11. One may not prepare an *'erub* for his adult child, his Hebrew slave, or his wife without their consent, for they may act as independent individuals.

[32]Neusner, *Mishnaic System of Appointed Times*, 83.

[33]If a gentile brings something into the Israelite sacred space, it is considered an intrusion into the space which cannot be moved, just like Israelite belongings; tShab. 17:17.

courtyard accept the transformation of the area.[34] Therefore, the presence of a gentile resident sharing a courtyard with Israelites could be an issue of concern. The *sugyot* of interest to us assume that gentiles and Israelites live together in single courtyards, and the *'erub* with which our texts are concerned is the one formed by joining the units around a common courtyard. The issue under consideration is whether or not the gentile's presence in the courtyard is important for the Israelites who wish to transform the courtyard into part of one large private domicile: Does the presence of the gentile negate the possibility of transforming the courtyard into an extended, shared domicile or can the presence of the gentile simply be ignored?

Space in which only gentiles reside need not be transformed during the Sabbath; however, the presence of one Israelite in a courtyard neutralizes the gentile "nature" of an area.[35] Meir[36] considers gentiles to be equal residents in a courtyard in which Israelites dwell; therefore, an Israelite can establish his Sabbath-domicile in a courtyard, only if there are no gentiles in the area to interrupt the continuity of "Israelite space." Agreeing with this picture of the gentile, some held that if a gentile rented out his space in a courtyard to an Israelite, an *'erub* may be constructed in the courtyard.[37] On the other hand, Eliezer b. Jacob simply ignores the gentiles. Their presence in the courtyard is unimportant; they are "non-beings,"[38] who do not interrupt the continuity of "Israelite space."[39] The point of these views is the question of whether or not a

----

[34]MErub. 6:1-3.

[35]TErub. 5:19. Cf., tErub. 5:22.

[36]MErub. 6:1. However, see Goldenberg who suggests that the comment should not be attributed to Meir; Robert Goldenberg, *The Sabbath-Law of Rabbi Meir* (Ann Arbor: 1978), 63-66.

[37]TErub. 5:18.

[38]This idea of the gentile as a "non-being" functions here; however, in other contexts, such as saving a life on the Day of Atonement or, I assume even on the Sabbath, the humanity of the gentile is equal to that of an Israelite; see mYoma 8:7: If a building collapsed on the Day of Atonement, the rubble may be removed, if the people suspect that a person is trapped, even if the person is a gentile.

[39]MErub. 6:1. In mErub. 8:5, Meir again accepts the presence of a gentile as important. If an Israelite or a gentile left his house in a courtyard in order to observe the Sabbath in another town, his house restricts the other members of the courtyard, while Judah holds that the empty house is ignored. For an *'erub* within a courtyard to be valid, all those who live in all of the houses must participate. Meir holds that a house is considered part of the courtyard, even if no one is dwelling in it, while Yosi maintains that an empty house does not affect the situation. Both assume that the gentile and the Israelite affect the courtyard in the same way. Yosi states that a gentile's empty house affects the *'erub* because he might return during the Sabbath; Bartinoro, *loc. cit.* However, an empty house belonging to an Israelite is ignored because the Israelite would not be able to return to his house on the Sabbath. Simeon adds that if the Israelite left his house in the courtyard to visit his daughter on the Sabbath, his house not does affect the *'erub* because he has no intention of returning to his home until after the Sabbath. Thus, Meir and Yosi maintain that a gentile's presence

gentile may join with the Israelites so as to allow the Israelites to transform the area into usable space on the Sabbath. The problem seems to revolve around the conception that gentiles and Israelites may not act together in this distinctively Israelite activity of transforming the space, for this serves specific Israelite needs and accords with Israelite conceptions of the Sabbath.

iv

We saw above that with respect to the Land of Israel some held that there was a holiness which adhered to the Land independently of Israelites or gentiles and that, in some regards, even the latter had to act with this holiness in mind. This possibility is not expressed with regard to the periods of Appointed Times. From the point of view of our authors, the sacred times are holy only because Israelites mark them as holy; gentiles, therefore, are not expected to alter their activity, unless they come into contact with Israelites. Even when this interaction occurs, however, usually, it is the Israelite who alters his activity *vis-a-vis* the gentile, and not the other way around. Throughout, our texts consistently recognize that gentiles are not Israelites and that only the latter are affected by the advent of the periods of sacred time. In fact, the gentiles so completely stand outside of the system of holy time that Eliezer b. Jacob can allow the Israelite to ignore the presence of the gentile in the former's courtyard, when he sets about to create his *'erub*. Although the Israelite and the gentile shared a common courtyard, and therefore must normally recognize each other's presence, from this perspective of holy time, the gentile is deemed totally transparent, so as not to interfere with the Israelite's activities on the Sabbath. This position was challenged by those who believed that the presence of a gentile in a courtyard could prevent the transformation of the courtyard into an extended domicile. For them, the gentile was real and presented an obstacle to the Israelites' achieving their desired goals.

In virtually all cases, the gentile is expected to act in ways opposite to the ways in which the Israelite is expected to perform his duties. While the Israelites cease from certain activities on the Sabbath, unless they are performed in prescribed areas, the gentiles do not need to alter their activity. This suggests that it would have been obvious to a gentile, who was used to observing and interacting with Israelites, that something was different. The gentile would realize

---

in a courtyard prevents the Israelites from establishing a *'erub*, while Eliezer, and probably Judah, does not believe that the gentile's presence has any affect on the Israelite's practices.

that for a specific period of time, things, at least from the Israelites' perspective, had changed. Similarly, on the intermediate days of the Festivals, Israelite endeavors are placed into special categories, so that the Israelite may perform functions with regard to the gentile in which he may not engage with another Israelite, while at the same time, keeping intact the principle which limits the interactions between Israelites. Again, the gentiles would realize that the Israelites are treating them differently from the way in which they interact with other Israelites.

The situation during Passover is especially interesting. The Exodus from Egypt and the revelation at Sinai are seen as the foundational events of rabbinic culture. The cessation of the sacrificial cult brought the offering of the Pascal lamb, the central biblical rite, to an end. In order to compensate for this, the sages in Mishnah shifted the emphasis from the Bible's focus on the Passover-sacrifice to the eating of only unleavened bread. This meant that along with the Seder, eating unleavened bread and avoiding leaven became the central rites in marking the events which the authors of Mishnah-Tosefta considered to have created their culture. This explains why the rabbis picture the gentiles as the exact opposite of Israelites with regard to leaven.

TPis. 2:5-15 form one of the longest extended essays on the gentile outside of tractate *Abodah Zara*, and they deal exclusively with the gentile and leaven. TPis. 2:5-10 comprise a series of pericopae divided into three matched pairs in which the roles of the Israelite and the gentile in the first *suyga* of each set of pairs are reversed in the second pericope of the set: TPis. 2:5 discusses *ḥameṣ* found after Passover in wares in an Israelite's shop in which there are gentile workers, and tPis. 2:6 discusses *ḥameṣ* found after Passover in the wares in a gentile's shop in which there are Israelite workers. TPis. 2:7 discusses *ḥameṣ* found after Passover in an Israelite's shop in which there are gentile workers, and tPis. 2:8 discusses *ḥameṣ* found in a gentile's shop in which there are Israelite workers. TPis. 2:9 discusses *ḥameṣ* which an Israelite provided as security for the loan he took from a gentile, and tPis. 2:10 discusses *ḥameṣ* which a gentile provided as security for the loan he took from an Israelite. This essay draws a clear distinction between the gentile and the Israelite, based solely on the issue of *ḥameṣ*, and tPis. 2:5-10 demonstrate that the gentile is the *exact opposite* of the Israelite in regard to the matter of *ḥameṣ* and Passover. A gentile may own and use *ḥameṣ* during Passover, while an Israelite may not. Immediately after Passover, an Israelite may use the *ḥameṣ* which was in a gentile's possession during the sacred period, while immediately after Passover an Israelite may not use the *ḥameṣ* which was in an Israelite's possession during the sacred period.[40]

The boundaries set here, especially in tPis. 2:5-10, are drawn in terms of exact opposites, and this seems to be the point of the section. The expression of these principles through the extended essay, especially in the carefully drawn parallels in tPis. 2:5-10,[41] suggests that our authors were fascinated by the inversion of the roles of the gentile and the Israelite with regard to leaven during Passover. The idea that the "other" is the mirror-image, or direct opposite, is common among a variety of cultures, and it is significant that with regard to Passover, the holiday which was a remembrance of the foundational event of rabbinic culture, and leaven, one of the central rabbinic symbols of the holiday, is the distinction between the Israelite and the gentile drawn so sharply. In the mind of our authors, the clearest way to demarcate between the Israelite and non-Israelite with regard to this period of sacred time was in terms of *ḥameṣ*, and they took great pains carefully to work out the distinctions.[42]

Throughout the discussions of the gentiles and the Israelite periods of sacred times, we have seen that the focus is on ideas important to the authors of Mishnah-Tosefta. The gentile as non-Israelite figured prominently with regard to leaven and with regard to doing business on the intermediate days of Sukkot and Pesaḥ. The texts we have reviewed in this chapter do not tell us much about non-Israelites, nor do they exhibit any particular knowledge of them, or concern with them. In the bulk of these *sugyot*, the gentiles are dealt with solely in terms of concepts and ideas which were central to the rabbinic frame of reference with regard to the Israelite holidays: Not working on the Sabbath and abstention from leaven on Passover. In the latter instance, the discussions of the gentiles served to emphasize the unique characteristics of the Israelites during the period of time which the authors of Mishnah-Tosefta viewed as a remembrance of the events which created their culture and way of life.

----

[40]TPis. 1:12 states that an Israelite may use a gentile's *ḥameṣ* after Passover, and mPes. 2:2 states that an Israelite may derive benefit from a gentile's *ḥameṣ* which has remained over Passover.

[41]The discussion of using *ḥameṣ* as security for a loan appears in mPes. 2:3.

[42]See Barbara A. Babcock, *The Reversible World: Symbolic Inversion in Art and Society* (Ithaca: 1978). If we consider Mishnah-Tosefta to be intellectual creations which do not clearly distinguish between theoretical situations and actual situations, what the authors of Tosefta's essay did is not much different from the activities discussed in Babcock.

Chapter Eight:

Israelite Society and the Gentiles

i

The Torah maintains that the various peoples who inhabited the environment in which the ancient Israelites resided stemmed from different human ancestors. Noah's sons became the progenitors of a number of "clans, languages, and nations."[1] Lot's grandsons produced the Moabites and the Ammonites.[2] Ishmael fathered "a great nation,"[3] and "two nations" fought within Rebekah's womb:[4] Jacob became an ancestor of the Israelites,[5] while Esau produced the Edomites.[6] The desire to keep themselves and their kin distinct from these peoples stands behind the Patriarchs' seeking wives for their sons from their ancestral tribes.[7] As a result of the actions of the various nations towards the Israelites, prohibitions were set forth concerning the intermingling of the

----

[1]Gen. 10:1-31. Speiser notes that "biblical terminology uses 'people' ('m) primarily for a genetically related group, and 'nation' (gwy) largely for a political entity centered in a given locality. . . . For the purposes of national classification, therefore, it is thus gwy that is the more suitable term; hence the Table of Nations employs it repeatedly (Gen. 10:5, 20, 31-32), but dispenses with 'm altogether." Speiser therefore maintains that the basis of the divisions in Genesis was geographical; Ephraim A. Speiser, "Man, Ethnic Divisions of," in George A. Buttrick (ed.), *The Interpreter's Dictionary of the Bible: An Illustrated Encyclopedia* (Nashville and New York: 1962), III, 235-236. Compare, Daniel Sperber, "Nations, the Seventy," in Cecil Roth and Geoffrey Wigoder (eds.), *Encyclopedia Judaica* (Jerusalem: 1972), XII, 882-883. However, it does seem that there is a genetic factor at play, for we find various *sets* of tribes, each of which was descended from a single son of Noah.

[2]Gen. 19:36-38. Speiser comments, "Popular tales about neighboring peoples are encountered the world over. The product of traditional rivalries, local pride, and raw folk humor, they often tend to place the neighbor's character and origin in an uncomplimentary, if amusing, light;" Ephraim A. Speiser, *The Anchor Bible Genesis* (Garden City: 1983), 145.

[3]Gen. 21:18.

[4]Gen. 25:23.

[5]Jacob's name is changed to Israel, Gen. 32:29, so that "the Children of Israel" are literally Jacob's children.

[6]Gen. 36:9.

[7]Gen. 24; Gen. 26:34-35; Gen. 28:1-9.

"tribes."[8] These carried over into Mishnah-Tosefta, for even though some of our sages knew that the Ammonites, Edomites, Egyptians, and Moabites were no longer recognizable "tribes" in the second century of the common era,[9] the discussions of these "peoples" still appear in our texts,[10] as if their conversion to Judaism or their marriage to an Israelite were still possible.

Following the biblical paradigm, some of the sages treat the Israelites as a separate segment of humanity from the non-Israelites. The differences between the Israelite and the gentile are related to the ancestry of the various peoples, as well as to the unique religious and other cultural practices and beliefs of the various tribes.[11] Because YHWH created these distinct nations, it was obligatory for the Israelites to ensure that the boundaries between themselves and the other segments of humanity were recognized and maintained.

ii

The gentiles and Israelites represent two classes of human beings, so that a person or an ox that intended to kill a gentile but killed an Israelite is not punished for an act of pre-meditated murderer.[12] In addition, one text even maintains that although a gentile who kills a gentile or an Israelite is liable, an Israelite who kills a gentile is "exempt."[13] In an attempt to preserve the divisions among the nations who inhabit the world, the writers of our documents

----

[8]Deut. 23:4-9.

[9]MYad. 4:4.

[10]TQid. 5:4, tYeb. 8:1, mYeb. 8:3, mYad. 4:4, tYad. 2:16-17.

[11]However, as we shall see in the next chapter, when our authors view the gentile as an idolater, they seek to establish a much firmer division between the two peoples.

[12]In these *sugyot*, the distinction between the gentile and the Israelite parallels the division between human beings and other animals. If an ox rubbed against a wall and intended to kill a gentile but killed an Israelite, it is exempt from the punishment of death by stoning, which would have been applied to the animal if it had succeeded in killing its intended victim. The owner, however, is liable for the ransom-payment, mB.Q. 4:6. In tB.Q. 4:6, Judah states that the owner is not liable for the damages caused by the ox, while Simeon declares that he is liable. If, however, the ox were considered harmless, the owner is exempt for the ransom payment, and the ox is exempt from the death-penalty. In mSanh. 9:2 and tSanh. 9:2, the ox is replaced by a human being. The point of both texts is that Israelites and gentiles represent two sub-classes of human beings, so that killing a *human being* does not necessarily make one culpable for pre-meditated murder. One is guilty of pre-meditated murder only if he kills a member of the class which he intended to kill.

[13]TA.Z. 8:5. See Saul Lieberman, *Tosefeth Rishonim: A Commentary Based on Manuscripts of the Tosefta and Works of the Rishonim and Midrashim in Manuscripts and Rare Editions Part II Seder Nashim Nezikin Kadashim* (Jerusalem: 1938), 200 and Saul Lieberman, *HaYerushalmi Kifshuto* (Jerusalem: 1934), 188.

discourage sexual contact between Israelites and non-Israelites,[14] much like the biblical Patriarchs insisted that their sons marry women from their own ancestral tribes. In addition, some rabbis even attempted to regulate the marriage practices among the non-Israelite nations of the world.[15] While intercourse is one means of "acquiring" an Israelite woman and contracting a valid marriage,[16] intercourse between an Israelite and a gentile does not result in an acceptable relationship.[17] Furthermore, the children who are produced from the union of a gentile and an Israelite occupy a lesser status than the offsprings produced by the union of two Israelites.[18]

The Torah distinguishes between Hebrew and non-Hebrew slaves, limiting the years of service of the former and calling the latter "property for all time."[19] The idea that non-Israelite slaves may be "property," while Hebrew

----

[14]One who takes an Aramean woman as his lover will be punished by the zealots; mSanh. 9:6.

[15]TQid. 5:1. Segal suggests that the purity laws were one way to prevent marriage between Israelites and gentiles; however, below, chapter 11, we shall see that the issue of purity with regard to gentiles is complex, for the major categories of Israelite purity often did not apply clearly to gentiles; Alan F. Segal, *Rebecca's Children: Judaism and Christianity in the Roman World* (Cambridge and London: 1986), 125.

[16]MQid. 1:1.

[17]If a gentile or a slave had intercourse with an Israelite woman, they do not have a valid marriage contract. If they wish to marry after the slave is freed or the gentile converted, the marriage contract is a *maneh*, the sum for a non-virgin, tKet. 1:3. Along these lines, sexual relations with a Canaanite slave girl do not constitute an act of acquisition, so that she may not eat heave-offering; she can be acquired by only money, tKet. 5:1. If a gentile or a slave is suspected of having intercourse with an Israelite woman, he may not marry her if he converts or if the slave becomes a freeman. However, if they do marry, the marriage is not dissolved, tYeb. 4:6. If an Israelite man is suspected of having intercourse with a gentile woman or a slave, the same rules apply, mYeb. 2:8, tYeb. 4:6. The marriage is prohibited because it will appear to confirm the rumor of the suspected sexual contact. Along different lines, an Israelite may give his wife a conditional divorce, for he may state that she is not free to marry his father or brother, a slave or a gentile, or anyone with whom she may not contract a valid betrothal. This again stresses the point that a marriage between a gentile and an Israelite is unacceptable, mGit. 9:2. Cf., Yom Tov Lipmann, *loc. cit.*

[18]If a woman's betrothal is invalid and she is of a class of women who cannot contract a valid betrothal with anyone else within the Israelite community, her child takes on her status, and such is the case with a gentile woman, or a bondwoman, mQid. 3:12. However, an anonymous statement rules that if a gentile or a slave has intercourse with an Israelite, a male offspring is a *mamzer*. Simeon b. Judah, quoting Simeon, states that a *mamzer* is the offspring of one of the prohibited relationships mentioned in the Torah for which the punishment is "cutting off" if one violates the injunction, tQid. 4:16. MYeb. 7:5 states that if an Israelite woman were married to a priest, or if a woman of the priestly class were married to an Israelite, and they produced a daughter who married a slave or a gentile, any son produced from this latter union is considered a *mamzer*.

[19]Ex. 21:2-6, Lev. 25:39-46, and Deut. 15:12-18. Exodus and Deuteronomy specify that a Hebrew slave must be given the option of going free after six years of service, while Leviticus states that Hebrew slaves are freed during the Jubilee Year. Lev. 25:44-46 indicate that non-Hebrew slaves become their master's property, so that they can be bequeathed to the latter's descendants.

slaves remain independent "humans," is carried forward and expanded in our texts, for Hebrew slaves are acquired differently from Canaanite slaves, and each purchases his freedom in a distinct manner.[20] In addition, to the authors of Mishnah-Tosefta, gentile slaves cannot act independently of their masters, while Hebrew slaves may act as distinct human beings.[21] Similarly, the amount of compensation one is assessed for damage to a slave depends on whose slave it is and whether the slave was a Hebrew or a Canaanite.[22]

----

[20]Canaanite and Hebrew slaves are acquired by different means and may redeem themselves according to distinct methods. While a Hebrew bondman is acquired by money or a writ, and he acquires his freedom at the end of six years of service, at the arrival of the Jubilee year, or by his redeeming his outstanding value, mQid. 1:2, Meir states that a Canaanite bondman is acquired by money, a writ, or usucaption and that he acquires himself by money paid by others, or by a writ of indebtedness which he executes. Sages disagree and state that he acquires his freedom by money which he himself pays, or by a writ executed by someone besides the bondman, mQid. 1:3. On the issue of slavery see Ephraim E. Urbach, "The Laws Regarding Slavery as a Source for Social History of the Period of the Second Temple, the Mishnah and Talmud," in J. G. Weiss (ed.), *Papers of the Institute of Jewish Studies London* (Jerusalem: 1964), 1-94.

[21]MM.S. 4:4, an Israelite may give money to his Hebrew slaves and instruct them to purchase the second tithe; however, he may not do this with his Canaanite slaves because "their hand is as his hand." TErub. 6:11, an Israelite may prepare an *'erub* for his Canaanite slave with or without the slave's permission, while he must have the permission of his Hebrew slave. MErub. 7:6, one may not grant permission to share in a *shittuf* through his Canaanite slave because "their hand is as his hand;" however, he grants permission through his Hebrew slave. MB.Q. 9:10, while a Hebrew slave may keep lost items which he finds, those items which Canaanite slaves find belong to their masters. If an Israelite steals something in order to feed his dependents, including his Canaanite slaves, he does not have to make restitution. If he left them something which is subject to a mortgage and the terms of the agreement and payments are clear, his heirs must pay the debt. The Canaanite slaves do not appear in mB.Q. 10:1; they are mentioned only in tB.Q. 10:21.

[22]If a person inflicts bodily harm on another, he is liable for the injury, the pain, the cost of healing, the loss of time, and the indignity he caused, mB.Q. 8:1. When dealing with another Israelite's property, our texts do not draw a distinction between Israelite and non-Israelite slaves. Therefore, if an Israelite injures another's Hebrew or Canaanite slave but does not leave a wound, he is liable on all five counts. Judah states that one is not liable for causing indignity to a slave, mB.Q. 8:3. With regard to one's own slaves, the Mishnah distinguishes between Hebrew and Canaanite servants, while Tosefta does not. If one wounds his own Canaanite slave and leaves a wound, he is not culpable on any of the five counts; however, if he injures his own Hebrew slave, he is culpable for everything, except the loss of time he causes, mB.Q. 8:3 and mB.Q. 8:5. However, tB.Q. 9:10 rules that if one injures his own Canaanite slave, is liable for everything, except for the loss of time. Tosefta draws another distinction between Hebrew and Canaanite slaves, for injury done to a Hebrew slave is compensated according to the rules of damages, while injury done to a Canaanite slave is compensated by a fine. Therefore, if a person injures his Hebrew slave while they are alone, so that there are no witnesses, the slave may swear to the facts of the matter and collect damages. On the other hand, if one injured a Canaanite slave (Abraham Abele Ben Hayyim HaLevi Gombiner, *loc. cit.*, argues that this refers to someone else's Canaanite slave) when there were no witnesses present, the gentile slave may not collected damages because the damages in this case would be a fine, and one does not impose a fine on the testimony of the defendant alone, tB.Q. 9:21.

In discussing damages and torts, our texts again distinguish between cases involving Israelites and those between Israelites and gentiles. A different set of legal standards applies to each group of cases, for as one moves outside the group, the legal principles change.[23] For some, the fine points of Israelite law do not apply at all to gentiles: If a gentile's ox injures his fellow gentile's ox, the owner must pay full damages, no matter the ox's character, for the distinction between a dangerous ox and a harmless ox, which plays a large role in the discussions concerning damages done by an Israelite's ox, does not apply to a gentile's animal, even if the non-Israelite decides to live according to Israelite law.[24] Similarly, if an Israelite's ox gored a gentile's ox, the Israelite is not culpable for damages; however, if a gentile's ox gored an Israelite's ox, the gentile must pay for the damages.[25] An ox which is owned by a gentile and an Israelite is treated the same as an ox which is owned by an Israelite alone.[26]

The Israelites and gentiles occupied different places in the Israelite judicial system. A number of *sugyot* respond to the fact that there were two court systems, an Israelite and a gentile, which affected the Israelites in

----

[23]In the *gemara*, bB.Q. 38a, Abbahu explains that since the "sons of Noah" did not observe even the seven commandments which God placed on them, they were placed outside of the protection of Israelite civil laws. Kirzner writes: "As Canaanites did not recognise the laws of social justice, they did not impose any liability for damage done by cattle. They could consequently not claim to be protected by a law they neither recognised nor respected. . . . In ancient Israel as in the modern state the legislation regulating the protection of life and property of the stranger was . . . on the basis of reciprocity. Where such reciprocity was not recognised, the stranger could not claim to enjoy the same protection of the law as the citizen." E.W. Kirzner, *Baba Kamma: Translated into English with Notes, Glossary and Indices* in Isidore Epstein (ed.), *The Babylonian Talmud* (London: 1935), 211, n. 6. The phrase "children of the covenant" appears in mB.Q. 1:2 and 1:3. TB.Q. 1:1-2 explain that in mB.Q. 1:2 the phrase is meant to exclude an ox belonging to an Israelite which gored an ox belonging to a gentile, and in mB.Q. 1:3 the phrase excludes gentiles, slaves, and anyone else who may not give valid testimony in court. Tosefta's comment seems to place its understanding of Mishnah into the category of "religious" differences. This specification may indicate that others did not view these texts in the same way.

[24]TB.Q. 4:2.

[25]MB.Q. 4:3. The text states that it makes no difference whether the gentile's ox was classified as harmless or dangerous; Cf., tB.Q. 4:1. In tB.Q. 4:3, Meir states that if a gentile's ox gored an Israelite's ox, the owner must pay the damages from his choicest possessions, whether or not the ox was deemed dangerous before it caused the injury. These rules reflect an idealized situation, for it is difficult to imagine that an Israelite could refuse to pay damages to a gentile, while requiring him to pay for damages done to an Israelite's property.

[26]Cf., mB.Q. 4:2. If a dangerous ox which is jointly owned by a gentile and an Israelite injures an ox which belongs to an Israelite, the owners must pay full damages. However, if the jointly owned ox were not considered dangerous before it injured the Israelite's ox, the owners pay half-damages, tB.Q. 4:1.

Palestine.[27] In matters of the taking of oaths or of giving testimony, gentiles were treated differently from Israelites.[28] Furthermore, a clear distinction is made between gentile and Israelite witnesses who might sign important Israelite documents, such as writs of divorce and writs of emancipation, and the gentile registries in which such documents were recorded and filed.[29]

While we might naturally expect our authors to be concerned about the proper slaughter of animals used for sacrifices, we learn that they also were interested in the proper slaughter of ordinary, profane food. In this context, there is a good deal of discussion concerning the role a gentile may play in this activity. The passages do not focus primarily on matters of idolatry or the pos-

----

[27]While an Israelite court may impose a divorce on a couple, a gentile court may not, unless it instructs the parties to do exactly what the Israelite court demands, so that in fact the divorce is enacted by the Israelite court, mGit. 9:8; Cf., Bartinoro, *loc. cit.* The same rules apply to the act of *halisah*, tYeb. 12:13. We know virtually nothing about the Israelite legal system except what we can deduce from Mishnah-Tosefta and *later* rabbinic documents. For these reasons, it is useless so speculate on how these ideas were put into practice, or if they were put into practice at all. Discussions of the legal institutions in the Tannaitic period are highly speculative, at best. See, Emil Schürer, *The History of the Jewish People in the Age of Jesus Christ (175 B.C.-A.D. 135)* edited by Geza Vermes, Fergus Millar, and Matthew Black (Edinburgh: 1979), II, 199-226 and the bibliography cited there. While this section focuses on the Sanhedrin, its implications for the entire legal system of Tannaitic Palestine are clear. See also, Shaye J.D. Cohen, *From the Maccabees to the Mishnah* (Philadelphia: 1987), 107-108 and Segal, 43-45.

[28]Gentiles cannot give testimony in an Israelite court, and if an Israelite imposes an oath on a gentile, the latter is exempt from fulfilling the oath, tShebu. 2:5; the text mentions women and children along with the gentile. We also learn that the gentile is included among those upon whom an oath may be imposed, but for whom they do not take an oath if they bring a claim in an Israelite court, tShebu. 5:10. Even outside the court, an Israelite could lie to a gentile under certain conditions. An Israelite may take a false oath before a gentile, tax-collector, or robber, tShebu. 2:14.

[29]Writs of divorce are not valid if drawn up in gentile registries; however, Simeon accepts them if they were prepared by valid judges, mGit. 1:5. A gentile may not deliver a bill of divorce from an Israelite husband to his wife, mGit. 2:5. The text also excludes the deaf-mute, imbecile, minor, and blind man; this is a standard configuration of ritually unfit persons. The point is emphasized in mGit. 2:6, which states that even if the gentile converted after he delivered the document, it still is not valid. The principle is that a gentile may not serve as an Israelite's agent; Cf., Bartinoro, *loc. cit.* A gentile may not give valid testimony which is required concerning the fact that the document was signed in his presence; Cf., Yom Tov Lipmann, *loc. cit* and Jacob Neusner, *A History of the Mishnaic Law of Women Part Four Sotah, Gittin, Qiddushin. Translation and Explanation* (Leiden: 1980), 137. Aqiba rules that all documents deposited in a gentile archive are valid, even if they contain the signatures of gentiles, while sages declare that divorce documents and writs of emancipation are invalid if they are filed in the archives of gentiles, tGit. 1:4. Elsewhere, sages' opinion appears anonymously, while Simeon disagrees and rules that divorce documents and writs of emancipation are valid if they are executed by an authorized sage, even if they are filed in a gentile archive, mGit. 1:5.

sibility that the gentile might somehow perform a religious ritual while slaughtering the meat;[30] rather, the topics relate to the proper methods of the slaughter of animals for ordinary food. While the sages' concern for these matters relates to some passages in the Torah, we learn from these pericopae that there were strict "Israelite" rules which had to be followed if the meat were to be eaten, and that the meat had to be prepared by an Israelite butcher or, at least, under his supervision. In general, meat prepared by a gentile was considered the same as meat torn by a beast, and such carrion was prohibited to Israelites.[31]

The concern with food is carried forward in other contexts. In general, Israelites could sell gentiles items which the former were forbidden to eat or to sell to one another. Therefore, the hip containing the sciatic nerve, Gen. 32:32,

----

[30]However, in mHul. 2:7, Eliezer maintains that unless a gentile states otherwise, anything he does is done to honor an idol. Cf., Jacob Neusner, *Eliezer ben Hyrcanus: The Tradition and the Man Part One: The Tradition* (Leiden: 1973), 382-383.

[31]By definition, only Israelites could properly slaughter animals; therefore, beasts slaughtered by gentiles were considered to be carrion, which conveyed uncleanness by carrying, mHul. 1:1. This text also states that slaughtering done by a deaf-mute, an imbecile, or a minor is not acceptable, unless the butcher was supervised by an adult Israelite male. Neusner notes that since "carrion imparts uncleanness to the person who carries it, Lev. 11:40," the specific reference to the fact that what the gentile slaughters conveys uncleanness by carrying "is redundant;" Jacob Neusner, *A History of the Mishnaic Law of Holy Things Part Three Hullin, Bekhorot. Translation and Explanation* (Leiden: 1979), 15. THul. 1:1 permits slaughtering by a Samaritan, an uncircumcised man, an Israelite apostate, but not by a *min* or a gentile. In mHul. 2:7, Eliezer states that an Israelite may not slaughter a gentile's beast for the gentile, while the anonymous opinion holds that such a slaughtering is valid. If a gentile finished the slaughtering begun by an Israelite, it is invalid, even if the gentile cut further than was necessary. If an Israelite completed the slaughtering of an animal begun by a gentile, by cutting further than necessary, the slaughtering is valid. If a gentile engages in an act of slaughtering, by cutting something which does not render the beast unfit for eating, and a Israelite comes and completes the slaughtering, the beast may be eaten, tHul. 1:2; Cf., Lieberman, *Tosefeth Rishonim*, II, 219. If an Israelite and a gentile both held the knife during the slaughtering, the slaughtering is acceptable, tHul. 1:3. If an Israelite holds the animal while the gentile slaughters it, the slaughtering is acceptable, tHul. 1:6. Gentiles need not observe the prohibition against slaughtering an animal and its young on the same day, nor the command to pour out the blood and cover it over, for these are applicable to only Israelites, tHul. 5:3 and tHul. 6:4. See Lev. 17:13-14 and Lev. 22:28. If an Israelite slaughters an animal for consumption by a gentile, he may not derive any benefit from it, tHul. 2:15. If a gentile slaughters an animal, an Israelite may derive some benefit from it, tHul. 2:15. An Israelite may derive benefit from meat found in the possession of gentiles, but he may not benefit from meat found in the possession of a *min*, tHul. 2:20. An Israelite must obey the rule against slaughtering an animal and its young on the same day, even if he slaughters something to be consumed by gentiles, tHul. 5:2. If an Israelite slaughtered a beast for a gentile, it conveys food-uncleanness while it still jerks. It conveys carrion-uncleanness only after it is dead or its head has been chopped off, mHul. 9:1. For some, mHul. 8:5, milk found in the stomach of a beast slaughtered by a gentile or in the stomach of carrion was forbidden; however, for others this was not a matter of concern, tHul. 8:12.

could be sold to gentiles under certain conditions, even though it could not be eaten by Israelites. However, it is clear that not everyone agreed on this point. For some, certain forbidden meats could not be sold to gentiles, while others held that an Israelite could sell to a non-Israelite virtually anything which an Israelite could not eat. Thus, at least for some, the different foods eaten by gentiles and Israelites illustrated and maintained the separation of the two groups.[32] This would, of course, have important implications for social interaction. However, in this context, the issue seems to be primarily economic, for the issues are what could be sold to gentiles and from which items an Israelite could "derive benefit." Some sages held that an Israelite merchant could benefit from items which he could not sell to Israelites, for he could vend them to gentiles.

Lev. 27:1-8 discuss the pledge of one's valuation,[33] and the language of the text makes it clear that the practice should apply to Israelites, alone.

----

[32]An Israelite may send a gentile a hip containing the sciatic nerve, "since its place is known." Tosefta specifies that the Israelite should not sell the hip to the gentile in the presence of another Israelite, so that the second Israelite not assume that the hip is fit for him to purchase from the gentile, mHul. 7:2 and tHul. 7:3. Bartinoro, *loc. cit.*, explains that the problem is that one Israelite may see another Israelite selling the hip to a gentile and assume that the nerve has been removed, so that he purchases the hip from the gentile. The poor state of the text makes the issues unclear; however, there is a difference between what one may do with the hip when selling it to an Israelite, who must obey the statutes in the Torah, and how one sells it to a gentile, who need not take the rules in the Torah seriously. An Israelite may not sell carrion or *terefah*-meat to a gentile, tHul. 7:3. The text is corrupt, and it is difficult to make sense of the reasons given in support of this ruling; Gary G. Porton, "Forbidden Transactions: Prohibited Commerce with Gentiles in Earliest Rabbinism," in Jacob Neusner and Ernest Frerichs (eds.), *"To See Ourselves as Others See Us" Christians, Jews, and "Others" in Late Antiquity* (Chico: 1985), 328. However, an Israelite cannot trust a gentile to purchase meat for him, for the gentile might purchase carrion, or he might simply steal the Israelite's money, tHul. 7:3. Unclean animals could be sold to gentiles, mNed. 4:3. An Israelite may purchase an egg from any source without worrying that it came from a prohibited bird. However, Israelites may not sell eggs from carrion-birds or *terefah*-birds to a gentile, unless they are cracked in a dish. Therefore, an Israelite may not buy an egg cracked in a dish from a gentile, tHul. 3:24. Cf., Porton, "Forbidden Transactions," 325.

[33]*YHWH spoke to Moses saying: "Speak to the Israelite people and say to them: 'When a man explicitly vows to YHWH the equivalent for a human being, the following scale shall apply: If it is a male from twenty to sixty years of age, the equivalent is fifty sheqels of silver by the sanctuary weight; if it is a female, the equivalent is thirty sheqels. If the age is from five years to twenty years, the equivalent is twenty sheqels for a male and ten sheqels for a female. If the age is from one month to five years, the equivalent for a male is five sheqels of silver, and the equivalent for a female is three sheqels of silver. If the age is sixty years or over, the equivalent is fifteen sheqels in the case of a male and ten sheqels for a female. But if one cannot afford the equivalent, he shall be presented before YHWH, and the priest shall assess him; the priest shall assess him according to what the vower can afford.'"*

While some of our authors applied the practice of "valuation" to gentiles, the rules were different, so that one could easily distinguish between Israelites and non-Israelites.[34]

In the same way, the texts draw a clear distinction between financial dealings among Israelites and those between Israelites and gentiles. An Israelite may lend to a gentile and collect interest on what he lends, and he may borrow money from a gentile and pay interest on the loan; however, one Israelite may not charge interest to another Israelite, or pay interest to him.[35] One may not

----

[34]While priests, Levites, Israelites, women and slaves may vow another's valuation or worth, and their valuation or worth may be vowed by others, mArakh. 1:1, Meir holds that the a gentile's valuation may be vowed, but that he cannot vow another's valuation. Judah rules that a gentile may vow another's valuation, but others cannot vow his valuation. Both agree that a gentile may vow another's worth and that his worth may be vowed by others, mArakh. 1:2. Whatever the reasoning behind Judah's and Meir's opinions, see bArakh. 5b., the force of their opinions is to place the gentile in a different category from the Israelite. Since a person's non-Israelite slaves are considered his property, he may devote part of them to the Temple, mArakh. 8:4.

[35]Money may be lent to, or borrowed from, gentiles or resident aliens at exceedingly high rates of interest. An Israelite may lend out a gentile's money with his knowledge, so that he acts an intermediary between a gentile and another Israelite with regard to a loan made on an exceedingly high rate of interest; however, if it were money which the gentile borrowed from an Israelite, it may not be lent to another Israelite with the first Israelite's knowledge, for this would be the same as the first Israelite's allowing his money to be lent to another Israelite at an exceedingly high rate of interest, mB.M. 5:6. Similarly, a gentile may borrow a *sheqel* and lend out a *seah*, but an Israelite may not, tB.M. 5:15. One *seah* equals two *sheqalim*; Herbert Danby, *The Mishnah: Translated from the Hebrew with Introduction and Brief Explanatory Notes* (London: 1933), 798. If an Israelite borrowed money from a gentile, another Israelite may not come to him and say, "Give it to me and I shall hand it over to him just as you would." However, he may ask the gentile to allow this to happen, tB.M. 5:16. The point is that if one Israelite takes over the loan from another Israelite without the gentile's intervention, it will appear as if the first Israelite has lent the money to the second Israelite at the exceedingly high rate of interest. However, if the first Israelite brings the second Israelite before the gentile and obtains the latter's permission, the first Israelite acts merely as agent of the gentile, who is considered to have made the loan; see Rashi's comment on bA.Z. 71b. When an Israelite pays a gentile his salary, he may not tell him to lend out the money on interest; however, a gentile may pay an Israelite his salary and tell him to lend it out on interest, tB.M. 5:19. The text adds that even though it is permitted for a gentile to tell an Israelite to lend the money out on interest, an Israelite should not do it, for the sake of appearances. The point seems to be that in this case the one making the loan acts as the other's agent and with his knowledge; therefore, in the first case, one could argue that the Israelite is making the loan at the exceedingly high rate of interest. In the second case, it would *appear* that the Israelite is making the loan at these rates of interest. This second case parallels the ruling in mB.M. 5:6. If an Israelite leaves money as a bailment with a gentile, the latter may loan it out; however, if a gentile left money as a bailment with an Israelite, the Israelite may not lend it, tB.M. 5:19. The same principle underlies these texts: A gentile may lend out his money or funds for which he has ultimate responsibility, while an Israelite may not lend such funds on interest. Because the guardian of an estate serves as the owner's agent, a gentile guardian of an Israelite's estate may not lend out money on interest, while the Israelite guardian of a gentile's estate may lend out the estate's funds, tB.M. 5:20. In the case of a loan between an Israelite and a gentile, another Israelite may guarantee the loan, even if the gentile charges interest, tB.M. 5:20.

engage in a contract on "iron terms"[36] with an Israelite, because it involves an exceedingly high rate of interest; however, one may engage in such a contract with a gentile.[37] The distinctions drawn here derive from the Torah, for Lev. 25:35-37 instruct an Israelite not to collect interest on a loan made to his brother,[38] Ex. 22:24 forbids an Israelite from collecting interest for the poor among YHWH's people, and Deut. 23:20-21 prohibit deducting interest from loans to Israelites, but allow one to deduct interest from loans to a foreigner, nkry. However, the prohibition against collecting on interest from fellow Israelites was often circumvented by the rabbinic authorities,[39] so that the distinctions drawn here conform to the biblical paradigm, which differentiated between "brothers" and non-brothers in Leviticus and between "brothers" and "foreigners" in Deuteronomy, so as to maintain the distinctions between the Israelites and the gentiles in the sphere of economic activity.

It is with regard to the matter of charging or collecting interest that one distinguishes between Israelites and gentiles, and the rather long essay on this subject in tB.M. 5:15-20 sets up the gentiles and the Israelites as exact opposites, in the same manner that the essay in tPis. 2:5-10 does with regard to leaven. In both instances, Tosefta presents the gentiles and the Israelites as mirror-images of each other on the basis of a central biblical symbol. With regard to Passover, gentiles may possess and eat leaven, while Israelites may not. Concerning loans, gentiles may charge interest and pay interest to Israelites, while Israelites may charge and pay interest to *only* gentiles. In both cases, the essays are created by replacing the words "Israelite" and "gentile" with each other, so that the essays contain matched pairs of statements which clearly create boundaries between the two groups.

The above rules regulate economic interaction between Israelites and gentiles and distinguish it from economic activity among Israelites; it does not

----

[36]Danby defines "iron terms" as "a species of contract in which A sells his flock to B on condition that B shares the profits with A until such time as he has made payment in full, B being solely responsible for all losses sustained. . . ;" Danby, 796.

[37]MB.M. 5:6 mentions only the flock, while tB.M. 5:14 mentions the flock and the field and adds that one may accept the field on "iron terms" even from an Israelite.

[38]*If your brother, being in straits, comes under your authority, and you hold him as though a resident alien, so that he remains under you, do not exact from him advance or accrued interest, but fear your God. . . . Do not lend him money at advance interest, or give him your food at accrued interest.*

[39]Hillel Gamoran, "The Talmudic Law of Mortgages in View of the Prohibition Against Lending on Interest," *Hebrew Union College Annual*, LII (1981), 153-162.

prohibit gentiles and Israelites from lending money to each other or from applying normal business practices to those loans. Such a distinction was probably necessary for the economic life of the society to continue, for Israelites had to have a ready source of loans, and it would have been difficult for Israelites to make loans to fellow Israelites if they could not count on a profit. Furthermore, given the chaotic state of the economy of the Roman empire at this time, Israelites who wished to secure loans with their property would need to turn to non-Israelites, for there were difficulties, according to the *halakhah*, with securing such loans from fellow Israelites. Therefore, by allowing the Israelites to make loans to, and to secure loans from, non-Israelites, the authors of Mishnah-Tosefta made necessary provisions for the economic realities of their world, while still maintaining the biblical restrictions. However, all of this is based on the fact that Israelites and gentiles represent two different peoples, and one marks this difference in financial transactions.

We also find several texts which focus on aspects of the social relationship between Israelites and non-Israelites. These too point to distinctions between these segments of humanity. A person should not be forced to live among gentiles. Although an Israelite man has control of his wife, he cannot force her to move with him from a town with an Israelite majority to a town whose population is primarily composed of non-Israelites. However, one may force his wife to move from a town which has a gentile majority to a town whose population is primarily Israelite.[40] On the other hand, in a city in which both Israelites and gentiles reside, the Israelites should collect money for the poor from both Israelites and gentiles and distribute the funds among both peoples, "for the sake of peace."[41] Similarly, Israelites should perform the burial rites for gentiles, and they should comfort gentiles who are grieving over the death of a loved one, "for the sake of peace."[42] At the same time, however, one may lie to a gentile tax-collector and claim that his produce is heave-offering.[43]

These *sugyot* assume that gentiles and Israelites live in close proximity to each other. While this is not an ideal situation, Israelites are told to make the best of the circumstances in which they find themselves. In an ideal world, Israelites would live only among other Israelites, and in theory, at least, one strove

----

[40]TKet. 12:5.
[41]TGit. 3:13.
[42]TGit. 3:14.
[43]TNed. 2:2. The reference to gentiles is missing from the parallel passages in mNed. 3:4.

to achieve that ideal. Because this is not a perfect world, however, the two peoples do live together. When this occurs, Israelites should strive to live at peace with their gentile neighbors. Furthermore, there are some social situations in which human needs take precedence over ethnic divisions. People in need are people in need, people who die need to be buried, and those who mourn need support, no matter to which ethnic group they belong. The purpose of these texts is to stress the humanity of all peoples and the need for creating a peaceful, cooperative society. This parallels Hanina's statement that Israelites should pray for the welfare of the government, "since but for fear of it humans would swallow up one another alive."[44] The view that one should support the ruling power and help others in need, however, did not exclude attempting to avoid paying one's taxes.

The integration of the Israelites into gentile society, at least outside of Palestine, is evidenced by the fact that outside of the Land of Israel, Israelites have names like gentiles, so that a divorce document from abroad may be accepted, even though it is signed with gentile sounding names. Also, a convert may take a gentile-sounding name.[45] Clearly, the ideal in Mishnah-Tosefta is for the Israelites to live at peace among the gentiles within Palestine and for the former to keep themselves distinct from their non-Israelite neighbors. While accepting the use of gentile names abroad, it is not clear that the authors of Tosefta would have approved of this practice within Palestine itself.

iii

Although gentiles represent a different segment of humanity from the Israelites, an Israelite who robs one is obligated to restore the stolen object to its owner. In fact, a stricter rule applies to an Israelite who steals from a gentile than to one who steals from another Israelite because of "the profanation of the Name" which occurs when an Israelite wrongs a gentile.[46] The Israelite should

---

[44]MAbot 3:2.

[45]TGit. 6:4.

[46]TB.Q. 10:15. With regard to gentiles and those who shepherd or raise small animals, one need not raise them from a pit, but one may not cast them into a pit, tB.M. 2:33. Neusner reads the text totally differently: "Gentiles and shepherds of small cattle and those who raise them do not make a difference one way or the other [in figuring out whose lost object to seek first];" Jacob Neusner, *A History of the Mishnaic Law of Damages Part Two Baba Mesia. Translation and Explanation* (Leiden: 1983), 40. While Neusner's translation follows the topic of Tosefta and the corresponding Mishnah, the translation I have presented is the one followed by the translators of the *gemara*. Those who shepherded small animals had little respect within the Israelite community, and they were often classified with gentiles as those about whom an Israelite need not be overly concerned, Cf., bA.Z. 13b, 26a, bSanh. 57a. Mishcon writes, "Most shepherds were known to practise robbery . . . ;" A. Mishcon, *Abodah Zarah: Translated into English with Notes, Glossary*

not provide the gentiles with a reason for degrading the Israelites or their culture/religion. The changes in Abram's and Sari's names occurred to indicate that they were the progenitors of "many nations,"[47] but later tradition, which obviously had problems with this comment, suggested that this meant that Abraham was the father of many converts to Judaism.[48] On the other hand, an Israelite must daily thank YHWH for not creating him as a gentile.[49]

While many of our texts assume that gentiles and Israelites lived together in courtyards, neighborhoods, and cities,[50] a few passages see them as different populations which should remain separate from one another.[51] Although the two groups may share some common practices, such as circumcision, the rites are considered to be fundamentally different.[52] The presence of a large

----

and Indices in Isidore Epstein (ed.), *The Babylonian Talmud* (London: 1935), 68, n. 9.

[47]Abram's name was changed to Abraham because he was to be the father of a multitude of nations, and Sari's name was changed to Sarah because she was to be the princess of "all who come into the world," tBer. 1:12-13. Meir can speak of the offspring of a gentile married to an Israelite or a slave as a distinct "nation," tQid. 5:11.

[48]Louis Ginzberg, *The Legends of the Jews* (Philadelphia: reprint, 1968), V, 232-233.

[49]TBer. 6:18. This difference finds expression in the fact that a gentile convert to Judaism should separate himself completely from his "former" family. If a proselyte and a gentile inherited property from their gentile father, the proselyte can tell his non-Israelite brother to take the property which pertains to the idol *before* it comes into the former's possession; after it has come into his possession, he must dispose of it, mDem. 6:10 and tDem. 6:12. If they inherit a bath-house, the convert may claim the profit from the weekdays and give the profits from the Sabbath to his gentile brother; however, if the gentile and the Israelite jointly purchased a gentile's house, the Israelite may not disavow ownership of the idolatrous items in the house. Similarly, if they jointly purchased a bath-house, the Israelite may not disavow a claim to the profits from the Sabbath; in short, if the Israelite purchased something from a gentile from which he knew he would profit through a violation of Israelite law, he may enjoy no benefit from his purchase, tDem. 6:13. Onqelos, the righteous convert, separated himself completely from his former family and cast his inheritance into the Salt Sea, tDem. 6:13.

[50]The importance of living within the Land of Israel is stressed by the statement that it is better to live among gentiles within the Land than among Israelites outside the Land, tA.Z. 4:3.

[51]If gentiles and Israelites live together in a city, and there are gentile guards and Israelite guards, designated produce and non-designated produce, designated guards and non-designated guards, the Israelites may claim a specific part of the city and designate the other part for the gentiles; however, they may not make the designation for specific places of business, tDem. 6:14. In an area which is populated by both gentiles and Israelites, one makes determinations concerning ritual and other matters following the majority of the population. If the population is evenly split, one must make the determination only after he is sure that he will not violate Israelite law or practice. Again, the general assumption is that Israelite laws do not apply to gentiles and that they represent two different "ethnic" units within a given geographic area, mMakh. 2:3-2:10. Cf., tToh. 5:2 which states that with regard to gentile urine mixed with other items, they determine the purity on the basis of the majority of the liquid.

[52]While Israelites' circumcision is valid, that of gentiles is not, mNed. 3:11.

gentile population in an area could cause certain Israelite customs to be suspended.[53] Similarly, gentiles may not be counted with Israelites in certain rituals,[54] and their objects may not be sanctified by Israelite prayers.[55] Because gentiles do not fall under YHWH's special care, there was some question concerning whether or not they would have a place in the world-to-come. Eliezer held that no gentile would receive this reward, while Joshua responded that the righteous among the gentiles would inherit a portion of the future world.[56] Even cosmic and social phenomena point to the essential difference between the two groups.[57] While we have discovered many instances in which gentiles and Israelites interacted freely with one another, we also discover passages which restrict their normal daily activity, especially in the area of business transactions.[58]

Gentiles were seen as powerful, and at times threatening; in fact, the fear of gentiles' harming Israelites could be used to encourage Israelites to follow their traditions.[59] Some of our authors realized that the Israelite officials

----

[53] If a body were found near the frontier or near a town in which the majority of the population were gentiles, they do not break the heifer's neck, mSot. 9:2; Cf., tSot. 9:1.

[54] Gentiles are not Israelites; therefore, they may not be included among those who recite the Grace after meals, mBer. 7:1.

[55] Although at the end of the Sabbath one recites a blessing over the lamp and spices, one may not recite a blessing over the lamp and spices of gentiles, mBer. 8:6. Exactly what is behind this rule is unclear, for the text also specifically states that one may not recite a blessing over the lamp and spices used for idolatry; therefore, the author(s) of this passage distinguished between items used by gentiles and those used in the worship of an idol. The *gemara* explains, bBer. 52b-53a, that the light of the gentile may have been used during the Sabbath. On bBer. 52b, Judah, in Rav's name, maintains that the reference to the spices refers to those used at a banquet, for all banquets are in the honor of idols. Hanina of Sura explains that the specific reference to spices used in idol-worship is meant to explain the reference to spices of gentiles. While the explanation of the gentile's lamp seems possible, the discussion of the gentile's spices is less than convincing. However, if an Israelite lights his lamp from a gentile's lamp, or if a gentile lights his lamp from an Israelite's lamp, one must recite a blessing over it, tBer. 5:31.

[56] An anonymous statement rules that the wicked among gentiles will not be judged and will not live in the world-to-come. Eliezer, citing Ps. 9:17, states that none of the gentiles will have a portion in the world-to-come. Joshua responds that the righteous among the gentiles will have a place in the world-to-come, tSanh. 13:2. Gentiles who sinned with their bodies are punished the same as Israelites who sinned with their bodies, tSanh. 13:4.

[57] When the sun is eclipsed, it is a bad omen for the nations of the world because they follow a solar calendar, tSuk. 2:6. When Israel experiences trouble and the nations of the world are at rest, the former ask YHWH to take note, tSot. 13:9. When the number of Israelites who accept charity from the gentiles increase, it is a bad sign for Israel, tSot. 14:10.

[58] Porton, 317-336.

[59] If one refuses to heed the words of the priest preparing for battle, his wife will be taken by gentiles, tSot. 7:22.

held tenuous power, for final authority resided with the gentile rulers.[60] While the members of the gentile government could be friendly, they could also be a menace.[61] Several texts presuppose the danger posed by gentile troops inside Israel and on her borders.[62] Although this view of the "harmful gentile" could

----

[60]Eliezer once had to report to a hegemon to be questioned about the charges of heresy brought against him, tHul. 2:24, and Gamliel had his authority confirmed in Syria by the governor, mEd. 7:7. The power held by the gentile authorities finds expression in other ways. If tax-collectors entered a house, everything within the house is considered unclean. However, the tax-collectors are believed if they said that they did not enter the house, even if a gentile is with them. However, they are not believed if they say that they entered the house, but did not touch anything. The exact wording of what the tax-collectors may say when accompanied by a gentile is unclear; see Danby, 726, n. 8; Jacob Epstein, *Introduction to the Text of the Mishnah* (Jerusalem: 1954), II, 825, n. 3; Hanokh Albeck, *The Six Orders of the Mishnah: Order Tohorot* (Tel Aviv: 1957), 322. Cf., above, Chapter Two, n. 191. The assumption seems to be that the gentiles have power over the tax-collectors; see Bartinoro on 'm ys 'mhn . . . in mToh. 7:6. This is stated explicitly in tToh. 8:5.

[61]Meir reports that in the School-house he and Aqiba were forced to recite the *Shema'* quietly because a quaestor was standing at the door, tBer. 2:13. If gentiles said to a group of Israelite women that they should give them one of their number to defile or they will defile each of them, the Israelites should not deliver the woman, tTer. 8:12. If the gentiles told a group of Israelites to deliver one of their number to be killed or they would execute all of them, the Israelites should not deliver one of their number, but rather, they should all be willing to die. But, if the gentile's specifically named an individual they wanted to kill, he should be given over to them. Judah suggests that this is the case only when the gentiles are outside the city. If they are inside the city, one assumes that they will kill the named Israelite and then murder all the rest of the people, tTer. 7:20. One method of execution favored by the government was beheading with a sword, which was considered shameful by the editors of Mishnah, mSanh. 7:3.

[62]Israelites set up guards around cities close to the border, so that gentiles would not invade the land and desecrate the seventh-year produce, tSheb. 4:7. They do not declare any town near the border to be an apostate city, so that gentiles will not break through and wipe out settlements in the Land of Israel, tSanh. 14:1. An Israelite may not extinguish a lamp on the Sabbath in order to save the lamp, wick, or oil. If he puts out the lamp for one of these reasons, he is liable for violating the Sabbath; however, one may put out a lamp because he is afraid of gentiles, thieves, or an evil spirit, or if a sick person wishes to sleep, mShab. 2:5. The point is that one may extinguish the lamp in order to prevent harm to a human being. Bartinoro's comment that the authors of Mishnah were afraid of the Persians, who only lit a fire on their festivals in their temples, is clearly incorrect. TErub. 3:5-8 raise the issue of the dangerous gentile in the context of violating the Sabbath. If gentiles attack an Israelite town in order to harm the Israelites, the latter may violate the Sabbath by going forth outside the town carrying weapons and fighting with them. If the gentiles do not threaten to spill Israelite blood, the latter may not engage in battle with the former or violate the Sabbath in any way. However, if the towns are close to the frontier, the Israelites may violate the Sabbath and engage in battle, even if the gentiles merely come to take spices or straw; Cf., Saul Lieberman, *Tosefta Ki-fshutah A Comprehensive Commentary on the Tosefta, Part III Order Mo'ed* (New York: 1962), 342. In the past, the Israelites had stored their weapons in a house near the city wall, but the confusion which resulted at the time of an attack led them to store the weapons in individual homes. If Israelite troops go forth to fight an optional battle, they should not besiege a gentile town less than three days before the Sabbath. But once they have begun the siege, they do not interrupt it, even on the Sabbath. Shammai ruled that siege-work could be constructed on the Sabbath. He cites Deut. 20:20, *[Only trees which you know do not yield food may be destroyed; you may cut them down for] constructing siege-works against the city that is*

no doubt be supported by the contemporary situation, our texts also point to the past as proof that the "Greek" rulers had mistreated the Israelites.[63]

The gentiles were feared not only because they held political and military power, but also because they were less "civilized" than the Israelites. This found expression in the gentiles' inability to control their sexual urges; however, some believed that monetary considerations could cause a gentile to curb his sexual desires.[64] It is interesting that we discover that under certain conditions Israelites may lie to gentiles.[65] Not only were gentile rulers and their armies considered to be dangerous, but some assume that any gentile who is in a posi-

----

waging war on you, until it has been reduced, in support of his opinion. We further read that a town besieged by gentiles, one threatened by a river, those aboard a ship sinking at sea, or a person running away from a gentile, robbers, or an evil spirit may violate the Sabbath in order to save himself. If a city is encompassed on the Sabbath by gentiles or a flood, the *shofar* may be sounded, mTan. 3:7. However, tTan. 2:12 does not mention the Sabbath; it states that if a town is besieged by gentiles or if one is pursued by gentiles, they may not fast. They may, however, sound the *shofar*. Because one fears gentiles, he is allowed to set up conditional *'erubin* and use the one which is away from the direction he believes the gentiles are taking, mErub. 3:5. Our texts also discuss the rules concerning the Sabbath-limit for one who has been forcibly removed from his town by gentiles, mErub. 4:1. The anonymous comment rules that he is allowed to move only four cubits around him from the place they put him. However, if they return him to his city, "it is as if he had never gone out." If they put him in another town, a cattle-pen, or a cattle-fold, Gamliel and Eleazar b. Azariah rule that he may traverse the whole area, while Aqiba and Joshua teach that he may move only four cubits.

[63]The 17th of *Tammuz* commemorates the day that Apostomus burned the scrolls of the Law and an idol was set up in the sanctuary, mTan. 4:6; Cf., tTan. 3:10. Eleazar b. Yosi reports that while he was in Rome he saw the curtain from the Temple upon which were bloodstains from the Day of Atonement, tKip. 2:16. During the wars with Vespasian and Titus, the wedding customs were altered, tSot. 15:8. It was also believed that the Greek kings blocked the roads, so that Israelites could not fulfill their obligation to go up to Jerusalem on the festivals, tTan. 3:7-8.

[64]If an Israelite woman were imprisoned for a capital offense, so that her gentile captors had no intention of setting her free, we assume that they raped her; however, if she were imprisoned for a civil offense, so that the gentiles wished her to be ransomed by her relatives, we assume that her gentile captors would not sexually abuse her, mKet. 2:9. The invading troops of gentiles were assumed to represent a threat to the sexual purity of Israelite women; however, the rules of testimony concerning a woman's purity were very liberal, mKet. 2:9 and tKet. 3:2. An Israelite should not leave cattle in a gentile's inn because non-Israelites were suspected of bestiality, Israelite women should not be left alone with gentiles because of the fear of rape, and a male Israelite should not be left alone with gentiles because they would probably inflict bodily harm upon him, mA.Z. 2:1. TA.Z. 3:2 expands on this and specifies that one may not even leave male animals with males and female animals with females. Also one does not give his small cattle to their shepherds.

[65]An Israelite may lie to a gentile robber and state that his fruit is heave-offering, tNed. 2:2.

tion to harm an Israelite will probably do so.[66] In addition, gentiles could not always be trusted.[67] When the opportunity arose, the Israelite was permitted to remember YHWH's statements concerning the punishments he would mete out to the gentile nations.[68]

iv

In the above passages, the Israelites and the gentiles are recognized as different groups of human beings, each with its own particular customs. Agreeing with some previous forms of Israelite thought, Mishnah-Tosefta sought to keep these different groups separate. To accomplish this, our *sugyot* prohibit sexual contact between the groups; define members of the two groups as comprising distinct categories of servants; and legislate distinctions in the financial,

----

[66]An Israelite should not go to a gentile barber, so Meir, unless the haircut is performed in a public place, so sages, mA.Z. 2:2, or he can watch the barber in a mirror, tA.Z. 3:5. Also, an Israelite should not use a gentile doctor, mA.Z. 2:2 and tA.Z. 3:4. The text states that Israelites may accept healing of property but not of their persons. Bartinoro, following the *gemara*, bA.Z. 27b, claims that mmwn refers to the Israelites' cattle. Elmslie states that it refers to "living property, cattle or slaves;" W.A.L. Elmslie, *The Mishna On Idolatry: 'Aboda Zara Edited with Translation, Vocabulary and Notes* (London: 1911), 29. TA.Z. 1:8, which is included in the section which deals with gentile fairs, states that an Israelite may go to a gentile fair in order to accept healing for property, but not healing for his person. While an Israelite may circumcise a gentile for purposes of conversion, Meir holds that a gentile cannot circumcise an Israelite, for the former are suspected of bloodshed. Sages hold that a gentile may be allowed to circumcise an Israelite only if others stand by him and supervise, tA.Z. 3:12. An Israelite should not be alone with a gentile in a toilet. Furthermore, if a gentile and an Israelite are walking together, the Israelite places the gentile on his right, so that he is nearest the gentile's left hand. Ishmael b. Yohanan b. Beroqa states that the Israelite should travel with a sword in his right hand and a staff in his left hand. If the two are going up or coming down a ramp or stairs, the Israelite should always be higher than the non-Israelite. Israelites should not bow before gentiles, lest the latter hit them on their heads, and when possible, they should walk a distance apart. If a gentile asks an Israelite where he is going, he should not tell him the route he plans to take, tA.Z. 3:4. TA.Z. 3:4 specifies that a female gentile should not cut the fetus from an Israelite's womb, nor should [s]he give the Israelite a cup of bitters; however, some held that a gentile woman was *trusted* to serve as a midwife for an Israelite woman. In tA.Z. 3:3, Meir rules that a gentile cannot serve as a midwife for an Israelite because non-Israelites are suspected of taking a life; sages respond that a gentile may serve as a midwife for an Israelite only if others supervise her. Similarly, a gentile could nurse an Israelite child in the latter's home; tA.Z. 3:3 adds with her permission, mA.Z. 2:1. If a gentile coerced an Israelite into taking another Israelite's possessions, the Israelite is not liable; however, the Israelite is liable if he freely takes another Israelite's possessions and hands them over to gentiles, tB.Q. 9:33.

[67]TPe. 4:1 states that one does not believe claims made by the poor among the gentiles.

[68]On Rosh HaShannah, a verse which refers to the punishments of the gentiles is read by itself, tR.H. 2:12.

social, and legal realms, in matters of food-preparation, and in several other areas. Whether or not the rabbis were able to put their theories into practice is not the issue. It is important that they believed there should be, or were, two different sets of social conventions and institutions: One applied to Israelites, especially when they interacted with one another. A second pertained to gentiles, specifically when they came into contact with Israelites.

One might argue that these distinctions relate to the "chosenness" or "holiness" of the Israelite nation; that is, that the distinctive character of Israelite thought stands behind these ideas. In an effort to maintain Israel as "a nation of priests, a Holy people,"[69] our authors endeavored to keep them separate from their non-Israelite neighbors. Furthermore, it was the Revelation at Sinai, a decidedly "religious" experience, which made Israel unique and which stands behind the rabbis' attempt to draw sharp boundaries between the Israelites and the gentiles.

While there is some truth in these claims, it is also likely that many of the sages in Mishnah-Tosefta believed that the distinctions they sought to maintain were built into the very structure of the universe. Some of our authors clearly viewed Israel and the rest of the nations of the world as stemming from different ancestors, and this led to the conclusion, at least for some of our writers, that the two groups had to be clearly distinguishable. Thus, while the idea of "chosenness" or "holiness" was important, it was equally relevant that the structure of the universe necessitated the separation of Israelites from gentiles.

The biblical paradigms were clearly important, and they are reflected in the terminology of several passages in Mishnah-Tosefta. Non-Israelite slaves were called Canaanite slaves, a phrase derived from the Torah and its concep-

---

[69]Neusner argues that the Pharisaic plan was based on their attempt to make the Israelites a nation of priests; therefore, they transferred many of the priestly prerogatives to the common Israelites. Jacob Neusner, *From Politics to Piety: The Emergence of Pharisaic Judaism* (Englewood Cliffs: 1973), especially, 146. Zohar phrases the issue slightly differently: "It may be said that one of the major (if not the major) goals of the sages' endeavor was to restore a sense of value and religious vitality to the life of the community at large, especially outside of the priesthood. One of their primary ways of accomplishing this was to stamp the principal areas of daily life with an element of ritual, which was intended to create the same kind of impression, in everyday life, as had been created by the elaborate rituals of the sanctuary; that is, it was to strengthen the people's sense of God's presence and of man's vital relationship with Him;" Zvi Zohar, "The Consumption of Sabbatical Year Produce in Biblical and Rabbinic Literature," in Harvey E. Goldberg (ed.), *Judaism Viewed From Within and From Without* (Albany: 1987), 101.

tions of reality.[70] The few discussions of the relationship of the Ammonites, Moabites, and Egyptians to the Congregation of Israel find their origin in the Torah, not in the social or political environments of the rabbis. Israelite thought, from the Bible onward, viewed the elements of the world as divided into unalterable categories, usually sets of opposites,[71] and it is likely that the desire to keep the People Israel distinct from the other nations of the world derives from this world-view, and not necessarily from uniquely Israelite ideas of "holiness" or "chosenness." Furthermore, it is common for groups to view members of other groups as a different sub-species of humanity, or even as non-human,[72] so that what the rabbis attempted to do and their view of the inherent differences between their people and the other peoples of the world is not unique. Although the separation of Israelites from non-Israelites has a long history in Israelite thought, it is not unique to Israelite thought, for the separation of "our" group from "their" group is a common feature of peoples throughout time and space.

----

[70]Urbach suggests that the term Canaanite slaves derives from Gen. 9:25-26: *And he said, "Blessed be YHWH, the God of Shem; Let Canaan be a slave to them. May God enlarge Japheth, and let him dwell in the tents of Shem; and let Canaan be a slave to them."* Urbach, 31.

[71]See, for example, Samuel Cooper, "The Laws of Mixture: An Anthropological Study in the Halakhah," in Goldberg, 55-74.

[72]Needham writes: "It is a frequent report from different parts of the world that tribes call themselves alone by the arrogant title 'man,' and that they refer to neighboring peoples as monkeys or crocodiles or malign spirits. When European voyagers explored the world, they often enough had a clear eye for physique, dress, and habitations, but they more often had a distorted or derogatory view of the moral aspects of exotic peoples. Typically, these strange societies had no religion, or no law, or no idea of the family or not even a true form of language to qualify them as truly human." Rodney Needham, *Primordial Characters* (Charlottesville: 1978), 5. William S. Green, "Otherness Within: Towards a Theory of Difference in Rabbinic Judaism," in Jacob Neusner and Ernest S. Frerichs, 49-69, especially, 49-51.

Chapter Nine:

Gentiles As Idolaters

i

We have seen that the separation between Israelites and gentiles was not absolute. In agricultural and business dealings, the two groups interacted, albeit according to specified norms and rules. A number of legal and financial procedures and protocols were designed to distinguish transactions among Israelites from those between gentiles and Israelites. Only in the area of sexual concerns, are the texts consistent in prohibiting contact between the Israelites and their neighbors. In general, then, in the areas we so far have studied, interactions between Israelites and gentiles were regulated, but not prohibited.

With regard to matters of idolatry, the texts take a different stance. The gentile *as idolater* is to be avoided. The Israelite must neither *actually* support and participate in, nor *appear* to support and participate in, the gentiles' worship of their gods. The desire to keep the Israelite separate from the gentile *as idolater* is based on the belief that the Israelites owe complete and exclusive allegiance to YHWH. From the point of view of these *sugyot*, the distinction between the Israelite and the gentile is that the former worship the one, true God, YHWH, while the latter revere idols, non-deities. Following the Bible's lead,[1] our authors work to prevent the Israelite from any manner of veneration of the foreign gods. In fact, Israelites are to express their appreciation to YHWH at locations from which idols have been removed.[2] The occasion for our documents' concern with this topic is the assumption by the authors of Mishnah-

----

[1] See especially, Ex. 20:2-6, Ex. 23:13, Ex. 23:24, Ex. 23:32-33, Ex. 34:12-16, Deut. 5:6-10, Deut. 7:1-5, Deut. 7:25-26, and Deut. 12:2-3.

[2] If an Israelite comes upon a place where an idol *used* to stand, he recites the following blessing: "Blessed is He who uprooted idolatry from the Land," mBer. 9:1. The version in tBer. 6:2 adds, "May it be your will, YHWH, our God, that idols shall be uprooted from all the places in Israel and the heart of your servants returned to your service." The version in Mishnah may relate to the holiness of the Land of Israel, which is challenged by the presence of idols within the borders of the Holy Land. Tosefta suggests that the idols presented a temptation to Israelites.

Tosefta that Israelites live in an environment in which contact with foreign gods and their devotees could occur with some regularity.[3]

Even though the sages of Mishnah-Tosefta had some knowledge of the gentiles' religious practices,[4] a portion of the material before us reflects the imagined picture that the sages had of idols and idolaters, so that Mishnah-Tosefta do not always evidence a sophisticated or realistic understanding of the non-Israelite religions which surrounded the Israelites in Palestine. For example, many rabbis assume that gentiles offer libations from virtually any amount of wine with which they come into contact. Also, the texts speak of Molech, a problematic figure in the Hebrew Bible, and an *Asherah*, also a biblical idol, in the same terms as they speak of Mercury. Again, biblical images and paradigms are simply projected into the sages' own world.

Urbach[5] and Lieberman[6] maintain that by the time of the writing of

----

[3]Neusner argues that with regard to idolatry, "Mishnah makes concrete and everyday the general conceptions in Scripture;" Jacob Neusner, *A History of the Mishnaic Law of Damages Part Four Shebuot, Eduyot, Abodah Zarah, Abot, Horayot. Translation and Explanation* (Leiden: 1985), 138. Urbach argues that the rabbinic concerns with idolatry date from after the Bar Kokhba War when the Israelites were forced to live in close proximity with gentiles; Ephraim E. Urbach, "The Rabbinical Laws of Idolatry in the Second and Third Centuries in Light of Archaeological and Historical Facts," *Israel Exploration Journal*, (1959), IX, 3, 157. See, also, David Flusser, "Paganism in Palestine," S. Safrai and M. Stern (eds.), *The Jewish People in the First Century: Historical Geography, Political History, Social, Cultural and Religious Life and Institutions* (Philadelphia: 1976), II, 1065-1100.

[4]Lieberman asserts that "the Rabbis had a fair knowledge of the rites and practices of idol worshipers and of the various regulations bearing on heathen divinities;" Saul Lieberman, *Hellenism in Jewish Palestine: Studies in the Literary Transmission Beliefs and Manners of Palestine in the I Century B.C.E.--IV Century C.E.* (New York: 1950), 115. Exactly how widespread or profound this knowledge was is unclear to me, and Lieberman's examples are not always convincing.

[5]Urbach claims that although the sages were not worried that the Israelites would practice idolatry, they were concerned that interaction with idolaters and idolatrous practices would corrupt the Israelites' morals: "The laws commanding Jews to have no social intercourse with Gentiles, and to keep away from all contact with their customs and activities, were most stringently enforced by those very Sages who were usually lenient in their interpretation of the laws about actual idolatry. The reason for this apparent paradox is that, while they had no fear that their contemporaries would go and worship pagan gods or take part in pagan rites, they were gravely perturbed by the danger to their national identity implicit in their social contact with the gentiles and the consequent moral corruption resulting from their forgetting the Law and Commandments. It was true that the idolatrous instinct had been eradicated long since; but the sensual passions were still very much alive;" Urbach, 241-242. The internal contradiction of these comments need not detain us.

[6]Lieberman writes that "[i]n the first centuries C.E. the Jews were so far removed from clear-cut idolatry that there was not the slightest need to argue and to preach against it. . . . They [the rabbis] were concerned with the heathen rites only in so far as they affected the social and commercial contact of the Jew with the gentile . . . ;" Lieberman, 120-121. Elsewhere he states that "[t]he Jewish teachers were primarily concerned with the practical rites of idolatry in so far as they

the Mishnah, in fact much earlier, there was no danger that the Israelites would practice idolatry, so that Mishnah-Tosefta were concerned with only social and economic issues; they were not designed to prevent the Israelites from actually worshipping idols or foreign deities. The claim that idols and idolatry held no attraction for Israelites at the end of the second century of the common era is untenable. It is true that when dealing with the gentile as idolater, the texts do focus their attention on disassociating the Israelite from the gentile primarily in the social and economic realms. However, as we have seen, Mishnah-Tosefta do not normally seek to *prevent* Israelites from engaging in normal economic or social intercourse with gentiles. Rather, as we shall see below, they focus on *separating* the Israelites from gentiles in the economic and social realms specifically when they knew, or believed, that religious activities impinged on these areas. Our authors differentiated between occasions when overtly religious activity within the spheres of social and economic life were evident and periods when they were not. The writers of Mishnah-Tosefta were able to distinguish between the gentile as farmer, merchant, borrower, lender, and the like, and the *gentile as idolater* who was also a farmer, merchant, borrower, lender, and the like. The distinction was important, for only when the gentile was overtly engaged in, or was presumed to be engaged in, the worship of his idol was he considered to be an idolater whom Israelites had to avoid. Therefore, those *sugyot* which seek *to prevent* the Israelite from interacting with gentiles do so when they perceive this interaction, not as normal social or economic intercourse, but as being part of the gentiles' religious activities. Contrary to the opinions of Urbach and Lieberman, at least in the minds of the authors of Mishnah-Tosefta, these texts are designed to prevent the Israelites from worshipping deities other than YHWH. They do not merely have social and economic importance.

ii

To prevent Israelites from engaging in idolatry, Mishnah-Tosefta present two sorts of requirements: 1) Israelites should not directly participate in the worship of idols by having contact with idols or anything related to them, and 2) Israelites should not appear to engage indirectly in idolatry by acting in a way

---

might affect the behavior of the Jews . . .;" Lieberman, 127. Again we need not be detained by the apparent inconsistency in these statements.

which promotes, or seems to promote, the gentile's worship. This includes increasing the joy gentiles experience during their holy days. Perhaps because the former principle is "obvious" and easier to define, Mishnah-Tosefta's major discussion of idolatry begins with the second topic. Tractate *Abodah Zarah* opens with an extended exposition of the rule that Israelites should not engage in business dealings with gentiles during the latter's festivals.[7] The separation between

----

[7]MA.Z. 1:3 and tA.Z. 1:4 define these festivals; however, their terminology differs. Compare the discussion in Mireille Hadas-Lebel, "Le paganisme à travers les sources rabbiniques des IIe et IIIe siècles, Contribution à l'étude du syncrétisme dans l'empire romain," Hildegard Temporini and Wolfgang Haase (eds.), *Aufstieg und Niedergang der römischen Welt* (Berlin & New York: 1979), II.19.2, 426-438, with W.A.L. Elmslie, *The Mishna on Idolatry 'Aboda Zara: Edited with Translation, Vocabulary and Notes* (Cambridge: 1911), 18-26. Lieberman, 239-241.

The exact days on which business is prohibited are unclear. MA.Z. 1:1 states that one may not do business with gentiles three days before their festivals. In mA.Z. 1:2, Ishmael prohibits doing business with gentiles three days before and three days after their festivals, while sages agree with mA.Z. 1:1 that one cannot do business with them three days before their festivals. In tA.Z. 1:1, Nahum the Mede says that in the diaspora communities, one may not engage in business with gentiles one day before their festivals. The anonymous text states that Nahum's opinion applies to only recurrent festivals; if the festival does not occur annually, the festival-day alone is the only day upon which an Israelite may not engage in business with a gentile. Furthermore, tA.Z. 1:1 limits the prohibition to transactions involving durable goods; however, if the items are perishable, one may engage in business with gentiles on their festivals. TA.Z. 1:13 takes an extreme position and claims that Israelites should not engage in business among themselves on gentile festival; however, see Saul Lieberman, *Tosefeth Rishonim: A Commentary based on Manuscripts of the Tosefta and Works of the Rishonim and Midrashim in Manuscripts and rare Editions* (Jerusalem: 1938), II, 187. In mA.Z. 1:1, Judah states that one may accept the repayment of a debt from a gentile on the latter's festival; however, the anonymous text rejects Judah's opinion because eventually the gentile will be happy that he has freed himself from his debt. In tA.Z. 1:1, Joshua b. Qorha states that in the case of a loan secured by a bond, one does not accept repayment from a gentile; however, if the loan were not secured by a bond, an Israelite may accept repayment from a gentile on the latter's holy day. Israelite workmen may work for a gentile in an Israelite's house on the gentile's festival; but they may not work in a gentile's house on the festival. Simeon b. Eleazar states that if the Israelite workman were hired by the day, he may not work with the gentile if it is the latter's festival, no matter in whose house he works. The Israelite may work only if he were hired for an extended period of time which incidentally includes the festival, and then he may work only in an Israelite's house on the gentile's festival. The context of tA.Z. 1:3 provides the concern with the festival; however, the festival is not specifically mentioned, so that the statement could have meant something very different in another context; Cf., Neusner, *Shebuot*, 143-144. In no case may an Israelite work for a gentile on something which is attached to the ground on the festival of his gentile employer. However, the Israelite employee of a gentile may work in a town other than one in which there is a festival on the latter's festival; Cf., Mitzpah Shemuel, tA.Z. 1:3. If an Israelite has completed manufacturing an item for a gentile before the latter's festival, he should not deliver the item on the latter's festival because it will bring joy to the gentile, tA.Z. 1:3. Similarly, an Israelite may not engage in business with a gentile who is going on a pilgrimage, but he may engage in business with one who is returning from a pilgrimage, mA.Z. 2:3. TA.Z. 1:15 states that one may do business with an Israelite who is going to, or returning from, a gentile's fair; however, one may not engage in

Israelites and non-Israelites on the latter's holy days becomes as complete as possible, for an Israelite should not even engage in frivolous conversation with gentiles, or seek them out to ask about their health. However, if an Israelite happens to meet a gentile on the latter's festival, the Israelite may ask after his health.[8] This probably relates to the idea, we encountered in the previous chapter, that Israelites should seek to live in a stress-free environment and should work to achieve a state of peaceful co-existence with their gentile neighbors.

Not only are there restrictions on business dealings between Israelites and gentiles and on casual, unnecessary contact between Israelites and non-Israelites on the latter's holy days, but also they occur in the context of normal day-to-day business transactions. Israelites must be careful not to supply

----

business with a gentile who is going to his fair. One may trade with the gentile only upon the latter's leaving the fair. If the idol in whose honor the festival is held is within a town, Israelites may engage gentiles in business outside of the town. Similarly, if the idol is outside of the town, those inside the town may engage in business with Israelites. TA.Z. 1:6 refers to a fair, yryd, and applies virtually the same rules as mA.Z. 1:4 does to an idol. If there is a fair inside a town, an Israelite may not enter the town, but may do business outside of the town. If the fair is outside the town, the Israelite may do business inside the town. However, if an Israelite is part of caravan, that is a group of people traveling through the town, that is permitted. On the other hand, tA.Z. 1:16 states that one should not travel with a caravan at all, even if one is afraid of darkness, gentiles, thugs, evil spirits, or the like. Given the context and the citation of Deut. 6:14, *Do not follow other gods*, this probably means that one should not join a caravan which is clearly going to a gentile fair. The relationship between the fair and the idol is made explicit in tA.Z. 1:7, which states that fairs held by the Empire or the Province are permitted; only fairs held in honor of an idol are prohibited. However, an Israelite merchant may do business in a town the day before, or the day after, a fair, for only the actual day of the fair is prohibited for doing business, tA.Z. 1:9. An Israelite may not travel a road to a town in which the idol who is the subject of the festival (the reference to the festival is derived from the context) resides, unless the road leads to places other than that specific town. In tA.Z. 1:5, Meir states that if there is a festival in a specific town, an Israelite may not travel to that particular town, or to villages in its vicinity, while sages state that only travel to that particular town is prohibited. If there is a festival within a city, an Israelite may not do business within shops which are adorned for the festival; however, he may do business inside shops which are not adorned for the festival, mA.Z. 1:4. Similarly, in a town in which some of the people celebrate the festival while others do not, one need avoid doing business only with those who are observing the festival, tA.Z. 1:4. An Israelite may redeem fields, vineyards, or male and female servants from gentiles, presumably on the latter's festival. Cf., MM.Q. 2:4 where the context is a discussion of the intermediary days of an Israelite festival. Here, in tA.Z. 1:8, the context suggests that the rule is restated with reference to the festivals of the gentiles. The negative in our text is clearly incorrect; Lieberman, *Tosefeth Rishonim*, II, 186. If an Israelite purchases anything at a gentile's fair, he may not use it, tA.Z. 3:19. Animals must be hamstrung, clothing and utensils are left to rot, money and metal are cast into the Salt Sea. Produce is poured out, burned, or buried. If one purchased an idol, he must crush it and scatter it to the winds, cast it into the sea, or use it for manure.

[8]TA.Z. 1:2. TA.Z. 1:3 states that Israelites do greet gentiles on the latter's festivals "for the sake of peace."

gentiles with items which the latter might use in their daily religious activities.[9] Thus, the care which an Israelite had to take to ensure that he did not aid a gentile in his worship affected everyday activities, as well as those on the latter's religious holidays.

In order to ensure that Israelites would avoid contact with idols or with any items associated with their worship or adoration, a number of texts establish criteria for what constitutes an idol or items associated with its worship. Various *sugyot* discuss how one determines whether or not a specific image is something which gentiles might adore, how one decides whether designs on rings or gems render these objects forbidden,[10] and under what circumstances a

----

[9]An Israelite may not sell a gentile fir-cones, white figs with stalks, frankincense (In tA.Z. 1:21 Judah b. Peterah limits the prohibition so a specific amount of frankincense; see Gary G. Porton, "Forbidden Transactions: Prohibited Commerce with Gentiles in Earliest Rabbinism," in Jacob Neusner and Ernest Frerichs (eds.), *"To See Ourselves as Others See Us:" Christians, Jews, "Others" in Late Antiquity* (Chico: 1985), 321, n. 16.) or a white cock on the latter's festivals. (But see Judah's comment in tA.Z. 1:21 that one may not sell a white cock, only if the gentile specifies that he plans to use it for idolatrous purposes.) Thus, an Israelite may not sell a gentile an item whose idolatrous use is specified; however, if no idolatrous use is specified, the item may be sold, mA.Z. 1:5. Meir forbids the sale of fine dates, Hazab dates or Nicalous dates. One can sell almost anything--pigs, dogs, and even wine--to a merchant, on the assumption that he will not make use of it himself, but will sell it to another. However, if the merchant states that he plans to use his purchase for the worship of an idol, he may not be sold even water or salt, tA.Z. 1:21. For a discussion of these texts see Porton, 321-323. In addition, see Hadas-Lebel, 446-450 and Saul Lieberman, "Palestine in the Third and Fourth Centuries," *Jewish Quarterly Review*, XXVI (1946), 173-174.

[10]In mA.Z. 3:1, Meir states that all images belonging to gentiles are forbidden, because they are worshipped once a year, while sages state that only those which hold a staff, a bird, or a sphere are forbidden. The *gemara*, bA.Z. 41a, states that the idols hold these objects to symbolize the fact that they rule the world. In tA.Z. 5:1, sages mention the same three items and add images which hold a sword, crown, ring, image, or snake. Simeon b. Gamliel forbids an idol which holds anything in its hand, mA.Z. 3:1. On mA.Z. 3:1, see Elmslie, 44-45. If an Israelite finds an idol's garment, he may use it; however, a fragment in the shape of a hand or a foot is prohibited, mA.Z. 3:2. If an Israelite finds an object in the shape of the sun, the moon, or a dragon, he must cast it into the Dead Sea, mA.Z. 3:3. Cf., tA.Z. 5:1 which adds that this applies also to the image of Isis or Seraphis. For a discussion of these matters see Hadas-Lebel, 413-422. In mA.Z. 3:3, Simeon b. Gamliel says if these shapes are found on worthless objects--tA.Z. 5:1 gives pitchers, water-pots, frying pans, kettles, bowls, mats, or rings as examples--the objects are permitted; however, if they are found on valuable objects--tA.Z. 5:1 gives silk nose-rings, bracelets, and earrings as examples-- the objects are prohibited. Yosi says that the objects should be broken apart and thrown to the winds or into the sea; but the anonymous "they" seem to object to this. If the image on a ring projects from the ring's surface, an Israelite cannot derive benefit from it; if the image does not standout, the Israelite may derive benefit from the ring. A ring on which there is a seal may be used as a signet-ring. Judah prohibits the use of a signet-ring on which the image has been incised; however, the ring may be worn. If the seal projects from the ring's surface, it may be used as a signet-ring, but it may not be worn. Similarly, a ring on which there is a figure may be used as a signet-ring. A gem made into a figure of a dragon is prohibited, but one on which a dragon is suspended may be used, if the dragon is removed, tA.Z. 5:2. Hadas-Lebel, 413-426; Urbach, 158, 229-230, 238.

gentile's idol is prohibited.[11] Because Israelites must avoid not only the idol but also anything associated with it,[12] we find methods for determining whether or not specific items should be viewed as related to the idol or its adoration. Specifically, our texts present detailed discussions of statutes of Mercury and the stones found near them,[13] pedestals erected for the honor of the Emperor,[14]

----

[11]MA.Z. 4:4 forbids a gentile's idol under any circumstances, but an Israelite's idol is forbidden only after it has been worshipped. TA.Z. 5:4 states that a gentile's idol is not prohibited until it has been worshipped, while tA.Z. 5:3 states that an Israelite's idol is forbidden, even if it has not been worshipped. Cf., Urbach, 159-161.

[12]If a field is fertilized with manure belonging to an idol, or with manure from an animal which has been fed with produce belonging to an idol, the field must lie follow, tA.Z. 6:1. Wool stamped with the wood from an idol must be burned. And, one may not make a lament with pipes which belong to an idol; however, one may use pipes which were rented from the State, even if they were used in the worship of an idol. One may not rent space on ships belonging to idols, but one may rent space on ships belonging to the State. One may not contribute to charity-collectors collecting on behalf of an idol, unless they are employed by the State, tA.Z. 6:1. An Israelite should not tell another Israelite to wait for him near the idol of such-and-such, for the Israelite should not mention an idol's name; in support of its statement, tA.Z. 6:11 quotes Ex. 23:13: *Make no mention of the names of other gods; they shall not be heard on your lips.* Any place or item which is associated with an idol should be called by a name which is insulting or derogatory, tA.Z. 6:4. If one purchases metal filings from a gentile and finds an idol among the filings, the idol may be discarded, and the filings used. Hills or mountains which gentiles worship are permitted, but items which are on them are prohibited, mA.Z. 3:5. TA.Z. 6:8 adds that those Israelites who worship these hills or mountains should be stoned. The same is true if they worship a man, even though the man is permitted. On hills and mountains, see Hadas-Lebel, 408-409. On metal filings, see Urbach, 229.

[13]For example, one cannot benefit from stones used as offerings to statues of Mercury; on Mercury see Hadas-Lebel, 403-405; Elmslie, 74. In mA.Z. 4:1, Ishmael and sages dispute exactly how one tells whether or not stones near a statue of Mercury were used in the worship of the idol; Cf., Gary G. Porton, *The Traditions of Rabbi Ishmael Part I: The Non-Exegetical Materials* (Leiden: 1976), 162-164. Ishmael holds a different opinion in tA.Z. 6:14. In fact, one may not derive benefit from anything on a statue of Mercury, tSanh. 14:11. If an Israelite brought stones from a statue of Mercury, they are prohibited; however, if a gentile brought stones from a statue of Mercury, they are permitted. A heap of stones dedicated to Mercury which has been ripped down is permitted, tA.Z. 6:14. TA.Z. 6:15 applies Prov. 26:8 to those Israelites who worship Mercury: *Like a pebble in a sling, so is paying honor to a dullard.* If one pays honor to an evil person, it is as if he worshipped Mercury, tA.Z. 6:16. If one gives into his evil impulse, it is as if he worshipped Mercury, tA.Z. 6:17. One who teaches Mishnah to an evil disciple is like one who worships Mercury, tA.Z. 6:18. Although an Israelite may use coins, clothing, or other objects left on the statue's head, he may not benefit from produce left for the statue, for these items were placed on the altar before YHWH in the Temple, mA.Z. 4:2. TA.Z. 6:12 repeats part of mA.Z. 4:2 and adds that any utensils used for the idol's body are prohibited, while those not used for its body are permitted. Any utensils associated with idolatry which the idol's priest sold are permitted. TA.Z. 6:13 specifies that clothes found on the idol are forbidden, whether or not the idol is dressed in them, while clothes found near the idol are not prohibited, unless the idol had been clothed in them. While mA.Z. 4:2 probably refers to a statue of Mercury, tA.Z. 6:13 makes a general statement about any idol and then repeats it with specific reference to a statue of Mercury. TA.Z. 6:13 states that "others" teach that even the coins and utensils found on the topmost of the heap of stones dedicated to Mercury are forbidden. Hadas-Lebel, 403-405, 450-452. The Roman Mercury was related to the Greek Hermes. On Hermes and "stone-gods" in Greece, see Martin P. Nilsson, *A History of Greek Religion*

Asherot and the wood derived from them,[15] Molech[16] and hides "pierced at the

----

translated by F.J. Fielden (New York: 1964), 109-110. H.J. Rose, *Religion in Greece and Rome* (New York: 1959), 244-245. On Mercury as the god of merchants, see Georges Dumézil, *Archaic Roman Religion* translated by Philip Krapp (Chicago and London: 1970), II, 439-440.

[14]The pedestals erected at the time of the Hadrianic wars are forbidden, tA.Z. 5:6. If the greater part of a pedestal is damaged, it is permitted, tA.Z. 5:8. An Israelite should not climb up a pedestal, even to disfigure it, tA.Z. 6:10. Urbach claims that the rabbis were consistent in their adamant rejection of the emperor cult and anything related to it; Urbach, 238-239. Cf., Hadas-Lebel, 422-426.

[15]On the *Asherah*, see Hadas-Lebel, 409-412; Elmslie, 60-61. The rabbinic discussions of the *Asherah* must derive from the appearance of the term in the Bible. See the bibliography in William G. Dever, "Asherah, Consort of Yahweh? New Evidence from Kuntillet 'Ajrud," *Bulletin of the American Schools of Oriental Research* (1984), Summer, 255, 39-48. Walter A. Maier, III, *'Asherah: Extrabiblical Evidence,* (Atlanta: 1987). There are three types of *Asherot*: If a tree were planted for purposes of idolatry, it is forbidden; if a tree were trimmed for idolatry, any new growth must be removed; if a tree were one under which a gentile placed an idol and then desecrated it, it is permitted. An *Asherah* is also defined as any tree under which there is an idol, while Simeon defines an *Asherah* as any tree which is worshipped, mA.Z. 3:7. The anonymous statement in tA.Z. 6:8 defines an *Asherah* as any tree which gentiles worship and guard and whose fruit they do not eat. Simeon b. Eleazar points to three [sic!] specific trees within the Land of Israel which are *Asherot*: A carob tree in Kefar Qesem, a carob tree in Kefar Pigshah, and a sycamore tree in Rano and in Carmel. Büchler suggests that we could have three trees if we eliminate the conjunction "and" before Carmel; Adolph Büchler, "The Levitical Impurity of the Gentile in Palestine Before the Year 70," *Jewish Quarterly Review*, New Series, XVII (1926-1927), 66, n. 203. Israelites should avoid sitting in the shade of a tree which was considered an *Asherah* or passing under it, mA.Z. 3:8; however, one who sits or passes under an *Asherah* does not become unclean. Although lettuce may not be sown under an *Asherah*, vegetables may be planted under one in the rainy season, but not during the summer, mA.Z. 3:8; Yosi forbids planting under an *Asherah* even during the rainy season. Cf., tA.Z. 6:8 in which Simeon b. Eleazar says that one may never plant seeds or vegetables under an *Asherah*. Israelites could not derive benefit from the wood of an *Asherah*: The wood could not be used in an oven, so that a new oven had to be destroyed; an old one had to cool before it could be used. Bread baked in such an oven could not be used. The wood could not be used in a loom, and garments woven in such a loom could not be used, mA.Z. 3:9. A field which has been plowed with a plow made from the wood of an *Asherah* must lie fallow, tA.Z. 6:1. An *Asherah* becomes invalidated if it is trimmed and the trimming does not benefit the tree, mA.Z. 3:10; Cf., tA.Z. 6:9. An Israelite cannot trim an *Asherah* for any reason, tA.Z. 6:9. For the *lulab* one may not use a palm-branch or a myrtle branch from an *Asherah*; similarly, the *etrog* may not come from an *Asherah*, mSuk. 3:1, mSuk. 3:3, and mSuk. 3:5. The hyssop for the rite of the Red-Heifer cannot come from an *Asherah*, tPar. 11:6.

[16]Again the rabbinic discussions of Molech derive from his appearance in the Bible. See George C. Heider, *The Cult of Molek: A Reassessment* (Sheffield: 1985); Geza Vermes, "Leviticus 18:21 in Ancient Jewish Bible Exegesis," in Jakob J. Petuchowski and Ezra Fleischer (eds.), *Studies in Aggadah, Targum and Jewish Liturgy in Memory of Joseph Heinemann* (Jerusalem: 1981), 108-124. If one claims that causing one's seed to be given to Molech means that an Israelite should not marry a non-Israelite, so that the child will be raised as an idolater, he is silenced, mMeg. 4:9. One who gives his seed to Molech is liable only if he has given his seed and

heart."[17] Even every-day activities are discussed with this concern in mind, for one should not bend over to pick up coins which have fallen in front of an idol, unless he turns his back to the object of gentile worship.[18]

Buildings in which an idol resides are "defiling,"[19] and gardens associated with foreign gods should be avoided.[20] Similarly, Israelites should not help gentiles build a structure which may hold an image, such as a basilica, a scaffold, a stadium, or a tribunal; however, they may aid them in building a bath-house, as long as they do not participate in erecting the place where the idol actually will be placed.[21]

----

caused the child to pass through the fire, tSanh. 10:4-5.

[17]Hadas-Lebel, 444-446 and Lieberman, 119. "Hides pierced at the heart" are forbidden. Simeon b. Gamliel forbids the hides only if they have a round cut; mA.Z. 2:3. TA.Z. 4:6 adds that a "hide pierced at the heart" is one in which there is a perforation at the heart which looks like a peep-hole. If the cut is straight, the hide is permitted. Cf., mA.Z. 5:9. If an Israelite takes a vow to eat a "hide pierced at the heart," it is not binding, mNed. 2:1.

[18]TA.Z. 6:4. Similarly, in a public place, one should not bend down toward an idol in order to drink from a spring, but one should turn his back to the idol and drink from the spring, tA.Z. 6:5. If water shoots forth from a figure, one should not place his mouth on the pipe; rather, he should collect the water in his hand and drink from it, tA.Z. 6:6.

[19]TA.Z. 6:3: One who pokes his head or the greater part of his body into an idol's temple becomes unclean. A clay vessel whose airspace opens up to the inside of an idol's temple is unclean. Benches and chairs whose greater part has been placed inside an idol's temple are also unclean. If an Israelite dedicated his house to an idol, it imparts uncleanness to anyone who enters it. If a public road passes through it, it imparts uncleanness only to those on the road. If one erects his house near an idol's temple, the whole house imparts uncleanness to anyone who enters; however, if a temple were erected near an Israelite's house, the whole of the house does not impart uncleanness to those who enter, tA.Z. 6:1. If an Israelite sells his house to an idol, he must cast the money he received for it into the Salt Sea; however, if gentiles forcibly took over his house and placed an idol in it, he may keep any proceeds he received, and he may file records of the transaction in the public archives, tA.Z. 6:2. If an Israelite's house adjoins an idol's temple, the common wall is deemed to be divided in half, tA.Z. 3:6. If an Israelite's house which adjoins a idol's shrine fell down, the Israelite cannot rebuild, unless he moves four cubits away from the shrine, mA.Z. 3:6; tA.Z. 6:2 states merely that the Israelite may rebuild his house. If the Israelite rebuilds the house, it returns to its original condition; if the wall is built by others, only that wall imparts uncleanness. If an Israelite's house shares a common wall with an idol's shrine, the wall conveys uncleanness like a creeping thing. Aqiba says it is in the same class as a menstruating woman, mA.Z. 3:6. Cf., mShab. 9:1 where Aqiba also equates an idol with a menstruating woman. If a house were built for an idol, it is forbidden to an Israelite. If it were decorated or remodeled for an idol, the house is permitted to an Israelite if the decoration or what was added is removed. If the redecorated house never contained an idol, it is permitted at once to the Israelite, mA.Z. 3:7; the same distinctions are applied to stones and trees.

[20]An Israelite may not use a garden or a bath-house which is associated with an idol if he must express gratitude for its use; however, if the garden or bath-house is associate with an idol and also belongs to a private individual, the Israelite may use it, mA.Z. 4:3.

[21]MA.Z. 1:7; Urbach, 160-162.

Furthermore, an Israelite may not attend an amphitheater if it is the site of idolatry,[22] a ruling which would interfere with the normal social interaction between Israelites and gentiles. Professional interaction which related to matters of health or the care of young children was also limited by our texts.[23] However, an Israelite is allowed to do things decreed by the State, even if an idol is associated with them. This allowed the Israelites to function in a setting dominated by a government which supported the worship of foreign deities.[24]

On the other hand, gentiles have the power to desecrate their objects of worship, so that Israelites may come into contact with, and benefit from, such items. The rabbis picture the gentiles as fickle with regard to their images. They suggest that non-Israelites might not attempt to retrieve an idol which has been washed away by a flood, or that they might sell a valuable image for a profit. Furthermore, they picture the gentiles as desecrating some of their images. It is clear that in the minds of the authors of Mishnah-Tosefta, gentiles do not necessarily exhibit undying loyalty to specific images or deities. In general, the texts imply that gentiles do not take the worship of their deities as seriously as the Israelites do, or should, take their worship of YHWH.[25]

----

[22]Meir states that an Israelite may not enter a gentile's amphitheater because of idolatry, while sages say that the prohibition against entering because of idolatry applies only when the gentiles are actually making a sacrifice to an idol. If they are not sacrificing to an idol, an Israelite may not enter because one should not sit among the insolent, tA.Z. 2:5. This is a reference to Ps. 1:1, *Happy is the man who has not followed the counsel of the wicked, or taken the path of sinners, or joined the company of the insolent.* This is expanded in tA.Z. 2:6, which states that if one goes to a stadium or a camp to see a performance of sorcerers, enchanters, clowns, mimics, buffoons, or the like, he takes his seat among the insolent. While an Israelite may go to an amphitheater because the State requires him to do so, he may not take account of what is going on, tA.Z. 2:7. While some hold that one who watches gladiators fighting is guilty of bloodshed, Nathan permits an Israelite to watch gladiators because he will call out to save the loser's life, and he can provide evidence for a woman's claim that her husband died in the theater. However, the Israelite may not go for the entertainment, tA.Z. 2:7.

[23]Israelites cannot support idolaters; therefore, an Israelite woman may not assist a gentile woman in childbirth, or serve as a nurse for a gentile baby. However, a gentile may serve as a midwife for an Israelite and may nurse an Israelite child, mA.Z. 2:1 and tA.Z. 3:3. Some of these rules concern the fear that the gentile might harm the Israelite or her child. Probably out of fear of what the gentile will teach the Israelite, an Israelite does not allow a gentile to serve as his child's teacher, nor may one leave his child alone with a gentile, tA.Z. 3:2; however, the latter prohibition may relate to the fear that the gentile will harm the young Israelite.

[24]See, above, notes 12 and 22.

[25]By desecrating an idol, one also negates the "sanctity" of anything associated with the idol, mA.Z. 4:4. One gentile can desecrate any gentile's idol, while an Israelite cannot desecrate a gentile's object of worship. Only the one who places the object in the category of the sacred can remove it from that category, and the rabbis assume that gentiles often do this. In tA.Z. 5:4, Rabbi states, in Jacob's name, that an Israelite cannot nullify an idol which he has made, and Simeon b. Menassia states that an Israelite's idol is never subject to nullification, tA.Z. 5:7, for this is a trans-

iii

The sages assumed that gentiles would make a libation to their gods with any wine which was available to them.[26] The texts, therefore, evidence almost an obsession with keeping the Israelites from having contact with any wine that might have been poured out in honor of a foreign deity.[27] At the point that the liquid from the grapes was considered wine, an Israelite had to beware of touching it.[28] Even the permissibility of an Israelite's aiding a gentile in gathering grapes becomes a matter of dispute,[29] as does the use of grapes themselves;

----

gression which cannot be overcome. An Israelite may have a gentile negate an idol before it comes into the former's possession, tA.Z. 5:3. A gentile desecrates an idol by breaking parts of it, even small parts, mA.Z. 4:5. Rabbi and sages dispute whether or not the sale of an idol by a gentile constitutes desecration of the idol. TA.Z. 5:7 states that one nullifies an idol by damaging it with a hammer, or pushing it over and breaking it. TA.Z. 5:6 contains two statements, both based on Deut. 7:25--*You shall consign the images of their gods to the fire; you shall not covet the silver and gold on them and keep it for yourselves, lest you be ensnared thereby; for that is abhorrent to YHWH your God*--which disagree over whether or not an Israelite may benefit from an idol which a gentile has nullified. If a gentile sold an idol to people who worship it, it is prohibited; however, if he sold it to people who would not worship it, it is permitted, tA.Z. 5:5. If a wreck fell on an idol, if a river swept it away, or if thugs grabbed it, it is prohibited only if its owner seeks it; if he does not look for it, it is permitted, tA.Z. 5:5. If an idol were abandoned for no good reason, it is considered abandoned and profane, and Israelites may derive benefit from it; however, if it were abandoned at a time of war, for example, it is still considered forbidden to Israelites, mA.Z. 4:6. See Urbach, 230-232.

[26]We even find a discussion of whether or not invading troops would "defile" wine in a city: If a band of gentiles entered a city during times of peace, all open bottles of wine in the city are prohibited; however, if it were a time of war, all the wine is permitted, mA.Z. 5:6.

[27]Wine was associated with the god Jupiter; Georges Dumézil, *Fêtes romaines d'été et d'automne* (Paris: 1975), 87-107; Dumezil, *Archaic*, 185-186. On libation-wine see Elmslie, 69: "In the Mishna, however, the phrase [libation-wine] covers not only actual libation-wine, but also any wine which a heathen has touched, or has had the opportunity of touching when in no danger of being seen to do so by a Jew." On the relationship between Dionysus and wine see Walter F. Otto, *Dionysus: Myth and Cult* translated by Robert B. Palmer (Bloomington and London: 1965), 143-151. Otto notes that wine was used as "a metaphor for the god himself;" Otto, 146.

[28]Libation-wine is prohibited in any amount, mA.Z. 5:8-9. Because gentile wine is not considered wine until it flows down into the vat, an Israelite may tread the grapes with a gentile, mA.Z. 4:8, and may purchase the contents of a trodden wine-press from a gentile, mA.Z. 4:9. Also, Israelites and gentiles may work together at each other's wine-press during certain stages of the wine-making process, tA.Z. 7:2. However, even the lees, wet or dry, derived from gentile-manufactured wine are forbidden to Israelites, tTer. 10:13. On the wine-press, see Elmslie, 68-69.

[29]An anonymous statement holds that the Israelite may not gather grapes with a gentile, mA.Z. 4:9, while Meir rules that they may gather grapes together in new jars, as long as the gentile remains in the Israelite's sight, tA.Z. 7:1. Albeck suggests that once the gentile has defiled the grapes, the Israelite may aid him, as long as they have not become libation-wine; Hanokh Albeck, *The Six Orders of the Mishnah: Seder Neziqin* (Tel Aviv: 1953), 338. Cf., Elmslie, 70-71 and Bartinoro, *loc. cit.*

however, the issue here may be that the Israelite is aiding in the eventual defilement of a crop growing in the Holy Land.[30]

The sages' imagination forced them to deal with the presumably unlikely possibilities that a gentile might fall into a vat of Israelite wine,[31] that gentile-made wine might fall into a vat of Israelite wine,[32] or that one might unexpectedly find wine in vessels or utensils. In general, libation-wine contaminates vessels and utensils which then can transmit the contamination to other liquids which might be poured into them, so that we find a number of passages which deal with vessels which actually or potentially contained libation-wine, especially in the context of the market-place.[33]

----

[30]Meir forbids an Israelite from deriving benefit from a gentile's grape seeds or grape skins, while sages forbid these only when they are wet, mA.Z. 2:4.

[31]T.A.Z. 7:4 states that any wine which touches the gentile is forbidden. If a gentile fell into an Israelite's vat of wine, the Israelite may not drink the wine; he must sell it, mA.Z. 4:10. Similarly, if a gentile went down to remove the grapes from an Israelite's vat, all of it must be sold to gentiles. If the gentile measured the wine with a reed, flicked a hornet out of the vat with a reed, or patted the mouth of a frothing jar, the Israelite may not drink the wine; he must sell it. However, if in anger, a gentile threw a jar into an Israelite's wine-vat, the wine is permitted for drinking, mA.Z. 4:10.

[32]If libation-wine fell into a vat, the anonymous ruling is that everything in the vat is prohibited. Simeon b. Gamliel rules that the wine in the vat, with the exception of the libation-wine, may be sold to gentiles, mA.Z. 5:10.

[33]If an Israelite pours wine from his container into a gentile's jar, the wine in the Israelite's container is permitted, while the wine in the other container is prohibited, mA.Z. 5:7. TA.Z. 7:17 states that if a gentile sent a flagon with a drop of wine in it to an Israelite, the Israelite selling the wine fills up the flagon and accepts the full price for the wine and does not concern himself with the fact that there was a drop of libation-wine in the container. If a gentile were carrying grapes in a basket or a jar to a wine-press and liquid squirted out of the press onto the grapes in the gentile's basket, they are permitted, tA.Z. 7:5. If one purchased pressed grapes from a gentile and found in the container holes which contained wine, it is prohibited, tA.Z. 7:5. If an Israelite held out a clay vessel which he thought contained oil, but afterwards discovered that it contained wine, the wine must be sold to gentiles. Similarly, if a market supervisor tasted wine in a cup and then poured it back into the jug, or tasted it through a siphon, so that some drops fell back into the jug, the wine in the jug is forbidden, tA.Z. 7:6. An Israelite must make sure that his measuring-funnel is free of wine which he has poured into a gentile's flask before he uses the funnel to place wine into an Israelite's container. TA.Z. 7:18 states that an Israelite may not pour wine from one jar to another by placing the spout against the lips, or below the lips, of the jars. Rabbi rules that the vat, ladle and siphon of gentiles are permitted, while sages prohibit these, tA.Z. 8:1. Rabbi agrees with sages that gentiles' jars are prohibited, for they are made for holding liquids, while the others are not. A gentile's stone wine-press which was coated with pitch may be scoured and used by an Israelite. Rabbi says a wooden wine-press may also be scoured, but sages say that the pitch must be completely removed. In any case, an earthenware wine-press may not be used by an Israelite, even if the pitch has been removed, mA.Z. 5:11. Meir forbids an Israelite from deriving benefit from gentile skin-bottles or jars, even if they contain Israelite wine, while sages permit their use, mA.Z. 2:4. TA.Z. 4:9 states that an Israelite may benefit from a water-tank on wheels and from the Israelite wine collected in a gentile's leather-bottles; however, the Israelite may not drink the wine or the water. Simeon b.

These *sugyot* present the picture of gentiles regularly purchasing Israelite-wine. In light of what we saw above, this seems to present a problem, for Israelites normally were forbidden from providing items to gentiles which the latter would use in their religious acts. However, here the texts assume that Israelite merchants regularly supply wine to gentile customers and that Israelites also prepare wine for gentiles. In fact, some of them contain rulings which allow for a fairly easy trade in wine.[34] Other passages outline several daily economic activities in which the Israelite might come into contact with libation-wine: Wine might be used for a dye,[35] might appear among items which one Israelite sold to another Israelite,[36] might be used as a surety for a loan[37] or in its

----

Godea testified in the name of Rabban Gamliel that the Israelite wine could be drunk; however, "they" rejected his opinion. An Israelite may use new jars belonging to gentiles, but not old ones. If an Israelite pours out the water from a jar into one in which a gentile has placed water and the former washes the jar, he may place wine or oil in it. If the gentile collected wine in a jar, the Israelite must soak it in water for three days, seventy-two hours, then he may put wine into it. An Israelite may place wine into a gentile's jar in which the latter has collected Israelite wine, pickling brine, or plain brine, tA.Z. 4:10. Hadrianic vessels are prohibited, mA.Z. 2:3, and one cannot derive any benefit at all from them, tA.Z. 4:7; see Elmslie, 31. Simeon b. Gamliel, in the name of Joshua b. Qopesai, rules that animal skins belonging to gentiles may be made into mats for cattle. If the skins have been scrapped, sealed or covered with pitch, the Israelite may not use them. However, if the Israelite supervised the gentile while he worked the skin and covered it with pitch, the Israelite may collect wine or oil in the skin, tA.Z. 4:10.

[34]If an Israelite sells wine to a gentile, he must fix its price before he measures it out into the gentile's vessels, mA.Z. 5:7, for it becomes contaminated by the vessel, so that the Israelite could not derive a profit from it. TA.Z. 7:17 states that an Israelite may set the price for which he wishes to sell wine to a gentile, even if he is going to dry out the measuring instruments at a future time. A merchant needs to be less concerned with these matters than does a common Israelite. If an Israelite carefully prepared wine belonging to a gentile and left it in the latter's keeping in a house open to the public, Israelites may drink the wine, if the location is inhabited by both gentiles and Israelites. If only gentiles live in the area, Israelites may not drink the wine, unless the one who prepared the wine assigned a guard to watch it; however, the guard need not sit and watch the wine continually, mA.Z. 4:11. TA.Z. 7:9 adds that if it is assumed that the Israelite will spend the night in a certain place, the wine is forbidden, for the gentile might offer a libation with it. The assumption of mA.Z. 4:11 is that the wine was prepared by an Israelite, so that it is permitted as long as the gentile has not made a libation with it, Cf., tA.Z. 7:7. If an Israelite put wine into a gentile's domain and the jug is sealed or locked, the wine is permitted; but if not, it is forbidden, tA.Z. 7:7. If an Israelite carefully prepares wine for a gentile and the latter writes a document stating that the Israelite has purchased and paid for the wine, it is permitted, even though it is in the gentile's domain. However, if in the gentile's opinion the Israelite has not purchased the wine, the wine is prohibited, mA.Z. 4:12; Cf., tA.Z. 7:8.

[35]If one gave his wool to a gentile to dye, he need not worry that the gentile uses libation-wine in the dye, unless the gentile presents him with a detailed bill which makes it clear that libation-wine was used, tA.Z. 7:11.

[36]If one sells his friend produce and tells him that it is libation-wine, that which has been consumed is permitted, but the rest must be returned to the seller, and the money is returned to the purchaser, tM.S. 3:12.

[37]TA.Z. 7:7.

repayment,[38] or might be used as a payment for services.[39] In addition, some texts treat the problem of libation-wine contaminating foods on which it has fallen[40] or liquids with which it has become mixed.[41]

A full range of business[42] and social settings[43] in which a gentile

----

[38]If a gentile owes money to an Israelite, the latter may collect from funds which the former received from the sale of libation-wine or the sale of an idol. However, the gentile may not deliver the wine or idol as payment, or inform the Israelite that he will sell the forbidden items in order to pay off the debt, t.A.Z. 7:16.

[39]If a gentile offered wine in payment for services, the Israelite may ask for the value of the wine instead of the wine, as long as the wine has not come into his possession, t.A.Z. 7:16.

[40]If libation-wine fell onto grapes which were whole, they may be washed off and used. If enough libation-wine to leave a flavor fell on figs or dates, they are prohibited. However, if the wine fell on dried figs, they may be eaten by Israelites, mA.Z. 5:2. This is based on the following general rule: Whatever derives benefit from the flavor of the libation-wine is prohibited; whatever does not derive benefit from the flavor of the wine is permitted.

[41]If any amount of libation-wine is mixed with other wine, or if libation-water is mixed with other water, the mixture is forbidden, no matter the amount of libation-wine. If libation-wine is mixed with water, the mixture is forbidden if the wine leaves a taste, mA.Z. 5:8. The general rule is that if similar liquids are mixed together, the mixture is prohibited. If dissimilar liquids are mixed together, the mixture is prohibited only if the forbidden liquid leaves a taste.

[42]An Israelite cannot be hired by a gentile to help with his libation-wine; however, if the gentile hired the Israelite for some specific work, and while they were working he asked him to move a jar of libation-wine, the Israelite may do so. I assume that it could be argued that moving the libation-wine was an incidental act for which the Israelite was not receiving any specific pay, so that he derived no benefit from it; Cf., Elmslie, 76-77 and bA.Z. 65b. Similarly, an Israelite cannot hire out his pack animal for the transportation of libation-wine; however, a gentile may place his flagon of libation-wine on an animal which he has hired from an Israelite for another purpose, mA.Z. 5:1. If an Israelite hires a worker to work with him in preparing permitted wine for half a day and prohibited wine for half a day, and they are poured into one jar, the wine is prohibited. If they are put into separate containers, the permitted wine is permitted, and the prohibited wine is prohibited, t.A.Z. 7:10. If a gentile hires a worker to work with him near evening, and he tells him to move a flagon of libation-wine from one place to another, the Israelite make accept pay, even though he should not have entered into the agreement in the first place, t.A.Z. 7:10. One may give his worker a *denar* and tell him to purchase wine for his meal with it without worrying that the person will purchase libation-wine, t.A.Z. 7:10. T.A.Z. 7:10 discusses wine which Israelites and gentiles bring for sale in the market. If one is weighing grapes on a scale or pressing wine into a jar and some of the wine flows over the gentile's hand, the wine is permitted to the Israelite, t.A.Z. 7:3. If an Israelite left his wine in the presence of a gentile and informed him that he would be gone for a specific amount of time, the wine is prohibited. However, if the gentile did not know exactly how long the Israelite would be gone, the wine is permitted, mA.Z. 5:3-4. The anonymous text and Simeon b. Gamliel differ over the exact amount of time the Israelite may be gone. An Israelite may leave his wine in his store and go off to town and remain there for a considerable time without affecting the wine's status, as long as he does not inform the gentile that he is going, or if he locks the store, t.A.Z. 7:12. Similarly, an Israelite may leave his wine on a boat, as long as he does not inform the gentile that he is leaving, or as long as the boat does not cast off without the Israelite. If the Israelite has a jug of wine tied to his bed, and the gentile does not know about it, the wine is permitted. Judah states that it is prohibited if the Israelite was gone long enough for a hole to be drilled and plugged up in the jug, t.A.Z. 7:13.

might conceivably be left alone with Israelite wine were also imagined and discussed by the rabbis. The moral obligation an Israelite had to aid the gentile's ass which is struggling under a burden did not extend to his touching the libation-wine which the animal might be carrying.[44] Even the existence of converts among the Israelites generated concern for wine which one might inherit from one's gentile parent.[45]

In dealing with libation-wine, our sages covered almost every arena of activity, real or imagined, in which an Israelite could possibly come into contact with wine which *might* have been offered to an idol or foreign god. As much as any other topic, this is one which exercised the rabbis' imagination.

iv

The isolation between Israelites and *gentiles as idolaters* was further maintained by forbidding the Israelite from eating or "deriving benefit from" a number of gentile foods because they might possibly contain wine, or a wine-product, or because they might in some way be related to the worship of an idol. Thus, according to some, certain types of fish-brine, cheese, vegetables, bread, oil, meat, and even milk were forbidden to Israelites as food or as a source of "benefit." An Israelite who was concerned with the rabbis' opinions would be leery about dining in a gentile's house or at a gentile's affair.[46] In addition, because Israelites could not even "derive benefit" from these food items, certain forms of business transactions were also closed. Israelite shops could not sell certain products prepared by gentiles, nor could Israelites purchase many food items sold by gentiles.[47]

----

[43]If an Israelite and gentile were eating together and there were jars of wine on the table and on a serving-table, if the Israelite leaves the room, he may not drink the wine on the table when he returns. If an Israelite told the gentile to mix himself a cup of wine while the former left the room, all the wine is forbidden. Another opinion holds that any bottles of wine which were open when the Israelite left room are prohibited, and sealed bottles are forbidden if the Israelite were gone for a long time, mA.Z. 5:5.

[44]TB.M. 2:27.

[45]If one inherits libation-wine from a gentile, he may sell it to another gentile before he takes possession of it; however, once he has taken possession of the libation-wine, the money he receives from its sale is prohibited, tA.Z. 3:16.

[46]Any Israelite who attends a gentile's banquet is considered to have participated in an idolatrous practice, tA.Z. 4:6.

[47]Aqiba prohibits meat which comes out of an idolatrous temple, but permits meat before it enters the idol's temple, mA.Z. 2:3. Meir forbids Israelites from eating or "deriving benefit" from fish-brine and Bithynian cheese, while sages allow an Israelite to derive benefit from these, mA.Z. 2:4. On Bithynian cheese see Elmslie, 35 and 43. While Joshua forbids gentile cheese to Israelites, Ishmael seems to question this position, mA.Z. 2:5 and tSheb. 5:9; see Porton, *Ishmael*, 159-161. TA.Z. 4:11 prohibits gentile cheese which has not been curdled in the presence of Israelites. The

V

The texts before us draw a complex picture of the legislation concerning the daily intercourse of Israelites with gentiles. On the one hand, when discussing the gentile as idolater, the exclusive nature of the allegiance the People Israel owed YHWH predominated. That is, Israelites had to avoid contact with gentiles if that association could, in any manner, be seen as contributing to, or condoning, the worship of foreign deities. This concern with the worship of YHWH and the covenant between YHWH and his people led the rabbis to at-

---

cheese is permitted if it were curdled in the presence of an Israelite, even if a gentile prepared it. An Israelite may not enjoy benefit from milk which a gentile gathered without the supervision of an Israelite, mA.Z. 2:6; however, the Israelite may sit on one side of the corral and the gentile on the other and bring the milk to the Israelite, tA.Z. 4:11, and an Israelite may even drink such milk, mA.Z. 2:7. The issue might be that an unsupervised gentile would give the Israelite milk from a forbidden animal. An Israelite may not enjoy benefit from bread which a gentile has baked, unless it was prepared in the presence of an Israelite, mA.Z. 2:6; but Cf., tA.Z. 4:11 and tSheb. 5:9. If the Israelite baked the dough, it is permitted to him, even if it were kneaded by a gentile, tA.Z. 4:11. Some prohibited benefiting from oil which gentiles had prepared, although Judah and his court permitted gentile oil, mA.Z. 2:6, an opinion rendered by a standing vote according to tA.Z. 4:11; Cf., tSheb. 5:9. Israelites could not benefit from vegetables which have been stewed or pickled into which gentiles normally put wine or wine-vinegar, mA.Z. 2:6. TA.Z. 4:8 adds that one cannot derive any benefit whatsoever from the stewed or pickled vegetables which contain gentile wine or vinegar. Similarly, an Israelite could not derive benefit from minced fish, brine which does not contain fish, or hilek-fish, drops of asafoetida, or sal-conditum, mA.Z. 2:6, or locusts that come out of a shop-keeper's basket, mA.Z. 2:6. According to mA.Z. 2:7, an Israelite may eat or drink milk which a gentile milked under an Israelite's supervision, honey from a honey comb, pickled vegetables into which they do not normally put wine or vinegar, unminced fish--defined by tA.Z. 4:11 as any fish in which the head and the backbone are discernible--brine containing fish--defined by tA.Z. 4:11 as any brine in which one or two kilbit-fish are floating--a whole leaf of asafoetide or pickled olive-cakes. Yosi states that the olives cannot be sodden olives. Only locusts that come from a shop are permitted. An Israelite is permitted a piece of meat on which there is a sign on all of it or on part of it, even if the sign is on only one piece in a hundred, tA.Z. 4:11. In tA.Z. 4:8, we read that sodden olives sold at the door of gentile bath-houses are prohibited for eating, but one may derive benefit from them. Yosi states that an Israelite may not derive benefit from them because gentiles normally pour vinegar on them. Israelites are permitted caper-fruit, leeks, liverwort, boiled water, and parched corn prepared by gentiles, tA.Z. 4:11. However, an Israelite is not permitted an egg which was roasted by a gentile, tA.Z. 4:11. The roasted egg must have something to do with idolatry, for elsewhere an Israelite may buy eggs from gentiles as long as they are in their shell, so that he can determine the type of bird which laid the egg. Israelites may not purchase from gentiles eggs cracked in a dish because they sell gentiles eggs from forbidden birds only after they have cracked them in a dish, tHul. 3:24; see Porton, "Forbidden Transactions," 325.

tempt to ensure the separation of the Israelite from the "non-gods" who existed in their world and from those who worshipped these "false" deities. The implications of these rulings were broad, for they would have forced the Israelite to look at every business dealing and social encounter as a possible source of direct worship of an idol or of providing indirect support of its adoration.

On the other hand, at least as Mishnah-Tosefta describe the situation, gentiles and Israelites lived in close proximity and regularly interacted in the economic, political, and social spheres of life. Not only do the texts describe the Israelites and non-Israelites as employing one another and working together, but they also assume that they jointly owned property. Furthermore, we have seen that while Israelites should not provide gentiles with items which the latter might use in their religious practices, the Israelites could merely take the gentiles at their word that the items were not destined to be used in the worship of their deities. And a vendor of wines or anything else could sell items to non-Israelites fairly easily, without worrying too much about the use to which the items would be put. Moreover, it appears that Israelites regularly prepared wine for gentiles, while at the same time the authors of Mishnah-Tosefta assume that gentiles would make a libation to their deities with virtually any amount of wine with which they came into contact. Finally, we have seen that events or activities sponsored by or controlled by the State were permitted, even if idols were associated with them. This points to the "practical" side of the legislation in Mishnah-Tosefta in which they took account of the fact that Israelites should live at peace with the ruling power. Although against idolatry, Mishnah-Tosefta did not encourage the Israelites to work for the overthrow of the Roman government which supported the adoration of foreign deities. This parallels the idea, we saw above, that Israelites should strive to live at peace with their gentile neighbors and the ruling authority.

The sages of Mishnah-Tosefta desired to separate the Israelite from the gentile *as idolater*, and they were able to distinguish the gentile *as idolater* from the gentile as farmer, merchant, lender, etc. However, our texts do not exhibit sophisticated knowledge of contemporary religious practices, and, at least at times, the old biblical images and paradigms predominate. In general, Mishnah-Tosefta are concerned with idolatry primarily from the point of view of keeping the Israelites separate from it. Idolatry is important *primarily* as something to be avoided by Israelites, and not necessarily as an activity in which non-Israelites engage. While the texts know that non-Israelites worship idols, this is not their primary characteristic; it is only important in certain specific circumstances, such as on their holidays, when it might impinge on Israelite activity or interfere with the normal interactions of Israelites and non-Israelites. The rabbis do not exhibit a keen interest in, or fascination with, gentile religious practices in themselves; rather, they are viewed only from their perceived impact on daily Israelite-gentile activity.

Mishnah-Tosefta display a rather practical attitude toward the gentiles as idolaters. On the one hand, Israelites must avoid any direct or indirect contact with gentile religious rites. On the other hand, the texts assume that gentiles and Israelites regularly interacted, so that the concern with avoiding idolatry did not *predominate* in determining how the two groups should interrelate. While the regulations in Mishnah-Tosefta could have resulted in the Israelites' scrutinizing every contact with a gentile to ensure that the former would not support the latter's religious practices, the texts support the view that unless it is clear that the gentile is engaging in religious activity, the Israelites need not be concerned with interacting with non-Israelites. Mishnah-Tosefta assume that the natural course of life in Palestine necessitated daily interaction and co-operation among Israelites and gentiles, and the documents sought to make this possible. They did this by separating the gentile *as idolater* from the gentile *qua* gentile. The former had to be avoided; the latter did not. Furthermore, the authors of Mishnah-Tosefta seem to have assumed that the individual Israelite could determine when the gentile was an idolater, so that much of the concern with idolatry was internalized. Just as the Israelite distinguished his grain by his own activity, so he could decide, in most cases, whether or not he was contributing to a gentile's religious activity. In both instances, the decision was left to the individual Israelites, albeit they made them in accordance with specific guidelines and rules. Again, we discover that the concern with idolatry is an internal Israelite matter, which is described from the Israelite point of view and discussed in terms of importance to Israelites. The goal was to avoid idolatry, while at the same time existing and flourishing in an environment which necessitated daily contact with idols and their worshipers, and which was dominated by a ruling power which supported the worship of gods other than, or in addition to, YHWH, and the authors of Mishnah-Tosefta reached their goal.

Chapter Ten:

The Jerusalem Temple and the Gentiles

i

The Jerusalem Temple and its cult were a central topic of concern for the authors of Mishnah-Tosefta, so that they found it necessary to deal with the gentile in relationship to them. Although viewed at times as idolaters, gentiles were also seen as possible worshipers of YHWH. While Mishnah-Tosefta permit the gentiles to bring voluntary sacrifices to the Temple, the matter of the Temple and the relationship of non-Israelites to it are a complex issue.

The treatment of the Temple and its cult in Mishnah-Tosefta is an imagined description, for the realities of which it speaks concerning the cultus had ceased to exist about a century an a half before the documents were finally edited. The detailed discussions of the sacrificial rules had no setting in which to be realized, and it is unclear whether our writers believed that such a setting would soon come into being. With the Temple in ruins, it appears that the authors of Mishnah-Tosefta reverted to the Torah, specifically to Leviticus and Numbers, as their source of information, mythology, and ideology concerning the rituals associated with the Ethnic Shrine.[1] As Neusner notes, "if the division of Holy Things wants to say something other than is found in Leviticus and Numbers . . . it is difficult to specify what that might be in detail. Although the division does not depend entirely on the facts given in scripture, its dependence is so nearly complete that we may say there can have been no division of Holy Things without the specified verses of the Pentateuch."[2] Although none of

----

[1]For detailed discussions of the descriptions of the Temple and cult as found in Mishnah-Tosefta, see Emil Schürer, *The History of the Jewish People in the Age of Jesus Christ (175B.C-A.D. 135)*, New English Version Revised and Edited by Geza Vermes, Fergus Millar, Matthew Black (Edinburgh: 1979), II, 237-313 and Shmuel Safrai, "Temple," in Shmuel Safrai and Menahem Stern (eds.), *The Jewish People in the First Century: History, Geography, Political History, Social Cultural and Religious Life and Institutions* (Philadelphia: 1976), II, 865-907. Alfred Edersheim, *The Temple, Its Ministry and Services as They Were at the Time of Jesus Christ* (London: 1959).

[2]Jacob Neusner, *A History of the Mishnaic Law of Holy Things Part Six. The Mishnaic System of Sacrifice and Sanctuary* (Leiden: 1980), 34. Neusner also writes: "The principle consequence of our analysis remains the simple fact that Mishnah has chosen to amplify every theme of scripture's laws on Holy Things except for the ones dealing with the priesthood. But the chief message of our division is that there should *be* a division of Holy Things," 34. "*Mishnah*

Mishnah's or Tosefta's editors would have witnessed personally the activities in the Temple, there surely were descriptions available to them of what actually transpired within the Temple's precincts. Such accounts, however, were either ignored or subsumed under Scripture's images and categories. The authors of Mishnah-Tosefta seem to have chosen to remember and to describe the Temple in Jerusalem in idealized terms based on Scripture, and if they possessed information about the daily workings of the actual Temple, this too was cast in terms of Scripture's pictures. We have seen that biblical paradigms have appeared throughout our material, so that the authors' reverting to Scripture's images of the cult is neither unusual, nor unexpected. In other instances, however, the biblical paradigms were modified or set alongside human activity in the authors' Palestinian environment. With regard to the events within the Temple, this could not have occurred because there were not any which were contemporaneous with the writers of Mishnah-Tosefta. In this instance, there was nothing in the life-experiences of the authors to set alongside Scripture's descriptions or images, and perhaps this is the reason that Scripture's ideas and concepts are so prevalent with regard to this topic. However, with regard to the gentiles, the sages do appear to have modified the Torah's teachings, for they allow gentiles voluntarily to worship YHWH, through limited participation in the cultus at Jerusalem.

Although the Temple in Jerusalem lay in ruins and its cult was no longer practiced, in one sense the cult had not actually ended: It continued to exist in the sages' minds. They treated the cult with the same care, detail, and vitality with which they discussed the Sabbath, the family laws, or the laws of damages. In fact, Mishnah-Tosefta make a powerful statement about the continuity of Scripture and the unimportance of the events taking place in the world around them: "[I]t is as if our division chooses not only to ignore its world and the potentialities for the exegesis of contemporary times, but also to turn itself backward toward Leviticus and other relevant passages in Scripture."[3] More than in any other context, our authors here look for a "restabilization of a society

----

constitutes a statement on the meaning of Scripture, not merely a statement of the meaning of Scripture," 34-35. Neusner writes that he is "struck by the insistence of Mishnah upon the letter of Scripture, its obsession with detail and clearcut effort to say only what Scripture has supplied warrant for saying: choice of topics, mode of interpretation," 45. "So far as there is a ritual process of sacrifice, therefore, it is not described in Mishnah, but in Scripture. . . . Time and again all we find in our division is an amplification of secondary implications of Scripture, never a confrontation with the primary assertions or fundamental ideas thereof," 276.

[3]Neusner, 281.

which has been profoundly upset by the loss of its Temple, then of the city, and of all hope of access to the Temple-site."[4] Neusner argues, however, that the authors' purpose was to solidify their authority among the People Israel: "The cosmic order is not to be replicated. But it can at least be studied in sages' words. The Temple cannot be regained. It can at least be remembered in vivid detail supplied by sages. . . . It is with the sage who knows . . . the rules of the cult that one who wants to experience the cult must identify."[5]

Because Mishnah-Tosefta explicitly draw on Scripture for their discussion of the Temple and its cult, it seems advisable to turn to the Torah in order to explicate the meaning of Israel's cult which stands behind the *sugyot* we shall discuss below. Of course, it is dangerous merely to transfer biblical ideas into the period of Mishnah's editing, so that we must proceed with caution.

It has been suggested that in the Hebrew Bible the Temple in Jerusalem was considered YHWH's residence, and it was here that YHWH directly met his people: "It is from heaven that God's power originates, but it is from the Temple that the deity appears and gives strength to the people."[6] In discussing the rules for the construction of the altar in Ex. 20:22-26, Levine suggests that God's coming to the altar was dependent on the correctness of the rites practiced there, for "improper rites may persuade the deity not to frequent certain sites, and he may come to despise them."[7] In short, it is possible for the authors of our texts to have thought that the correctness of the rites connected with the Jerusalem cult determined whether or not YHWH was present among his people. Although writing in a time when the Temple no longer stood, and in a culture which had developed ways of approaching YHWH without the Temple, its priesthood, or its cult,[8] when writing about the Temple and its cultus, the biblical mythology could still hold sway among the rabbis. Whether looking back to the time when the Temple stood, or looking forward to a time when it would be

----

[4]Neusner, 282.

[5]Neusner, 289.

[6]Baruch A. Levine, "On the Presence of God in Biblical Religion," in Jacob Neusner (ed.), *Religions in Antiquity: Essays in Memory of Erwin Ramsdell Goodenough* (Leiden: 1970), 82. Safrai writes: "The Temple . . . constituted primarily the divine dwelling-place of the God of Israel which set them apart from other nations;" Safrai, 906.

[7]Levine, 79.

[8]See Jacob Neusner, *A Life of Yohanan Ben Zakkai: Ca. 1-80 C.E.*, Second Edition, Completely Revised (Leiden: 1970); Baruch M. Bokser, *The Origins of the Seder: The Passover Rite and Early Rabbinic Judaism* (Berkeley and Los Angeles: 1984); Zvi Zohar, "The Consumption of Sabbatical Year Produce in Biblical and Rabbinic Literature," in Harvey E. Goldberg (ed.), *Judaism Viewed from Within and from Without* (Albany: 1987), 75-106.

rebuilt, our authors clearly believed that YHWH had to be approached through an exacting ritual. If the People Israel wished to approach the God of Israel at his Holy Residence, they had to follow all of the long established rules of protocol and etiquette. If the sages of Mishnah-Tosefta believed that inappropriate activity at the Temple could drive YHWH from their presence, they also thought that the presentation of sacrifices by non-Israelites would not alienate YHWH, or drive him from the Temple.

In Scripture's terms, the cultic rules were given to Israel by YHWH, and they applied only when those two entities were to meet, so that access to the altar/Temple was limited to Israelites. Even if gentiles might wish to bring offerings to YHWH, they most likely could not approach the altar.[9] This finds expression in post-biblical times in the fact that gentiles could not move past the outermost rampart of the Temple Mount, a datum attested to by Mishnah, Josephus, and the remains of two Greek inscriptions.[10] However, Mishnah-Tosefta also contradict the apparently exclusively Israelite nature of the biblical cult, for some sources claim that gentiles participated in pilgrimages to the Temple and offered sacrifices there.[11] The problem is that we do not know how the authors of Mishnah-Tosefta thought this was to occur, or how they envisioned the actual participation of the gentiles in the offering of their sacrifices.[12]

By the common era, the Temple and its cult occupied a dual role in the minds of the Israelites. On the one hand, it represented the religious center of the people. It was here that humans approached YHWH. Above, we saw that non-Israelites had to respond to some degree to the holy nature of the Land of Israel. Below, we shall discover that the gentile could also respond to the sacred

----

[9]Lev. 22:25 states that *Israelites* should not bring offerings from foreigners to the altar which implies that access to the altar/Temple was limited to Israelites. It is significant that the term "gentile" does not appear in the indexes to Roland de Vaux, *Ancient Israel Volume 2: Religious Institutions* (New York: 1965) or Menahem Haran, *Temples and Temple-Service in Ancient Israel: An Inquiry into the Character of Cult Phenomena and the Historical Setting of the Priestly School* (Oxford: 1978). But, see below, note 13.

[10]Safrai, 866.

[11]Safrai, 878: "Tradition and practice rendered Gentile sacrifices acceptable; often, particularly on feast-days, Gentiles could be seen in the Temple. They came to prostrate themselves before God, to hear the Torah and to bring their offerings." Cf., Shmuel Safrai, "Relations Between the Diaspora and the Land of Israel," in Shmuel Safrai, Menahem Stern, David Flusser and William C. van Unnik (eds.), *The Jewish People in the First Century: Historical Geography, Political History, Social, Cultural and Religious Life and Institutions* (Philadelphia: 1974), I, 199-201.

[12]Nowhere do the texts explain how the gentile was to bring his offering to the altar without moving past the Temple's outer precincts.

nature of YHWH through the Temple cult.[13]   From this point of view, the Temple in Jerusalem is seen as the residence of YHWH, the God of the Israelites, the Deity to whom gentiles could also express adoration. Josephus and Philo found in the Temple symbols of the entire cosmos, including both its earthly and heavenly realms, and others saw it as a source of blessing for Israelites and gentiles alike.[14]   However, one scholar has suggested that the gentiles participated in the Jerusalem cult because "the originally very close connection between faith and worship often turns out to be [superficial]," and "to offer sacrifice at some famous sanctuary was very often no more than an expression of a piety that had become cosmopolitan, an act of courtesy towards the nation or city concerned. . . ."[15]   Thus, one could argue that when Mishnah-Tosefta permit gentiles to bring sacrifices to the Israelite Temple, the texts reflect a general Hellenistic phenomenon, for foreigners regularly brought offerings to the deities of cities which they visited, without exhibiting any long term or profound allegiance to these gods. Or, one could claim that in the minds of the authors of Mishnah-Tosefta, the gentiles' coming to the Temple and worshipping YHWH through participation in the sacrificial cult served to testify to YHWH's sacredness and his pervasiveness. I see no way to discover which of these explanations is appropriate. The voluntary nature of gentiles' worship corresponds to the idea that Israelites were also free to chose not to fulfill their role as Israelites, by refusing to follow the rabbinic rules and interpretations of Scripture. Human beings have free will; therefore, just as Israelites were free to stray from the worship of YHWH, so also gentiles were free to acknowledge him. It is also possible, that both of these ideas stand behind the *sugyot* below, and that the sages' allowing the participation of the gentiles in the cult of YHWH simply was made easier by the Hellenistic environment in which they lived.

From another point of view, however, the Temple represented the political center of the Israelite ethnic group. It is assumed that governmental administrative institutions were established in the Temple's courtyards.[16] In addition, the Temple treasury, which our sources describe as large and sufficiently funded, financed the expenses of the Temple and the communal needs of Jerusalem.[17]   Safrai also claims that the Temple was "a place for the cultivation,

---

[13]The Bible itself *may* assume that non-Israelites would participate in the sacrifices offered to YHWH; Schürer, 309. Josephus also records that gentiles made offerings to YHWH in Jerusalem; Schürer, 310-313.

[14]Safrai, II, 906.

[15]Schürer, 309.

[16]Safrai, II, 865.

[17]Safrai, II, 879.

preservation and dissemination of the holy scriptures and of historical narratives and genealogies" and that the Temple housed the "official" version of the Bible against which all other copies were evaluated.[18] As the Ethnic Shrine and the social, economic, political, and mythological focal point of the People Israel, the gentiles could not contribute to the Temple's upkeep, for they were not part of the people whom the Shrine represented. Interestingly, even though the gentiles could not contribute to the Temple's upkeep, they could separate some agricultural gifts, such as the heave-offering, which went to the priests. This suggests that in the minds of some of the authors of Mishnah-Tosefta, the Temple served as an ethnic symbol, while its major functionaries, the priests, did not. This may be a result of a rabbinic anti-priestly polemic, or it may reflect the view that the priests served YHWH and did not possess, at least for some of the writers of Mishnah-Tosefta, a distinctively Israelite nature. While the gentiles could approach YHWH through a limited number of rituals at the Temple, they could not merge with the People Israel by treating the Temple as their ethnic symbol.

The Temple, like the Land of Israel,[19] is a multivaried phenomenon. On the one hand, it was an Israelite institution. From this point of view, gentiles could come into only limited contact with it, and they could not contribute to its maintenance. On the other hand, the Temple represented a path to YHWH and a means of acknowledging his sovereignty and holiness. From this point of view, the gentiles could participate in its cultus. However, we have seen above that our sources recognize and seek to maintain distinct political and social systems for the gentiles and the Israelites, and this applies in the area of Temple ritual as well. When the texts permit the gentiles to bring sacrifices to the Temple, they limit the types of sacrifices which non-Israelites may bring, and some of the sages do not apply certain cultic categories--such as refuse, remnant, and the like--to their offerings. Furthermore, the rites which the gentiles could perform over their animal-offerings were limited, for they could neither lay their hands on their sacrifices, nor wave them before YHWH.

----

[18]Safrai, II, 905; Cf., Saul Lieberman, *Hellenism in Jewish Palestine: Studies in the Literary Transmission Beliefs and Manners of Palestine in the I Century B. C. E.--IV Century C. E.* (New York: 1950), 85-86. We know that passages from the Torah were first read publicly during some of the holiday services at the Temple, so even if Safrai has exaggerated its role, the Temple still served as the "official" center for the transmission of God's word. On the role of the priests as transmitters of Revelation, see Gary G. Porton, "Midrash: Palestinian Jews and the Hebrew Bible in the Greco-Roman Period," in Hildegard Temporini and Wolfgang Haase (eds.), *Aufstieg und Niederganag der römischen Welt* (Berlin and New York: 1979), II.19.2, 113-114.

[19]See above, Chapter Six.

ii

Gentiles could bring only voluntary offerings to the Temple;[20] they could not offer the obligatory sacrifices. Therefore, non-Israelites could not bring the bird-offering of one who has flux or a woman after child-birth, a sin-offering, or a guilt-offering.[21] However, it was unclear whether or not the complex system of rules which apply to Israelites' sacrifices applied to those of non-Israelites. The question under dispute between Meir and Yosi was whether the person who offered the sacrifice determined its sacred status, or whether the fact that the offering was brought to YHWH's residence determined its sacredness.[22] Even for the sacrifices they brought, gentiles[23] could not perform the rite of the "laying on of hands,"[24] or the rite of waving an offering before

----

[20]On the gentiles' bringing offerings to the Temple, see Adolf Büchler, "The Levitical Impurity of the Gentile in Palestine Before the Year 70," *Jewish Quarterly Review*, New Series, XVII (1926-1927), 31-38; Schürer, 309-313. Cf., Gedalyahu Alon, *Jews, Judaism and the Classical World: Studies in Jewish History in the Times of the Second Temple and Talmud* translated by Israel Abrahams (Jerusalem: 1977), 165-167.

[21]Vow-offerings and freewill-offerings were accepted from gentiles, mSheq. 1:5. In tSheq. 1:7, Yosi states that Israelites accept from gentiles freewill-offerings of burnt-offerings, peace-offerings, birds, meal-offerings, wood, incense, and salt. Aqiba states that only their burnt-offerings and peace-offerings were accepted. We also learn that gentiles could not give freewill-offerings for the upkeep of the Temple; however, if they sanctified something for the Temple, the sanctification was valid.

[22]In mZeb. 4:5, Meir held that sacrifices brought by gentiles are not subject to the rules of Refuse, Remnant, uncleanness, location, and time, for the status of the person who made the offering determined whether or not it was a sacred offering, according to Israelite law. Yosi maintained that the determining factor was that the offerings were brought before YHWH in the Temple, so that the complex rabbinic laws applied, no matter who made the offering. Part of Meir's comment is attributed to Simeon in tZeb. 5:6, and then the whole is repeated anonymously. I attribute the whole opening of mZeb. 4:5 to Meir, for it seems to me that in the passage, Yosi responds to Meir's whole statement; see, however, Jacob Neusner, *A History of the Mishnaic Law of Holy Things Part One Zebahim. Translation and Explanation* (Leiden: 1978), 83. Yosi appears in both texts, but with a slightly different comment attributed to him in each passage. Simeon at first declares that Israelites cannot benefit from the gentiles' offerings, that their offerings are not subject to the law of sacrilege, and that they do not impart the status of a substitute on animals which may be designate as substitutes, but that they do require a drink-offering; however, later on in the passage Simeon "concedes" that the gentiles' sacrifices are subject to the laws of sacrilege, if they were brought for the upkeep of the Temple. TMe'. 1:18 has an anonymous statement which reads that the egg of a turtle dove, the crop of fowl, and the offerings of gentiles are not available for use and are not subject to the law of sacrilege.

[23]Along with deaf-mutes, imbeciles, minors, blind men, slaves, agents, and women.

[24]MMen. 9:8, tMen. 10:13. The *gemara*, bMen. 93a, explains that the deaf-mute, imbecile, and minor are disqualified because they do not know what they are doing. The gentile is disqualified because Lev. 1:4 reads, *the children of Israel*. The references to *his hand* in Lev. 3:2 and Lev. 3:8 exclude the agent or a man's wife. As we saw above, the gentile often appears in the

YHWH,[25] both of which were limited to healthy adult Israelite males. If a gentile sent his whole-burnt-offering from beyond the sea along with the drink-offering, these are accepted. And, Israelites may pay for the drink-offering out of the community funds, if the gentile did not provide it.[26] If a gentile brought peace-offerings and gave them to an Israelite, the Israelite eats them. If he gave them to a priest, the priest eats them.[27]

While the gentiles could not pay the *sheqel*-tax to support the ethnic shrine of the Israelites, the Temple in Jerusalem, they could dedicated a beam to a synagogue.[28] The *sheqel*-tax was imposed on only Israelites, to pay for the upkeep of the ethnic symbol, and the gentiles could not make this contribution, either from the point of view of the rabbis, or from the point of view of the Roman administration.[29]

While we saw above that the holiness inherent in the Land of Israel led the rabbis to allow the gentiles to bring certain agricultural offerings which were destined for the priests, the same did not hold true for priestly gifts taken from animals, for unlike the Land, animals do not possess an inherently sacred nature. Therefore, the priestly gifts were not taken from animals which gentiles slaughter,[30] nor was the first-fleece given from sheep belonging to gentiles.[31]

----

context of these other "disqualified" individuals, for none of them have the status of an adult Israelite male. Here we learn is that a gentile is not subject to the rules of the Torah, which are generally viewed as having been addressed to healthy adult Israelite males.

[25]TMen. 10:17. TMen. 10:17 parallels tMen. 10:13.

[26]MSheq. 7:6.

[27]TSheq. 3:11.

[28]If a gentile sanctified a beam for use in a synagogue and on it wrote "for the Name," they store it away if he meant the Holy Name. If he said the beam was for the sake of the synagogue, they planed off the reference to the Name and used the rest of it, tMeg. 2:16.

[29]On the *sheqel*-tax see E. Mary Smallwood, *The Jews Under Roman Rule: From Pompey to Diocletian* (Leiden: 1976), 124-125. Michael Avi-Yonah, *The Jews of Palestine: A Political History from the Bar Kokhba War to the Arab Conquest* (New York: 1976), 49-50. Schurer, 270-274. Safrai, II, 880-881.

[30]If the animal belongs to a gentile, the priestly gift is not taken when the animal is slaughtered, tHul. 9:3. If an Israelite slaughters a gentile's beast for the gentile, he is exempt from giving the priestly gifts, mHul. 9:1. However, if an Israelite slaughters his own animal for a gentile to eat, the Israelite is liable for the priestly gifts, tHul. 9:2. However, priestly gifts are not subject to sanctity, so that if a priest sold them to a gentile or threw them to the dogs, there is no penalty, tHul. 9:9. If an Israelite shares the ownership of an animal with a gentile, he must bring proof of the joint ownership, if he does not wish to pay the priestly gifts, mHul. 10:3. On the priestly gifts, see Schurer, 257-270.

[31]If an Israelite bought fleece from a gentile, he is exempt from the requirement of giving the first fleece to the priest, mHul. 11:2. If an Israelite sheared a gentile's sheep, the first fleece is not taken, for the animal belongs to a gentile, tHul. 10:2.

The firstling of the herd and flock was given to the priests, so that the gentiles were also excused from this offering.[32]

iii

From the point of view of our authors, gentiles could *voluntarily* choose to recognize YHWH's sovereignty over the world and the obligations which all humans owed to him. For this reason, gentiles could bring voluntary offerings to the Temple. Even when they brought these offerings, however, the complex rules which applied to the offerings of Israelites were not applied to them. Non-Israelites were not permitted to perform the detailed rituals expected of Israelites. Thus, even though both groups might approach the Temple with their offerings to YHWH, they did so differently. First, the access of the

----

[32]Many of our discussions of this offering assume that the gentile was unconcerned with this matter, so that the Israelite who purchased an animal from a gentile had to determine whether or not the animal had given birth before she was purchased. If an Israelite bought the unborn young of an ass, mBekh. 1:1, or a cow, mBekh. 2:1, from a gentile, sold these to a non-Israelite, jointly owned these with a gentile, had received the young of a gentile's animal to rear, or had given the young of his animals to a gentile to rear, the laws of firstlings do not apply because the gentile is not subject to these restrictions. Mishnah cites Num. 3:13, *all the firstborn in Israel*, and states that the law applies to only Israelites and not to others. Cf., tBekh. 1:1 and 2:1. Similarly, if an Israelite received the flock from a gentile on "iron terms," the offsprings are exempt from the law of firstlings, but not the offsprings of their offsprings. If the contract stipulated that the offsprings stand in place of the mother, their offsprings are exempt, but not the offspring of their offsprings. Simeon b. Gamliel rules that all of the offsprings are exempt because the gentile has a lien on all of them, mBekh. 2:4; Cf., tBekh. 2:5. Ishmael explains how one can tell if the beast he bought from a gentile had already given birth, so that the Israelite will know whether an animal born while he owns the mother is a firstling, mBekh. 3:1 and tBekh. 2:11. See Gary G. Porton, *The Traditions of Rabbi Ishmael Part One: Non-Exegetical Materials* (Leiden: 1976), 173-176. Simeon b. Gamliel states that if an Israelite bought a nursing beast from a gentile, he can be assured that the animal is nursing its own young, so that he knows that the animal has already born an offspring, mBekh. 3:2, tBekh. 2:14, tBekh. 2:16. Others seemed to have assumed that the matter might be in doubt, tBekh. 2:14. The Shammaites rule that an Israelite cannot be numbered along with priests in an single company for the consumption of a firstling, while the Hillelites, or Aqiba, permit even gentiles to be numbered along with the priests. TBekh 3:15 attributes this rule to Aqiba, while mBekh. 5:2 attributes it to the Hillelites. See Jacob Neusner, *The Rabbinic Traditions About the Pharisees Before 70* (Leiden: 1971), II, 245-246. Once a quaestor saw an old ram. When he asked why the ram had been allowed to grow so old, he was told that it was a firstling, so that it could not be slaughtered unless it suffered a blemish. The quaestor took a knife and slit its ear, whereupon the sages permitted its slaughter. The quaestor then slit the ears of other firstlings, but sages did not permit these animals, mBekh. 5:3. If a gentile set aside the firstborn of an ass, they notify him that he is not obligated to do so, and they set the gentile's animal to work, or they shear it, in order to show that it does not have the status of a firstling, tTer. 4:13.

gentiles to the Temple was limited, for they could not pass the outer rampart. This means that gentiles and Israelites would occupy different spaces around the Temple.[33] Second, the gentiles could bring only a few types of sacrifices, so that Israelites could bring a series of offerings not permitted to the gentiles. Third, gentiles and Israelites did not perform the same rituals with regard to their offerings. In addition, the gentiles could not support the Temple's upkeep, and priestly gifts were not taken from animals owned by gentiles. Because the Temple was the Ethnic Shrine, the symbol of the People+Land+YHWH, it could be supported by only Israelites. The gentiles' support of the priesthood was complex, for they could separate the heave-offering, even though this was given to the priests, because it acknowledged the holiness of the Land. However, priestly dues were not taken from gentiles' animals, because these possessed no inherent holiness. This distinction implies that the sages of Mishnah-Tosefta wanted at least to limit the gentiles' support of the priesthood.

Again we see that the gentile has a complex relationship to a central symbol of the sages who produced Mishnah-Tosefta. On the one hand, the sovereignty of YHWH is such that the gentiles may, and perhaps should, be cognizant of it, so that they may approach him through the rites performed at the Jerusalem Temple. On the other hand, the gentile cannot respond to YHWH and the Temple in the same manner that Israelites do. For this reason, our authors set out requirements which differentiate between Israelites and gentiles. The sovereignty and holiness of YHWH is maintained, and the uniqueness of his people, the Israelites, is also upheld. This also points to the complexity of the meaning of the Temple for the sages, for at one and the same time it was a Ethnic symbol and the residence of the Ruler of the Universe, the Sovereign of all peoples.

----

[33]It is interesting that our sources do not explain how the gentiles' offerings were transported to the altar, given the fact that the gentiles were not suppose to have been able to move from the Temple Mount into the Courts; Safrai, 866.

Chapter Eleven:

Israelite Purity and the Gentiles

i

Scripture conceives of impurity as "an external force which adheres to a person or object," and of purification as "an attempt to alienate impurity." According to this view, impurity is something from which people "divest themselves."[1] Because, as Levine suggests, YHWH would unleash his demonic wrath against anyone who approached his presence without taking the necessary precautions, specifically, freeing him/herself from impurity, it was essential for humans to approach the altar in a state of ritual cleanness, and for only those to stand before YHWH who were permitted to do so in the first place.[2] The severe penalties for those who committed cultic offenses resulted from the fact that YHWH "was extremely concerned about his purity as a resident deity."[3] In addition, Levine argues that the Israelites placed the blood on the doorposts and the lintels in Egypt because the *mashit* "was conceived as a distinct force which, once unleashed, was not controllable, even by Yahweh himself."[4] Thus, there were impure forces in the universe from which YHWH had to be protected, and this lies behind the biblical notions of impurity. In fact, Levine argues that the ritual on the Day of Atonement, described in Lev. 16, was designed to "protect" YHWH and the area immediately surrounding him from "the incursion of impurity which would penetrate the sanctuary. . . ."[5] According to Levine, a person who became impure by means of committing an offense against YHWH "introduced a kind of demonic contagion into the community." In order for the community to be restored to its proper state, the contagious person had to be

----

[1] Baruch A. Levine, *In the Presence of the Lord: A Study of Cult and Some Cultic Terms in Ancient Israel* (Leiden: 1974), 63.

[2] Levine, 70f.

[3] Levine, 72.

[4] Levine, 75.

[5] Levine, 74.

purified. And YHWH's residing in the community could be assured only if the community remained in "an extreme degree of purity."[6]

Levine has argued that the biblical concern with impurity and purity centered around protecting YHWH. Because YHWH's residence was the sanctuary, it was a concern primarily of the priests, for they alone approached YHWH in the Temple. Furthermore, if we accept Levine's conception of "impurity" as a force which "threatens" YHWH, we can understand why the idea of purity became a matter of sectarian concern among the various groups of Israelites in the first centuries of the common era. In fact, Smith suggests that different ideas of "purity" were major factors used by various groups to distinguish among themselves.[7] Therefore, discussions of purity generally occur in connection with disagreements among various elements within the Israelite community.[8] Neusner suggests that the issue arose among the several Israelite groups--the *yahad* of Qumran, the early Church, the Pharisaic *haburah*, the rabbis--because they either claimed to be the New Temple--YHWH's Residence--or to be entitled to the priestly prerogatives.[9] Because each group exercised its claim to the same Temple/Residence of YHWH and its prerogatives, each struggled with the others over the issue of purity. Concerns with purity and impurity, then, are most important for those among whom YHWH dwells, and among those who may come in contact with him.

Because the gentiles, by definition, made no demands on, or for, the Temple and were not conceived of as a people among whom YHWH dwelt, purity does not become a major issue in the Israelite discussions about them. Following Smith and Neusner, the concern for purity in Mishnah-Tosefta derives from the rabbis' attempt to turn the People Israel into a nation of priests;

----

[6]Levine, 75. We should note that Levine's discussion of impurity stands in opposition to that of Kaufmann, who saw impurity as a state of being; Yehezqal Kaufmann, *History of the Israelite Faith* (Jerusalem: 1952), I, 525-33, 539-45. Kaufmann's work is extensively discussed by Levine, 77-91.

[7]Smith writes: "Differences as to the interpretation of the purity laws and especially as to the consequent question of table fellowship were among the principle causes of the separation of Christianity from the rest of Judaism and the early fragmentation of Christianity itself. The same thing holds for the Qumran community and, with Pharisaic tradition, the *haburah*. They are essentially groups whose members observe the same interpretation of the purity rules and therefore can have table fellowship with each other;" Morton Smith, "The Dead Sea Sect in Relation to Ancient Judaism," *New Testament Studies*, VII (1960), 347-360. Compare Shaye J.D. Cohen, *From the Maccabees to the Mishnah*, (Philadelphia: 1987), 124-173, especially 129-131.

[8]Jacob Neusner, *The Idea of Purity in Ancient Judaism: The Haskell Lectures, 1972-1973* (Leiden: 1973), 111. Neusner quotes Smith with approval.

[9]Neusner, 112.

therefore, rules which originally applied to mainly the priestly caste are now placed upon the entire Israelite community. This would exclude the gentiles, who, according to our authors, were not part of YHWH's people.

Douglas, however, disagrees with Neusner and Smith. She suggests that the purity rules in the Bible form part of a "symbolic system" which "set up the great inclusive categories in which the whole universe is hierarchised and structured."[10] Therefore, she argues that cultic purity, sexual purity, and agricultural rules against mixtures are interrelated, so that the concern with purity affected every segment of biblical Israelite society.[11] Therefore, they should not be seen, even in the Bible, as solely a priestly issue. Douglas further argues that "the temple stands for the pure consecrated body of the worshiper and that the rules which protect the sanctuary from defilement repeat by analogy the rules which protect the purity of the human body from wrong food and wrong sex, and the people of Israel from false gods." However, Douglas does agree that this picture of the universe was "taught by the priests."[12] Similarly, she agrees that "[t]he holiness of the Temple is a focal point of the purity rules of the biblical legacy" and that "in later periods, sectarian communities constituted themselves in relation to the Temple and revived purity rules to signify their apartness and holiness."[13] However, Douglas claims that "any sect tends to define itself by purity rules whether a biblical corpus lies at hand or not."[14]

When we look at the discussions of the gentile from the point of view of the Israelite purity laws, Levine, Neusner, and Smith seem to be correct. As we shall see below, most of the purity rules do not apply to gentiles; they are internal ethnic matters. Because the non-Israelites did not make any claims on the Temple, and did not claim to constitute a community in which YHWH dwelt, the Israelite purity laws were irrelevant to them, for as Levine has argued, the origin of the Israelite concept of impurity derives from a desire to protect YHWH and his residence. Because we have seen that the rules which were designed to protect the Israelites from, in Douglas' words, "wrong food and wrong sex" did apply to the gentiles, her analogy from the purity rules concerned with the Temple to these matters appears to be too simplistic. Although we find no explicit descriptions of how the gentiles were to bring their freewill-offerings to YHWH, or how they were to prepare for that activity, it is likely

----

[10]Mary Douglas, "Critique and Commentary," in Neusner, 139.
[11]Douglas, 139.
[12]Douglas, 140.
[13]Douglas, 141.
[14]Douglas, 141.

that they had to undergo the same purification and preparatory rituals as did the Israelites. This would also explain why gentiles were restricted in their access to the Temple Mount. However, because YHWH did not dwell among the non-Israelites, nor did they normally approach his Temple, they did not need to follow the Israelite purity rules in their daily lives.

ii

The sectarian nature of the concern for purity in Mishnah-Tosefta finds expression in the fact that many of the purity rules do not apply to gentiles. Gentiles *qua* gentiles do not necessarily covey uncleanness.[15] Because gentiles do not form a segment of the People Israel, the laws of skin-disease and mildew do not apply to the former.[16] The semen of an Israelite causes uncleanness, while a gentile's semen does not, and for some the blood of a gentile similarly does not pollute.[17] In the same way, a gentile's corpse does not convey un-

----

[15]A vessel which touches a gentile does not become unclean, tAhil. 1:4; Jacob Neusner, *A History of the Mishnaic Law of Purities Part Four Ohalot. Commentary* (Leiden: 1974), 33-34. Neusner writes that the gentile is "not subject to uncleanness at all. . . ." Also, if a gentile touches a corpse, utensils which touch the gentile are clean, tAhil. 1:4. Similarly, the flux of a gentile does not produce uncleanness, tZab. 2:1. Segal maintains that the purpose of the purity laws was "to keep Israel from close contact with Gentiles . . ." and that this was based on biblical ideas, for these derive from the priestly ideas of purity in relationship to the sanctuary. Alan F. Segal, *Rebecca's Children: Judaism and Christianity in the Roman World* (Cambridge and London: 1986), 125-126. However, I do not see how Segal's interpretation fits our sources.

[16]Gentiles cannot contract uncleanness from the signs of skin-disease, mNeg. 3:1. Bright spots on gentiles are clean, even after they convert to Judaism, mNeg. 7:1. Cf., tNeg. 2:14-15. A non-Israelite's garments may not contract uncleanness from mildew or skin-disease, mNeg. 11:1. Cf., tNeg. 7:10 and tNeg. 7:15. Similarly, their houses cannot contract uncleanness from mildew, mNeg. 12:1. Cf., tNeg. 7:15. If one side of a house belongs to a gentile and the other side to an Israelite, the house is not affected by mildew, tNeg. 6:4.

[17]If a gentile woman discharges the semen of an Israelite, it is unclean; however, if an Israelite woman discharges the semen of a gentile, it is clean, mMiq. 8:4. TMiq. 6:7 states that the urine which is discharged is unclean. The point is that an Israelite's semen may cause uncleanness, while the rules of uncleanness do not apply to a gentile, or his semen. The Shammaites ruled that the blood discharged by a gentile woman is clean, mNid. 4:3 = mEd. 5:1. The Shammaites hold that because the laws of purity and impurity do not apply to gentiles, the blood of these women is pure and does not render other things impure, even though elsewhere, others have held that gentile women are considered to be women with flux. The Hillelites, on the other hand, consider gentile women to be like a woman with flux, so that any moist flow--blood, urine or spittle--render things unclean. Cf., Hanokh Albeck, *The Six Orders of the Mishnah: Seder Tohorot* (Tel Aviv: 1957), 387; Bartinoro, *loc. cit.*; Jacob Neusner, *The Rabbinic Traditions About the Pharisees Before 70* (Leiden: 1971), II, 299-300. Adolph Büchler, "The Levitical Impurity of the Gentile in Palestine Before the Year 70," *Jewish Quarterly Review*, New Series, XVII (1926-1927), 9-13. Büchler, 14, *assumes* that both the Shammaites and the Hillelites considered the menstruating gentile woman "as defiling to a certain degree." On the basis of an "authentic" report on yA.Z. 36b,

cleanness by carrying.[18] Only Israelites, among whom YHWH dwells, or who might wish to approach frequently YHWH's residence, needed to concern themselves with these matters. In their concern with grave-areas, the rabbis seem to have excluded the gentile because they realized that they had no control over the non-Israelites.[19] Furthermore, the water from the Red-Heifer should not be sprinkled on gentiles, for the ritual is not appropriate for them.[20] Also, certain immersion-pools which were constructed by gentiles were permitted to be used by Israelites for cleansing from certain types of impurities.[21]

On the other hand, some texts assume that gentiles are impure and transmit impurity. However, the reasons for these assumptions vary, and they

----

Büchler, 15, "dates" the origin of the law which declared gentile women to defile like menstruating Israelite women to "the time of the Hellenists," with a renewal "some time before the year 17/18." Alon argues that the point of this text is to state that "a non-Jewess is not susceptible to a menstruant's uncleanness, even under Rabbinic law;" Gedalyahu Alon, "The Levitical Uncleanness of the Gentiles," reprinted in Gedalyahu Alon, *Jews, Judaism and the Classical World*, translated by Israel Abrahams (Jerusalem: 1977), 162. In tNid. 5:5, the Shammaites state that the blood which flows from a gentile woman is the blood of a wound and not like menstrual blood. In line with the Shammaite assumption that the laws of purity apply to only Israelites, we read that blood stains which come from gentile women are clean, mNid. 7:3. If an Israelite woman loans her shift to a gentile and discovers a blood stain on it when it is returned, she may claim that the stain comes from the gentile woman, so that the garment is not declared unclean, mNid. 9:3 and comment of Bartinoro.

[18]MNid. 10:4 and tNid. 9:14.

[19]MOhol. 17:3. The text has some problems. We read that if a gentile plows, he does not make a grave-area, "for the law of the grave-area does not apply among Samaritans." Cf., Neusner, *Ohalot*, 323. Cf., tSheb. 3:13 which mentions both gentiles and Samaritans and states that the rabbis made decress only in places where they could enforce them.

[20]TPar. 12:11.

[21]Outside the Land of Israel, a gentile's immersion-pool may be used by an Israelite who suffers a pollution, even if there is a swipe-well, which is considered to be drawn-water. In some cases, mMiq. 3:4, persons who suffer a pollution may be purified by drawn-water. A gentile's immersion-pool within the Land of Israel but outside the town-gate may be used by menstruant women. Bartinoro, *loc. cit.*, explains that the immersion-pools outside of the gates are not popular, so that many people will not come by them and fill them with drawn water or otherwise make them unfit. Those within the town-gate may be used by those who suffer a pollution, mMiq. 8:1. The point of the passage is that there are situations in which one can use a gentile's immersion pool. With regard to pools inside the Land but outside a city gate, these pools are considered permissible even for a menstruant woman, a major source of impurity for which the punishment is "cutting off" if the woman does not correctly purify herself. In tMiq. 6:1, Meir states that the immersion-pools outside the gates are fit for purification from all types of uncleanness, while those inside the city gates are unfit for use. Judah holds that those inside the gate are fit for those who suffer a nocturnal emission, and those outside the gate are fit even for a menstruant woman. With reference to an immersion-pool of the house of Anath of Rome, Hananyah b. Tardyion declared it unfit because he claimed that gentiles had emptied water into it during the night, tMiq. 6:3.

are limited to specific types of impurity. There are two possible explanations of this inconsistency. Some of the sages could have believed that particular categories of impurity applied to all humans and were not related to Israel's ethnicity. Or, some could have held that the close contact between gentiles and Israelites could pose a threat to YHWH and his continued presence among the Israelites within the Land of Israel. With regard to the residences of gentiles, they are considered to be unclean because the authors of Mishnah-Tosefta seem to have assumed that gentiles buried the corpses of aborted children near their homes. Thus, these dwellings are unclean not because gentiles are inherently unclean, but rather because these locations have been polluted by corpses[22] through the gentiles' "uncivilized" activities. Because gentile women[23] do not

----

[22]MOhol. 18:7 rules that the dwelling-places of gentiles are unclean. TAhil. 18:6 notes that any gentile, whether a slave, servant-girl, eunuch, a child past puberty, or a gentile married to a Samaritan make his/her dwelling subject to the laws of the gentile dwelling-place. If a gentile male lived alone in the house for forty days, (this opinion is anonymous in Mishnah but is attributed to Abbah Yudan of Sidon in Eliezer's name in tAhil. 18:7) the house must be examined; if a woman lived with the gentile, the house need not be examined, for it is assumed to be unclean. The status of holy things is suspended because of the gentile dwelling-place, and Yosi b. Judah states that "they" burn the heave-offering which comes into an area designated as a gentile dwelling-place, tAhil. 18:7. This is the assumed meaning of the passage when it is quoted in yTer. 8:9; see comment of Moses Margalioth, *loc. cit.* and Neusner, *Ohalot*, 344. If an Israelite woman or slave watched the house, it need not be examined, for we assume that they would have prevented the burial of an abortion; Cf., Bartinoro, *loc. cit.* TAhil. 18:8 adds that if the guard died and the gentile stayed there forty days, it is assumed to be unclean. If one enters and leaves the place, it is assumed to be clean because it is guarded. The place may be guarded by a slave, a woman, or a child nine years old and one day. If the male lived alone, it is possible that a woman visited him and buried her abortion there. If a woman lived with the male, we *assume* that she buried an abortion. An anonymous statement reads that deep drains and foul water must be examined. When the examination takes place, an Israelite must enter before a priest; if the priest enters first, he becomes unclean, tAhil. 18:10. The Shammaites rule that dung-heaps and loose earth must be examined, while the Hillelites maintain that an area into which a weasel or pig can go must be examined, mOhol. 18:8. These rules do not apply to colonnades, unless one lives in the colonnade, tAhil. 18:11, and Simeon b. Gamliel adds that these restrictions do not apply to a gentile's city which lies in ruins, mOhol. 18:9. Furthermore, these rules do not apply to Arabs' tents, field-huts, fruit-shelters, simple tents, summer-houses, gate-houses, the open space in a courtyard, a bath-house, an armory, or the camp grounds of a legion, mOhol. 18:10. TAhil. 18:12 states that feedsheds, granaries, bath-houses, water-houses, gate-houses, the open space in a courtyard, the fruit-shelters, way stations for travelers, field-huts, hedged-in-places, huts, and tents are not subject to these rules. Rabbi declares fortifications and a legion's campground unclean, but sages declare them clean. Judah declares the armory and the weapons-hut unclean, but Yosi declares them clean. Gate-houses and the airspace of the courtyard are unclean, if they are joined to the dwelling-place. Summer-houses do not fall under these rules. The rules do not apply to a store, unless the gentile actually lives in the store. A gentile's dwelling remains unclean, even if it has been destroyed, tAhil. 18:11. We further learn that these rules do not apply outside of the Land of Israel, where the rabbis' authority does not extend, tAhil. 18:11.

[23]Along with Samaritan women and imbeciles.

follow the rabbinic rules concerning vaginal flows, all spittle found in a town in which there was a gentile woman is unclean.[24] Some commentators connect this ruling with the statement that gentiles always transmit impurity like those with flux.[25] Some also use this ruling to explain the statement that if thieves entered a house, only in the part of the house where they walked are the foodstuffs, liquids, and items in open vessels considered to be unclean, while if a gentile[26] were with them, everything is considered to be unclean.[27] Similarly, the impurity of a gentile is assumed when we read that if one moves or stumbles against millstones in the midst of which are gentiles, the Israelite suffers *midras*-uncleanness.[28] The point here seems to be that the gentile is assumed to suffer from flux and that the millstones are movable.

In the same manner, an Israelite who buys vessels from a gentile craftsman suffers *midras*-uncleanness and corpse uncleanness.[29] What to do with domestic items which have been purchased from gentiles becomes a matter of concern; however, the texts are less than clear. Some ruled that domestic items purchased from non-Israelites had to be purified in the manner appropriate to the material out of which they were made. A parallel version states that if the Israelite knows that the utensils have not been used, he must only immerse them.

----

[24]MToh. 5:8.

[25]TZab. 2:1. In interpreting mToh. 5:8, Bartinoro, following Maimonides, states that because gentile women are all considered to be women with flux, their spittle is unclean; Bartinoro on kl. Albeck follows this line of reasoning; Albeck, 317. Slotki connects this ruling with the fact that these women do not follow the rabbinic rules concerning menstruation; Israel W. Slotki, *Tohoroth: Translated into English with Notes* in Isidore Epstein (ed.), *The Babylonian Talmud* (London: 1948), 388, n. 9.

[26]Or a woman.

[27]MToh. 7:6. See Bartinoro on the second appearance of 'm ys 'mhn and Slotki, 397, n. 10. This assumption also appears as an explanation for the statement that a gentile's corpse does not covey uncleanness by carrying; see Bartinoro on mNid. 10:4 and Albeck, 406. However, see Simeon in tNid. 9:14, who claims that the rule is a result of the fact that the scribes, not Scripture, are the source for the idea that a corpse conveys uncleanness by carrying. Alon argues that this rule has nothing to do with corpse-uncleanness; rather it deals with a gentile with flux-uncleanness. Simeon actually "refers to the Gentile's uncleanness in his life-time (the impurity of one that had a flux) and declares him clean of this defilement;" Alon, 149-150, n. 3.

[28]TAhil. 9:2. Neusner, *Ohalot*, 195; Saul Lieberman, *Tosefeth Rishonim: A Commentary based on Manuscripts of the Tosefta and Works of the Rishonim and Midrashim in Mansucripts and rare Editions Part III Kelim-Niddah* (Jerusalem: 1939), 120. Cf., tToh. 6:11.

[29]TToh. 8:9. See, Saul Lieberman, *Tosefeth Rishonim: A Commentary based on Manuscripts of the Tosefta and Works of the Rishonim and Midrashim in Mansucripts and rare Editions Part IV Mikwaoth-Uktzin* (Jerusalem: 1939), 85-86.

He needs to purify them more fully only if he has knowledge that they have actually been used with forbidden edibles.[30] If the first statement refers to *only* those utensils which have been used by the gentile, then the source of impurity is the food, and not the gentiles and their environment. However, if the first text means that all of the vessels must be extensively purified, then the source of impurity must be the gentiles and/or their environs.[31]

The inherent impurity of the gentile is assumed in the context of his coming into contact with an Israelite's heave-offering. Because of a gentile, heave-offering is rendered unclean and needs to be burned. However, gentiles do not always render the Temple or its offerings unclean.[32] But, we do know that the gentiles, like those who suffered from corpse-uncleanness, were excluded from the Temple-court;[33] however, we also have seen that gentiles could make voluntary offerings at the Temple in Jerusalem.

A bath-house with gentile attendants is unclean when its filters open onto private property, but is clean when its filters open onto public property.[34] One may not place his vessels in the "windows" of the keeper of the bath-house because the gentile keeper knows that he will be questioned about the things left with him.[35]

iii

Schürer wrote that ". . . a gentile--as a non-observer of the laws of purification--was unclean, and that consequently all intercourse with him was defiling. . . . [T]his [Acts 10:28] must not indeed be misunderstood to the extent

----

[30]If an Israelite purchases utensils from a gentile, they may be cleaned in their customary manner. A knife needs only to be polished, but a spit must be heated until it is white-hot, mA.Z. 5:12. TA.Z. 8:2 states that if the Israelite knows that the utensils have not been used, he need only immerse them. The Israelite rinses with cold water cups and flasks which he knows have been used. Pitchers, water-kettles, frying pans, or kettles are rinsed in boiling water. Knives, spits, and gridirons must be heated to white-hot. Anything used before it has been polished, is permitted if it has been scalded, immersed, or made white-hot.

[31]Cf., Alon, 153.

[32]TZab. 2:1; Lieberman, *Tosefeth Rishonim*, IV, 123. Cf., mTer.8:11 and tTer. 1:14, where it is assumed that a gentile can defile heave-offering; Cf., Alan J. Peck, *The Priestly Gift in Mishnah: A Study of Tractate Terumot* (Chico: 1981), 241-245.

[33]In delineating the various levels of purity connected with the Temple's environs, we learn that the Rampart is holier than the Temple Mount, for no gentile or one who has contracted corpse uncleanness may enter inside the Rampart, mKel. 1:8.

[34]TMiq. 6:4.

[35]TToh. 8:8.

of supposing that there was an absolute prohibition of all intercourse, yet it does mean that ceremonial uncleanness was incurred by such intercourse."[36] Schurer continues by stating that the uncleanness of the gentile placed "a heavy burden" on an Israelite "who was faithful to the law. . . ."[37] Schurer's view, that the gentile was unclean because he did not adhere to the rabbinic purity laws, was rejected by both Buchler[38] and Alon,[39] and our analysis supports their rejection. Furthermore, the passages which speak of the interactions of Israelites with non-Israelites generally pay little, if any, attention to the question of becoming unclean through mutual contact.

Bůchler opened his classic article on the Levitical impurity of the gentile by rejecting Schůrer's conclusions. Bůchler realized that on the basis of all the evidence, one must conclude that the gentiles *qua* gentiles were not considered to be impure, and that interactions between Israelites and non-Israelites were not restricted because of the supposed impurity of gentiles. However, Bůchler saw that while the gentile was not inherently impure, some of the texts clearly considered gentile women to be unclean, while others attributed ritual impurity to gentile males. Bůchler explained this apparent contradiction by arguing that the rabbinic views had changed through time; therefore, he set out to date the various rabbinic rulings concerning the gentile's impurity. He concluded that while the Temple was standing, the gentile was not considered to be ritually impure because impurity was a matter of concern only with regard to those who wished to make offerings in the Temple.[40] Bůchler dated the decision to consider gentile women as defiling like menstruous women to "the time of the Hellenists," with a renewal "some time before the year 17/18."[41] Basing

----

[36]Emil Schürer, *A History of the Jewish People in the Time of Jesus Christ* translated by Sophia Taylor and Peter Christie (New York: 1891), II, 1, 54. Cf., Emil Schürer, *The History of the Jewish People in the Age of Jesus Christ (175 B.C.-A.D. 135)* A New English Version Revised and Edited by Geza Vermes, Fergus Millar, and Matthew Black (Edinburg: 1979), II, 81f.

[37]Schürer, 55.

[38]Bůchler, 1-2.

[39]Alon, 154.

[40]Bůchler wrote: "[L]evitical impurity was not attributed to the Gentile in Jerusalem in Temple times; . . . the intercourse between Jew and Gentile was neither wholly prevented nor even restricted thereby; . . . the non-observance by the Gentile of the rules of the levitical purity had nothing to do with any actual levitical impurity of his, and . . . its defiling effect was the same as that of the same degree of levitical impurity of the Jew, or even less, as it affected exclusively the priest on duty, the Temple, the Jew specially purified for the sacrifice, and the sacrificial meal,--nobody and nothing beyond," 2.

[41]Bůchler, 15, 39-47.

himself on Josephus' account of the gentiles in Jerusalem during Herod's administration, Büchler dated this law between 37b.c.e. and 6c.e., and he argued that it was designed to protect the priests from contracting ritual impurity from the many gentiles then resident in Jerusalem.[42] The sages ruled that this impurity was transmitted to gentile males "about the year 1," but "it affected only the high priest and the priests on duty in the Temple."[43] On the basis of mPes. 8:8, he dated the equating of the impurity of a gentile with the impurity of a corpse to the Hillelites[44] sometime "between the years 20 and 60."[45] However, between the years 40 and 50, none of these rules prevented normal trade between Israelites and gentiles.

Büchler saw further development to have taken place among some of the sages who flourished during the second century in Galilee, for some of them accepted the fact that a gentile woman was always treated as a menstruous woman and that gentile men always suffered from the defilement of a corpse; however, he does not consider these rulings to be "the direct continuance of the same practice in Judea."[46] Büchler concluded that "shortly before 60" the Hillelites and Shammaites "resolved" to ascribe to the gentile the impurity of a "Jew who has an issue," in order to counteract sodomy; however, the outbreak of the Great Revolt in 66 prevented the rule from being applied in practice.[47] Therefore, the rules enacted later by the Galilean sages marked a new stage, not a continuation of older rulings. Furthermore, these stricter rulings were not accepted by all, for we find a number of sources which describe the gentiles and Israelites as eating together in the former's homes, without the latter being defiled.[48]

Writing in 1926, Büchler, like his contemporaries, uncritically followed a literal reading of the rabbinic texts. By combining Josephus and Philo with the *entire* corpus of rabbinic literatures, Büchler believed that he could place each statement attributed to a specific sage in its historical framework. If we set aside Büchler's "historical" reconstruction as being the result of a historically naive and literarily pre-critical reading of the sources, it is clear that he saw in the texts much the same things that we have seen. Gentiles were not viewed as inherently

---

[42]Büchler, 46.
[43]Büchler, 46.
[44]Büchler, 16-21.
[45]Büchler, 46-47.
[46]Büchler, 49-50.
[47]Büchler, 80.
[48]Büchler, 52-57.

impure, at least in many of the texts. In fact, only a limited number of passages attributed any impurity to them. Furthermore, Büchler consistently realized that the interaction between Israelites and gentiles was, for the most part, neither limited nor restricted, so that even if some held that the latter were impure, this had little practical effect in the daily interactions of the two groups. In addition, he argued that the issue of impurity originated as a matter centered around the Temple and the priests, and that it was not applied to the non-Israelites because they did not come into contact with either the cult or its supervisors.

Alon set out to refute Büchler's claims. Against Büchler, Alon argued that the impurity of the gentiles "is one of the early Halakhot, current . . . a long time before the destruction of the Temple." The gentiles' uncleanness derived from "the Halakhic tradition that ascribes levitical uncleanness to the idol itself and to its attendants." Alon argued that the uncleanness of the gentiles "led to definite consequences in the transactions between Jews and other peoples;" however, "since . . . this Halakha was not essentially absolute and fixed, Jews did not refrain from having dealings with non-Jews, even in circumstances in which they might contract and impart uncleanness."[49] On the other hand, Alon wrote that "the early Sages were inclined to deny Gentiles the fitness to become defiled,"[50] even though gentiles were prohibited from entering the Temple from "the beginning of the Second Temple period."[51] Alon explained the contradictions in the rabbinic texts by claiming that the sages far removed from the origin of these rules tended "to set aside the early tradition concerning the levitical impurity of the Gentile status and to restrict the laws flowing therefrom."[52]

Alon's comments are less perceptive than those made by Büchler. Even if we set aside Alon's uncritical historical reconstructions, his conclusions still present problems. We have seen that the authors of Mishnah-Tosefta were able to distinguish between the gentile *as idolater* and the gentile as farmer, merchant, and the like. For this reason, it is doubtful that any uncleanness associated with idols would be transferred to *all* non-Israelites. Furthermore, claiming that later generations rejected the laws of previous generations because they did not understand the "origins" of the earlier rules seems to beg the question. First, it assumes the reliability of the attributions of sayings, especially the chronology of the sayings, without attempting to establish it. Second, it assumes that all later generations were fully aware of what earlier generations had decided.

----

[49]Alon, 147-148.
[50]Alon, 165.
[51]Alon, 166.
[52]Alon, 180.

Third, if changes did occur, Alon would attribute them to a later generation's ignorance of an earlier generation's intentions, rather than to a conscious decision of the later sages to reject, or to change, the rulings of their predecessors. This assumes that later generations would blindly follow the decisions of their forefathers.

At this point, several conclusions seem clear: 1) The gentiles *qua* gentiles were not considered unclean in many of the *sugyot* of Mishnah-Tosefta. 2) Social interaction between Israelites and non-Israelites was not severely restricted because of the impurity of the gentiles. 3) Many of the purity rules did not apply to gentiles. However, 4) some of the passages do attribute forms of ritual uncleanness to gentiles. Throughout this volume we have argued that a chronological reconstruction of the discussions of the gentile is doomed to failure. However, by setting the question of the gentiles' uncleanness in the context of Mishnah-Tosefta's scheme of ritual impurity, we can uncover some important information, not addressed by previous studies on this question.

MKel. 1:1-4 contain a list of the most severe sources of Israelite uncleanness, the "fathers of uncleanness:" 1) Semen, 2) one who has contracted corpse-uncleanness, and 3) the one who suffers from a skin-disease during the periods of the completion of his purification rites and the eighth day render humans and vessels and their contained air-space unclean by contact. These do not render something unclean by carrying them without making direct contact. 4) One who has intercourse with a menstruating woman conveys uncleanness to what is above or beneath him. 5) A Zab's flux, 6) his spittle, 7) his semen, 8) his urine, and 9) a menstruating woman's blood render things above them unclean, and they render unclean by carrying or touching. 10) A Zab renders a couch unclean. 11) The female Zab renders one who has intercourse with her unclean. 12) One with a skin-disease renders unclean by merely entering a house, and 13) a corpse is the most severe source of uncleanness.

It is striking that taken as a whole, Mishnah-Tosefta differentiate between the Israelite and non-Israelite by applying the "fathers of uncleanness" to only the former. Gentile semen, unlike that of an Israelite, 1, is not a source of uncleanness. Although a gentile corpse does render unclean, it does so to a lesser degree than an Israelite corpse, for a vessel which touches one who has touched a gentile corpse is not rendered unclean, against 2. A gentile cannot contract a skin-disease, against 3 and 12. There was a disagreement concerning the blood of gentile women, so that 4 and 9 were held by some *not* to apply to gentiles. There was also some question concerning whether or not the laws of the Zab--5, 6, 7, 8, 10, 11--applied to the gentile, for we read that the gentile does not become unclean through flux; however, they are to be treated like one with flux in all matters. The text seems to say that although the laws of flux do not apply to non-Israelites, we treat them as if it did. Along these lines, we have noticed that only a few of those texts which speak of the normal interactions between Israelites and gentiles express a concern for the impurity or purity of the non-Israelite.

When we turn to those *sugyot* which deal with the gentile from the point of view of the purity laws, we notice the same ambiguity and inconsistency we have seen in every other category with which Mishnah-Tosefta are concerned. On the one hand, the major categories of uncleanness do not apply to gentiles. On the other hand, these sources of uncleanness are relevant when dealing with non-Israelites, for some do affect the non-Israelite, even if not in the same way that they apply to Israelites. It is clear, therefore, that based on what our texts explicitly state, any generalizations concerning the gentile as a source of impurity must be rejected. While clearly there was an attempt to place the gentile outside of the major categories of the Israelites' purity laws, the ambiguous nature of the gentile did not allow this plan fully to succeed. On one level, the purity laws were Israelite; on another level, they affected all human beings.

While the relationship of the gentile to the Israelite purity laws is ambiguous, some sense can be made of this situation. Part of the solution lies in the biblical passages which served as the bases for the discussions in Mishnah-Tosefta. Lev. 15:16-17 state that a male becomes unclean by an emission of semen and that any cloth or leather upon which the semen falls also is unclean. The male and the cloth or leather must be washed, and they remain unclean until evening. These verses are contained in a collection of statements which YHWH told Moses to tell the *Children of Israel*, so that they could be seen as applying to only Israelites. The laws concerning skin-diseases appear in Lev. 13:2-44 and Lev. 14:2-32. These rules are also addressed to the *Children of Israel*, and their Israelite nature is made even clearer by the fact that the priest plays an crucial role in determining the nature of the skin-disease, in deciding when the individual is clean and unclean, and in performing the rituals which purify the unclean individual. Lev. 15:19-30 discuss the menstruating woman. These rules are also addressed to the *Children of Israel*, so that they could be seen as exclusively Israelite concerns. However, we have seen some ambiguity with regard to this category of uncleanness in Mishnah-Tosefta. Some of the concern may revolve around the fact that an Israelite may not have intercourse with a woman who is considered to be a menstruating woman; therefore, applying these rules to the non-Israelite females, or claiming that they are always considered to be menstruating, may be a symbolic way of regulating sexual activity with them, so that Douglas may not be completely incorrect in connecting "wrong sex" and purity.

Num. 19:11-22 deal with the uncleanness derived from touching a corpse, and their major concern is that the person made unclean by the corpse will defile YHWH's sanctuary. If this occurs, the person "shall be cut off from the congregation." Since Num. 19:11 refers to the corpse of any person, it is easy to see how a gentile corpse would be a source of contamination. However, by claiming that a gentile's corpse does not defile in exactly the same way as does an Israelite's corpse, our authors are able to maintain the position that Israelites and gentiles are not equal human beings, but represent different "types" within the human family. The central role of YHWH's sanctuary in this regard is expressed in our sources by the fact that neither the gentile nor the one who suffers from corpse-uncleanness may go pass the outer rampart on the Temple Mount.

From the biblical sources, it is easy to conclude that the purity rules are an internal Israelite concern. If we are correct that these rules derive from the context of the cult/altar, and if Levine is correct that they were originally designed to protect YHWH, the exclusive Israelite nature of these rules becomes even clearer.

It is with respect to the Zab, the person with flux, that the ambiguity comes to the forefront. Lev. 15:2-15 deal with the Zab. Again this is addressed to the *Children of Israel*, and in order to complete the cleansing process, one must appear before YHWH with offerings, which are given to the priest for him to place on the altar. The ambiguity of the application of these rules to the gentile is the most interesting, for while our text recognizes that the rules *do not apply* to gentiles, we treat them *as if they did*. It is possible that this inconsistency derives from the situation in which the authors of Mishnah-Tosefta found themselves. On the one hand, the purity rules are an internal Israelite matter, and only Israelites come under their framework. If Israelites and gentiles formed two separate entities in Palestine, this scheme need not be altered. If the two groups did not come into contact with each other and if the non-Israelites did not approach the Temple, the purity rules need not be applied to the gentiles. However, we have seen that Israelites and gentiles continually interacted on several levels. We have also seen that gentiles could even approach YHWH through their freewill-offerings. Although Mishnah-Tosefta do not tell us how the gentiles had to prepare themselves in order to bring a freewill-offering to the

Temple, it is likely that they had to be concerned with their ritual purity. Furthermore, when gentiles wished to enter the Israelite community through conversion, their state of ritual impurity became a matter of concern.

But, what about the normal gentiles and their daily interaction with normal Israelites? Obviously, some rabbis were not concerned with the ritual purity of gentiles with regard to their daily interaction with Israelites. However, other sages did perceive a problem in this area, and it is possible that the conflicting statements about the laws of flux reflect these differing views. On the one hand, all agreed that the Israelite purity laws affected only Israelites; on the other hand, daily interaction between Israelites and gentiles could be influenced by these rules, so that Israelites should be cautious when dealing with non-Israelites. It is possible that the ambiguity with regard to the laws of the person with flux represents an attempt to regulate social interaction between the gentiles and Israelites by those who took seriously the ethnic nature and the social implications of the Israelite purity laws. On the one hand, these rules applied only to Israelites; on the other hand, they could be an effective means of regulating, or preventing, interaction between Israelites and gentiles. Thus, even though the laws of a person with flux applied to only Israelites, gentiles were treated as if they suffered from this source of uncleanness. In this way, the unique relationship between the Israelites and the laws of uncleanness were maintained, while at the same time social interaction between Israelites and gentiles was regulated, at least by some sages, according to a native Israelite category. It appears that we have before us a collection of rulings from different sages with different views on how Israelites should interact with gentiles, and this accounts for the contradictions and inconsistencies we have discovered.

Chapter Twelve:

The Gentiles as Non-Israelites

i

This study has described and analyzed a significant number of passages in Mishnah-Tosefta which mention the gentiles. It has noted that the non-Israelites are not the subject of a major division of our documents. Nor, we have seen, did they engender unique literary creations or receive a distinctive treatment in these collections. The gentiles were an element in the sages' environment, to be catalogued, interpreted, and regulated through the existing categories of rabbinic deliberation. But the gentiles in no case define an area of legislation unto themselves.[1] The authors of Mishnah-Tosefta were parochial in their outlook. Not only did they view everything from their own point of view, but also they limited their attention to matters they believed were essential in constructing and defining the People Israel and in maintaining their unique character. The gentiles were an issue for attention primarily because they, actually or potentially, came into contact with the People Israel or the latter's ethnic symbols or institutions. And, it is in terms of these symbols and institutions that the gentiles are discussed. The treatment of the gentiles has been rabbinized in the sense that it has been framed in the same literary terms and around the same basic symbols and concepts which were used for the other topics taken up in Mishnah-Tosefta. This means that we see the gentiles through the eyes of the authors of these documents, and that we know about them only what the sages behind Mishnah-Tosefta thought was important from their point of view, and according to their agenda. We see the gentiles only in light of YHWH, his Land, his People, and his Residence. We do not see them on their own terms. We see the non-Israelites primarily only as a counterpart to the Israelites.

The discussions of the gentile in Mishnah-Tosefta derive from three sources: 1) The Torah, 2) the sages' imagination, and 3) the rabbis' Palestinian environment. We have encountered several *sugyot* in which the biblical images

---

[1] A significant amount of the legislation concerning idols and idolatry in Mishnah-Tosefta deals with Israelites, and not with gentiles.

of the non-Israelite inform the passages in Mishnah-Tosefta. For example, our texts consistently refer to a non-Israelite servant as a "Canaanite," an image perhaps derived from Gen. 9:25-26.[2] Moreover, on the basis of Deut. 23:4-9, the sages discuss the entrance of biblical peoples, such as Moabites, Edomites, Ammonites, and Egyptians, into the congregation of Israel, mYeb. 8:3 and tYeb. 8:1. Furthermore, the *Asherah* of the Bible and the biblical Molech are as real to the rabbis of Mishnah-Tosefta as the Roman god, Mercury. In light of the role that biblical ideas and conceptions played in the formulation of the ideas in Mishnah-Tosefta, we encounter exactly what we expect to find.[3]

Distinguishing those matters in Mishnah-Tosefta which resided only, or primarily, in the minds of the authors of these texts from those which existed in the world outside of the sages' imagination is difficult, if not impossible. However, the rabbis' attempt to regulate the marriage practices *among* the gentiles, mQid. 4:3 and tQid. 5:1, to limit situations in which Israelites had to follow the rulings of the *gentile* courts, mGit. 9:8 and tYeb. 12:13, to legislate the business practices of *non-Israelite* merchants, tA.Z. 2:1, to set the amount of compensation *gentiles* should pay for injury done to an Israelite, mB.Q. 4:3, tB.Q. 4:1, and tB.Q. 4:3, and to require *gentiles* to free a slave they had purchased from an Israelite, tA.Z. 3:16, most likely reflect wishful thinking on the part of the sages and not the actual authority they had in these situations. Furthermore, the stereotyping of the gentiles as dangerous, tTer. 8:12, mA.Z. 2:1 and tA.Z. 3:3, sexually "uncivilized," mA.Z. 2:1 and tA.Z. 3:2, and untrustworthy, tPe. 4:1 and tDem. 5:2, are intellectual constructions, which need not reflect "reality."

Clearly, the Bible and the rabbinic imagination are important elements in the descriptions of the gentiles found in Mishnah-Tosefta. However, the content of the *sugyot* we have reviewed suggests that the catalyst for these discussions was the presence of the non-Israelites in the rabbis' Palestinian environment. We have seen that those statements which are attributed to known sages are assigned primarily to rabbis who lived during the period following the Bar Kokhba revolt, a time when the gentile population, and its influence, in Palestine achieved new importance.[4] Furthermore, virtually all of the *sugyot* we have encountered assume that gentiles and Israelites regularly interacted with one anoth-

----

[2]Ephraim E. Urbach, "The Laws Regarding Slavery as a Source for Social History of the Period of the Second Temple, the Mishnah and Talmud," in J. G. Weiss (ed.), *Papers of the Institute of Jewish Studies London* (Jerusalem: 1964), 31.

[3]Jacob Neusner, *Judaism: The Evidence of Mishnah* (Chicago: 1981), 167-229.

[4]However, as we saw above, the predominance of these sages may be simply a result of the editorial process of these documents; see above, Chapter Five, n. 193.

er on a daily basis. On the one hand, as we saw above, the sages attempted to regulate the gentiles as well as the Israelites, while on the other hand, they recognized the authority that the gentile rulers had over their own lives, mEd. 7:7. While the sages viewed the gentiles in abstract stereotypic terms, they also saw them as individuals whom they had to support and with whom the Israelites had to live in peace, tPe. 3:1, mSheb. 4:3, tGit. 3:13, and tGit. 3:14. In addition, as we saw above,[5] some of the discussions about the gentiles and wine are based on imagined realities, while others are derived from the practical needs of the Palestinian economy.

The rabbinic comments on the gentiles paint a varied and complex picture of the non-Israelites, and it seems to reflect the diversity of the situation which confronted, or was imagined by, the authors of Mishnah-Tosefta. *Abodah Zarah* devotes a good deal of attention to the gentiles as idolaters, worshipers of divinities other than YHWH, perhaps the feature which most readily comes to the minds of most of us when we hear the term "gentile." But Mishnah-Tosefta recognize the gentiles as much more than idolaters. They are also farmers, landowners, and tenants, who could perhaps own a parcel of the Land of Israel, work her soil, and benefit from her crops. They are merchants and customers, who trade in produce grown on the Land or in goods which are susceptible to the Israelite purity laws, agricultural gifts, and other dietary restrictions. And, they are neighbors, fellow citizens, rulers, soldiers, and commoners, who must function along with the Israelites in the legal, political, economic, and social systems of Palestine which fall under YHWH's concern and which the rabbis interpret and regulate according to his Revelation at Sinai.

We have, then, limited, highly selective and interpreted descriptions of the gentiles. The picture is not, however, one-sided, for it reflects both the gentiles as they existed solely in the minds of the rabbis, and the gentiles as the rabbis saw them in everyday life. In fact, it is the complexity and inconsistency of the image of the non-Israelite which is one of the most striking facts we have encountered. The gentiles are not merely projections from the Bible, imagined or theoretical "others," or "normal" human beings. They are all three. This depiction of the gentile, however, does not demand the rabbis' interest and attention on its own terms. It is important only because it served the authors of Mishnah-Tosefta as a means of defining the People Israel. Throughout, we have seen that the one point made over and over again is that the gentiles are not Israelites. For this reason, rules which apply to Israelites do not apply to non-

----

[5]Chapter Nine.

Israelites, and common activities are performed in dissimilar ways by members of each group. Gentiles were of interest to the rabbis because they interacted with Israelites on a daily basis, and the sages treated them in such a way so as to make the distinctions between Israelites and gentiles clear and definite. It appears, then, that the discussions of the gentiles provided the rabbis with a means of constructing and defining the People Israel as an ethnic unit, so that the rabbis dealt with the non-Israelites in the same manner that all other peoples deal with their neighbors.

ii

For about a decade, a significant number of anthropologists and sociologists have focused their attention on ethnic groups, and their results provide us with an useful instrument for understanding the data amassed in this study. Although the specialists have not reached agreement on a single definition of an ethnic group, or the reasons that such units come into being, a review of some of the most commonly accepted descriptions does bring to light a number of consistencies.

The larger point all these studies make is that peoples, nations, ethnic groups, tribes, cultures, and the like do not exist in vacuums. Each unit interacts with other sets and subsets of peoples on various levels and in several contexts, and each grouping's identity is partially created and influenced by these contacts.[6] Each community understands itself, at least partially, in terms of the other society. In order to act, humans must categorize, classify, and symbolize all reality, including themselves, and, as Needham argues, the creation of "binary opposites is an elementary and universal mode of classification."[7] Although, this need not be the case, for there is no inherent reason for a classification system to stop at the creation of pairs or opposites,[8] it is common for an aggregate of individuals to divide the human community into "us" and "them." And, ethnicity is one way by which a group of persons sets itself apart in order to understand itself and others, so that it might function in interactive situations.

----

[6]Barth writes, ". . . ethnic distinctions do not depend on an absence of social interaction . . ., but are quite to the contrary often the very foundation on which embracing social systems are built." Fredrik Barth, *Ethnic groups and Boundaries: The Social Organization of Cultural Difference* (Bergen-Oslo: 1969), 10.

[7]Rodney Needham, *Symbolic Classification* (Santa Monica: 1979), 32. Cf., Rodney Needham, *Primordial Characters* (Charlottesville: 1978), 35.

[8]Needham, *Symbolic Classification*, 57-58.

We have seen that Mishnah-Tosefta make no clear distinctions among the various types of non-Israelites. Romans, Greeks, Syrians, Egyptians, and the like are classified merely as gentiles, *goyim* or *nokrim*. While the rabbis differentiated among various types of Israelites of whom they disapprove,[9] they had one term for all non-Israelites, whether idolaters or farmers, liars or trustworthy, Greek or Roman. While internally "we" might be variegated, from "our" point of view, "they" form an undifferentiated "them." The world's population was divided into two peoples, "us" and "them." And, over and over again our sources made this point: Gentiles are not Israelites; all of them are different from us. Thus, the lack of differentiation among the various peoples whom the rabbis encountered is what we would expect.

Ethnicity is primarily "a sorting device" which develops "only out of a confrontation with and differentiation from 'others' to whom a different identity is ascribed."[10] Devereux further suggests that the statement "A is not a non-X (they) is prior to the statement A is an X (we)," so that "specifications as to what constitutes ethnic identity develop only after an ethnic group recognizes the existence of others who do not belong to the group."[11] Thus, according to Devereux, a "we" cannot describe itself until after it has identified and classified a "they," a "not-we," so that ethnic identity cannot develop unless one unit comes into contact with, creates, or presupposes the existence of another assemblage of people.

Devereux's insights mean that while the rabbis did not need to have extensively dwelt upon the gentiles, they could not have ignored them. If the sages wished to develop a definition of the People Israel, they had to make reference to the non-Israelites. Both Devereux and Needham imply that attempting to treat the Israelites without any mention of the non-Israelites would have been doomed to failure. Therefore, the discussions of the gentiles appear in Mishnah-Tosefta for at least two reasons: 1) On the practical level, Israelites and gentiles daily confronted one another in Palestine, or were presumed to have done so by the rabbis, so that rules and procedures had to be set forth to regulate their inter-

----

[9]William S. Green, "Otherness Within: Toward a Theory of Difference in Rabbinic Judaism," in Jacob Neusner and Ernest S. Frerichs (eds.), *"To See Ourselves as Others See Us" Christians, Jews, "Others" in Late Antiquity* (Chico: 1985), 57-59.

[10]George Devereux, "Ethnic Identity: Its Logical Foundations and Its Dysfunctions," in George De Vos and Lola Romanucci-Ross, *Ethnic Identity: Cultural Continuities and Change* (Palo Alto: 1975), 48.

[11]Devereux, 54.

action. This was of immediate importance because both groups interacted with important elements in the rabbis' symbolic system, such as the Land of Israel, the Israelite periods of sacred time, and the Temple, and the rabbis had to explain how these units should differ in their responses to those entities. 2) On a theoretical level, the rabbis could not have constructed a definition of the People Israel, or clearly delineated the ways in which they were to relate to one another and to the central symbols and institutions of their group, without reference to those who stood outside the ethnic unit. This explains why documents as parochial, and at times as theoretical, as Mishnah-Tosefta took up the question of the gentiles at all, without treating them as a topic unto themselves. Both Needham and Devereux imply that parochial texts can remain ethnocentric in their outlook and still be cognizant of the "other."[12]

To this point we have seen that a group of people derives its identity, at least partially, by contact with another group, or by setting itself off from another group. This means that if the gentiles had not existed, the rabbis and the Israelites would have had to invent them.[13] Furthermore, we have argued that the authors of Mishnah-Tosefta could not have totally excluded discussions of the gentile from their texts, even when their primary concern was to define and to regulate the Israelites' daily activity. Throughout this volume, we have referred to the Israelites of Mishnah-Tosefta as an ethnic group, and it is now our task to explain the meaning of this designation and the appropriateness of applying it to the Israelites of Mishnah-Tosefta.

There is little agreement among scholars concerning the major elements of an ethnic unit, so that it is virtually impossible to set forth a universally accepted definition of ethnicity, or to compile a list of the essential characteristics of an ethnic group. However, if we focus on elements which find a place in the descriptions of several different scholars, we discover that they can be applied to the Israelites of Mishnah-Tosefta, as they are presented in the *sugyot* we have examined. The point here is that when one views the references to the Israelites in Mishnah-Tosefta in light of the discussions of the gentiles, the former look very much like one of the ethnic groups under discussion by contemporary anthropologists and sociologists.

----

[12]Similarly, Michael Fischer states that "ethnicity is a process of inter-reference between two or more cultural traditions and that these dynamics of intercultural knowledge provide reservoirs for renewing human values." Michael M.J. Fischer, "Ethnicity and the Post-Modern Arts of Memory," in James Clifford and George E. Marcus (eds.), *Writing Culture* (Berkeley and Los Angeles: 1986), 201.

[13]Cf., Green, 52.

An important element of ethnicity is the group's sense of itself as a unified set of individuals or subgroups which share characteristics not possessed by other human aggregates. In brief, an ethnic unit views itself as being different from other collections of humans. Barth writes that an ethnic group "has a membership which identifies itself and is identified by others as constituting a category distinguishable from other categories of the same order."[14] Similarly, Bessac argues that an ethnic group is "a group of people who . . . have a sense of common identity."[15] In a like manner, Enloe writes that ethnicity "refers to a peculiar bond among persons that causes them to consider themselves as a group distinguishable from others."[16] Throughout, the passages we have analyzed point to the belief held by the authors of Mishnah-Tosefta that the Israelites were different from the gentiles. In fact, this seems to have been one of the major reasons that the discussions of the non-Israelites were included in these documents.

While the specialists agree that ethnic groups have a sense of themselves which sets them off from other groups, there is less agreement concerning the basis of this self-perception. Several scholars have argued that a shared ancestry is important in the group's conception of itself. Chester Hunt and Lewis Walker stress the importance of ancestry in defining an ethnic group: "An ethnic group is a collection of people whose membership is largely determined by ancestry . . . ."[17] Similarly, Berreman quotes and accepts H.S. Morris, who states that an "ethnic group consists of people who conceive of themselves as being alike by virtue of a common ancestry, real or fictitious. . . ."[18] De Vos also points to the importance of a common ancestry for an ethnic group's sense of itself. In one place he lists "common ancestry" as one among the "set of traditions" which an ethnic group holds in common.[19] Keyes and van den Berghe hold an extreme position on this point and have placed concerns with descent at the center of their definitions of ethnicity. Keyes has written that "ethnicity . . .

----

[14]Barth, 11.

[15]Frank D. Bessac, *Current Anthropology*, V, 4 (October 1964), 293.

[16]Cynthia H. Enloe, *Ethnic Conflict and Political Development* (Boston: 1973), 15.

[17]Chester L. Hunt and Lewis Walker, *Ethnic Dynamics: Patterns of Intergroup Relations in Various Societies* (Homewood: 1974), 3.

[18]Gerald D. Berreman, "Race, Caste, and Other Invidious Distinctions in Social Stratification," in Norman R. Yetman, *Majority and Minority: The Dynamics of Race and Ethnicity in American Life*, Fourth Edition (Boston: 1985), 23.

[19]George De Vos, "Ethnic Pluralism: Conflict and Accommodation," in De Vos and Romanucci-Ross, 9. Elsewhere, he writes that ethnicity is "primarily a sense of belonging to a particular ancestry or origin and of sharing a specific language or religion;" 19.

derives from a cultural interpretation of descent." However, descent need not be biological; rather, "descent presupposes socially validated parent/child connection."[20] For Keyes, "kin selection provides the underlying motivation that leads human beings to seek solidarity with those whom they recognize 'as being of the same people,' or as 'sharing descent.'" However, Keyes does admit that recognition of descent "is predicated upon the cultural construal of what characteristics indicate that others do or do not belong to the same people as oneself."[21] Because Keyes argues that ethnicity is based on descent, he can claim that an individual may belong to more than one, or to no, ethnic group.[22] Similarly, van den Berghe argues that ethnicity, like race, is an extension of the idiom of kinship and that it is in reality an "attenuated form" of kin selection.[23] We have seen that ancestry and "descent" play an important role in the Israelites' conception of themselves. The group's preferred name for itself, Children of Israel, that is Jacob, testifies to this fact. In addition, we saw that from the biblical period onward, the Israelite tradition connected the different peoples of the world with different ancient ancestors. Furthermore, we saw that one of the few points on which the texts were completely consistent was in their rejection of sexual unions between Israelites and gentiles.[24]

While some have placed ancestry at the center of their descriptions of ethnicity, others have argued that ethnic groups form units because they share a common culture. However, this matter has given rise to some differences of opinion. Scholars like Enloe, Rose, and Yetman are among those who place the idea of a shared culture at the center of their discussions of ethnicity. Enloe writes that "the content of the bond [which units a ethnic group] is shared culture. . . ."[25] Similarly, Rose writes that "groups whose members share a unique social and cultural heritage passed on from one generation to the next are known as *ethnic groups*. Ethnic groups are frequently identified by distinctive patterns of family life, language,[26] recreation, religion, and other customs that cause

----

[20]Charles F. Keyes, *Ethnic Change* (Seattle & London: 1981), 5.

[21]Keyes, 6.

[22]Keyes, 6.

[23]Pierre L. van den Berghe, "Race and Ethnicity: A Sociobiological Perspective," in Yetman, 56.

[24]De Vos, 9, has written that endogomy is a "usual" characteristic of an ethnic group.

[25]Enloe, 15.

[26]Raoul Narroll places a common language at the center of his discussions of ethnicity. Raoul Narroll, "On Ethnic Unit Classification," *Current Anthropology* V, 4 (October, 1964), 286. The issue of a common language for Israelites in Palestine is rather complicated. For a summary of the situation, see Eric M. Meyers and James F. Strange, *Archaeology, the Rabbis, and Early Christianity* (Nashville: 1981), 62-91.

them to be differentiated from others."[27]   And, Yetman argues that an ethnic group is socially defined on the basis of cultural characteristics: "Ethnicity, or the sense of belonging to a particular ethnic group, thus implies the existence of a distinct culture or subculture in which group members feel themselves bound together by common history, values, attitudes and behaviors--in its broadest sense, a sense of peoplehood--and are so regarded by other members of society."[28]   Barth, however, argues that the shared culture is a *result*, rather than a "definitional characteristic," of the ethnic group's organization,[29] and Knutsson rejects the idea that one can define an ethnic group in terms of "cultural content."[30]   Whether or not the idea of a shared culture creates the ethnic group or is the result of the creation of the ethnic group begs the question, and this is an insolvable problem, unless one takes a reductionist position with regard to either ethnicity or culture.   Furthermore, the disagreement among scholars concerning the definition of culture further complicates the matter and stands in the way of any solution to the problem of which came first, the ethnic group or its shared culture.[31]   Despite these problems, it does seem correct to claim that an ethnic group is marked by its shared culture, and we now must turn to the problem of culture in Mishnah-Tosefta.

For our purposes, White and Spiro provide us with a workable explanation of culture.   White's definition of culture derives from the realization that there are "things or events consisting of or dependent upon symboling,"[32] that

----

[27]Peter I. Rose, *They and We: Racial and Ethnic Relations in the United States*, Third Edition (New York: 1981), 7.

[28]Norman R. Yetman, "Introduction: Definitions and Perspectives," in Yetman, 6.

[29]Barth, 1.

[30]Karl E. Knutsson, "Dichotomization and Integration: Aspects of Inter-ethnic Relations in Southern Ethiopia," in Barth, 99.

[31]Although almost thirty years old, Leslie A. White's essay indicates the variety of definitions and conceptions of the term "culture."   Leslie A. White, "The Concept of Culture," in M.F. Ashley Montagu (ed.), *Culture and the Evolution of Man*, (Oxford: Reprint 1972), 38-64. In his textbook on cultural anthropology, William A. Haviland writes that "[c]ulture consists of the abstract values, beliefs, and perceptions of the world that lie behind a people's behavior, and which that behavior reflects. These are shared by the members of a society, and when acted upon they produce behavior considered acceptable within that society. Cultures are learned, through the medium of language, rather than inherited biologically, and the parts of a culture function as an integrated whole;" William A. Haviland, *Cultural Anthropology*, Fourth Edition (New York: 1983), 29. Similarly, Richard A. Barrett defines culture as "the body of learned beliefs, traditions, and guides for behavior that are shared among members of any human society. The key word is *learned;*" Richard A. Barrett, *Culture and Conduct: An Excursion in Anthropology* (Belmont: 1984), 54.

[32]White, 41.

is, their meaning is not derived from sensory perceptions alone.[33] "Culture . . . is a class of things and events, dependent upon symboling considered in an extrasomatic context."[34] White argues that one should examine each element of culture, each symbolate, "in terms of its relationships to other symbolates or symbolate clusters."[35] In this way, White wishes to separate the study of culture from a consideration of the symbolates' relationship to human beings: "If we treat them [symbolates] in terms of their relationship to the human organism . . . these things and events become *human behavior* and we are doing *psychology*."[36] White argues that the study of culture allows us to explain *why* people do one thing and not another, while the study of human behavior merely describes *how* individuals or groups act.[37] The important points in White's discussion are his emphasis on symbolizing and his stress that the interrelationship of the symbolates is more important than the relationship of each symbolate to the human actor. However, White's desire to separate anthropology from psychology has forced him to place too high a barrier between the human and culture. And, White's discussion on the relationship of human action to culture is less than clear. His statement that "a people's behavior is a response to, a function of, their culture"[38] does not help much.

Spiro's discussion of culture and the person solves the problem of the relationship of the human being to culture, especially in light of the nature of the material we encounter in Mishnah-Tosefta. Spiro writes, "'culture' designates a cognitive system, that is, a set of 'propositions,' both descriptive (e.g., 'the planet earth sits on the back of a turtle') and normative (e.g., 'it is wrong to kill'), about nature, man, and society that are embedded in interlocking higher order networks and configurations."[39] Spiro's formulation has the advantage of providing a link between human activity and culture, which is missing from White's analysis. If symbolizing is an activity of the human mind, it follows that even in White's formulation a culture must be a creation of the human intellect. As Spiro states, "cultural doctrines, ideas, values, and the like exist in the minds of social actors . . . . [S]ince [cultural symbols] neither possess nor

---

33White, 60, n. 6.
34White, 46.
35White, 44.
36White, 44.
37White, 53.
38White, 53.
39Melford E. Spiro, "Some Reflections on Cultural Determinism and Relativism with Special Reference to Emotion and Reason," in Benjamin Kilborne and L.L. Langness (eds.), *Culture and Human Nature: Theoretical Papers of Melford E. Spiro* (Chicago: 1987), 32.

announce their meanings, they must be found in the minds of the social actors."[40] The important element here is that while the symbolates exist outside of the human mind, the meanings they attain is a human creation; therefore, they can be studied from the point of view of the humans who created them.

The culture which finds expression in the normative and descriptive propositions of Mishnah-Tosefta is dominated by a religious outlook.[41] Defining religion is at least as difficult as defining either culture or ethnicity, and there is little scholarly consensus on its meaning.[42] However, for our present purposes, it is sufficient to accept Spiro's definition of religion "as an institution consisting of culturally patterned interaction with culturally postulated superhuman beings."[43] Granting the facts that Spiro's definition is limited in scope and that it does not apply to everything scholars and non-scholars have called religion, Spiro's claim that not everything and anything people have labeled as religion need to be covered by one definition[44] is correct, for it is possible, if not probable, that phenomena which some have called religion have been labeled incorrectly. Even if Spiro's definition is inadequate for all purposes, it does point to an essential element of the religion of the rabbis who stand behind Mishnah-Tosefta, for they clearly built their religious world-view around their conceptions of YHWH. While claiming that Mishnah-Tosefta present a culture influenced by religion, we do not mean to assert that the culture is only religious. In fact, some of the inconsistencies we find in the treatment of the gentiles may result from the fact that a given symbolate has both a religious, and a nonreligious, ethnic meaning.

In the terms set forth above, Mishnah-Tosefta present a cultural system which is based, at least in part, upon the sages' understanding of YHWH and his relationship to the universe. This culture rests upon the interrelationship of sym-

----

[40]Melford E. Spiro, "Collective Representations and Mental Representations in Religious Symbol Systems," in Kilborne and Langness, 161-162.

[41]De Vos, 14, has stated that religion may be the dominant factor in a particular group's construction of its ethnicity. Kokosalakis has written that "it is the unique juxtaposition of religion, ethnicity, and identity which makes for the essential dimension of Jewish Culture;" N. Kokosalakis, *Ethnic Identity and Religion: Tradition and Change in Liverpool Jewry*, (Washington: 1982), 2.

[42]See, for example, Jonathan Z. Smith, *Imagining Religion* (Chicago and London: 1982). Jonathan Z. Smith, *Map is not Territory* (Leiden: 1978). John H. Morgan, *Understanding Religion and Culture: Anthropological and Theological Perspectives* (Washington: 1979).

[43]Melford E. Spiro, "Religion: Problems of Definition and Explanation," in Kilborne and Langness, 197.

[44]Spiro, "Religion," 189-190.

bolates to which the rabbis have ascribed meaning, based, at least partially, upon their concepts of YHWH and his relationship to the world. This culture, in the terms of Mishnah-Tosefta, serves to maintain, and is maintained by, the Israelite ethnic group. The group's identity is partially expressed by setting it off from the gentiles, defined as those who do not share the same cultural system as the Israelites, who, the Israelites claim, do not ascribe the same meanings to the same symbolates as do the Israelites, and who, according to Mishnah-Tosefta, do not relate to these symbolates in the same ways that Israelites do.

Although we cannot definitely know the intentions of the authors of Mishnah-Tosefta, the reasons they compiled these texts, or the purposes they intended them to serve,[45] it is not unreasonable to suggest that one of the results of, if not one of the reasons for, the editing of these documents was the creation of a coherent cultural system which in turn led to a rabbinic definition of the Israelite People as an ethnic group, in the terms discussed above. This would have been a necessary task, for as Fischer notes "ethnicity is something reinvented and reinterpreted in each generation . . . . Ethnicity is not something that is simply passed on from generation to generation, taught and learned. It is something dynamic . . . ."[46] Ethnic boundaries are altered in response to varying and changing internal and external factors. Also, different ethnic units, or sub-units within a larger ethnic group, construct boundary-systems of different strengths and intensities. This means that the several boundary systems within any single ethnic unit may also differ in their flexibility and that not all members of an ethnic group need to agree on the *exact* nature of each boundary. This explains why the distinctions drawn between Israelites and gentiles in Mishnah-Tosefta are not always absolute, even within specific categories, or with regard to specific symbols. The flexibility and fuzziness of ethnic boundaries permit them to function in the full range of human activities and interactions. The variety and disagreement exhibited by the discussions in Mishnah-Tosefta, therefore, are not atypical of other attempts to draw ethnic boundaries.[47]

It is contended, therefore, that Mishnah-Tosefta contain the description of the People Israel as an *ethnic group* based on a particular culture, as defined above. There is no doubt that for periods of time while Mishnah-Tosefta were in their penultimate stage, nationalistic movements arose among the Israelites of

----

[45]On the variety of theories concerning these questions, see Jacob Neusner, *The Modern Study of the Mishnah* (Leiden: 1973).

[46]Fischer, 195.

[47]On boundary-systems, see Yehudi A. Cohen, "Social Boundary Systems," *Current Anthropology*, X, 1 (February: 1969), 103-126.

Palestine.[48]   However,   Mishnah-Tosefta do not provide the intellectual or practical programs for nationalism or nationalistic movements as generally understood by the scholars. Whatever political agenda one might find in Mishnah-Tosefta, a major theme in them advises the Israelites to live at peace with the gentile political powers. While the authors of Mishnah-Tosefta sought control

----

[48]On this matter, see Fergus Millar, "Empire, Community and Culture in the Roman Near East: Greeks, Syrians, Jews, and Arabs," *Journal of Jewish Studies* XXXVII, 2 (Autumn: 1987), 143-148. Much of the theoretical literature on nations and nationalism argues that nations are a product of the "modern" world, although it disagrees over exactly when the "modern" world begins. Gellner defines nationalism as "a theory of political legitimacy, which requires that ethnic boundaries should not cut across political ones, and in particular that ethnic boundaries within a given state . . . should not separate the power-holders from the rest;" Ernest Gellner, *Nations and Nationalism* (Oxford: 1983), 1. Gellner holds, however, that nationalism can be found only in the modern world, for pre-modern "agrarian-literate" societies were incapable of achieving nationalism because they could not create a situation in which the "high culture" was shared by all; Gellner, 2-18, 138. Anderson defines a nation as "an imagined political community--and imagined as both inherently limited and sovereign." It is characterized as "imagined" because "the members of even the smallest nation will never know most of their fellow-members, meet them, or even hear of them, yet in the minds of each lives the image of their communion." Because any community larger than "primordial villages of face-to-face contact" are imagined, this alone does not serve to mark a nation as unique. It is the style of the imagination which differentiates various types of imagined communities; Benedict Anderson, *Imagined Communities: Reflections on the Origin and Spread of Nationalism* (London: 1983), 15. Nations are limited because none of them views itself as encompassing all of humanity; there is always another nation on the other side of a national border. Anderson contrasts "sovereignty" to divinely-ordained hierarchical dynastic realms, so that this aspect reflects the period in the history of the West when nationalism came into vogue. Nations are communities because "the nation is always conceived as a deep, horizontal comradeship;" Anderson, 16. Nationalism did not arise until the end of the idea that "a particular script-language offered privileged access to ontological truth," the end of the societies organized around "high centers--"monarchs who were persons apart from other human beings and who ruled by some form of cosmological (divine) dispensation, and the distinction between cosmology and history became accepted by human beings;" Anderson, 17-40; summarized on 40. In addition, Anderson argues that nations could not arise until the invention of the printing press which allowed for the creation of "national print languages," which served to unite various language-groups into differentiated units; Anderson, 41-49. In Anderson's words, "The lexicographic revolution in Europe . . . created, and gradually spread the conviction that languages (in Europe at least) were, so to speak, the personal property of quite specific groups . . . and moreover that these groups, imagined as communities, were entitled to their autonomous place in a fraternity of equals;" Anderson, 80-81. Breuilly, on the other hand, argues that "nationalism is, above all else, about politics, and . . . politics is about power;" John Breuilly, *Nationalism and the State* (New York: 1982), 1-2. Nationalism develops, according to Breuilly, from the ideas that a nation "with an explicit and peculiar" character exists, that the nation's values "take priority over all other interests and values," and that the "nation must be as independent as possible. This usually requires at least the attainment of political sovereignty;" Breuilly, 3. See, also, Michael Palumbo and William O. Shanahan (eds.), *Nationalism: Essays in Honor of Louis L. Snyder* (Westport: 1981).

over the Israelites and gentiles, they did not envision this being done by over-throwing the Roman political system; rather, they sought to function as one eth-nic element within Rome's political structures. The ethnicity of the Israelites as described in Mishnah-Tosefta becomes clear when we focus our attention on the descriptions of the gentiles in these documents, and now we must turn to this matter.

iii

In Mishnah-Tosefta, the gentile is primarily the "other." At times the term *goy* symbolizes that part of humanity not represented by the term *benai ys-rael*. In other places, the gentile is merely one of the several groups who oc-cupies the Land of Israel, but who does not adhere to the rabbinic practices, such as tithing. As the "other," gentiles may be characterized as dangerous and sexually deviant. In a word, they are "uncivilized." In many, perhaps the major-ity of the *sugyot*, however, the gentile is merely one element within the popula-tion of Palestine to whom the Israelites had to relate. What is important about the discussions of the interactions between Israelites and non-Israelites is that Mishnah-Tosefta present these activities as distinctive from the ways in which Israelites act towards one another. For example, different rules of damages app-ly in cases between Israelites and non-Israelites from those which are relevant to situations which involve only Israelites.

Most of what is described above concerning the discussions of the gentiles in Mishnah-Tosefta can be found with reference to the interactions of ethnic groups. We have seen that Needham and Devereux maintain that a group needs to set itself in opposition to another aggregate, and Needham claims that dividing the human population into two groups, "us" and "them," is a character-istic of human thought. It is also common for members of an ethnic group to create stereotypes of those outside their unit,[49] often claiming that the outsiders are uncivilized, dangerous, or even non-human. In Needham's words, "It is a frequent report from different parts of the world that tribes call themselves alone by the arrogant title 'man,' and that they refer to neighboring peoples as monkeys or crocodiles or malign spirits."[50] Yetman writes that "ethnic groups are inherently ethnocentric, regarding their own cultural traits as natural, correct, and superior to those of other ethnic groups, who are perceived as odd, amusing,

---

[49]Hunt and Walker, 5.
[50]Needham, *Primordial Characters*, 5.

inferior, or immoral."[51] Similarly, Babcock's work on cultural reversal presents numerous examples in which the "other" is pictured as the exact opposite of the members of the group drawing the comparison.[52]

The detailed protocols concerning the interactions of Israelites and gentiles in specific settings are also characteristic of ethnic groups. The differences which an ethnic group sees between itself and another human aggregate have ramifications in all the areas of human activity, so that the interactions between the two groups is highly regulated.[53] Along these lines, we have found discussions concerning how an Israelite treats a gentile who eats in his house, which gentile professionals an Israelite may employ, how one deals with gentile employees and employers, how gentiles and Israelites should interact in the market-place, and the like. The prohibition of sexual activity between the two groups also reflects this, as well as other characteristics, of ethnicity. Because of the concern by the authors of Mishnah-Tosefta for the religious symbols and institutions of their culture, this is an area which receives much attention. For this reason, our texts devote a good deal of space to regulating the ways in which gentiles respond to the Land of Israel and her crops, the Israelite holy days, the Temple and its cult, and YHWH.

The point of this analysis is important: The descriptions of the gentiles found in Mishnah-Tosefta, the regulations placed upon their interaction with the religious symbols of Israelite culture, and the limitations placed on their interactions with Israelites are not unique to our texts. Nor do they point to some distinctive characteristics of the Israelites, their religion, or their sacred texts. Rather, the treatment of the gentiles in Mishnah-Tosefta parallels, in general and in particular terms, the ways in which any ethnic group treats those outside its unit. The Israelites' description of the gentile as expressed in Mishnah-Tosefta is decidedly common-place, when viewed from the perspective of the interaction of ethnic units throughout the world and throughout history.

----

[51]Yetman, 7.

[52]Barbara A. Babcock (ed.), *The Reversible World: Essays in Symbolic Inversion* (Ithaca: 1978).

[53]Barth writes that the formation of ethnic groups leads to "a systematic set of rules governing inter-ethnic social encounters, a structuring of interactions, a set of prescriptions governing situations of contact and allowing for articulation in some sectors or domains of activity and a set of proscriptions on social situations preventing inter-ethnic interaction . . . ;" Barth, 15-16. Cf., Haaland, 61.

iv

Above, we claimed that the Israelite culture found in Mishnah-Tosefta is heavily influenced by the religious ideas of their authors. It is obvious that one way we can learn about these ideas is to turn to the study of the important symbolates of this culture: YHWH, the Land of Israel, Sacred Time, the People Israel, and the Temple and its cult. These are religious ideas because, in Spiro's terms, they are derived from their relationship to the rabbis' ideas about YHWH. Normally, these symbolates have been approached through examining the ways in which the Israelites respond to them. However, by addressing these symbols through the patterns of behavior Mishnah-Tosefta allow to the gentiles, we can also learn a good deal about them. The following analyses must remain tentative, for we do not yet have thorough studies of these symbolates, so that it is impossible to compare the conclusions reached here with those which might be drawn if we had studied all of the discussions of these symbolates throughout Mishnah-Tosefta.

There is no doubt that YHWH has a special relationship to the People Israel, and Mishnah-Tosefta are intent upon making him the exclusive object of worship among the Israelite people, so that the main thrust of the discussions of the gentiles' religious practices is to keep the Israelites from worshipping, appearing to worship, or contributing to the worship of foreign deities. YHWH himself is seldom discussed in these texts. His attributes and activities are presumed throughout, but they are infrequently detailed. Similarly, the direct responsibilities that humans have toward YHWH and their relationship to him most often are expressed in Mishnah-Tosefta in terms of the other basic symbolates: The Land, the People, the Holy Times, and the Temple. However, the exclusiveness of YHWH's relationship to the Israelites finds some expression in the discussions of the gentile.[54] Objects owned by gentiles may not be used in the worship of YHWH, nor may YHWH's blessings be called upon them, mBer. 8:6 and tBer. 5:31. The issue here is probably that these objects do not belong to YHWH's people, so that they were unfit to be used in the worship of YHWH or to receive his blessing .

Most relevant in the present context is tMeg. 2:16:[55] "If a gentile sanctified a beam for a synagogue and on it was written 'For the Name,' they

----

[54]Gentiles may not be included in the recitation of the Grace after meals, but neither may women, slaves, or minors, mBer. 7:1-2, so that this is irrelevant to our discussion.

[55]A slightly different version appears on bArakh. 6a. Cf., Saul Lieberman, *Tosefta Kifshutah: A comprehensive Commentary on the Tosefta Part V, Order Mo'ed* (New York: 1962), 1156.

examine him. If he vowed it for the 'Holy Name,' they store it away. If he vowed it for the sake of the synagogue, they plane off the Name, store away the chips, and use what is left of the beam." The force of the passage is that the gentile cannot dedicate something to YHWH, or apply YHWH's name to an object dedicated to the synagogue. The beam could be used only if it were not dedicated to YHWH. On the other hand, the gentiles were allowed to bring freewill-offerings to the Temple, so that some of the sages believed that the non-Israelites were free to worship YHWH if they chose.

A major symbolate in the framework of Mishnah-Tosefta is the Land of Israel. Above, we examined the meanings of the Land for the Torah's authors, as well as for the sages. Several points are relevant in the present context. For some, the Land was to be an exclusive Israelite possession, and we have encountered texts which seem to question the right of the gentiles to own property in the Land of Israel. Much of what Mishnah-Tosefta have to say about the Land and its produce is derived from the beliefs that the Land of Israel belongs to YHWH and that it is holy. The agricultural gifts which the Israelites separated from their crops were a means of recognizing YHWH's ownership of the Land. In the Torah, it appears that *all* of the agricultural gifts were related to this single idea. However, our examination of the gentiles in this context suggests that the authors of Mishnah-Tosefta had attributed more than one meaning to some of the agricultural gifts. On the one hand, many sages held that the gentile, like the Israelite, could recognize YHWH's stewardship of the Land of Israel through the separation of the heave-offering and the tithes. On the other hand, the gentile could not separate the gifts for the poor, such as the gleanings, forgotten sheaves, or "corners." Apparently, in the sages' minds, these gifts had become ethnic obligations only. While in the Torah they reflected the fact that YHWH owned the Land and cared for the poor, in Mishnah-Tosefta they reflected only the Israelites' responsibility to care for one another. This seems to be reason that the gentile could validly separate some of the agricultural gifts, but not others. The Land, in Mishnah-Tosefta, is a means of expressing YHWH's greatness *and* a phenomenon through which the ethnic unity of the People Israel is maintained. Only from the former point of view could the Land be a medium through which the gentiles could approach YHWH if they chose. Furthermore, while some rabbis believed that gentiles could validly separate tithes and heave-offerings, others did not. The point here appears to be that for some sages, the sacred nature of the Land of Israel which was derived from its relationship to YHWH was important no matter who worked the soil and benefited from its produce. For others, however, the Land was sacred only for

Israelites; therefore, only Israelites were required to separate the agricultural gifts.

The situation with regard to the gentiles' relationship to the Israelites' periods of Sacred Time is fairly straight forward. The two periods of time which receive the most attention are the Sabbath and Passover. Overall, the gentiles have no responsibility on their own for observing the Israelite periods of sacred time. The rites, rituals, and alterations of normal activity, which are incumbent upon Israelites, do not apply to gentiles. However, if gentiles come into contact with an Israelite, especially on the Sabbath, the former must alter their actions, so that the Israelites' observance of the Sabbath may have an effect on the gentiles' ability to pursue their normal activities. Limiting the observance of the Sabbath exclusively to the Israelites reflects a conscious choice by the rabbis. In the Torah, the Sabbath has both a cosmic and an ethnic meaning. In Genesis and Exodus, one rests on the Sabbath because YHWH rested when he finished creating the universe. However, in Deuteronomy, Israelites rest because they were once slaves in the Land of Egypt. The sages' decision to apply the Sabbath-restrictions to only Israelites reflects their following Deuteronomy's ethnic explanation of the Sabbath, for the universal view of Genesis and Exodus could have caused matters to have been worked out differently.

When the Israelite restriction on working on the Sabbath is applied to gentiles, it is done so because the issue is the work, and not who performs it. Furthermore, these restrictions are applied only from the Israelite point of view and only when the activity impinges, or might impinge, upon the Israelites. This means that the concerns with the gentiles' working on the Sabbath focus on the relationship of ideas of work and rest to the Israelite. This may explain why one may benefit from a gentile's activity, if it were done without any regard for the Israelite.[56] The ethnic character of the Sabbath would have been obvious to all, for Israelites alone altered their activity on the Sabbath, even with regard to gentiles with whom they might have come into contact.[57]

The ethnic quality of Passover is also emphasized in Mishnah-Tosefta. We have seen that the abstention from possessing or eating leaven became the central features of Passover for the sages of Mishnah-Tosefta. The texts which

----

[56]There is, however, the curious case in mShab. 24:1 and tShab. 17:20 in which an Israelite is allowed to give his purse to a gentile to carry, so that he not violate the Sabbath if he is traveling with a gentile on a Friday afternoon.

[57]Note, however, tMo'ed 2:14-15 which tell us that Gamliel permitted Israelites to sit on the chairs near gentile shops on the Sabbath, even though it might appear that they were engaging in business.

discuss the gentile make it clear that an Israelite is a person who does not possess leaven during Passover, while the gentile is one who does retain leaven during this period. In fact, the gentile is pictured as the mirror-image of the Israelite, with the possession of leaven being the crucial element which distinguishes the two peoples. Thus, the periods of sacred times become a uniquely Israelite manner of approaching YHWH and of distinguishing between the Israelites and the non-Israelites. The treatment of the gentiles in this context serves solely as a means of differentiating them from the Israelites.

When we examine the Temple and its cult from the perspective of the discussions of the gentile in Mishnah-Tosefta, it becomes clear that it is a symbolate with multiple meanings. The two relevant meanings for our purposes are the Temple as YHWH's residence and the Temple as the Israelites' ethnic shrine. As the ethnic shrine of the Israelites, the gentiles had limited access to its precincts. Furthermore, they could not contribute to its upkeep by dedicating items for its repair, or by paying the half-*sheqel* tax. These restrictions on the gentiles' activity with regard to the Temple probably derive both from the concept of the Temple as an ethnic shrine and from the idea that YHWH was first and foremost the divinity of the Israelites. However, we have seen above that even gentiles could express their adoration for YHWH through separating the heave-offering and the tithes. This finds expression in the fact that gentiles were allowed to bring freewill-offerings to the Temple, and that the Israelite community could support these offerings, by providing the drink-offerings, if the gentiles had not supplied them. The point here is that gentiles were allowed *limited* access to YHWH through the Temple. However, even when the gentiles brought offerings, the complex rules which applied to the Israelites' offerings were not applied to the gentiles' sacrifices. The result was that even when gentiles presented offerings to YHWH, they did so differently from the way in which Israelites would have made those same sacrifices.

Above all else, Mishnah-Tosefta focus on the nature of the People Israel, and this concern stands behind most of the discussions of the gentile. We have discovered that while Israelites and gentiles both work the Land of Israel, they do so differently. Israelites could not work the soil in the seventh year, while gentiles could. Israelites were required to separate a number of agricultural gifts for use by the poor among them, but these were not required of non-Israelites. Some held that the laws of the fourth year applied to gentiles, while others limited its applicability to Israelites alone. It appears that the laws of mixed-kinds also did not apply to gentiles. Furthermore, only Israelites were required to separate the dough-offering.

Two points should be made. First, despite the fact that Israelites and gentiles had to follow different practices when planting and harvesting their fields, the texts assume that they might jointly own property, buy and sell land from each other,[58] or rent property to, and from, each other. Therefore, the differences in agricultural practices did not prevent their interaction in the sphere of agriculture, they only regulated it. Second, in many cases, the different ways in which the gentiles and Israelites treated their harvested grain would not be obvious to the gentiles; they were internal Israelite matters. This suggests that it was important only from the Israelites' point of view to mark out their uniqueness. For example, an Israelite might purchase grain from a gentile and then separate the tithe after he left the gentile's presence, so that the gentile might never know that the Israelite had treated his grain differently from grain he would have purchased from another Israelite.

The distinctions between Israelites and gentiles is further drawn in the discussions of the holy days in three ways. First, the gentiles receive little attention in this major division of Mishnah-Tosefta. Second, in the treatment of Passover, the holiday which revolves around the creation of the People Israel, the sharpest distinctions between the Israelites and the gentiles are drawn. Bokser[59] has demonstrated that the rabbis' central concern with reference to Passover was with leaven, and it is exactly here that the differences between Israelites and non-Israelites are most sharply drawn in our texts. Third, during the intermediate days of Passover and Sukkot an Israelite may engage in activities with gentiles in which he may not be occupied with another Israelite. This means that when Israelites and non-Israelites met each other during the Israelite holidays, the gentiles would see that they were being treated differently from Israelites.

With reference to the gentiles' celebrations on religious occasions, the lines between Israelites and non-Israelites were sharply drawn. The authors of Mishnah-Tosefta did every thing they could to prevent the Israelites from participating in, or appearing to engage in, any form of worship of a deity other than YHWH. It would have been obvious to the gentiles that during their periods of religious activity they were treated differently by the Israelites than they were treated at other times. Mishnah-Tosefta seek to make it clear that from their point of view, the religious gentiles were completely distinct from Israelites.

----

[58]Some held that gentiles could not own property in the Land of Israel, but much in Mishnah-Tosefta assumes that they did.

[59]Baruch M. Bokser, *The Origins of the Seder: The Passover Rite and Early Judaism* (Berkeley: 1984).

In the minds of the authors of Mishnah-Tosefta, gentiles and Israelites were totally different peoples, originating from different ancient ancestors. They could not intermarry, nor could they engage in sexual activities with each other. Furthermore, different laws and regulations concerning testimony in the courts, damages, and the like applied to each group. Furthermore, our texts indicate that the rabbis believed they could, or should be able to, regulate the business activities of the gentiles, as well as those of the Israelites. Again, this is an area of activity in which the gentiles would recognize that they were treated differently from Israelites, *if any* of the rules in Mishnah-Tosefta were actually put into practice. In the area of financial transactions, the Torah emphasized that Israelites could not charge interest to or collect interest from other Israelites. And it is regard to the matter of interest that Mishnah-Tosefta distinguish between Israelites and non-Israelites. Like in the case of leaven and Passover, here with regard to the charging and collecting of interest Mishnah-Tosefta present the gentiles as the mirror-images of the Israelites. An Israelite may charge interest to and collect interest from gentiles; the former may not engage in these financial activities with other Israelites.

When the gentiles approached the Temple or sought to participate in its cult, they would have been cognizant of the fact that they were different from Israelites. They would have been barred from entering certain areas of the Temple Mount, they were limited in the sacrifices and offerings they could present to YHWH, and they were restricted in the rites they could perform over their sacrifices. It would have been obvious to all that Jerusalem's Temple was an Israelite institution, and that YHWH was primarily a deity of only the Israelites. When this is combined with the legislation in Mishnah-Tosefta concerning the gentiles' religious practice, it would have been clear to both gentiles and Israelites that they represented two completely different religions.

Perhaps the most complex area to understand revolves around the Israelite purity laws. On the one hand, the Israelite purity laws did not apply to the gentiles. Of course, this would have meant nothing to the non-Israelites. On the other hand, some held that gentiles were to be treated as if they were unclean. Whether or not either of these positions would have been obvious to the gentiles is unclear. However, the two positions would have caused the Israelites to treat the gentiles very differently. If the latter position held, social interaction between the groups would have been limited, while the former position would have resulted in easy daily social intercourse. Perhaps the disagreement in this area reflects the fact that while some wished to limit severely the interaction between Israelites and non-Israelites, others realized that this could not be done.

The need to deal with the actual situation in Palestine is evident throughout our documents, and it may apply here.

From the point of view of the authors of Mishnah-Tosefta, Israelites were different from gentiles, and these differences had important ramifications in all areas of activity. In fact, it appears that one of the major reasons that the gentiles appear in our texts at all is to make this point and to serve as means for setting forth the ethnic borders of the Israelites: Israelites treat the crops that grow in the Land of Israel in their own way, they observe their own periods of sacred time and ignore those of others, they engage in sexual activity with only other Israelites, they have their own court system, they have their own rules of damages, they alone perform all the rites at the Temple in Jerusalem, and they alone are concerned with the ritual purity of only other Israelites. When they come into contact with gentiles, so that they interact with them, they are constantly aware that they are dealings with non-Israelites, so that all of their activities may be different from those which occurred when they dealt with other Israelites.

v

To summarize: One best understands the ways in which the gentiles are discussed in Mishnah-Tosefta by recourse to the information we have about they ways in which ethnic groups form themselves and respond to the outsiders. From this perspective, the treatment of the gentiles in Mishnah-Tosefta is completely expected and normal. The discussions of the gentiles do not reflect anything unique to the Israelites, their culture, or their religious beliefs; they are merely the result of an ethnic group's attempt to understand itself, and to set itself off from those with whom it shares territory. Throughout, the gentiles are presented only from the Israelites' point of view; the former have no inherent importance in themselves.

Our texts are complex, and the discussions of the gentiles reflect this complexity. On the one hand, some of our material suggests that the rabbis had complete control over all of the Israelites and gentiles in Palestine. Others even indicate that gentiles have no rights to property within the Land of Israel and that gentiles and Israelites should remain entirely separate. On the other hand, other passages indicate that whatever the ideal might have been, Israelites and gentiles lived close to one another and interacted on a daily basis, and this interaction should be allowed to occur: Wine merchants do not have to worry about selling wine to gentiles, even though we assume that they will make a libation with any wine with which they come into contact. Israelites should not sell gentiles any item which they might use to worship their deities; however, one believes them if they say that they will not use the item they have purchased in this manner. An Israelite should not attend the amphitheater, but he may if required to do so by the State. Above all, Israelites should attempt to create a peaceful environment in which they and gentiles might live together.

In whatever ways they interacted or remained apart, the point of Mishnah-Tosefta is that Israelites constantly had to be aware of the fact that they were different from gentiles. This was not a value judgment. It was what it meant to be an Israelite, and this is the overriding point of the images of the gentile which appear in Mishnah-Tosefta.

Bibliography

Albeck, Hanokh. *The Six Orders of the Mishnah: Seder Nashim.* Tel Aviv: 1959.

_____. *The Six Orders of the Mishnah: Seder Neziqin.* Tel Aviv: 1953.

_____. *The Six Orders of the Mishnah: Seder Qodashim.* Tel Aviv: 1957.

_____. *The Six Orders of the Mishnah: Seder Tohorot.* Tel Aviv: 1957.

_____. *The Six Orders of the Mishnah: Seder Zeraim.* Tel Aviv: 1957.

Alon, Gedalyahu. "The Levitical Uncleanness of the Gentiles." Gedalyahu Alon, *Jews Judaism and the Classical World.* Translated by Israel Abrahams. Jerusalem: 1977.

Anderson, Benedict. *Imagined Communities: Reflections on the Origin and Spread of Nationalism.* London: 1983.

Anonymous. *Mishna Codex Parma (De Rossi 138). An Early Vowelized Manuscript of the Complete Mishna Text.* Jerusalem: 1970.

Asher, Moshe Baer. *Mishna Codex Paris. Paris 328-329.* Jerusalem: 1973.

Avery-Peck, Alan. *Mishnah's Division of Agriculture: A History and Theology of Seder Zeraim.* Chico: 1985.

Avi-Yonah, Michael. *The Jews of Palestine: A Political History from the Bar Kokhba War to the Arab Conquest.* New York: 1976.

Babcock, Barbara A. *The Reversible World: Symbolic Inversion in Art and Society.* Ithaca: 1978.

Barrett, Richard A. *Culture and Conduct: An Excursion in Anthropology.* Belmont: 1984.

Barth, Fredrik. *Ethnic Groups and Boundaries: The Social Organization of Cultural Difference.* Bergen-Oslo: 1969.

Beer, Georg. *Faksimile-Ausgabe des Mischnacodex Kaufmann A 50 mit der Ungarischen Akademie der Wissenschaften in Budapest.* Jerusalem: 1968.

Berreman, Gerald D. "Race, Caste, and Other Invidious Distinctions." Norman R. Yetman, *Majority and Minority: The Dynamics of Race and Ethnicity in American Life.* 21-39.

Bessac, Frank D. *Current Anthropology.* V. 4. October: 1964. 293-294.

Blom, Jan-Petter. "Ethnic and Cultural Differentiation." Fredrik Barth. *Ethnic Groups and Boundaries: The Social Organization of Cultural Difference.* 74-85.

Bokser, Baruch M. *The Origins of the Seder: The Passover Rite and Early Rabbinic Judaism.* Berkeley and Los Angeles: 1984.

Bonacich, Edna. "Class Approaches to Ethnicity and Race." Norman R. Yetman, *Majority and Minority: The Dynamics of Race and Ethnicity in American Life.* 62-78.

Boon, James A. *Other Tribes, Other Scribes: Symbolic Anthropology in the Comparative Study of Cultures, Histories, Religions, and Texts.* Cambridge: 1982.

Breuilly, John. *Nationalism and the State.* New York: 1982.

Brooks, Roger. *Support for the Poor in the Mishnaic Law of Agriculture: Tractate Peah.* Chico: 1983.

Bruner, Edward M. *Text, Play and Story: Proceedings, American Ethnological Society.* Washington: 1984.

Büchler, Adolf. "The Levitical Impurity of the Gentile in Palestine Before the Year 70." *Jewish Quarterly Review.* New Series. XVII. 1926-1927. 1-81.

Cashdan, Eli. *Hullin: Translated into English with Notes, Glossary and Indices.* Isidore Epstein. *The Babylonian Talmud.* London: 1948.

Clifford, James and George E. Marcus. *Writing Culture.* Berkeley & Los Angeles: 1986.

Cohen, Abner. "Variables in Ethnicity." Charles F. Keyes. *Ethnic Change.* 306-332.

Cohen, Shaye, J.D. *From the Maccabees to the Mishnah.* Philadelphia: 1987.

Cohen, Yehezkel. *The Attitude to the Gentile in the Halacha and in Reality in the Tannaitic Period.* Unpublished doctoral dissertation. Hebrew University. Jerusalem: 1975.

Cohen, Yehudi A. "Social Boundary Systems." *Current Anthropology.* X. 1. February. 1969. 103-126.

Cooper, Samuel. "The Laws of Mixture: An Anthropological Study in Halakhah." Harvey E. Goldberg. *Judaism Viewed From Within and From Without: Anthropological Studies.* Albany: 1987. 55-74.

Danby, Herbert. *The Mishnah: Translated from the Hebrew with Introduction and Brief Explanatory Notes.* London: reprint 1964.

Davies, William D. *The Gospel and the Land: Early Christianity and Jewish Territorial Doctrine.* Berkeley and Los Angeles: 1974.

de Vaux, Roland. *Ancient Israel Volume 2: Religious Institutions.* New York: 1965.

Dever, William G. "Asherah, Consort of Yahweh? New Evidence from Kuntillet 'Ajrud." *Bulletin of the American Schools of Oriental Research.* Summer. 1984. 255. 39-48.

Devereux, George. "Ethnic Identity: Its Logical Foundations and Its Dysfunctions." George De Vos and Lola Romanucci-Ross, *Ethnic Identity: Cultural Continuities and Change.* 42-70.

De Vos, George. "Ethnic Pluralism: Conflict and Accommodation." George De Vos and Lola Romanucci-Ross. *Ethnic Identity: Cultural Continuities and Change.* 5-41.

De Vos, George and Lola Romanucci-Ross. *Ethnic Identity: Cultural Continuities and Change.* Palo Alto: 1975.

Douglas, Mary. "Critique and Commentary." Jacob Neusner. *The Idea of Purity in Ancient Judaism.* 137-142.

Dumézil, Georges. *Archaic Roman Religion.* Translated by Philip Krapp. Chicago and London: 1970.

_____. *Fêtes romaines d'été et d'automne.* Paris: 1975.

Edersheim, Alfred, *The Temple, Its Ministry and Services as They Were at the Time of Jesus Christ.* London: 1959.

Elmslie, W.A.L. *The Mishna on Idolatry 'Aboda Zara: Edited with Translation, Vocabulary, and Notes.* Cambridge: 1911.

Enloe, Cynthia H. *Ethnic Conflict and Political Development.* Boston: 1973.

Epstein, Jacob N. *Introduction to the Text of the Mishnah.* Second Edition. Tel Aviv: 1964.

_____. *Prolegomena ad Litteras Tannaiticas: Mishna, Tosephta et Interpretationes Halachicas.* Edited by E.Z. Melamed. Tel Aviv: 1958.

Essner, Howard S. "The Mishnah Tractate 'Orlah: Translation and Commentary." William S. Green, *Approaches to Ancient Judaism Volume III: Text as Context in Early Rabbinic Literature*. 105-148.

Fischer, Michael M.J. "Ethnicity and the Post-Modern Arts of Memory." James Clifford and George E. Marcus. *Writing Culture*. 194-233.

Flusser, David. "Paganism in Palestine." Shmuel Safrai and Menahem Stern. *The Jewish People in the First Century: History, Geography, Political History, Social Cultural and Religious Life and Institutions*. 1065-1100.

Gager, John G. *The Origins of Anti-Semitism: Attitudes Toward Judaism in Pagan and Christian Antiquity*. New York and Oxford: 1985.

Gamoran, Hillel. "The Talmudic Law of Mortgages in View of the Prohibition Against Lending on Interest." *Hebrew Union College Annual*. LII. 1981. 153-162.

Gellner, Ernest. *Nations and Nationalism*. Oxford: 1983.

Gereboff, Joel D. *Rabbi Tarfon: The Tradition, the Man, and Early Rabbinic Judaism*. Missoula: 1979.

Ginzberg, Louis. *The Legends of the Jews*. Philadelphia: Reprint 1968.

Goldberg, Abraham. "The Mishna--A Study Book of Halakha." Shmuel Safrai. *The Literature of the Sages First Part: Oral Tora, Halakha, Mishna, Tosefta, Talmud, External Tractates. Compendia Rerum Iudaicarum ad Novum Testamentum. Section Two*. 211-251.

Goldberg, Abraham. "The Tosefta--Companion to the Mishna." Shmuel Safrai. *The Literature of the Sages First Part: Oral Tora, Halakha, Mishna, Tosefta, Talmud, External Tractates. Compendia Rerum Iudaicarum ad Novum Testamentum. Section Two*. 283-302.

Goldenberg, Robert. "The Jewish Sabbath in the Roman World up to the Time of Constantine the Great." Hildegard Temporini and Wolfgang Haase, *Aufstieg und Niedergang der römischen Welt*. II.19.1. 414-444.

_____. *The Sabbath-Law of Rabbi Meir*. Ann Arbor: 1979.

Green, William S. *Approaches to Ancient Judaism: Theory and Practice*. Missoula: 1978.

_____. *Approaches to Ancient Judaism Volume III: Text as Context in Early Rabbinic Literature*. Chico: 1981.

_____. "Otherness Within: Towards a Theory of Difference in Rabbinic Judaism." Jacob Neusner and Ernest S. Frerichs. *"To See Ourselves as Others See Us" Christians, Jews, "Others" in Late Antiquity*. 49-69.

_____. *Persons and Institutions in Early Rabbinic Judaism*. Missoula: 1977.

_____. *The Traditions of Joshua Ben Hananiah, Part One: The Early Legal Traditions*. Leiden: 1981.

_____. "What's in a Name?--The Problematic of Rabbinic 'Biography.'" William S. Green. *Approaches to Ancient Judaism: Theory and Practice*. 77-96.

Haaland, Gunnar. "Economic Determinants in Ethnic Processes." Fredik Barth. *Ethnic Groups and Boundaries: The Social Organization of Cultural Difference*. 53-73.

Haas, Peter. *A History of the Mishnaic Law of Agriculture: Tractate Maaser Sheni*. Chico: 1980.

Haberman, A.M. *The Mishnah with the Commentary of Maimonides. First Edition: Naples 1492*. Jerusalem: 1930.

Hadas-Lebel, Mireille. "Le paganisme à travers les sources rabbiniques des IIe et IIIe siècles, Contribution à l'étude du syncrétisme dans l'empire romain." Hildegard Temporini and Wolfgang Haase. *Aufstieg und Niedergang der römischen Welt.* II.19.2. 397-485.

Hallo, William W. "New Moons and Sabbaths: A Case-study in the Contrastive Approach." *Hebrew Union College Annual.* XLVIII. 1977. 1-18.

Haran, Menahem. *Temples and Temple-Service in Ancient Israel: An Inquiry into the Character of the Cult Phenomena and the Historical Setting of the Priestly School.* Oxford: 1978.

Haviland, William A. *Cultural Anthropology.* Fourth Edition. New York: 1983.

Havivi, Abraham. "Mishnah Hallah Chapter One: Translation and Commentary." William S. Green. *Approaches to Ancient Judaism Volume III: Text as Context in Early Rabbinic Judaism.* 149-184.

Heider, George C. *The Cult of Molek: A Reassessment.* Sheffield: 1985.

Hengel, Martin. *Judaism and Hellenism: Studies in their Encounter in Palestine during the Early Hellenistic Period.* Translated by John Bowden. Philadelphia: 1974.

Hoffman, Lawrence A. "Introduction: Land of Blessing and 'Blessings of the Land.'" Lawrence A. Hoffman. *The Land of Israel: Jewish Perspectives.* 1-23.

_____. *The Land of Israel: Jewish Perspectives.* Notre Dame: 1986.

Hunt, Chester L. and Lewis Walker, *Ethnic Dynamics: Patterns of Intergroup Relations in Various Societies.* Homewood: 1974.

Jaffe, Martin. *Mishnah's Theology of Tithing: A Study of Tractate Maaserot.* Chico: 1981.

Jastrow, Marcus. *A Dictionary of the Targumim, the Talmud Babli and Yerushalmi, and the Midrashic Literature.* New York: Reprint 1971.

Kanter, Shamai. *Rabban Gamaliel II: The Legal Traditions.* Chico: 1980.

Kasovsky, Chayim Y. *Thesaurus Mishnae Concordantiae Verborum quae in Sex Mishnae ordinibus Reperiuntur.* Tel Aviv: 1967.

Kaufmann, Yehezqal. *History of the Israelite Faith.* Jerusalem: 1952.

Keyes, Charles F. *Ethnic Change.* Seattle and London: 1981.

Kilborne, Benjamin and L.L. Langness. *Culture and Human Nature: Theoretical Papers of Melford E. Spiro.* Chicago: 1987.

Kimelman, Reuven. "Birkat Ha-Minim and the Lack of Evidence for an Anti-Christian Jewish Prayer in Late Antiquity." E.P. Sanders. *Jewish and Christian Self-Definition Volume Two: Aspects of Judaism in the Graeco-Roman Period.* Philadelphia: 1981. 226-244.

Kirzner, E.W. *Baba Kamma: Translated into English with Notes, Glossary and Indices.* Isidore Epstein. *The Babylonian Talmud.* London: 1935.

Knutsson, Karl E. "Dichotomization and Integration: Aspects of Inter-ethnic Relations in Southern Ethiopia." Fredik Barth. *Ethnic groups and Boundaries: The Social Organizat-ion of Cultural Difference.* 86-100.

Kohler, Kaufmann. "Amorites In Rabbinical and Apocryphal Literature." Isidore Singer. *The Jewish Encyclopedia.* New York: Reprint ND. I. 529-530.

Kohut, Alexander. *Aruch Completum sive Lexicon vocabula et res, quae in libris targumicis, Talmudicis et Midraschicis continentur, explicans auctore Nathane filio Jehielis.* New York: Reprint ND.

Kokosalakis, N. *Ethnic Identity and Religion: Tradition and Change in Liverpool Jewry.* Washington: 1982.

Lehrman, S.M. *Shebi'ith: Translated into English with Notes.* Isidore Epstein. *The Babylonian Talmud.* London: 1948.

Levine, Baruch A. *In the Presence of the Lord: A Study of Cult and Some Cultic Terms in Ancient Israel.* Leiden: 1974.

_____. "On the Presence of God in Biblical Religion." Jacob Neusner. *Religions in Antiquity: Essays in Memory of Erwin Ramsdell Goodenough.* 71-87.

Levine, Robert A. and Donald Campbell, *Ethnocentrism: Theories of Conflict, Ethnic Attitudes and Group Behavior.* New York: 1972.

Levy, Jacob. *Worterbuch uber die Talmudim und Midraschim.* Darmstadt: Reprint 1963.

Lieberman, Saul. *Greek in Jewish Palestine: Studies in the Life and Manners of Jewish Palestine in the II-IV Centuries C.E.* New York: 1942.

_____. *HaYerushalmi Kifshuto.* Jerusalem: 1934.

_____. *Hellenism in Jewish Palestine: Studies in the Literary Transmission Beliefs and Manners of Palestine in the I Century B.C.E.--IV Century C.E.* New York: 1950.

_____. "Palestine in the Third and Fourth Centuries." *Jewish Quarterly Review.* New Series. XXXVI. 1946. 329-370.

_____. "Palestine in the Third and Fourth Centuries." *Jewish Quarterly Review.* New Series. XXXVII. 1946. 31-54.

_____. *Tosefeth Rishonim: A Commentary based on Manuscripts of the Tosefta and Works of the Rishonim and Midrashim in Manuscripts and rare Editions.* Jerusalem: 1938.

_____. *Tosefta Ki-fshutah A Comprehensive Commentary on the Tosefta: Order Zera'im, Part I.* New York: 1955.

_____. *Tosefta Ki-fshutah: A Comprehensive Commentary on the Tosefta: Order Zera'm, Part II.* New York: 1955.

_____. *Tosefta Ki-fshutah: A Comprehensive Commentary on the Tosefta: Part III Order Mo'ed.* New York: 1962.

_____. *Tosefta Ki-fshutah: A Comprehensive Commentary on the Tosefta: Part IV, Order Mo'ed.* New York: 1962.

_____. *Tosefta Ki-fshutah: A Comprehensive Commentary on the Tosefta: Part V Order Mo'ed.* New York: 1962.

_____. *The Tosefta According to Codex Vienna, with Variants from Codices Erfurt, London, Genizah Mss. and Editio Princeps (Venice 1521) Together with References to Parallel Passages in Talmudic Lit erature and A Brief Commentary: The Order of Mo'ed.* New York: 1962.

_____. *The Tosefta According to Codex Cienna, with Variants from Codex Erfurt, Genizah Mss. and Editio Princpets (Venice 1521) Together with References to Parallel Passages in Talmudic Literature and a Brief Commentary: The Order of Zera'im.* New York: 1955.

Lightstone, Jack N. "R. Sadoq." William S. Green, *Persons and Institutions in Early Rabbinic Judaism.* 49-148.

_____. *Yose the Galilean: I. Traditions in Mishnah-Tosefta.* Leiden: 1979.

_____. "Yose the Galilean in Mishnah-Tosefta and the History of Early Rabbinic Judaism." *Journal of Jewish Studies.* 1979.

Lowe, W.H. *The Mishnah on Which the Palestinian Talmud Rests: Edited for the Syndics of the University Press from the Unique Manuscript Preserved in the University Library of Cambridge.* Cambridge: 1883.

Maier, Walter A. III. *'Asherah: Extrabiblical Evidence.* Atlanta: 1986.

Mandelbaum, Irving. *A History of the Mishnaic Law of Agriculture: Kilayim.* Chico: 1982.

Meeks, Wayne. *The First Urban Christians.* New Haven: 1983.

Meyers Eric M. and James F. Strange. *Archaeology, the Rabbis, and Early Christianity.* Nashville: 1981.

Millar, Fergus. "Empire, Community and Culture in the Roman Near East: Greeks, Syrians, Jews, and Arabs." *Journal of Jewish Studies.* XXXVII, 2. Autumn: 1987. 143-164.

Mishcon, A. *Abodah Zarah: Translated into English with Notes, Glossary and Indices.* Isidore Epstein. *The Babylonian Talmud.* London: 1935.

Morag, Shelomo. *The Mishna Tactates Neziqin Qodashim Teharoth. Codex Jerusalem Heb 4 1336. A Mansucript Vocalized According to the Yemenite Tradition.* Jerusalem: 1970.

Morgan, John H. "Clifford Geertz: An Interfacing of Anthropology and Religious Studies." Morgan, John H. *Understanding Religion and Culture: Anthropological and Theological Perspectives.* 1-14.

_____. *Understanding Religion and Culture: Anthropological and Theological Perspectives.* Washington: 1979.

Narroll, Raoul. "On Ethnic Unit Classification." *Current Anthropology.* V. 4. October: 1964. 283-291.

Needham, Rodney. *Primordial Characters.* Charlottesville: 1978.

_____. *Symbolic Classification.* Santa Monica: 1979.

Neusner, Jacob. *The Bavli and Its Sources: The Question of Tradition in the Case of Tractate Sukkah.* Atlanta: 1987.

_____. *Christianity, Judaism and Other Greco-Roman Cults, Studies for Morton Smith at Sixty: Part Four: Judaism after 70, Other Greco-Roman Cults, Bibliography.* Leiden: 1975. IV.

_____. *Development of a Legend: Studies on the Traditions Concerning Yohanan ben Zakkai.* Leiden: 1970.

_____. *Eliezer ben Hyrcanus: The Tradition and the Man.* Leiden: 1973.

_____. *From Mishnah to Scripture: The Problem of the Unattributed Saying.* Chico: 1984.

_____. *From Politics to Piety: The Emergence of Pharisaic Judaism.* Englewood Cliffs: 1973.

_____. *A History of the Mishnaic Law of Appointed Times Part Five. The Mishnaic System of Appointed Times.* Leiden: 1983.

_____. *A History of the Mishnaic Law of Appointed Times Part Four Besah, Rosh Hashshanah, Taanit, Megillah, Moed Qatan, Hagigah. Translation and Explanation.* Leiden: 1983.

_____. *A History of the Mishnaic Law of Appointed Times Part One Shabbat. Translation and Explanation.* Leiden: 1981.

_____. *A History of the Mishnaic Law of Appointed Times Part Three Sheqalim, Yoma, Sukkah. Translation and Explanation.* Leiden: 1982.

_____. *A History of the Mishnaic Law of Appointed Times Part Two Erubin, Pesahim. Translation and Explanation.* Leiden: 1981.

_____. *A History of the Mishnaic Law of Damages Part Five. The Mishnaic System of Damages.* Leiden: 1985.

_____. *A History of the Mishnaic Law of Damages Part Four Shebuot, Eduyot, Abodah Zarah, Abot, Horayot. Translation and Explanation.* Leiden: 1985.

_____. *A History of the Mishnaic Law of Damages Part One Baba Qamma. Translation and Explanation.* Leiden: 1983.

_____. *A History of the Mishnaic Law of Damages Part Three Baba Batra, Sanhedrin, Makkot. Translation and Explanation.* Leiden: 1984.

_____. *A History of the Mishnaic Law of Damages Part Two Baba Mesia. Translation and Explanantion.* Leiden: 1983.

_____. *A History of the Mishnaic Law of Holy Things Part Four Arakhin, Temurah. Translation and Explanation.* Leiden: 1979.

_____. *A History of the Mishnaic Law of Holy Things Part One Zebahim. Translation and Explanation.* Leiden: 1978.

_____. *A History of the Mishnaic Law of Holy Things Part Six. The Mishnaic System of Sacrifice and Sanctuary.* Leiden: 1980.

_____. *A History of the Mishnaic Law of Holy Things Part Three Hullin, Bekhorot. Translation and Explanation.* Leiden: 1979.

_____. *A History of the Mishnaic Law of Holy Things Part Two Menahot. Translation and Explanation.* Leiden: 1978.

_____. *A History of the Mishnaic Law of Purities Part One Kelim. Chapters One Through Eleven.* Leiden: 1974.

_____. *A History of the Mishnaic Law of Purities Part Four Ohalot. Commentary.* Leiden: 1974.

_____. *A History of the Mishnaic Law of Women Part Five. The Mishnaic System of Women.* Leiden: 1980.

_____. *A History of the Mishnaic Law of Women Part Four Sotah, Gittin, Qiddushin. Translation and Explanation.* Leiden: 1980.

_____. *A History of the Mishnaic Law of Women Part One Yebamot. Translantion and Explanation.* Leiden: 1980.

_____. *A History of the Mishnaic Law of Women Part Three Nedarim, Nazir. Translation and Explanation.* Leiden: 1980.

_____. *A History of the Mishnaic Law of Women Part Two Ketubot. Translation and Explanation.* Leiden: 1980.

_____. *The Idea of Purity in Ancient Judaism: The Haskell Lectures, 1972-1973.* Leiden: 1973.

_____. *Invitation to the Talmud: A Teaching Book. Revised and Expanded Edition Including Hebrew Texts.* New York: 1984.

_____. *Judaism in Society: The Evidence of the Yerushalmi, Toward the Natural History of a Religion.* Chicago and London: 1983.

_____. *Judaism: The Classical Statement. The Evidence of the Bavli.* Chicago and London: 1986.

_____. *Judaism: The Evidence of the Mishnah.* Chicago and London: 1981.

_____. *A Life of Yohanan Ben Zakkai: Ca. 1-80 C.E.* Second Edition. Completely Revised. Leiden: 1970.

_____. *The Modern Study of the Mishnah.* Leiden: 1973.

_____. *The Rabbinic Traditions About the Pharisees Before 70.* Leiden: 1971.

_____. *Religions in Antiquity: Essays in Memory of Erwine Ramsdell Goodenough.* Leiden: 1970.

_____. *The Talmud of the Land of Israel, Vol. 35: Introduction: Taxonomy.* Chicago and London: 1983.

_____. *There We Sat Down: Talmudic Judaism in the Making.* New York: 1978.

_____. *Torah: From Scroll to Symbol in Formative Judaism.* Philadelphia: 1985.

_____. *The Tosefta: Its Structure and Its Sources.* Atlanta: 1986.

_____. *The Tosefta. Translated from the Hebrew Second Division Moed (Appointed Times).* New York: 1981.

Neusner, Jacob and Ernest S. Frerichs. *"To See Ourselves as Others See Us: Christians Jews, "Others" in Late Antiquity.* Chico: 1985.

Newman, Louis. *The Sanctity of the Seventh Year: A Study of Mishnah Tractate Shebiit.* Chico: 1983.

Nilsson, Martin P. *A History of Greek Religion.* Translated by F.J. Fielden. New York: 1964.

Orlinsky, Harry M. "The Biblical Concept of the Land of Israel." Lawrence A. Hoffman. *The Land of Israel: Jewish Perspectives.* 27-64.

Otto, Walter F. *Dionysus: Myth and Cult.* Translated by Robert B. Palmer. Bloomington and London: 1965.

Palumbo, Michael and William O. Shanahan. *Nationalism: Essays in Honor of Louis L. Snyder.* Westport: 1981.

Peck, Alan J. *The Priestly Gift in Mishnah: A Study of Tractate Terumot.* Chico: 1981.

Porton, Gary G. "According to Rabbi Y: A Palestinian Amoraic Form." William S. Green. *Approaches to Ancient Judaism I: Theory and Practice.* 173-188.

_____ "The Artificial Dispute: Ishmael and 'Aqiva." Jacob Neusner. *Chritianity, Judaism and Other Greco-Roman Cults, Studies for Morton Smith at Sixty: Part Four: Judaism after 70, Other Greco-Roman Cults, Bibliography.* 18-29.

_____ "Forbidden Transactions: Prohibited Commerce with Gentiles in Earliest Rabbinism." Jacob Neusner and Ernest S. Frerichs. *"To See Ourselves as Others See Us" Christians, Jews, "Others" in Late Antiquity.* 317-336.

_____ "Midrash: Palestinian Jews and the Hebrew Bible in the Greco-Roman Period." Hildegard Temporini and Wolfgang Haase. *Aufstieg und Niedergang der römischen Welt.* II.19.2. 103-138.

_____ "The Pronouncement Story in Tannaitic Literature: A Review of Bultmann's Theory." Robert C. Tannehill. *Pronouncement Stories. Semia.* XX. 1981. 81-99.

_____ *The Traditions of Rabbi Ishmael Part Four: The Materials as a Whole.* Leiden: 1982.

_____ *The Traditions of Rabbi Ishmael Part One: The Non-Exegetical Materials.* Leiden: 1976.

_____ *The Traditions of Rabbi Ishmael Part Two: Exegetical Comments in Tannaitic Collections.* Leiden: 1977.

Primus, Charles. *Aqiva's Contribution to Law of Zera'im.* Leiden: 1977.

_____. "The Borders of Judaism." Lawrence A. Hoffman. *The Land of Israel: Jewish Perspectives.* 97-108.

Purvis, James D. "The Samaritans and Judaism." Robert A. Kraft and George W.E. Nickelsburg. *Judaism and its Modern Interpreters.* Atlanta: 1986. 81-98.

Rose, H.J. *Religion in Greece and Rome.* New York: 1959.

Rose, Peter I. *They and We: Racial and Ethnic Relations in the United States.* Third Edition. New York: 1981.

Rubenstein, Margaret Wenig. "A Commentary on Mishnah-Tosefta Bikkurim Chapters One and Two." William Green. *Approaches to Ancient Judaism Volume III: Texts as Context in Early Rabbinic Literature.* 47-88.

Safria, Shmeul. *The Literature of the Sages First Part: Oral Tora, Halakha, Mishna, Tosefta, Talmud, External Tractates.* Philadelphia: 1987.

_____. "Relations Between the Diaspora and the Land of Israel." Shmuel Safrai and Menahem Stern. *The Jewish People in the First Century: Historical Geography, Political History, Social, Cultural and Religious Life and Institutions.* I. 184-215.

_____. "The Temple." Shmuel Safrai and Menahem Stern. *The Jewish People in the First Century: History, Geography, Political History, Social Cultural and Religious Life and Institutions.* II. 865-907.

Safrai, Shmuel and Menahem Stern. *The Jewish People in the First Century: Historical Geography, Political History, Social, Cultural and Religious Life and Institutions. Volume One.* Philadelphia: 1974.

_____. *The Jewish People in the First Century: Historical Geography, Political History, Social, Cultural and Religious Life and Institutions. Volume Two.* Philadelphia: 1976.

Sanders, E.P. *Paul and Palestinian Judaism: A Comparison of Patterns of Religion.* Philadelphia: 1977.

Sarason, Richard. *A History of the Mishnaic Law of Agriculture. Section Three: A Study of Tractate Demai.* Leiden: 1979.

_____. "The Significance of the Land of Israel in the Mishnah." Lawrence A. Hoffman, *The Land of Israel: Jewish Persepctives.* Notre Dame: 1986. 109-136.

Schaefer, Peter. "Research into Rabbinic Literature: An Attempt to Define the Status Quaestionis." *Journal of Jewish Studies.* XXXVII. 2. Autumn, 1986. 139-152.

Schiffman, Lawrence H. "At the Crossroads: Tannaitic Perspectives on the Jewish-Christian Schism." E.P. Sanders. *Jewish and Christian Self-Definition Volume Two.* Philadelphia: 1981. 115-156.

_____. *Who Was A Jew: Rabbinic and Halakhic Perspectives of the Jewish-Christian Schism.* Hoboken: 1985.

Schürer, Emil. *The History of the Jewish People in the Age of Jesus Christ (175 B.C.-A.D. 135).* Edited by Geza Vermes, Fergus Millar, and Matthew Black. Edinburgh: 1973-1979.

_____. *A History of the Jewish People in the Time of Jesus Christ.* Translated by Sophia Taylor and Peter Christie. New York: 1891.

Segal, Alan, F. *Rebecca's Children: Judaism and Christianity in the Roman World.* Cambridge: 1986.

_____. *Two Powers in Heaven: Early Rabbinic Reports about Christianity and Gnosticism.* Leiden: 1977.

Slotki, Israel W. *Tohoroth: Translated into English with Notes.* Isidore Epstein. *The Babylonian Talmud.* London: 1948.

_____. *Yebamoth, Translated with Notes, Glossary and Indices.* Isidore Epstein. *The Babylonian Talmud.* London: 1936.

Smallwood, E. Mary. *The Jews under Roman Rule: From Pompey to Diocletian.* Leiden: 1976.

Smith, Jonathan Z. *Imagining Religion.* Chicago and London: 1982.

_____. *Map Is Not Territory: Studies in the History of Religions.* Leiden: 1978.

Smith, Morton. "The Dead Sea Sect in Relation to Ancient Judaism." *New Testament Studies.* VII. 1960. 347-360.

Speiser, Ephraim A. *The Anchor Bible Genesis.* Garden City: 1983.

_____. "Man, Ethnic Divisions of." George A. Buttrick. *The Interpreter's Dictionary of the Bible: An Illustrated Encyclopedia.* Nashville and New York: 1962. III. 235-242.

Sperber, Daniel. "Nations, the Seventy." Cecil Roth and Geoffrey Wigoder. *Encyclopedia Judaica.* Jerusalem: 1972. XII. 882-886.

_____. *Roman Palestine: 200-400, The Land.* Ramat-Gan: 1978.

Spiro, Melford E. "Collective Representations and Mental Representations in Religious Symbol Systems." Benjamin Kilborne and L.L. Langness. *Culture and Human Nature: Theoretical Papers of Melford E. Spiro.* 161-184.

_____. "Religion: Problems of Definition and Explanation." Benjamin Kilborne and L.L. Langness. *Culture and Human Nature: Theoretical Papers of Melford E. Spiro.* 187-222.

_____. "Some Reflections on Cultural Determinism and Relativism with Special Reference to Emotion and Reason." Benjamin Kilborne and L.L. Langness. *Culture and Human Nature: Theoretical Papers of Melford E. Spiro.* 32-58.

Steinsaltz, Adin. *The Essential Talmud.* Translated by Chaya Galai. New York: 1976.

Stemberger, Gunter. "Die Beurteilung Roms in der rabbinischen Literatur." Hildegard Temporini and Wolfgang Haase. *Aufstieg und Niederganag der romischen Welt.* II.19.2. 338-396.

Temporini, Hildegard and Wolfgang Haase. *Aufstieg und Niedergang der römischen Welt.* II.19.1 and II.19. 2. Berlin and New York: 1979.

Urbach, Ephraim E. "The Laws Regarding Slavery as a Source for Social History of the Period of the Second Temple, the Mishnah and Talmud." J.G. Weiss. *Papers of the Institute of Jewish Studies London.* Jerusalem: 1964. I. 1-94.

_____. "The Rabbinical Laws of Idolatry in the Second and Third Centuries in Light of Archaeological and Historical Facts." *Israel Exploration Journal.* 1959. IX. 3. 149-165.

_____. "The Rabbinical Laws of Idolatry in the Second and Third Centuries in the Light of Archaeological and Historical Facts." *Israel Exploration Journal.* 1959. IX. 4. 229-245.

van den Berghe, Pierre L. "Race and Ethnicity: A Sociobiological Perspective." Norman R. Yetman. *Majority and Minority: The Dynamics of Race and Ethnicity in American Life.* 54-61.

Vermes, Geza. "Leviticus 18:21 in Ancient Jewish Bible Exegesis." Jakob J. Petuchowski and Ezra Fleischer. *Studies in Aggadah, Targum and Jewish Liturgy in Memory of Joseph Heinemann.* Jerusalem: 1981. 108-124.

Weiner, David. "A Study of Mishnah Tractate Bikkurim Chapter Three." William S. Green. *Approaches to Ancient Judaism Volume III: Text as Context in Early Rabbinic Judaism.* 89-104.

White, Leslie A. "The Concept of Culture." M. F. Ashley Montagu. *Culture and the Evolution of Man*. Oxford: Reprint, 1972. 38-64.

Yetman, Norman R. "Introduction: Definitions and Perspectives." Norman R. Yetman. *Majority and Minority: The Dynamics of Race and Ethnicity in American Life*. 1-20.

_____. *Majority and Minority: The Dynamics of Race and Ethnicity in American Life*. Fourth Edition. Boston, Sydney, London, Toronto: 1985.

Zahavy, Tzvee. *The Mishnaic Law of Blessings and Prayers: Tractate Berakhot*. Atlanta: 1987.

_____. *The Traditions of Eleazar ben Azariah*. Missoula: 1978.

Zakas, Nissin. *Mishnah Zera'im. The Six Orders of the Mishnah with Variant Textual Traditions from the Manuscripts of Mishnah Including the Genizah Fragments and the First Editions*. Jerusalem: 1971.

Zevin, Shlomo J. "Aretz-Israel." *Encyclopedia Talmudica: A Digest of Halachic Literature and Jews law from the Tannaitic Period to the Present Time Alphabetically Arranged*. Translated by David B. Klein. Edited by Harry Freedman. Jerusalem: 1978. III. 1-68.

Zohar, Zvi. "The Consumption of Sabbatical Year Produce in Biblical and Rabbinic Literature." Harvey E. Goldberg, *Judaism: Viewed from Within and from Without*. 75-106.

Zuckermandel, Moses. *Tosephta: Based on the Erfurt and Vienna Codices with Parallels and Variants*. Jerusalem: Reprint 1963.

Index of Biblical Passages

Index of Mishnaic Passages

1:5   126, 128, 150, 154, 246
1:6   67, 128, 150, 153
1:7   115, 249
1:8-9   198
1:8   127, 128, 150, 154, 198
1:9   115, 123
2:1   115, 123, 236, 237, 250, 286
2:2   123, 128, 135, 150, 151, 154, 237
2:3   115, 119, 123, 126, 127, 149, 151, 153, 154, 244, 249, 253, 255
2:4   128, 150, 151, 154, 252, 255
2:5   126, 149, 153, 154, 255
2:6   115, 119, 123, 256
2:7   127, 150, 154, 256
3:1   150, 151, 154, 246
3:2   246
3:3   150, 151, 154, 246
3:4   129, 149, 153
3:5   128, 149, 150, 153, 247
3:6   249
3:7   248, 249
3:8   124, 248
3:9   248
3:10   248
4:1   149, 153, 247
4:2   247
4:3   249
4:4   115, 247, 250
4:5   150, 251
4:6   151, 251
4:8   115, 251
4:9   115, 251

4:10   151, 154, 252
4:11   127, 151, 155, 253
4:12   115, 151, 253
5:1   115, 254
5:2   151, 254
5:3-4   254
5:3   127, 151, 154
5:4   127, 151, 155
5:5   115, 255
5:6   115, 251
5:7   115, 252, 253
5:8-9   251
5:8   254
5:9   249
5:10   151, 155, 252
5:11   128, 151, 155, 252
5:12   115, 276

Index of Toseftan Passages

Index of Rabbinic Masters

Index of Scholars

Index of General Subjects